"Hate speech is always with us, but the internet supercharged its developmental process. Formerly, voices crying out in the desert of hate largely went unheard, but the internet now provides a ready audience of fellow haters. Learn about the birth, nourishment, life, and death of hate speech in this impressive book."

William Crano, *Oskamp Distinguished Professor in Psychology, Claremont Graduate University, Claremont, California, USA*

"The very idea of a community of haters may seem paradoxical. Yet such is the extraordinary reality of our digital world. This carefully researched volume traces the emerging norms, innovative practices, and intensified cultures of online hate with which we must now contend, and challenges researchers – and society – to identify constructive new directions."

Sonia Livingstone, *Professor, London School of Economics, and Director of Digital Futures for Children, London, UK*

"With a novel focus on 'social process perspectives' – such as the ways in which online hate can be a bonding experience for the haters – this timely book offers a vital resource for understanding and addressing the complexities of contemporary online discourse."

Jonathan Zittrain, *Professor of Law, Computer Science, and Public Policy, Harvard University, Cambridge, Massachusetts, USA*

SOCIAL PROCESSES OF ONLINE HATE

This book explores the social forces among and between online aggressors that affect the expression and perpetration of online hate. Its chapters illustrate how patterns of interactive social behavior reinforce, magnify, or modify this expression. It also considers the characteristics of social media that facilitate social interactions that promote hate and facilitate relationships among haters. Bringing together a range of international experts and covering an array of themes, including woman abuse, antisemitism, pornography, radicalization, and extreme political youth movements, this book examines the specific social factors and processes that facilitate these forms of hate and proposes new approaches for explaining them.

Cutting-edge, interdisciplinary, and authoritative, this book will be of interest to sociologists, criminologists, and scholars of media, communication, and computational social science alike, as well as those engaged with hate crime, hate speech, social media, and online social networks.

Joseph B. Walther is the Bertelsen Presidential Chair of Technology and Society, and Distinguished Professor of Communication at the University of California Santa Barbara, California, USA.

Ronald E. Rice is the Arthur N. Rupe Chair in Social Effects of Mass Communication, and Distinguished Professor of Communication at the University of California Santa Barbara, California, USA.

SOCIAL PROCESSES OF ONLINE HATE

Edited by Joseph B. Walther and Ronald E. Rice

Routledge
Taylor & Francis Group

LONDON AND NEW YORK

Designed cover image: © Graham Glass/Joseph B. Walther and Ronald E. Rice

First published 2025
by Routledge
4 Park Square, Milton Park, Abingdon, Oxon OX14 4RN

and by Routledge
605 Third Avenue, New York, NY 10158

Routledge is an imprint of the Taylor & Francis Group, an informa business

© 2025 selection and editorial matter, Joseph B. Walther and
Ronald E. Rice; individual chapters, the contributors

The right of Joseph B. Walther and Ronald E. Rice to be identified as the
authors of the editorial material, and of the authors for their individual
chapters, has been asserted in accordance with sections 77 and 78 of the
Copyright, Designs and Patents Act 1988.

British Library Cataloguing-in-Publication Data
A catalogue record for this book is available from the British Library

ISBN: 978-1-032-75047-7 (hbk)
ISBN: 978-1-032-75042-2 (pbk)
ISBN: 978-1-003-47214-8 (ebk)

DOI: 10.4324/9781003472148

Typeset in Sabon
by Apex CoVantage, LLC

We wish to express our immense gratitude to Sandra Walther and Claire B. Johnson, for their patience and support.

CONTENTS

FIGURES

TABLES

CONTRIBUTORS

Steven Bethard is Associate Professor at the School of Information at the University of Arizona, Tucson, Arizona, USA, with courtesy appointments in linguistics, cognitive science, computer science, and applied mathematics. Steven Bethard previously worked as an assistant professor of computer and information science at the University of Alabama at Birmingham and as a postdoctoral researcher at Stanford University's Natural Language Processing Group, Johns Hopkins University's Human Language Technology Center of Excellence, KULeuven's Language Intelligence and Information Retrieval group in Belgium, and the University of Colorado's Center for Language and Education Research. He got his Ph.D. in computer science and cognitive science from the University of Colorado Boulder, Colorado, USA. Bethard's research interests include natural language processing and machine learning theory and applications, including modeling the language of time and timelines, normalizing text to medical and geospatial ontologies, and information extraction models for clinical applications.

Jeremy Blackburn is Associate Professor, Department of Computer Science, Binghamton University, State University of New York, New York, USA. Jeremy Blackburn joined the Department of Computer Science at Binghamton University in fall 2019. Jeremy is broadly interested in data science, with a focus on large-scale measurements and modeling. His largest line of work is in understanding jerks on the Internet. His research into understanding toxic behavior, hate speech, and fringe and extremist Web communities has been covered in the press by *The Washington Post*, the *New York Times*, *The Atlantic*, *The Wall Street Journal*, the BBC, and *New Scientist*, among others. Prior to his appointment at Binghamton, Jeremy was an assistant professor in the Department of Computer Science at the University of Alabama at Birmingham, USA. Prior to that, Jeremy was an associate researcher at Telefonica research in Barcelona, Spain.

Adam Burston is a Ph.D. candidate in sociology at the University of California, Santa Barbara, USA, with an emphasis in information, technology, and society. His work lies at the intersection of social movements, technology, and identity. His dissertation, "Radicalization vs. Resistance and Recommitment: Why Conservative Youth Accept or Reject Extremism," focuses on the strategies that right-wing student activists employ to radicalize their moderate peers as well as the ideological shifts in right-wing movements that enable formerly marginalized communities to participate. Before Adam came to UC Santa Barbara, he was a research associate with Carnegie Mellon University's Department of Engineering and Public Policy and a volunteer crisis counselor with Pittsburgh Action Against Rape.

Kevin Coe is a professor in the Department of Communication at the University of Utah, Utah, USA. Professor Coe's research employs both quantitative and qualitative methods to better understand political communication, news media, and public opinion. He is the coauthor of two books, *The Ubiquitous Presidency: Presidential Communication and Digital Democracy in Tumultuous Times* (Oxford, 2021, with Joshua Scacco) and *The God Strategy: How Religion Became a Political Weapon in America* (Oxford, 2010, with David Domke), as well as numerous research articles. Professor Coe teaches courses on media, strategic communication, political communication, and content analysis. He is from Tacoma, Washington, and is a product of the Tacoma Public Schools.

Walter S. DeKeseredy is Anna Deane Carlson Endowed Chair of Social Sciences, Director of the Research Center on Violence, and Professor of Sociology at West Virginia University, West Virginia, USA. He is also an adjunct professor in Monash University's Gender and Family Violence Prevention Center. DeKeseredy has published 28 books, over 130 scientific journal articles, and close to 120 scholarly book chapters on violence against women and other social problems. In 2008, the Institute on Violence, Abuse and Trauma gave him the Linda Saltzman Memorial Intimate Partner Violence Researcher Award. He also jointly received the 2004 Distinguished Scholar Award from the American Society of Criminology's (ASC) Division on Women and Crime and the 2007 inaugural UOIT Research Excellence Award. In 1995, he received the Critical Criminologist of the Year Award from the ASC's Division on Critical Criminology & Social Justice (DCCSJ), and in 2008, the DCCSJ gave him the Lifetime Achievement Award. In 2014, he received the Critical Criminal Justice Scholar Award from the Academy of

Criminal Justice Sciences' (ACJS) Section on Critical Criminal Justice, and in 2015, he received the Career Achievement Award from the ASC's Division on Victimology (DOV). In 2017, he received the Impact Award from the ACJS's section on Victimology and the Robert Jerin Book of the Year Award from the ASC's Division on Victimology. In 2022, he was named an ASC Fellow, received the Praxis Award from the DCCSJ, and received the 2022 Robert Jerin Book Award from the ASC's DOV.

Oeendrila Lahiri Gerold is a postdoctoral researcher in the online misogyny project funded by the Bavarian Institute for Digital Transformation (BIDT) at the University of Munich (LMU), Munich, Germany. Her research focuses on feminist resistance and religious nationalism in the digital space. Her training is interdisciplinary, with a focus on colonial and postcolonial studies.

Kate Kenski is a professor in the Department of Communication and School of Government and Public Policy at the University of Arizona, Tucson, Arizona, USA, where she teaches political communication, public opinion, and research methods. Prior to teaching at the University of Arizona, she was a senior analyst at the Annenberg Public Policy Center at the University of Pennsylvania. She is coauthor of *The Obama Victory: How Media, Money, and Message Shaped the 2008 Election* (2010, Oxford University Press) and *Capturing Campaign Dynamics: The National Annenberg Election Survey* (2004, Oxford University Press). She is coeditor of *The Oxford Handbook of Political Communication* with Kathleen Hall Jamieson. Dr. Kenski has over 70 publications in venues such as the *American Behavioral Scientist, Communication Research, Human Communication Research,* the *International Journal of Public Opinion Research,* the *Journal of Applied Social Psychology,* and *Public Opinion Quarterly.* Her current research focuses on social media and incivility, gender and politics, and presidential campaigns. She is the vice chair of the International Communication Association's Political Communication Division.

Jordan Kraemer is Director of Research at the Center for Technology and Society, Anti-Defamation League (ADL). Jordan Kraemer is a media anthropologist, with expertise studying digital platforms, social inequality, gender, and urban life. She currently directs research on hate and harassment online at the ADL's Center for Technology and Society. She is the author of a forthcoming book on social and mobile media among an emerging middle class in Berlin from Cornell University Press. Her work has also been published in *Catalyst: Feminism, Theory, Technoscience; Global Perspectives; Anthropological Quarterly;* and *Fast Company,* among others. Previously, she was an SSRC Just Tech grantee and a Mellon Postdoctoral Fellow at Wesleyan University and taught feminist and queer technology studies at NYU Tandon

School of Engineering. Jordan holds a Ph.D. in cultural anthropology from UC Irvine.

Binny Mathew is Machine Learning Scientist at the Center for Technology and Society, ADL, New York, USA. Binny Mathew is a natural language processing researcher, with an interest in online hate speech and counter measures. Prior to joining the ADL, he was part of CNERG at the Indian Institute of Technology, Kharagpur, West Bengal, India. His work has been published in several top-tier computer science and data science conferences, including PNAS, AAAI, ECML-PKDD, The WebConf (WWW), CSCW, ICWSM, and WebSci. He has also contributed multiple high-quality datasets and models to the research community. Binny received his Ph.D. in social computing from IIT Kharagpur in 2022.

Tanushree Mitra is an assistant professor in the Information School at University of Washington. Her research interests are in social computing, where she combines ideas from both computer science and social science to uncover insights about social life online via large datasets. Currently, one major focus of her research is understanding and designing defenses against problematic information in online social platforms. Her work employs a range of interdisciplinary methods from the fields of human computer interaction, data mining, machine learning, and natural language processing. From August 2017 to 2020, she was an assistant professor in the Department of Computer Science at Virginia Tech. She earned her Ph.D. in computer science from Georgia Tech. Currently, Dr. Mitra is also an adjunct affiliate of University of Washington Department of Computer Science and Engineering, an affiliate faculty of the Center for an Informed Public, and a cofounding director of RAISE, a Center for Responsibility in AI Systems and Experiences.

Shruti Phadke is a researcher at the University of Texas at Austin, Texas, USA, with a Ph.D. in information science from the University of Washington. Her research focuses on computationally understanding participation, social knowledge construction, and resource mobilization in online communities of problematic information. Her research benefits from multiple methodological approaches ranging from statistics, causal machine learning, natural language processing, and qualitative methods. Her research has received two Best Paper Honorable Mention awards at CSCW and the Best Paper Award at ICWSM 2022.

Stephen A. Rains is a professor of Communication at the University of Arizona. His research is situated in the areas of health communication, social influence, and communication and technology. He is interested in better understanding how and why messages influence people, particularly in health contexts and when using communication technologies. His work in recent years has primarily focused on social support, though he routinely studies digital coping, incivility, persuasion resistance, and related topics. He is especially interested in leveraging computational social science techniques to explore the dynamic communication processes involved in these phenomena.

Stephen C. Rea is a senior researcher with the Critical Internet Studies Institute (https://www.publicinterestinter.net/). A cultural anthropologist, Stephen's research expertise is in digital culture, with a focus on trust and community. His projects have included multi-year ethnographic research on South Korean online gaming culture, digital consumer financial services in the global South and the United States credit union system, the social and legal implications of automated decision-making systems, fairness and ethics in crowd work labor markets, engineering ethics education, and online hate and harassment and digital extremism on social media. Stephen's work has been published in *American Anthropologist*, the *Journal of the Royal Anthropological Institute*, *Signs and Society*, and *Law & Policy*, among others. He has held academic appointments as a visiting assistant professor at Bucknell University; a lecturer at the University of California, San Diego; a postdoctoral scholar at the University of California, Irvine, California, USA; and a research assistant professor at the Colorado School of Mines. He worked as a senior researcher for the Center for Technology and Society at the ADL. He received his Ph.D. in anthropology from the University of California, Irvine, California, USA, in 2015.

Ronald E. Rice is Arthur N. Rupe Chair in Social Effects of Mass Communication and Distinguished Professor of Communication at the University of California Santa Barbara, Santa Barbara, California, USA. Ronald E. Rice has been an officer in both the International Communication Association and the Academy of Management and was elected president (2006–2007) and fellow (2010) of the International Communication Association (ICA). He was honored with the ICA Steven Chaffee Career Achievement Award (2015), a Fulbright Award in Finland (2006), and was the Wee Kim Wee Visiting Professor, and then University Visiting Professor, of the School of Communication and Information at Nanyang Technological University in Singapore (2007–2010). He holds an honorary doctorate from the University of Montreal. He has conducted research and published widely in communication science, public communication campaigns, computer-mediated communication systems, research methodology, organizational and management theory, information systems, information science and bibliometrics, and social networks. His publications have won awards for best dissertation from the American Society for Information Science, 17 times for best paper from the International Communication Association, National Communication Association, Broadcast

Education Association, Conference on Computer-Supported Collaborative Work, Academy of Management, and Russian Communication Association, and a book award from the Health Communication Division of ICA. He has coauthored or coedited *Public Communication Campaigns* (1st ed. in 1981, 2nd ed. in 1989, 3rd ed. in 2001, and 4th ed. in 2012, Sage), *The New Media: Communication, Research and Technology* (1984, Sage), *Managing Organizational Innovation* (1987, Columbia University Press), *Research Methods and the New Media* (1988, The Free Press), *The Internet and Health Communication* (2001, Sage), *Accessing and Browsing Information and Communication* (2001, MIT Press), *Social Consequences of Internet Use: Access, Involvement and Interaction* (2002, MIT Press), *The Internet and Health Care: Theory, Research and Practice* (2006, Erlbaum), *Media Ownership: Research and Regulation* (2008, Hampton Press), *Organizations and Unusual Routines* (2010, Cambridge University Press), and *The Oxford Handbook of Digital Technology and Society* (2020, Oxford University Press).

Yotam Shmargad is an associate professor in the School of Government and Public Policy at the University of Arizona. His research focuses on understanding how digital platforms shape social and political life in the United States. He uses a mix of statistical and computational techniques, including social network analysis, online data collection, virtual experimentation, machine learning, and econometric methods. His research speaks to questions about how social media dampen certain disparities while magnifying others and how social media can both fuel political polarization and incivility and extinguish their flames. Shmargad's work has appeared in the *Journal of Politics*, *Political Communication*, the *Journal of Information Policy*, the *Journal of Political Marketing*, the *Journal of Interactive Marketing*, *PLOS One*, *Social Science Computer Review*, and the *Journal of the Association for Information Science and Technology*, among other venues.

Gianluca Stringhini is an associate professor in the Electrical and Computer Engineering Department at Boston University, holding affiliate appointments in the Computer Science Department, in the Faculty of Computing and Data Sciences, in the BU Center for Antiracist Research, and in the Center for Emerging Infectious Diseases Policy & Research. In his research, Gianluca applies a data-driven approach to better understand malicious activity on the Internet. Through the collection and analysis of large-scale datasets, he develops novel and robust mitigation techniques to make the Internet a safer place. His research involves a mix of quantitative analysis, (some) qualitative analysis, machine learning, crime science, and systems design. Over the years, Gianluca has worked on understanding and mitigating malicious activities like malware, online fraud, influence operations, and coordinated online harassment. He received multiple prizes, including an NSF CAREER Award in 2020, and his research won multiple Best Paper Awards. Gianluca has published over 100 peer-reviewed papers, including several at top computer security conferences like IEEE Security and Privacy, CCS, NDSS, and USENIX Security, as well as at HCI, and Web conferences such as IMC, ICWSM, CHI, CSCW, and WWW.

Stephanie Tom Tong is a professor in the Communication Department at Wayne State University, Detroit, Michigan, USA. She is Director of the Social Media and Relational Technologies (SMART; http://www.smartlabswayne. com/) Labs, which investigates how technology affects the ways people communicate across a variety of contexts, including romance, families, friendships, personal health, and online hate. Her work has been supported by the National Science Foundation, the National Communication Association, and the Central States Communication Association.

Anton Törnberg is an associate professor in the Department of Sociology and Work Science at the University of Gothenburg, Gothenburg, Sweden. His research chiefly focuses on the radical right movement online, particularly radicalization processes and violent extremism, by combining computational methods with qualitative approaches. He is currently involved in a research project that addresses the far right online and the interplay between online discourses and offline action.

Petter Törnberg is an assistant professor of computational social science, University of Amsterdam, Amsterdam, the Netherlands. In addition to his work at the University of Amsterdam, Petter Törnberg holds appointments at the University of Neuchâtel, Neuchâtel, Switzerland, and is Associate Professor of Complex Systems at Sweden's Chalmers University of Technology. His concerns revolve around how digital technology is reshaping our politics, media, and cities. He uses computational methods and digital data to examine the consequences of datafication, platformization, and AI from a critical perspective.

Sahana Udupa is a professor of media anthropology at the University of Munich (LMU), Germany, where she directs the research program "For Digital Dignity." She is the author of *Making News in Global India* (Cambridge University Press) and *Digital Unsettling: Decoloniality and Dispossession in the Age of Social Media* (New York University Press, with E.G. Dattatreyan) and is coeditor of *Digital Hate: The Global Conjuncture of Extreme Speech* (Indiana University Press) and *Media as Politics in South Asia* (Routledge). She is the recipient of the Joan Shorenstein Fellowship at Harvard University, the Francqui Chair in Belgium, and European Research Council grant awards.

Joseph B. Walther holds the Bertelsen Presidential Chair in Technology and Society at the University of California, Santa Barbara, where he is a distinguished professor of communication and former director of the Center for Information Technology and Society. A Fulbright Scholar, Fellow of the International Communication Association, and Distinguished Scholar in the National Communication Association, he is one of the leading theorists in the area of computer-mediated communication, with numerous behavioral science studies to his credit. His research focuses on the impact of interpersonal and intergroup dynamics on the attitudes and behaviors people develop via mediated interaction in personal relationships, groups, and interethnic conflict, as well as the reduction of prejudice. Prior to his position at UC Santa Barbara, he has held regular or visiting faculty positions at several prestigious universities in the United States, Europe, and Asia, in the fields of communication, social psychology, education, and information science. Professor Walther was recognized with the Charles Woolbert Awards from the National Communication Association on two occasions, for articles that have led to reconceptualizations of communication phenomena and have stood the test of time.

ACKNOWLEDGMENTS

We wish to acknowledge the support of the following generous and extremely talented people.

The Arthur N. Rupe Foundation and Mark C. Henrie, its President, provided funding for the conference though its endowment of the Arthur N. Rupe Professor in the Social Effects of Mass Communication (held by Professor Rice), in the UCSB Department of Communication. Through the endowment, they have helped sponsor a diverse range of biennial Rupe Conferences (see *http://www.comm.ucsb.edu/news-events/annual/rupe*), covering environmental communication, media industry and regulation, and the cosponsored Conference on Social Processes of Online Hate.

Mark and Susan Bertelsen and the President of the University of California generously helped to establish the Bertelsen Presidential Chair in Technology and Society (held by Professor Walther). The Bertelsens are UCSB alumni and UCSB Trustees and provide long-standing support of the Center for Information Technology and Society and other campus endeavors.

Acknowledgments are also due to the Berkman Klein Center for the Internet and Society at Harvard University, which supported Professor Walther as a visiting scholar in its Institute for Rebooting Social Media. Embedded in Harvard Law School, the Center's focus on the consequences of social media's design and governance, and the seeking of social justice through research, interaction with industry, policy, and the law, provided many useful lessons and outstanding connections that helped shape this work. So did many helpful conversations with scholars at nearby Boston University and at Northeastern University's Network Science Institute.

Professor Sharon Tettegah, Associate Vice Chancellor for Diversity, Equity, and Inclusion, and the Director of the Center for Black Studies Research at

UCSB, supported this research and the May 2023 conference since they were but a whisper and supported several students working with us on exploratory research.

We are thankful to the following from the UC Santa Barbara Department of Communication: Michelle Fredrich, Financial Assistant and event-planning wizard; Lindsay Miller, graduate student, conference assistant, and probably the fastest learner of the arcane UCSB financial and travel software; Audrey Francis, office assistant and a master of professional detail and cheerfulness; Vivian Hsaio, social media intern and creative designer of the conference posters and flyers; and Tammy Affifi, Professor and Chair, inspirational and energetic supporter and leader. Thanks to Graham Glass, Social Media Associate, UC Santa Barbara, Department of Communication for producing the book cover image, from the initial design by Walther and Rice.

Walter S. DeKeseredy, author of a chapter in this book, helped promote our book proposal to Routledge Books; Thomas Sutton, the publisher for the Criminology and Criminal Justice series for Routledge Books, provided immediate support and helpful advice, as did Jessica Phillips, Editorial Assistant, Criminology and Criminal Justice, Routledge Books; and the copyeditor Sutapa Mazumder and indexer Connie Angelo.

1

INTRODUCTION TO *SOCIAL PROCESSES* *OF ONLINE HATE*

Joseph B. Walther and Ronald E. Rice

In 1971, Murray Davis wrote an article in the *American Journal of Sociology*, titled "That's Interesting!" He argued that a lot of research may be good, and incrementally useful, but it is not necessarily *interesting*. What makes research interesting, he wrote, is when it defies intuition. When it asserts something that is the opposite of common knowledge. When it expresses a premise that conflicts with the accepted premises and then derives from these premises predictions and hypotheses that must be true if the premise is correct. Among the ways that research can be interesting, according to Davis, are the following:

- What seems to be a disorganized phenomenon is actually an organized phenomenon.
- What seems to be an individual phenomenon is in reality a holistic phenomenon.
- What seems uncorrelated is correlated.
- What is bad is in some way good.

That's interesting, according to Davis. We would add, to investigate that, and substantiate it, is not only interesting, it's important as well. Potentially groundbreaking. Paradigm-shifting.

Each of the scholars whose work appears in this volume is interesting. Their work is groundbreaking and paradigm-shifting. Each of them has discovered ways to prove that the production and propagation of hate messages on social media are not individual acts, not uncorrelated, not disorganized, but part of various social processes and systems. That people produce racist messages, sexist messages, and harassment, not only, or not even primarily,

DOI: 10.4324/9781003472148-1

to inflict harm to victims. Hate posters do it to engage in collective behavior, to get attention and admiration, to fit in, to advance a comforting (if deviant) virtual community, to perpetuate and respond to the negotiation of social norms, to entertain each other, and even to share in the fun of disparaging other people. It seems distasteful and misguided, if not downright evil, even to think about this form of verbal terrorism as being a source of fun for those who do it, but once you think it and ask yourself if it makes sense, you can't unthink it anymore.

The scholars whose work follows have found different ways of understanding how the spreading of hate online is not necessarily something that is expelled from the inside out, from a person's inner core of racism, distorted masculinity, personality, or that they are "bad actors," or that their messages are necessarily directed at an individual or group target. Rather, we learn from their work what the gratifications are that might appeal to anyone whose ego is threatened, who could use a scapegoat, who is otherwise depleted materially or emotionally, or who is afraid (justifiably or not) of being replaced, contaminated, or eliminated. Who finds that taking the role of a victim, or a prospective victim among other prospective victims, is comforting. And that being snarky, or witty, or clever, or scary, gets them liked by others who are willing to echo their sentiments. Gets them upvoted. Retweeted. Friended. Followed.

Of course, there has always been prejudice and there have always been hate messages, and social media didn't breathe them into existence. But social media changed the equation. The means of production. The affordances for exposing thoughts to others and being exposed to others' thoughts. The ease of collaboration. The ability to find and follow like-minded others. The ability to craft spontaneous-looking messages, sometimes in sequence, quite strategically and deliberately.

From a social processes approach to online hate, in some respects, the behavior is some weird manner of sport. A sport that requires no particular training or ability (and as several chapters show, the skills can be learned as one progresses on the team), where the team members support one another, where there are dozens or hundreds or even thousands of cheering spectators who applaud the players with Likes and Hearts and Upvotes and Retweets and cross-platform links, and fans, many of whom take their turns on the field as well.

Although we do not address what causes hate in the first place, we contend that the ebb and flow of its expression online is primarily influenced through social processes, not individuals and not personality traits. We cannot afford to allow ourselves to explain the expression of online hate as a product of a specific person's psychopathology or any other individual characteristics. We cannot afford to consider it sufficient to explain online hatred as merely a modern manifestation of existing in-group/out-group antipathies that simply manifest in new digital ways. To assume that it is a small number of atypical individuals. To assume that the people who write it and share it are evil. The reason we cannot afford to do this is that the mistake has been made before. If we simply dismiss its creators as bad actors or racists, we overlook subtle yet ultimately powerful social factors, magnified through social interactions and redistributed through digital social media, that can lead individuals into doing things they otherwise might not. A recent study titled "Anyone can become a troll: Causes of trolling behavior in online discussions" (Cheng et al., 2017) found that there are two triggers that can lead anyone to post hostile messages online: Being in a really bad mood and seeing other people posting hostile messages. So we do not dare attribute online aggression to a minority of inherently bad actors. We cannot afford to repeat the mistake of assuming there are only a small number of neo-Nazis (Woolf, 2008); there were only 60 Nazis in 1920, but there were 8.6 million Nazis by 1945, because of social pressures – because the dark corners of defamation and denigration seep into the mainstream, and because the opportunity to participate in a collective that allowed people to feel good about themselves by being superior to others can, for many, be almost too good to resist.

Nor do we address the question of whether online hate leads to offline aggression, although that outcome, and other harms befalling the victims of hate, implicitly drive our concern over the phenomenon itself (see Tong, this volume, for considerations of other outcomes). Understanding the social bases and effects of hate was for a time the utmost preoccupation of post-WWII social sciences. Might online hate stimulate desensitization to human suffering, a reinforcement of a sense of moral superiority, rationalizing peremptory self-defense to imagined threats, or ultimately to murder and hate crimes? Is physical aggression a byproduct or an outgrowth of the cultivation of social acceptance, community, and attention that, as several chapters in this book argue, may be at the heart of online hate messaging? On these questions, unfortunately, the implications of a social processes approach to online hate are mixed.

We know that online hate messaging can certainly provide logistical and operational communication that *facilitates* real-world, physical confrontations (Wahlström & Törnberg, 2021). Yet for all the bravado and calls for action that hate messages often express, as Törnberg and Törnberg (this volume) describe, the online discussions of White Nationalists more often reflect their resignation over the multiracial state of the society. Rather than plot offline aggression, Stormfront members verbally deconstruct just how the deplorable status quo came to be and what actions could have averted it but were not, in fact, taken.

We do not dismiss the possibility that participation in online hate messaging increases the propensity for offline violence, although we think it is important to learn more about when and why such a linkage may exist.

One possibility is that an individual's continued public espousal of hate in social media generates "self-effects" (see Valkenburg, 2017), a process by which individuals magnify the extremity of their own attitudes merely by expressing them to others, and by seeing those attitudes displayed in text and images. Add to self-effects the power of socially generated positive reinforcement in the form of social approval messages from others online (see, e.g., Walther et al., 2011, 2022), and it is even more likely that the hateful beliefs and attitudes one may have held mildly at some point become more extreme, even radicalized, through continued interaction (see, e.g., Burston, this volume).

Perhaps participation in online hate triggers predispositions toward violence that a small number of people possess (e.g., Dunbar & Molina, 2004; Lee et al., 2022). Such is the prospect of "stochastic terrorism" (Jones, in press; Nelson, 2022; Rae et al., this volume) by which influential individual(s) publicly "demonize and dehumanize groups of people" (Jones, in press, p. 1) in deliberate but implicit and ambiguous terms that hate group participants echo and amplify. Even if most participants do not perceive them as an actual call for violent action, a few extreme outliers do so, and it is these few who commit violence. According to Jones (in press, pp. 1–2):

> Researchers theorize that stochastic terrorism is nevertheless capable of statistical analysis the results of which positively correlates violence to hate speech; murders increase even if it cannot be determined when, where or how a particular murder will occur. Stochastic terrorism is the raison d'etre of hate groups.

Understanding this complex causal chain, and the role of online hate messages within it, is part of what makes an urgent case for understanding online hate as the culmination and reification of social processes.

Although the mechanisms by which online hate leads to offline aggression remain subject to further study, it appears that this kind of eventuality is the exception and not the rule. The authors of the chapters in this book argue and illuminate that, to a great extent, online hate posters are in the online hate business largely to have their own kind of enjoyment, to compete for status, cultivate a community, immerse themselves in the sexually and religiously tinged aspects of their cultures, and even to provide comfort among themselves, and not necessarily with the primary intent to inflict harm and hurt onto others. We feel it deserves renewed priority now that the Internet and social media have resurrected and magnified by orders of magnitude the threat that hate presents to minorities in particular and to civil society at large. It's important. Potentially groundbreaking. Paradigm-shifting. It is *interesting*, as Murray Davis (1971) might say. And it is urgent.

Background for the Book

This edited book is the product of our own various social processes and long-term interests. On May 11, 2023, the coeditors held a full-day public conference at University of California, Santa Barbara, involving leading scholars whose work addresses a "social processes" approach to online hate (https://www.comm.ucsb.edu/news-events/annual/rupe#2023RupeCITS). The event was sponsored by the Center for Information Technology and Society, the Bertelsen Presidential Chair in Technology and Society (Professor Joseph B. Walther), the Arthur N. Rupe Chair in the Social Effects of Mass Media (Professor Ronald E. Rice), and the UCSB Center for Black Studies Research.

We carefully selected outstanding researchers to participate in the conference, based on their prior work's consideration of social processes. Each participant presented their work in a half-hour session, followed by a question-and-answer session. As part of the overall project leading toward the book, the presenters provided drafts of their papers a week before the conference. After the one-day conference, we convened a workshop the next two days, during which we devoted considerable attention to deeper analysis and feedback for each chapter draft that participants had prepared. Each of these sessions involved the author's initial expansion about their work, followed by prepared reviews from two other participants, followed by additional, open feedback amongst the group. These were not formal reviews as for a journal, nor were they required to be written. In the following months, the authors and editors shared multiple revisions with each other, refining the arguments and clarifying the analyses and results.

The Chapters

The result of this extensive process of personal and mediated interactions, comments and responses, clarifications and extensions, and digressions and elaborations is this collection of superb contributions on various aspects of the social processes of online hate. The chapters include:

"Making a Case for a Social Processes Approach to Online Hate" by Dr. Joseph B. Walther argues that the audience of online hate messaging is other online haters, more so than the ostensible victims who the messages refer to. Compelling anecdotes and empirical studies on the language, placement, and other characteristics of online hate suggest that its primary purpose is to entertain and nurture relations among haters. Social processes better explain online hate than do traditional, personality-based approaches.

"Foundations, Definitions, and Directions in Online Hate Research" by Dr. Stephanie Tom Tong provides a comprehensive overview of findings related to the prevalence of online hate, its various content and message characteristics, and the effects of online hate on those who experience it. It offers a new taxonomy of hate messaging behavior depending on the targets and the publicness of social media hate.

"Misogyny and Woman Abuse in the Incelosphere: The Role of Online Incel Male Peer Support" by Dr. Walter S. DeKeseredy describes how incels, or involuntarily celibate males, use online community to share their invectives against "Stacys" (women who resist their sexual advances) and "Chads" (men who are sexually active). The chapter applies male peer support theory to explain how, online, participants console each other and rationalize one another's hatred toward others.

"From Echo Chambers to Digital Campfires: The Making of an Online Community of Hate in Stormfront" by Drs. Anton Törnberg and Petter Törnberg examines participation in one of the longest-standing interaction sites explicitly for White Nationalists, Stormfront.org. They describe how Stormfront provides its participants community through storytelling, and how new participants' language converges over time toward that of veteran users, as their expressions and worldviews about other races and religions become uniformly extreme.

" 'Deal' of the Day: Sex, Porn, and Political Hate on Social Media" by Dr. Sahana Udupa and Oeendrila Lahiri Gerold begins with an account of fake auctions of Muslim women online in India unbeknownst to the women whose pictures were stolen. The essay and its original data analyses explore the overlapping social forces of religious majoritarianism, the pornification of online culture, and other factors that feed hatred toward Muslims and women online, veiled in techno-entertainment and fun.

"Digitally Mediated Spillover as a Catalyst of Radicalization: How Digital Hate Movements Shape Conservative Youth Activism" by Adam Burston offers an in-depth look at how college campus club members become radicalized through the influence of new members who previously participated in alt-right social media. The evolution and ultimate dissolution of a college chapter parallel its adoption of and participation in online hate.

" 'Hate Parties': Networked Antisemitism from the Fringes to YouTube" by Drs. Stephen C. Rea, Binny Mathew, and Jordan Kraemer investigates cross-platform hate, when users post messages on a fringe platform linking to and encouraging comments on a different, mainstream platform. The strongest antisemitic fringe postings are linked not to Jewish messages but to antisemitic YouTube videos, where individuals posted additional disparaging remarks. The chapter shows how hate producers use multiple social media platforms to evade restrictions on message content that is prohibited on some platforms but not on others to keep a single conversation going in different social spaces.

"Information Sharing and Content Framing Across Multiple Platforms and Functional Roles That Exemplify Social Processes of Online Hate Groups" by Dr. Shruti Phadke and Dr. Tanushree Mitra examines how traditional, offline hate groups use Facebook and Twitter/X to create an online ecosphere of hate, misinformation, and conspiracies to grow their movements, cultivate new recruits, and spread their dogma.

"Detecting Antisocial Norms in Large-Scale Online Discussions" by Drs. Yotam Shmargad, Stephen A. Rains, Kevin Coe, Kate Kenski, and Steven Bethard look at antisocial commenting on news sites generally and on social network platforms during the January 6, 2020 attack on the U.S. Capitol. They describe how norms for toxic postings emerge through the patterns of encouragements, or "upvotes," others' toxic comments receive, and the effects of upvotes on one's own continued toxic postings.

"Understanding the Phases and Themes of Coordinated Online Aggression Attacks" by Dr. Gianluca Stringhini and Dr. Jeremy Blackburn examines sequences of events and emergent activities that occur in organized, deliberate, group-based efforts to attack victims with hate postings. They describe five stages of these attacks that are planned and managed on fringe platforms but carried out on mainstream platforms and the feedback loops that enhance and celebrate the attacks on YouTube or as "Zoombombing" efforts.

References

Burston, A. (Chapter 7 this volume). Digitally mediated spillover as a catalyst of radicalization: How digital hate movements shape conservative youth activism.

Cheng, J., Bernstein, M., Danescu-Niculescu-Mizil, C., & Leskovec, J. (2017). Anyone can become a troll: Causes of trolling behavior in online discussions. In *Proceedings of the 2017 ACM conference on computer supported cooperative work and social computing* (pp. 1217–1230). https://doi.org/10.1145/2998181.2998213

Davis, M. S. (1971). That's interesting! Towards a phenomenology of sociology and a sociology of phenomenology. *Philosophy of the Social Sciences, 1*(2), 309–344. https://doi.org/10.1177/004839317100100211

Dunbar, E., & Molina, A. (2004). Opposition to the legitimacy of hate crime laws: The role of argument acceptance, knowledge, individual differences, and peer influence. *Analyses of Social Issues and Public Policy, 4*(1), 91–113. https://doi.org/10.1111/j.1530-2415.2004.00036.x

Jones, D. K. (in press). Stochastic terrorism, speech incantations, and federal tax exemption. *New Mexico Law Review.* Preprint available ahead of publication in SSRN. https://papers.ssrn.com/abstract=4343878

Lee, S. M., Lampe, C., Prescott, J. J., & Schoenebeck, S. (2022). Characteristics of people who engage in online harassing behavior. In *Extended abstracts of the 2022 CHI conference on human factors in computing systems* (pp. 1–7). https://doi.org/10.1145/3491101.3519812

Nelson, B. (2022, November 5). How stochastic terrorism uses disgust to incite violence. *Scientific American.* https://www.scientificamerican.com/article/how-stochastic-terrorism-uses-disgust-to-incite-violence/

Rae, S., Mathhew, B., & Kraemer, J. (Chapter 8 this volume). "Hate Parties": Networked antisemitism from the fringes to YouTube.

Stringhini, G., & Blackburn, J. (Chapter 11 this volume). Understanding the phases of coordinated online aggression attacks.

Törnberg, A., & Törnberg, P. (Chapter 5 this volume). From echo chambers to digital campfires: The making of an online community of hate within Stormfront.

Valkenburg, P. (2017). Understanding self-effects in social media. *Human Communication Research*, *43*(4), 477–490. https://doi.org/10.1111/hcre.12113

Wahlström, M., & Törnberg, A. (2021). Social media mechanisms for right-wing political violence in the 21st century: Discursive opportunities, group dynamics, and co-ordination. *Terrorism and Political Violence*, *33*(4), 766–787. https://doi.org/10.1080/09546553.2019.1586676

Walther, J. B., Lew, Z., Edwards, A. L., & Quick, J. (2022). The effect of social approval on perceptions following social media message sharing applied to fake news. *Journal of Communication*, *72*(6), 661–674. https://doi.org/10.1093/joc/jqac033

Walther, J. B., Liang, Y. J., DeAndrea, D. C., Tong, S. T., Carr, C. T., Spottswood, E. L., & Amichai-Hamburger, Y. (2011). The effect of feedback on identity shift in computer-mediated communication. *Media Psychology*, *14*(1), 1–26. https://doi.org/10.1080/15213269.2010.547832

Woolf, L. M. (2008). The holocaust: Lessons not learned. *Peace Psychology*, *17*(2), 16–20. http://faculty.webster.edu/woolflm/HolocaustLessonsNotLearnedF08.pdf

2

MAKING A CASE FOR A SOCIAL PROCESSES APPROACH TO ONLINE HATE

Joseph B. Walther

The production and dissemination of an online hate message in social media are typically thought of as acts of aggression, perpetrated by an individual, in order to antagonize certain targets. Although "We don't usually think of online harassment as a social activity," according to Sarkeesian (2012; as cited in Marwick & Caplan, 2018, p. 545),

> we do know from the strategies and tactics that they used that they were not working alone, that they were actually loosely coordinating with one another. The social component is a powerful motivating factor that works to provide incentives for perpetrators to participate and to actually escalate the attacks by earning the praise and approval of their peers.

The expression of hate online is recognized as one of the biggest problems with social media: "major technology companies announced that they were taking unprecedented action against the hate speech . . . that had long flourished on their platforms . . . (yet) the level of online hate and harassment reported by users barely shifted" (Anti-Defamation League, 2018). Online hate includes racist, religious, anti-immigrant, or misogynistic comments and attacks on specific individuals' reputation, character, privacy, and safety. It takes forms indigenous to social media, such as doxxing, memes, and revenge porn, as well as conventional verbal attacks and threats based on race, ethnicity, gender, sexual orientation, political orientation, or other identity or personal characteristics.

There appear to be four major foci of research about online hate's proliferation in social media. These include (1) documenting the pervasiveness of online hate, (2) describing the contents and forms of hate messaging online,

DOI: 10.4324/9781003472148-2

(3) analyzing the effects of online hate on its victims, and (4) identifying the characteristics and motivations of people who propagate hate online, in efforts to explain the behavior. The first three areas appear to have occupied the most research attention to date. An overview of these foci and other trends in online hate research appears elsewhere in this collection (Tong, this volume). The focus of this chapter is on the fourth area – in particular, social motivations.

Why people express and propagate hate online and what motivations and gratifications impel people to create and share hateful social media postings have been understudied relative to the other research areas. There may be less attention to this question because people think the answer is simple and obvious: There are simply malicious people acting out, and U.S. free speech principles preclude stopping them. It seems, at least as far as the three other perspectives assume, that the problem is inherent and intractable and that there are bigots, racists, and "bad actors" in the world and online, who express their innate hatred as a more or less uninhibited expression of their feelings, to inflict suffering on the targets that are identified or alluded to in the messages.

An emerging, alternative explanation focuses on other motives and processes. This chapter develops the argument that online hate is produced as part of complex social processes among the hate messengers themselves. Exploring various social processes may provide a more comprehensive understanding of the production of online hate in social media. This perspective assumes that the patterns of interactive social behavior motivate, reinforce, magnify, and perpetuate the expression of hate online. Among its premises are the notion that online hate is socially organized; that is, it may be planned, managed, enacted, reinforced, diffused, and celebrated among networks of antagonists. It assumes that the production of hate messages has an audience, but it raises the question whether the audience is not only or even necessarily the ostensible victims of online hate messages but rather the "virtual community" of haters, themselves. It considers that hate is normalized and perpetuated through social support among hate posters. One line of argument even suggests that a primary purpose of hate messaging in social media is not necessarily to upset, insult, or terrorize those who appear to be the focus of the hate messages. Rather, the primary intended audience for online hate messages is other people who post online hate messages. The primary purpose of posting hate messages online is to garner social attention and social approval from other hate producers, to provide a sense of validation to one another, nurture their relationships and communities, and provide support and encouragement for one another. From this perspective, the individuals and groups that are the victims of online hate are often, tragically, collateral damage.

A social processes approach also considers the characteristics of social media that facilitate the social interactions leading to the collaborative creation and dispersion of hateful messages. Social media provide relatively unique methods and facilitate symbolic behaviors that streamline the generation of affirmations and congratulations for one's fellows' hostility. These and other new and provocative approaches to online hate have the potential to change our understanding of its production and its prevalence.

This chapter explicates several features and processes of online hate that demonstrate the vitality of a social processes approach to the phenomena. It will show that online hate messages often are delivered in venues and using symbolic codes that are unavailable or uninterpretable to the very targets that they denigrate, which supports the contention that hate messages' primary purpose is to commune with other hate posters in addition to, or even more so, than to antagonize victims.

The chapter follows with a discussion about the social organization of online hate, the existence of which gives further credence to the notion that hate is a social activity rather than the product of individuals' enmity. "Networked harassment" (Marwick, 2021) and cross-platform raids (see Stringhini & Blackburn, this volume) clearly indicate that online hate is often informally organized and coordinated among proponents, rather than being random, scattered, or coincidental dyadic activities, as one might expect them to be if online hate was simply intended to harm a victim or a social group. It will propose that a variety of socially based gratifications motivate, propel, and reinforce participation in the production and sharing of online hate. These include the suggestion that generating and spreading hate create enjoyment or fun, or solidarity and support, for those who engage in it. It describes the attraction to and easy conveyance of social approval signals in social media interactions, the getting of which may encourage the expression of hate and outrage among homophilous networked peers. It also considers research from related areas suggesting how beneficial social support processes emerge among hate producers in their encouragement and mutual exoneration of one another in hate communities. It follows by discussing how research that takes a social processes perspective may generate alternative means to mitigate online hate, and, finally, it addresses the question of whether online hate, as a social process, leads to offline confrontations and violence. Before laying out these observations and suggestions, however, is a short description of some more traditional explanatory perspectives about why people generate online hate and the identification of some shortcomings of those perspectives.

Traditional Explanations about the Production of Online Hate

Understanding the generation of online hate from a social processes perspective stands in contrast to a variety of individual-level trait-based and social identification-based approaches that are worth reviewing most briefly.

Individual Differences

The promulgation of online hate messaging is often attributed to individual differences, that is, to personality characteristics of the perpetrators. These characteristics may be as simple as the assumption that some people hold malevolent impulses (Quandt, 2018) or sadistic desires (Phillips, 2015). In other cases, they are more clinical, considering individual factors such as emotional instability; certain demographic characteristics and attitudes; and biases, prejudices, or the holding of stigmatizing beliefs and stereotypes that are often suggested to prime individuals toward hatred. "Unfortunately," according to a critique of trait-based research on hate production, "most of the literature on risk factors for hate-motivated behavior . . . lacks rigorous testing and empirical support" (Cramer et al., 2020; cf. Lee et al., 2022).

Some research indicates that individual differences are irrelevant and that "anyone can become a troll"; that is, ordinary people can easily be led to bully, harass, and insult others. As an example, an experiment by Cheng et al. (2017) employed 667 research participants recruited from Mechanical Turk and exposed them to comments from an online political discussion. Participants who they (1) exposed to other people's trolling, and (2) induced into a negative mood, were almost 200% more likely to write hate messages (e.g., "'What a dumb c***'" and . . . 'You're and idiot and one of the things that's wrong with this country'"; p. 1221) compared to participants in a control condition. This is not to suggest that online interaction causes individuals to become racists or bigots who would never otherwise be open to such attitudes. Rather, it is to suggest that once an individual takes the step into posting a hate message online, social processes may be a strong influence – perhaps the strongest – on their subsequent level of hate messaging. At the very least, interaction effects between dispositional tendencies, social media affordances, and social processes online can magnify the propensity to express hate online (and offline; see Woolf & Hulsizer, 2004).

Social Identification

In contrast to individual differences approaches lies social identification theory, which, in its simplest form, contends that people favor their in-group and denigrate an out-group. Identification with an in-group and seeing oneself as a member of that group improve one's esteem (Turner et al., 1987). People are attracted to the in-group and, by derivation, to all other in-group members, not because they know and like each other personally but because they all embody the central characteristics that the group values. Some theorists contend that members of an in-group can recognize some degree of inter-individual differences among in-group members, whereas others contend that in-group identification is depersonalized, that is, there is no salient individuality among in-group members, who are pragmatically interchangeable with one another, from this perspective. Attitudes and perceptions of out-groups, however, instill even greater depersonalization; out-groups seem homogenous, and their members are perceived to share (typically negative) stereotyped characteristics and motives uniformly (Hogg & Reid, 2006). Social identification moves a step further toward hate when the depersonalization of the out-group goes so far as to involve dehumanization, or the relegation of an out-group, or a race or ethnicity or sexual identity, as inherently inferior and subhuman (Haslam, 2006).

There is little question that in-group/out-group distinctions are strong and potentially powerful drivers of online hate perceptions and actions. Thus, for many online hate researchers, social identification theory suffices to explain the enmity that arises among haters toward those whom they hate. Hate messages that targets others, from this perspective, are the manifestation of in-group identification.

It can be said, however, that the social identification approach does not go far enough to explain the social dynamics of online hate, for several reasons. The expression of hate messages, from a social identification perspective, can be self-serving rather than socially dynamic. That is, one's declarations and denigrations of the out-group or of prototypical out-group members need not be public or provoke anyone's response to achieve their function. They merely must be made, in order for authors to stake their identity claims and to *self-categorize* (see Turner et al., 1987), that is, to perceive oneself as a group member like others. It is not necessary for social identification processes to occur for them to seek or participate in social interactions (although social interactions may reinforce the intergroup perceptions that have already been activated). Thus, hate messages in social media, from a strict interpretation of social identification theory, may be no more than soliloquies performed for oneself, or pubic testimonials, rather than influence messages. They may have esteem and belongingness value and affirm group membership, for oneself, whether or not they affect others, from a social identification perspective.[1] While numerous examples of online hate messages appear to satisfy the parameters of social identification (see below regarding in-group slang and symbols), it is theoretically likely that writing those in-group expressions may have dual purposes, both rededicating oneself to in-group identification while *also* facilitating social and interpersonal interactions, not just social identifications.

Intent to Harm

Whether more properly considered as a trait or as a state, the most common assumption in the literature and society at large is that individuals produce online hate messages out of an intention to antagonize, ostracize, or harm some target or victim. Aside from the group identification approach considered above, this assumption accompanies almost every consideration of online hate. The assumption seems to make so much intuitive sense that it is hardly challenged. Survey results about the prevalence of being victimized online suggest support for this contention:

> More than half of Americans younger than 30 (64%) have experienced online harassment, as have half of 30–59 year-olds, and a quarter of Americans older than 50; half of women (47%) say they think they have encountered harassment online because of their gender, whereas 18% of men who have been harassed online say the same. Similarly, about half or more Black (54%) or Hispanic online harassment targets (47%) say they were harassed due to their race or ethnicity, compared with 17% of White targets . . . 50% of lesbian, gay or bisexual adults who have been harassed online say they think it occurred because of their sexual orientation.
>
> (Vogels, 2021)

Nevertheless, the assumption that the sole or primary purpose of online hate is to harm victims becomes questionable when one considers other social motivations for the expression of hate. Alternative hypotheses come into view when we consider whether the primary audience for hate messages is other hate messengers.

Insulation: Of Haters, by Haters, for Haters

If hate proponents post messages in order to antagonize various targets, it stands to reason that the content of their messages should offer clearly hostile meanings to those targets and that they are posted in a way that is visible to those targets. However, at least two counterarguments exist. First, the anatomy of hate messages reveals considerable in-group symbology that is often unknown or uninterpretable by the targets. Second, hate mongers often retreat into more insulated virtual enclaves in which to post and share hate messages, where their supposed targets may be less and less likely to see their messages.

Symbology

Hate messages in social media often include symbols and phrases the meaning of which is understood almost exclusively among like-minded participants. Examples can be found in the international, pancultural list of racial slurs in the Racial Slur Database (http://rsdb.org/). A catalog of symbols and abbreviations that are frequently used by White Supremacists appears in the ADL's hate symbols database (ADL, n.d.; see also Qian et al., 2019). Certain graphics, such as the confederate flag or the Nazi *swastika*, are well recognized for White Supremacist connotations by insiders and outsiders alike. A simple rendering of what looks like the Iron Cross (✠) can suffice in the proper context. Other symbols, however, are more insidious and private, rendering them nearly indecipherable by outsiders, including the targets about whom the messages pertain. For instance:

> The number 14 is used by white supremacists as a shorthand reference to the so-called "14 Words," which is the most popular white supremacist slogan in the world: "We must secure the existence of our people and a future for white children."
>
> (ADL, n.d.)

The number 88 "is a white supremacist numerical code for 'Heil Hitler.' H is the eighth letter of the alphabet, so 88 = HH = Heil Hitler. One of the most common White Supremacist symbols, 88 is used throughout the movement." These coded elements often appear in messages, hashtags, and in the "handle" or username associated with a writer (see also De Koster & Houtman, 2008). A more subtle code construction consists of preceding and following someone's (((name))) with three parenthesis marks, which denotes that the subject is Jewish (see Hübscher & von Mering, 2022).

Cartoonish caricatures are also frequently used. Some are more universally understood, drawing on widespread, historical stereotypes, such as the so-called "Happy Merchant . . . a drawing of a Jewish man with heavily stereotyped facial features who is greedily rubbing his hands together" (ADL, n.d.). Others, such as Pepe the Frog, are more highly coded. Pepe the Frog is a green cartoonish character, often depicted as a sophisticate. Despite an emphatic disavowal of hate by the cartoon's original creator (Furie, 2016), social media users frequently appropriate the image for insertion in memes, for example, with Pepe the Frog nonchalantly overseeing cruelty to immigrants, Mexicans, Jews, or other minorities. These culturally coded symbols reinforce the identities of those who share them while excluding those who do not, including those to whom the hate messages in which they appear often refer.

Placement Venues

Widely accessible, mainstream social media platforms like X.com (formerly Twitter) and Facebook, with highly diverse user bases, are frequent venues for White Supremacist and other online hate promoters. "For white supremacists that want to make sport out of harassing people of color, Twitter is a 'target rich' environment . . . [with] lots of people of color to target," according to Daniels (2017). If we question whether harassing people is the primary goal of online hate and hypothesize that interaction among like-minded haters provides the primary reward, then diverse "target-rich" social media environments may be, in fact, less desirable arenas in which to exchange online hate. Some trends suggest that online hate mongers favor more insulated messaging venues, where prospective victims are less likely, rather than more likely, to go.

Insulation

Indeed, research documents the migration of online hate production from wide open conversational spaces into more secluded enclaves. Attempts by various social media platforms to deter online hate messaging seem not to reduce the presence of online hate on the Internet but only to chase it from one venue to another, farther and farther from view by those to whom it refers. For instance, Facebook's attempts to eliminate hate speech (and other offensive postings) have led the purveyors of hate messaging into more insulated virtual bunkers within Facebook itself. In 2018, when the platform removed postings or suspended individuals who violated rules against hate messaging, the activity "went underground": Many hate messengers, conspiracy mongers, and political extremists migrated from posting on public Facebook *pages* into posting within private Facebook *groups* (Albright, 2018). Despite the size of their membership, sometimes in the thousands or tens of thousands, participation in Facebook groups is by invitation only. They can be hidden from the general Facebook-using public. According to Albright (2018), "individual posts, photos, events, and files shared within these groups are generally not discoverable through Facebook's standard search feature or through the APIs that allow content to be retrieved from public pages." In other words, by using private Facebook groups, hate messages *about* various targets are hidden from likely being viewed *by* those very targets.

Content moderation and suspensions, or fear of them, drive whole communities to alternative platforms where moderation is either lax or deliberately nonexistent. Mitts (2021) reported that efforts by Facebook and Google to block or remove hateful and extremist content, and account suspensions on Twitter for similar reasons, corresponded to increased hate messaging on alternative, so-called "fringe" platforms that do not moderate the hate content (see Rae et al., this volume), including Gab Social and others. Individuals who had accounts both on Twitter and on Gab, Mitts showed, clearly showed migration from one platform to the other, accompanied by significant increases in messages that promote white supremacy and express hate toward minority groups. Gab welcomes people to the site by describing itself as "the home of free speech" (*Gab.com – Gab Social*, n.d.). It "takes pride in its openness to all types of content, including hate speech," according to Mitts (2021, p. 3). CNN described Gab as "a favorite of bigots and hate groups. People who get banned from mainstream sites like Twitter for hate speech or harassment sometimes end up on Gab" (Stetter & Murphy, 2018). Although there are discussion groups and hashtags that appear to support others, such as Jewish interests and BLM groups, there is easily found racist vitriol. As of this writing, for instance, there are seven discoverable variations on Gab of the username, HitlerWasRight, whose comments are, unsurprisingly, hateful.

One might suspect that the seclusion and insulation of hate messages from the targets that they denigrate is, for hate posters, merely an unfortunate byproduct of their needing to avoid stricter content moderation; that if hate posters had their preferences, they would post the same messages in more mainstream, "target-rich" environments rather than the fringe sites to which they have fled. The important point here, however, is that the hate messages persist in these fringe spaces, despite the far smaller likelihood that their targets will encounter them. If the sole purpose of online hate messages was to antagonize victims, then the scarce presence of prospective victims to read them would make posting hate messages quite moot and eventually extinguish. Their persistence, away from ostensible victims' eyes, challenges the notion that they are siloed from their targets by necessity alone.

Indeed, hate posters seem to take advantage of the relative separation from the presence of their messages' ostensible targets. ElSherief et al. (2018) discovered differences in the language between *directed hate* messages (that are addressed *to* specific targeted individuals) versus *generalized hate* messages (that express hate *about* particular groups or persons). The researchers found that, compared to directed hate, generalized hate messages more frequently used collective terms "such as Jews, Muslims, Christians, Hindus, Shia, Madina, and Hammas" (p. 47), as well as "they" rather than "we," as would be expected. But there were other, less intuitively obvious language differences, as well. Generalized hate messages *about* rather than *to* the targets also contained more references to killing, murder, and extermination. These findings strongly suggest that hate posters know to whom they are writing and that their audience is not the same as their targets in many very clear cases.

Audience Specification

It is also clear from hate messages' implicit and explicit indications of to whom they are addressed that they are meant for other hate posters. For instance, Gab hosts a variety of meme repositories the contents of which are often so derogatory about the people they target that it seems extremely unlikely that targeted groups and individuals would wish to peruse them. Beyond leaving it to chance, however, the visual and verbal contents of these entries often explicitly signal that they are addressed to an audience of white people, and what target group they denigrate. They are clearly labeled anti-Muslim, anti-Jewish, and the N**ger Meme Repository, among others. The example meme displayed in Figure 2.1 explicitly specifies its audience

FIGURE 2.1 Antisemitic Meme

and its target quite clearly: It is explicitly addressed to "WHITE MAN," saying that the Zionist Jew is out to "DESTROY YOU."

These virtual spaces clearly seem to be for the amusement of their creators and admirers only; the meme repositories do not comprise interactive message postings but, rather, consist of a display of the memes. In other words, they are not posted in a way that would intrude upon and antagonize someone involuntarily or by surprise. They are not presented *to* the targets.

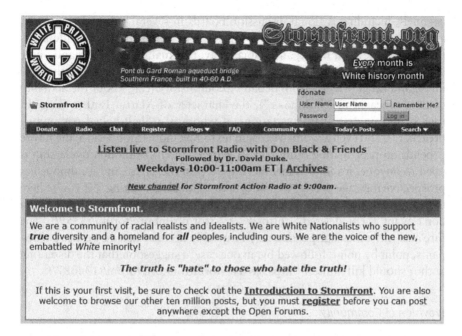

FIGURE 2.2   Stormfront.org Homepage

⚠ **Welcome: Guidelines for Posting**

Welcome to the Stormfront discussion board!

Our mission is to provide information not available in the controlled news media and to build a community of White activists working for the survival of our people.

FIGURE 2.3   Welcome to Stormfront Discussion Board

In these ways, extreme hate messengers migrate to channels that are more insulated not only from the mainstream but also from the very targets of their messages' denigration.

More obvious, deliberate insulation appears in traditional White Supremacists' online territories. Stormfront.org is "the oldest and most visited web-forum" for racist hate messaging, where Jewish, Black, and LGBTQ communities are the primary "'racial enemies'" (Scrivens et al., 2020, p. 217).[2] It displays a graphic on its homepage (Figure 2.2) saying, "WHITE PRIDE WORLD WIDE"; "We are White Nationalists," it says; "We are the voice of the embattled White minority!" (stormfront.org/forum).

There is no ambiguity that White Supremacists are its intended contributors and consumers (Figure 2.3). Its discussion boards offer hundreds of topical channels, including regional discussion boards in several national languages, and it claims to host over 13 million posts. The comments on the site focus primarily on Jewish; Black; and lesbian, gay, bisexual, transgender, and queer (LGBTQ) communities (Scrivens et al., 2020; Törnberg & Törnberg, this volume); and range widely, from debates about history (e.g., about the actuality of the holocaust or "holohoax"), the character of Martin Luther King, Jr. (one of the mildest characterizations of whom is a "half-baked communist preacher"), and even a women's forum (extolling motherhood, since the future depends on propagating more racially pure children). Although readership is open to anyone, it requires membership to post messages, and it admonishes prospective message posters to conform to its ideology, stating, "If you're here to argue with us, confine your posts to the 'Opposing Views' forum if you don't want them deleted" (https://www.stormfront.org/forum/t4359/). The rare anti-racist message posting may be quickly deconstructed by other participants, point by point, followed by, in one case, a suggestion that the dissenting author should kill himself (https://www.stormfront.org/forum/t134087/).

Provision of Community

Research on the appeal of Stormfront to its users suggests, again, that the social processes taking place among them are central. Positive social dynamics among the White Supremacist users themselves drives the platform's massive use, rather than any facility to antagonize minority targets within it. Research finds that some of its right-wing extremist users are stigmatized in their offline lives, when they espouse the views offline that Stormfront, in contrast, welcomes. As a result, Stormfront members "can express themselves freely, and generally feel accepted by the others" (De Koster & Houtman, 2008, p. 1166), experience camaraderie, and enjoy a sense of community. In some cases, they come to know each other as individuals and develop interpersonal relationships online, in ways more refined than simple in-group identification; some members remember one another's birthdays and offer support and comfort to one another in response to "unpleasant events in their offline lives" (p. 1167). We will return to the issue of relationships and community among hate producers later in this chapter. The platform is more dedicated to reciprocal discussion and denigration of others than to the delivery of messages or physical inflictions upon them. According to observers of a Dutch-speaking subgroup of Stormfront users, an occasional proponent who tries to recruit assistance among Stormfront colleagues to instigate offline harassment toward some target is rarely if ever successful in mobilizing accomplices. Other studies indicate that there may be two different types of Stormfront extremists, all of whom seem to share similar ideological beliefs: Those who are unlikely ever to engage in offline violence and a tiny minority who actually engage in physical violence offline. Interestingly, those who evolve into physical violence tend to post relatively *less* frequently in publicly accessible venues like Stormfront (Scrivens et al., 2023).

The point to be made here is that the online enclaves in which hate producers and consumers do so much of their messaging are relatively isolated from those about whom they post. This arrangement leads to the conclusion that their messaging is socially motivated for the benefit and enjoyment of persons like themselves rather than being intended for delivery to victims. Although there remains abundant hate and harassment in the "target-rich" environments of X/Twitter and other mainstream social media sites, the exodus of hate posters into more fringe social media venues that welcome hate messages strongly suggests that target practice is not the only point of online hate messaging. It may not even be the main point, considering the sense of commonality, camaraderie, and connection that virtual communities of hate mongers provide for each other. So, while a 2005 analysis of White Supremacist websites concluded that "it is impossible to know who the White supremacist writers perceived their audience to be" (Douglas et al., 2005, p. 70), that notion now seems implausible given the turn to social media and its ability to segment and insulate White Supremacists from both the mainstream and from their targeted populations. It seems far more likely that White Supremacists, in many online spaces, knowingly write for, and engage with, one another.

The Social Organization of Hate Attacks

When considering that there may be different audiences for online messaging, it stands to reason that there may be two kinds of online hate messages with two different purposes. One kind, as suggested above, promotes rewarding social interactions among online hate purveyors. Another kind of messages are crafted intentionally to be delivered to and to terrorize their victims, which is the traditional assumption about all online hate. Regarding the latter, Munger (2017) describes a method for detecting an individually targeted hate message in Twitter. If a message includes an ampersat (@ sign) connected to a specific username, that user is likely to be notified that their handle has been mentioned. They will see that they have been identified as a subject of the message. In Munger's work, a Tweet that combined the n-word, a second-person "you," and a @username was classified as a hate message.

While this type of message no doubt occurs frequently, it may not be as narrowly focused as it seems. As was the case in Munger's study, a great deal of what appear to be individually directed hate messages may, in fact, be primarily intended for a greater audience of hate perpetrators.

Consider how hashtags provide a means by which a hate poster can publicly deride a specific, named target, in a way that reaches many onlookers. Hashtags can both attract like-minded peers and repel outsiders, too (e.g.,

"#whitepower, #blackpeoplesuck, #nomuslimrefugees"; ElSherief et al., 2018, p. 44). Individuals also follow hashtags to get notifications (on their device's home screens, e.g., or each time they log into a platform) about the existence of new messages on the topic. In that manner, including a popular, controversial hashtag in a hate message increases the chances that targets *as well as accomplices* will see it.

Marwick (2021) provides compelling accounts showing how large groups of online haters collectively descend on individual targets in a coordinated manner, delivering "networked harassment." Networked harassment occurs when a group of online friends, followers, or online acquaintances, held together by hashtags, gaming channels, or other social network structures, gangs up on, "swarms," or "raids" an individual victim (see also Han et al., 2023). The individually targeted forms of harassment executed by members of such a collective can be quite severe, such as "doxxing (publishing personal information online), revenge porn (spreading intimate photos beyond their origins) . . . social shaming, and intimidation" (Marwick & Caplan, 2018, p. 544), as well as rape threats and death threats.

Marwick depicts networked harassment following these typical steps. It begins when one agent accuses some specific target individual of some offense that deserves retribution. The accusation may be echoed by other agents who substantiate the offense for a social-network-connected, ideologically similar audience online. These audience members then "send ad hominem attacks, insults, slurs, and in the worst cases, threats of death, rape, and violence to the accused (brigading, dogpiling, or 'calling out')" (Marwick, 2021, p. 5). A recent example describes how a university instructor scheduled a "provocatively titled . . . anthropology course . . . 'The Problem of Whiteness.'" A student (who had thousands of Twitter followers) derided the prospective course online, along with posting the instructor's photo and email address. The instructor's "inbox exploded . . . with vitriolic messages from dozens of strangers. One wrote that she was 'deeply evil.' Another: 'Blow your head clean off'" (Patel, 2023). The instructor cancelled the course.

Although these descriptions and anecdotes are compelling, the social aspects of online hate and networked harassment at broad scale are also empirically reflected in studies that employ tools for formal social network analysis. Large-scale analyses of who follows whom, who retweets whom, and how specific linguistic combinations cascade through a social media platform show the abstract interconnection among users, sometimes tens of thousands at a time (Jiang et al., 2022). The degree to which many potentially connected participants observe one another's postings is most probably low and is affected by the selection algorithms within social media platforms (see Bartley et al., 2021). Nevertheless, sophisticated "infodemiological analysis" has detected online hate communities within Twitter that exhibit greater organization over time, their degree of interconnectedness being influenced by events in the wider social and political world (Uyheng & Carley, 2021). Other network-analytic research that examined shared vocabulary, retweets, and interactions among users discovered "an online community of over 22,000 Twitter users whose online behavior directly advocates support for ISIS or contributes to the group's propaganda dissemination through retweets" (Benigni et al., 2017, p. 1). Facebook's hate detection and prediction systems analyze not only individuals' history of hate messaging to determine whether an account suspension might be appropriate but also the messaging of individuals' close social network ties to inform its predictions about the likelihood that an individual will violate behavioral standards by posting hate messages again (Halevy et al., 2022).

Whether networked harassment involves relatively small numbers of network participants or exceptionally large ideological groups, the very existence of networked harassment is further evidence that online hate is generally not the action of unconnected and uncoordinated "lone wolves" who may share the same ideology but who act autonomously motivated only by the desire for *Schadenfreude*. Even supposed lone-wolf terrorists, research shows, are connected to hate communities online (Weimann, 2012). The phenomenon of networked harassment demonstrates that online hate is a product of social processes, including normative social influences among and between hate posters, motivating them to act in systematic collective efforts, to preserve (their view of) the moral order in a loosely coordinated manner.

So far, this view of networked harassment describes the dynamics of participation as one-way attacks by group members on single targets who are the only observers of the attacks. Marwick's analysis of networked harassment does not consider that the mobilized network members do more than attack, concurrently but separately, when she says, "Networked harassment involves many individuals sending messages, emails, or phone calls within a relatively short amount of time" (Marwick, 2021, p. 8; Marwick & Caplan, 2018). Each of these media facilitates dyadic one-to-one messaging. The social factors involved in networked harassment do more than facilitate a temporally bound barrage of one-way hate messages, however. Social media and network characteristics facilitate the observation of each attack by others, displaying all antagonists' piled-on content. Indeed, elsewhere in Marwick's accounts, she suggests that audience members attack targets using channels that are public and in sight of one another. Said one of Marwick's interview informants, " 'One time I found a Reddit thread that was about bashing me'" (p. 8). Elsewhere, a U.S. Congressional representative who had criticized the prevalence of antisemitism on Twitter later reported, " 'the reply section of my post was flooded with hateful, antisemitic comments and images'" (Treene & O'Sullivan, 2023). The promulgation of networked harassment using social network sites clearly suggests that the participants are also part of the audience: They see how one another insults the target. It can only be by mutual observation that, as the quotation at the beginning of this chapter suggested, they "escalate the attacks by earning the praise and approval of their peers" (Sarkeesian, 2012).

Cross-Platform Hate Demonstrates Social Coordination

In addition to Marwick's description of networked harassment, other research demonstrates that online hate often appears as collective action through social coordination. Several studies document the operation of hate activities that operated across social media platforms. When an instigator plans and recruits collaborators within one platform, and they carry out an attack against targets on another platform, it is again clear that online hate is not a spontaneous act by isolated individuals but a result of coordinated social processes (see the chapters by Phadke & Mitra, this volume; and Rae et al., this volume). One of the most notorious multiplatform hate incidents, in 2014, became known as #Gamergate, a thumbnail summary of which (Eckert & Metzger-Riftkin, 2020, p. 273) indicates that it was a coordinated online harassment campaign . . .

> . . . specifically targeting women through a release of their personal information online, leading to massive and sustained attacks online and offline. #Gamergate was a reaction by misogynist video game enthusiasts against perceived favoritism towards women in gaming journalism. For months, harassers sent feminist activists and game developers Zoe Quinn, Anita Sarkeesian, and Brianna Wu abusive messages, defaced their online spaces, and hacked their accounts.

The campaign involved interaction across a variety of social media platforms, including 4chan, Twitter, Reddit, and Internet Relay Chat (Lewis et al., 2021; Tsapatsoulis & Anastasopoulou, 2019).

Other cases illuminate additional ways by which hate posters socially coordinate across specific platforms in well-worn patterns, using tacit, highly recognized signals. Mariconti et al. (2019) describe how "raids" by multiple attackers are instigated on 4chan against specific YouTube videos:

> A prototypical raid begins with a user finding a YouTube video and posting a link to it on a third party community, e.g., 4chan's /pol/.[3] In some cases, the original poster, or another user, might also write comments like "you know what to do." Shortly after, the YouTube video starts receiving a large number of negative and hateful comments.
>
> (p. 2)

Whether or not it seems so to the recipient of the hate messages, it is "obvious to an outside observer . . . that these comments are part of an organized attack." Such patterns have been well-documented and illuminated using temporal cross-platform analyses of postings (Hine et al., 2017). Even more social organization and social gratification may yet follow a raid: Raiders have been found to return to the 4chan space where the raid had originally been organized in order to brag to one another about their hate postings on YouTube (Mariconti et al., 2019; Stringhini & Blackburn, this volume). These findings indicate that many forms of networked harassment are more circular than they are linear: On top of posting hate messages where they are visible to the victim, the public, and one another, hate posters circle back to the original point where social organization instigated, presumably for "exchanging online 'high fives'" (Udupa, 2019, p. 3151).

In sum, a number of accounts and analyses point to the public nature of otherwise "directed" hate messages in which groups of hate posters act in a coordinated manner to instigate and execute a raid or swarm that targets a specific individual (see also Tong's typology, this volume). Even though they are created using affordances such as @usernames to increase the chances that their individual target sees them, in most cases they do not transmit their messages only privately to their target. They post them where others also see them, where others can observe, comment upon, "like" one another's hate postings, and even, at times, celebrate them together. It is therefore important to reconsider ElSherief et al.'s (2018) classification of online hate messages as *either* generalized *or* directed. When hate messages that target a specific target person are posted for an additional, wider audience, the reward from doing so comes not, or not only, from the infliction of trauma to a specific victim. Rather, the reward may also be the attention they get from like-minded peers, the social approval that they cull, and the *enhancement* to the recognition and status they hold as they torture their target. "Bullies are aggregated together and (increase) their popularity by following each other," asserted Tsapatsoulis and Anastasopoulou (2019, p. 3). Their "directed" hate messages are, in that sense, performative.

Social Gratifications of Online Hate

This chapter has alluded to various gratifications that the creators and disseminators of online hate messages may enjoy, derived from social interactions among haters themselves. These social gratifications may be so influential that the anticipation of their acquisition is among the primary motivators for participation in online hate. Such social gratifications, moreover, may serve as a powerful reinforcer, impelling hate posters to continue and perhaps escalate their production of online hate messaging and the social benefits it garners. Among these potential gratifications, the literature suggests, are having fun, acquiring social approval, and sustaining social support.

Fun

It is difficult to reconcile the revulsion most people experience when encountering online hate messages, with the notion that they are fun or funny in any way. Udupa (2019), however, convincingly argues that, from the perspective of participants who engage in public online attacks against others, having fun with others is a primary motivation and reward. In the context of Indian Hindu nationalism, Udupa contends, adherents find that its "exclusivist ideology is rendered acceptable and enjoyable" and it is made visible in online posts conveying "the visceral aspects of fun and enjoyment that constitute right-wing mobilization" (Udupa, 2019, p. 3144).

The efforts to have fun and be funny online, in the manner Udupa describes, account very well for features of online hate messages we recognize in other contexts as well. The original site of Udupa's inquiry involves a conflation of majority politics with religious discrimination in India, and this underlying dynamic may or may not be seen as strongly in other settings (such as far-right American Christian conservatives online). Nevertheless, in many online settings, antagonists lampoon, ridicule, or caricature their individual or identity group targets. They often attempt to be witty or over-the-top or make hyperbolic comparisons. Other examples in Udupa's account include publicly deriding an opponent by "creating memes, tweets, and Facebook texts to offer repetitive summaries of [one's own] ideology" and confronting "opposing views with an arsenal of stinging ridicule, accusations, and abuse, riding on a wave of online vitriol" (Udupa, 2019, p. 3150; see also Udupa & Gerold, this volume).

These fun activities are reinforced socially in several ways. Being funny is reflected in others' online comments and reactions to one's postings. Successfully impressing others is reflected in one's posts being shared, "liked," and going viral. These practices of fun, such as "fact-checking, argumentative confrontations, assembly, and aggression" (Udupa, 2019, p. 3144), it is worth noting, seem to describe very well many discussions within Stormfront, as well as in mainstream social media platforms when it is allowed to flourish there.

The meta-practice of fun in the propagation of online hate could hardly be clearer than in the cover screen introducing a meme collection on Gab, the "new n**ger meme repository" (Figure 2.4). It describes the contents of the collection as being "FUNNY AS HELL," and it encourages people to ask their friends to join the group.

There are analogous frames and states, in addition to the notion of "fun," which propel the exchange of ideas online that are repudiated by the public majority. Recent research suggests that participating in the propagation of online conspiracy theories garners emotional arousal and excitement. Moreover, "conspiracy theory very often goes hand in hand with racism – anti-Black racism, anti-immigrant racism, antisemitism and Islamophobia" (Schaefer,

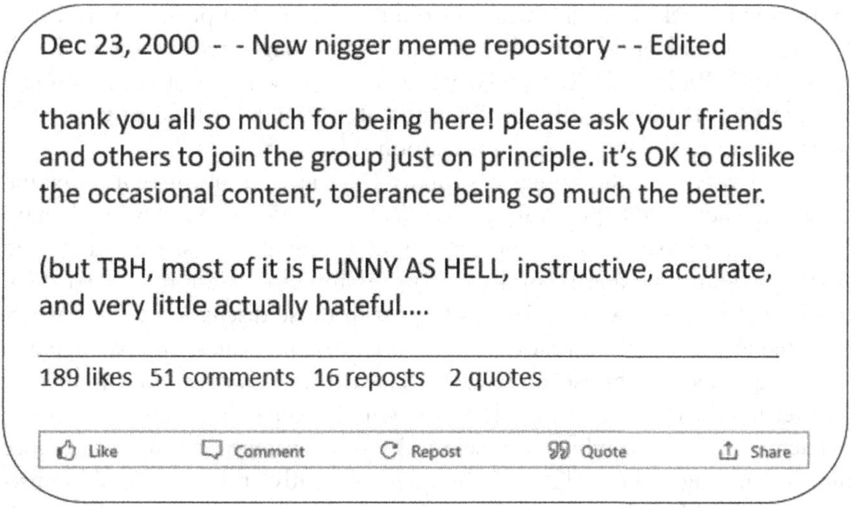

Dec 23, 2000 - - New nigger meme repository - - Edited

thank you all so much for being here! please ask your friends and others to join the group just on principle. it's OK to dislike the occasional content, tolerance being so much the better.

(but TBH, most of it is FUNNY AS HELL, instructive, accurate, and very little actually hateful....

189 likes 51 comments 16 reposts 2 quotes

🖒 Like   💬 Comment   🔁 Repost   99 Quote   ⬆ Share

FIGURE 2.4   Quoted Text from Welcome Screen for Gab's New N**ger Meme Repository, from https://gab.com/sopan123/posts/105431828772012713

2022; see also Jolley & Douglas, 2019). Conspiracy theorists revel in sharing with each other clues and so-called evidence that, they claim, reveal hidden meanings in otherwise well-known public statements and events. In doing so, they feel as though they are smarter than the vast majority of other people. They "encourage their followers to see themselves as the only ones with their eyes open," according to Schaefer (2022), who observes that conspiracy theorists endeavor not to find the most plausible interpretation of evidence but "the one that's most fun."

Social Approval Seeking and Getting

Recent scholarship has advanced a new theory of online hate that highlights very specific social processes as providing certain motivation and reinforcement for participating in hate messaging. A social approval theory of online hate (Walther, 2022) focuses on the way haters receive confirmation and social rewards for their actions, particularly through the streamlined process of communicating social approval that social media platforms readily afford.

Social media allow users to transmit social approval signals in a variety of ways. One can always comment on another's posting, stating agreement or appreciation in verbal prose, which increases message posters' satisfaction with online interactions (Sannon et al., 2017). Social media also frequently offer "one-click" generation of iconic social approval signals, such as the thumbs-up "like" in Facebook, the heart-shaped "favorite" in Twitter, the Upvote in Reddit, and similar signals (Hayes et al., 2016). People are motivated to seek these gratifications online and react in positive ways, psychologically and physiologically, when their messages receive them (Reich et al., 2022; Wolf et al., 2015). They are "social rewards" connoting "social acceptance" (Rosenthal-von der Pütten et al., 2019, p. 76), improving one's social standing and emotional gratification (Hayes et al., 2016).

Several recent studies suggest support for the contention that receiving these one-click social approval signals affects people's perceptions and behavior with regard to destructive messages online. One of these studies immersed participants in an experimental mock-up online discussion and asked them to select among pre-written Tweets to post in those discussions. The Tweets reflected either moral outrage messages or neutral messages, and participants were requested to choose the Tweet that would maximize the number of Twitter-like hearts that their selections would receive. The more hearts the participants received when they selected moral outrage messages, the more outrage messages they selected subsequently (Brady et al., 2021). A nonexperimental field study replicated these findings by examining naturally occurring patterns on Twitter. Researchers identified Tweets reflecting "moral outrage" (comprising hate messages or other messages that also reflected "emotions such as anger, disgust, and contempt . . . blaming people/events/things, holding them responsible, or wanting to punish them"; Brady et al., 2021, p. 2) and the number of hearts those messages spontaneously received from other Twitter users. Results indicated that the number of hearts the outrage expressions received on one day was positively associated with the number of outrage messages their authors posted the next. A somewhat similar study found that individuals who retweeted a negative fake news story about a politician from the opposite political party than their own came to dislike that politician more as a function of the number of hearts their retweet received (Walther et al., 2022).

Another study examined the effect of receiving upvotes or downvotes to one's toxic comments on Reddit. In short, upvotes encouraged more frequent toxic messages (Shmargad et al., 2020). More detail and additional studies by the authors of that research appear in this volume's chapter by Shmargad et al. These studies provide important, empirical evidence suggesting that social factors impel the expression of online hate through the seeking and getting of social approval signals through symbols that are somewhat unique to social media platforms.

Social Support

Another form of social approval and affiliation that may arise in the production and propagation of online hate appears as social support among hate producers. In the research literature, social support is communication and deed-doing by which people provide help, consolation, information, and empathy toward other people facing trauma, illness, or distress. Social support, effectively delivered, is associated with a number of psychosocial aspects of well-being and improvements in self-esteem and coping. This "prosocial" activity seems far-removed from the negativity of online hate, unless we consider the perceptions of threat and danger and the offline stigmatization experienced by people who engage in conventionally antisocial behavior such as hate messaging.

The application of social support theory to those engaged in conventionally antisocial behavior is only recently coming into view. Previously, DeKeseredy and his associates (see DeKeseredy & Schwartz, 2013) have developed a version of social support theory that explains the perpetration of domestic violence by men toward female relationship partners in offline settings. This line of work has been developed through expensive research, the complexities of which are beyond the bounds of this particular chapter. The crux of the theorizing may well apply beyond domestic violence, however. It holds that participants in these actions communicate with one another about the process. They teach each other how to do it. Most importantly, they help each other rationalize the actions and exonerate one another for engaging in them. They provide empathy and understanding to one another for behaviors that are often reacted to with disgust and abhorrence in their normal social circles.

These notions of social support among people who may be unlikely to find support elsewhere in their lives, and the emotional benefits of receiving it, map onto some of what we see in online hate communities as well. Recall the description of Stormfront participants described earlier in this chapter, who "can express themselves freely, and generally feel accepted by the others" (De Koster & Houtman, 2008, p. 1166), and, as we said, experience camaraderie, and enjoy a sense of community. DeKeseredy and Schwartz (2016) applied these principles to one form of online hate, the exchange of image-based involuntary sexual abuse, commonly referred to as "revenge porn." Although this phenomenon is frequently thought of as a dyadic targeted phenomenon, in which one individual terrorizes a single victim, it is distinctly social in several respects: First, such photos are only effective in humiliating their target when they are widely shared and linked to a distinctly social process. Second, as DeKeseredy and Schwartz discovered, there are online communities the members of which archive, curate, and mutually aid one another in their efforts to spread these specimens widely, and complement one another for having contributed. Recent research shows similar patterns of social support among *incels* – involuntarily celibate men who resent and espouse violent derision toward women – across multiple social media such as YouTube and discussion boards (DeKeseredy, this volume). These networks of support, empathy, and community provide significant attraction and gratification for engaging socially in online hate with other participants.

Implications for Intervention Research

Understanding the social processes conducive to the production of online hate may provide potentially valuable insights for how to try to reduce its prevalence. As the opening of this chapter indicated, the three most frequently studied areas in online hate research include documenting its pervasiveness, describing the contents, and examining its effects on recipients. These approaches follow from a presumption that the impetus to produce and post online hate is a given, a natural, and intractable outcome of personalities and previously developed intergroup enmity. As such, research and development related to "content moderation" seek to discern what the most effective ways are of making it go away through persuasion (Hangartner et al., 2021; Munger, 2017), deletion, and/or various punishments such as account suspension (see for review Schoenebeck et al., 2021; for a review of different countries' content restrictions and enforcements, see Gillespie, 2018), rather than by intervening in or disrupting social processes.

Approaching online hate as a social process suggests alternative approaches, and future research should investigate possible social-process-based interventions. For instance, if hate producers are motivated by attention and social approval, interventions such as "shadow banning" (see Jaidka et al., 2023) may thwart them, making a "user invisible to every other user, while to the offender it appeared as everything was functioning normally . . . [but] getting no reactions from anybody else" (Gillespie, 2022, p. 487) and thereby depriving hate message posters of the social attention that fuels their activity.[4] Such measures might be even more effective if they were to be coupled with recommendations from social network analyses: Blocking a single, critical individual – a node in a hate network – should reduce the propagation of hate messaging (Alorainy et al., 2022).

Other technical approaches might reduce cross-platform hate raids, following suggestions by Rae et al. (this volume): Social media platforms can "refuse entry" to their site by users from coming to their platform from a site that is known to foment raids. "Referrer log data" additionally show if such users arrive to one's site after typing in its address, or whether (as in the case of a cross-platform raid) users come via a link that was posted on their other site (see Burton & Walther, 2001).

In contrast, at least in countries and on platforms where unfettered freedom of expression is valorized, reducing the propagation of online hate messaging may be beyond platforms' ability to affect. Remedies to online hate, especially hate toward women, may be needed in offline societal, legal, and educational mores (DeKeseredy, this volume). Attitudes leading to the production of online hate messaging may be embedded in complex, multilayered structures involving majoritarianism, religious stereotypes, cultural values, and pornification of gender relations, as argued by Udupa and Gerold (this volume). It may be that online hate is a reflection rather than a cause of increasingly negative political partisanship (Abramowitz & Webster, 2016). This is not a suggestion that the investigation of the causes and remedies of online hate is futile. To give up the search is to give up on further understanding of an undesirable side of human nature. To give up is to become complacent over the potential magnification of extremism, the continued acceptance of discrimination and injustice, and the potential for violence that may be an indirect result of increasingly hateful communication.

A social processes approach to the social gratifications that play a large role in individuals' motivations to post online hate can be criticized as drawing focus away from the real hurt and the damage that are done in the lived experiences of its victims, although the approach is not intended to devalue those individual experiences. The possibility was raised, above, that people who are the targets of socially organized online hate may be collateral damage, if indeed the production of online hate is largely about hate producers trying to impress, gain favor, develop solidarity, act like, and/or entertain others in a community of like-minded peers. It does not acknowledge the amount of pain that people feel and the endangerment to their life sometimes, whether such outcomes were the non-primary motivations for online hate or fodder for collective *Schadenfreude*. The seriousness of the outcomes of online hate on its victims, individually, collectively, and societally, underlies the very impetus for theorizing and studying the phenomenon, no matter what its motivational genesis is.

Acknowledgments

This chapter was completed while the author was supported as Visiting Scholar to the Institute for Rebooting Social Media in the Berkman Klein Center for Internet & Society at Harvard University. Sincere thanks to Ron Rice for generously detailed and invaluable feedback during several iterations of this chapter, and to Yotam Shmargad, Anton Törnberg, and Jordi Weinstock for their constructive suggestions.

Notes

1 Although the social identification literature occasionally references processes such as the *interactive model of opinion formation* to describe how social interaction can lead to self-categorization (Postmes et al., 2005), the role of social interaction is neither necessary or sufficient for the activation of self-categorization within the general theory: As Thomas et al. (2010, p. 8) explain,

> [S]ocial identities shape individual behaviour not because of conformity to external pressures; they shape behaviour because they become internalized aspects of 'self', and because their normative dimensions shape our perceptions of what is right and proper and thus our expectations of others' views and behaviour. Consistent with these points, we argue that similar processes underpin the formation of identities that are commonly seen as either prosocial

(those that promote inter-group cooperation, social harmony and/or social equality) or hostile (those that promote inter-group aggression, prejudice or hostility.

Although they later argue "that interaction plays a key role, as the medium through which social ideologies may be aired and socially validated" (p. 8), this assertion involves no different processes than those described elsewhere in an *interpersonal* communication process in which social identification plays no part (see Duck et al., 1991).

2 For those unfamiliar with hate narratives against these groups, Scrivens et al. (2020, pp. 218–219) note:

> Jews, for example, have been subject to extensive criticism by the radical right, particularly by racist leaders who label Jews as "the source of all evil," the spawn of the Devil himself, conspiring to extinguish the White race and breed them out of existence – through "Jew-controlled" government, financial institutions, and media . . . Black communities, too, have been the primary target of much of the hateful sentiment expressed by the radical right. Blacks have been constructed as "mud races" and the descendants of animals created before Adam and Eve; "savages" who viciously rape White women and take jobs away from White communities; and the foot soldiers of conspiring Jews. . . . Adherents of this male-dominated movement have also categorized anyone who is not heterosexual as "contaminated" and "impure," by maintaining not only that the gay rights movement is the killer of the traditional White family and the cultural destruction of the White race.

In the views of some neo-Nazi and White Supremacist groups, Jews are "the central enemy, with African Americans, Latinos, and Asians as merely pawns of the Jews" (p. 228).

3 4chan hosts anonymous messaging in a number of topical channels or discussion boards. The /pol/, or "politically incorrect" board, "has often been linked to the alt-right movement and its rhetoric of hate and racism" according to Hine et al. (2017, p. 1). Their analyses provide a sense of the nature of /pol/ by noting, among other findings, that posts containing the n-word appear about 120 times an hour.

4 In addition to shadow banning, there are similar but less extreme measures to reduce exposure of hateful messages using algorithmic "interventions surreptitiously made by the platform, leaving the user thinking they are participating normally, while other users see less of them," thereby throttling the attention they might get. These include posts being "recommended less; or only to certain kinds of users, such as to followers only; or for a shorter time" (Gillespie, 2018, p. 487).

References

Abramowitz, A. I., & Webster, S. (2016, March). The rise of negative partisanship and the nationalization of U.S. elections in the 21st century. *Electoral Studies, 41*, 12–22. https://doi.org/10.1016/j.electstud.2015.11.001

ADL. (2021, March 22). *Online hate and harassment: The American experience.* https://www. adl.org/resources/report/online-hate-and-harassment-american-experience-2021

ADL. (n.d.). *Hate on display: Hate symbols database.* https://www.adl.org/resources/hate-symbols/search

Albright, J. (2018, November 16). The shadow organizing of Facebook groups. *Medium.* https://medium.com/s/the-micro-propaganda-machine/the-2018-facebook-midterms-part-ii-shadow-organization-c97de1c54c65

Aloramy, W., Burnap, P., Liu, H., Williams, M., & Giommoni, L. (2022). Disrupting networks of hate: Characterising hateful networks and removing critical nodes. *Social Network Analysis and Mining, 12*(1), 27. https://doi.org/10.1007/s13278-021-00818-z

Bartley, N., Abeliuk, A., Ferrara, E., & Lerman, K. (2021). Auditing algorithmic bias on Twitter. In *13th ACM web science conference 2021* (pp. 65–73). https://doi.org/10.1145/3447535.3462491

Benigni, M. C., Joseph, K., & Carley, K. M. (2017). Online extremism and the communities that sustain it: Detecting the ISIS supporting community on Twitter. *PLoS One, 12*(12), e0181405. https://doi.org/10.1371/journal.pone.0181405

Brady, W. J., McLoughlin, K., Doan, T. N., & Crockett, M. (2021). How social learning amplifies moral outrage expression in online social networks. *Science Advances, 7*(33), eabe5641. https//doi.org/10.1126/sciadv.abe5641

Burton, M. C., & Walther, J. B. (2001). The value of web log data in use-based design and testing. *Journal of Computer-Mediated Communication, 6*(3), JCMC635. https://doi.org/10.1111/j.1083-6101.2001.tb00121.x

Cheng, J., Bernstein, M., Danescu-Niculescu-Mizil, C., & Leskovec, J. (2017). Anyone can become a troll: Causes of trolling behavior in online discussions. In *Proceedings of the 2017 ACM conference on computer supported cooperative work and social computing* (pp. 1217–1230). https://doi.org/10.1145/2998181.2998213

Cramer, R. J., Fording, R. C., Gerstenfeld, P., Kehn, A., Marsden, J., Deitle, C., King, A., Smart, S., & Nobles, M. R. (2020, November 9). Hate-motivated behavior: Impacts, risk factors, and interventions. *Health Affairs Blog.* https://www.healthaffairs.org/do/10.1377/hpb20200929.601434/full/

Daniels, J. (2017, October 19). Twitter and white supremacy, A love story. *Dame Magazine.* https://www.damemagazine.com/2017/10/19/twitter-and-white-supremacy-love-story/

De Koster, W., & Houtman, D. (2008). 'Stormfront is like a second home to me': On virtual community formation by right-wing extremists. *Information, Communication & Society, 11*(8), 1155–1176. https://doi.org/10.1080/13691180802266665

DeKeseredy, W. S. (Chapter 4 this volume). Misogyny and woman abuse in the incelosphere: The role of incel male peer support.

DeKeseredy, W. S., & Schwartz, M. D. (2013). *Male peer support and violence against women: The history and verification of a theory.* Northeastern University Press.

DeKeseredy, W. S., & Schwartz, M. D. (2016). Thinking sociologically about image-based sexual abuse: The contribution of male peer support theory. *Sexualization, Media, & Society, 2*(4), Article 4. https://doi.org/10.1177/2374623816684692

Douglas, K. M., McGarty, C., Bliuc, A.-M., & Lala, G. (2005). Understanding cyberhate: Social competition and social creativity in online white supremacist groups. *Social Science Computer Review, 23*(1), Article 1. https://doi.org/10.1177/0894439304271538

Duck, S., Rutt, D. J., Hurst, M. H., & Strejc, H. (1991). Some evident truths about conversations in everyday relationships: All communications are not created equal. *Human Communication Research, 18*(2), 228–267. https://doi.org/10.1111/j.1468-2958.1991.tb00545.x

Eckert, S., & Metzger-Riftkin, J. (2020). Doxxing, privacy and gendered harassment. The shock and normalization of veillance cultures. *Medien & Kommunikationswissenschaft, 68*(3), Article 3. https://doi.org/10.5771/1615-634X-2020-3-273

ElSherief, M., Kulkarni, V., Nguyen, D., Wang, W. Y., & Belding, E. (2018). Hate lingo: A target-based linguistic analysis of hate speech in social media. In *Proceedings of the Twelfth International AAAI Conference on Web and Social Media* (p. 10). https://arxiv.org/pdf/1804.04257

Furie, M. (2016, October 13). Pepe the Frog's creator: He was never about hate. *TIME.* https://time.com/4530128/pepe-the-frog-creator-hate-symbol/

Gab.com – Gab Social. (n.d.). Retrieved April 6, 2023, from https://gab.com/

Gillespie, T. (2018). Regulation of and by platforms. In *The SAGE handbook of social media* (pp. 254–278). SAGE Publications Ltd. https://doi.org/10.4135/9781473984066

Gillespie, T. (2022). Reduction/borderline content/shadowbanning. *Yale Journal of Law and Technology*, 24(1), 476–492. https://heinonline.org/HOL/P?h=hein.journals/yjolt24&i=476

Halevy, A., Canton-Ferrer, C., Ma, H., Ozertem, U., Pantel, P., Saeidi, M., Silvestri, F., & Stoyanov, V. (2022). Preserving integrity in online social networks. *Communications of the ACM*, 65(2), 92–98. https://doi.org/10.1145/3462671

Han, C., Seering, J., Kumar, D., Hancock, J. T., & Durumeric, Z. (2023). *Hate raids on Twitch: Echoes of the past, new modalities, and implications for platform governance* (arXiv:2301.03946). arXiv. https://doi.org/10.48550/arXiv.2301.03946

Hangartner, D., Gennaro, G., Alasiri, S., Bahrich, N., Bornhoft, A., Boucher, J., Demirci, B. B., Derksen, L., Hall, A., Jochum, M., Munoz, M. M., Richter, M., Vogel, F., Wittwer, S., Wüthrich, F., Gilardi, F., & Donnay, K. (2021). Empathy-based counterspeech can reduce racist hate speech in a social media field experiment. *Proceedings of the National Academy of Sciences*, 118(50), e2116310118. https://doi.org/10.1073/pnas.2116310118

Haslam, N. (2006). Dehumanization: An integrative review. *Personality and Social Psychology Review*, 10(3), 252–264. https://doi.org/10.1207/s15327957pspr1003_4

Hayes, R. A., Carr, C. T., & Wohn, D. Y. (2016). One click, many meanings: Interpreting paralinguistic digital affordances in social media. *Journal of Broadcasting & Electronic Media*, 60(1), Article 1. https://doi.org/10.1080/08838151.2015.1127248

Hine, G. E., Onaolapo, J., De Cristofaro, E., Kourtellis, N., Leontiadis, I., Samaras, R., Stringhini, G., & Blackburn, J. (2017). *Kek, cucks, and god emperor Trump: A measurement study of 4chan's Politically Incorrect forum and its effects on the web* (arXiv:1610.03452). arXiv. https://doi.org/10.48550/arXiv.1610.03452

Hogg, M. A., & Reid, S. A. (2006). Social identity, self-categorization, and the communication of group norms. *Communication Theory*, 16, 7–30. https://doi.org/10.1111/j.1468-2885.2006.00003.x

Hübscher, M., & von Mering, S. (Eds.). (2022). *Antisemitism on social media*. Routledge. https://doi.org/10.4324/9781003200499

Jaidka, K., Mukerjee, S., & Lelkes, Y. (2023). Silenced on social media: The gatekeeping functions of shadowbans in the American Twitterverse. *Journal of Communication*, 73(2), 163–178. https://doi.org/10.1093/joc/jqac050

Jiang, J., Ren, X., & Ferrara, E. (2022). *Retweet-BERT: Political leaning detection using language features and information diffusion on social networks*. https://doi.org/10.48550/ARXIV.2207.08349

Jolley, D., & Douglas, K. (2019, March 14). Conspiracy theories fuel prejudice towards minority groups. *The Conversation*. http://theconversation.com/conspiracy-theories-fuel-prejudice-towards-minority-groups-113508

Lee, S. M., Lampe, C., Prescott, J. J., & Schoenebeck, S. (2022). Characteristics of people who engage in online harassing behavior. In *Extended abstracts of the 2022 CHI conference on human factors in computing systems* (pp. 1–7). https://doi.org/10.1145/3491101.3519812

Lewis, R., Marwick, A. E., & Partin, W. C. (2021). "We dissect stupidity and respond to it": Response videos and networked harassment on YouTube. *American Behavioral Scientist*, 65(5), 735–756. https://doi.org/10.1177/0002764221989781

Mariconti, E., Suarez-Tangil, G., Blackburn, J., De Cristofaro, E., Kourtellis, N., Leontiadis, I., Serrano, J. L., & Stringhini, G. (2019). "You know what to do": Proactive detection of YouTube videos targeted by coordinated hate attacks. *Proceedings of the ACM on Human-Computer Interaction*, 3(CSCW), Article 207. https://doi.org/10.1145/3359309

Marwick, A. E. (2021). Morally motivated networked harassment as normative reinforcement. *Social Media + Society*, 7(2), 20563051211021378. https://doi.org/10.1177/20563051211021378

Marwick, A. E., & Caplan, R. (2018). Drinking male tears: Language, the manosphere, and networked harassment. *Feminist Media Studies*, 18(4), Article 4. https://doi.org/10.1080/14680777.2018.1450568

Mitts, T. (2021). *Banned: How deplatforming extremists mobilizes hate in the dark corners of the internet*. https://www.dropbox.com/s/iatnxn5gtq48fxu/Mitts_banned.pdf?dl=0

Munger, K. (2017). Tweetment effects on the tweeted: Experimentally reducing racist harassment. *Political Behavior*, 39(3), Article 3. https://doi.org/10.1007/s11109-016-9373-5

Patel, V. (2023, July 3). At UChicago, a debate over free speech and cyberbullying. *The New York Times*. https://www.nytimes.com/2023/07/03/us/university-of-chicago-whiteness-free-speech.html

Phadke, S., & Mitra, T. (Chapter 9 this volume). Inter-platform information sharing, roles, and information differences that exemplify social processes of online hate groups.

Phillips, W. (2015). *This is why we can't have nice things: Mapping the relationship between online trolling and mainstream culture*. MIT Press.

Postmes, T., Haslam, S. A., & Swaab, R. I. (2005). Social influence in small groups: An interactive model of social identity formation. *European Review of Social Psychology*, 16(1), 1–42. https://doi.org/10.1080/10463280440000062

Qian, J., ElSherief, M., Belding, E., & Wang, W. Y. (2019). Learning to decipher hate symbols. In *Proceedings of the 2019 conference of the North American chapter of the association for computational linguistics: Human language technologies (long and short papers)* (Vol. 1, 3006–3015). https://doi.org/10.18653/v1/N19-1305

Quandt, T. (2018). Dark participation. *Media and Communication*, 6(4), 36–48. https://doi.org/10.17645/mac.v6i4.1519

Rae, S., Mathhew, B., & Kraemer, J. (Chapter 8 this volume). 'Hate Parties': Networked antisemitism from the fringes to YouTube.

Reich, S., Schneider, F. M., & Heling, L. (2022, April 12). Zero likes – symbolic interactions and need satisfaction online. *Computers in Human Behavior*, 80, 97–102. https://doi.org/10.1016/j.chb.2017.10.043

Rosenthal-von der Pütten, A. M., Hastall, M. R., Köcher, S., Meske, C., Heinrich, T., Labrenz, F., & Ocklenburg, S. (2019). "Likes" as social rewards: Their role in online social comparison and decisions to like other people's selfies. *Computers in Human Behavior*, 92, 76–86. https://doi.org/10.1016/j.chb.2018.10.017

Sannon, S., Choi, Y. H., Taft, J. G., & Bazarova, N. N. (2017). What comments did I get? How post and comment characteristics predict interaction satisfaction on Facebook. *Proceedings of the International AAAI Conference on Web and Social Media*, 11(1), Article 1. https://doi.org/10.1609/icwsm.v11i1.14930

Sarkeesian, A. (2012, December 4). *Anita Sarkeesian at TEDxWomen 2012*. YouTube. https://www.youtube.com/watch?v=GZAxwsg9J9Q

Schaefer, D. (2022, July 5). Buying into conspiracy theories can be exciting – that's what makes them dangerous. *The Conversation*. http://theconversation.com/buying-into-conspiracy-theories-can-be-exciting-thats-what-makes-them-dangerous-184623

Schoenebeck, S., Haimson, O. L., & Nakamura, L. (2021). Drawing from justice theories to support targets of online harassment. *New Media & Society*, 23(5), 1278–1300. https://doi.org/10.1177/1461444820913122

Scrivens, R., Davies, G., & Frank, R. (2020). Measuring the evolution of radical right-wing posting behaviors online. *Deviant Behavior*, 41(2), 216–232. https://doi.org/10.1080/01639625.2018.1556994

Scrivens, R., Wojciechowski, T. W., Freilich, J. D., Chermak, S. M., & Frank, R. (2023). Comparing the online posting behaviors of violent and non-violent right-wing extremists. *Terrorism and Political Violence*, *35*(1), 192–209. https://doi.org/10.1080/09546553.2021.1891893

Shmargad, Y., Coe, K., Kenski, K., & Rains, S. A. (2020). Social norms and the dynamics of online incivility. *Social Science Computer Review*, *40*(3), Article 3. https://doi.org/10.1177/0894439320985527

Shmargad, Y., Coe, K., Kenski, K., & Rains, S. A. (Chapter 10 this volume). Detecting anti-social norms in large-scale online discussions.

Stetter, B., & Murphy, P. P. (2018, October 28). What's gab, the social platform used by the Pittsburgh shooting suspect? *CNN Business*. CNN. https://www.cnn.com/2018/10/27/tech/gab-robert-bowers/index.html

Stringhini, G., & Blackburn, J. (Chapter 11 this volume). Understanding the phases of coordinated online aggression attacks.

Thomas, E., Smith, L., McGarty, C., & Postmes, T. (2010). Nice and nasty: The formation of prosocial and hostile social movements. *Revue Internationale de Psychologie Sociale*, *23*(2–3), 17–55. https://www.academia.edu/30264950/Nice_and_Nasty_The_Formation_of_Prosocial_and_Hostile_Social_Movements

Tong, S. T. (Chapter 3 this volume). Foundations, definitions, and directions in online hate research.

Törnberg, A., & Törnberg, P. (Chapter 5 this volume). From echo chambers to digital campfires: Constructing intimate community of hate within Stormfront.

Treene, A., & O'Sullivan, D. (2023, February 10). Congressman who raised issue of anti-semitism on Twitter says he was bombarded with antisemitic tweets. *CNN*. https://www.cnn.com/2023/02/10/tech/congressman-antisemitism-twitter/index.html

Tsapatsoulis, N., & Anastasopoulou, V. (2019). Cyberbullies in Twitter: A focused review. In *2019 14th international workshop on semantic and social media adaptation and personalization (SMAP)* (pp. 1–6). https://doi.org/10.1109/SMAP.2019.8864918

Turner, J. C., Hogg, M. A., Oakes, P. J., Reicher, S. D., & Wetherell, M. S. (1987). *Rediscovering the social group: A self-categorization theory*. Blackwell.

Udupa, S. (2019). Nationalism in the digital age: Fun as a metapractice of extreme speech. *International Journal of Communication*, *13*(0), Article 0. https://ijoc.org/index.php/ijoc/article/view/9105

Udupa, S., & Gerold, O. L. (Chapter 6 this volume). 'Deal' of the day: Sex, porn, and political hate on social media.

Uyheng, J., & Carley, K. M. (2021). Characterizing network dynamics of online hate communities around the COVID-19 pandemic. *Applied Network Science*, *6*(1), Article 1. https://doi.org/10.1007/s41109-021-00362-x

Vogels, E. A. (2021, January 13). The state of online harassment. *Pew Research Center: Internet, Science & Tech*. https://www.pewresearch.org/internet/2021/01/13/the-state-of-online-harassment/

Walther, J. B. (2022). Social media and online hate. *Current Opinion in Psychology*, *45*, 101298. https://doi.org/10.1016/j.copsyc.2021.12.010

Walther, J. B., Lew, Z., Edwards, A. L., & Quick, J. (2022). The effect of social approval on perceptions following social media message sharing applied to fake news. *Journal of Communication*, *72*(6), Article 6. https://doi.org/10.1093/joc/jqac033

Weimann, G. (2012). Lone wolves in cyberspace. *Journal of Terrorism Research*, *3*(2), Article 2. https://doi.org/10.15664/jtr.405

Wolf, W., Levordashka, A., Ruff, J. R., Kraaijeveld, S., Lueckmann, J.-M., & Williams, K. D. (2015). Ostracism online: A social media ostracism paradigm. *Behavior Research Methods*, *47*(2), 361–373. https://doi.org/10.3758/s13428-014-0475-x

Woolf, L. M., & Hulsizer, M. R. (2004). Hate groups for dummies: How to build a successful hate-group. *Humanity & Society*, *28*(1), Article 1. https://doi.org/10.1177/016059760402800105

3

FOUNDATIONS, DEFINITIONS, AND DIRECTIONS IN ONLINE HATE RESEARCH

Stephanie Tom Tong

Although the advent of social media has helped people forge meaningful connections, it has also fueled an accompanying rise in online incivility, harassment, hate, and extremism. Online hate has become a topic of concern among intellectuals, activists, organizations, and governments attempting to uncover its underlying causes and combat the effects it has on individual well-being, online communities, and civic life. The public consideration being paid to this issue is paralleled by increased scholarly attention from researchers who have been investigating the role of the Internet – and social media spaces more specifically – in the generation, diffusion, and effects of online hate.

The research on online hate falls roughly into four foci: (1) Benchmarking its pervasiveness across social media, (2) describing the content and nature of the messaging, and how social media enable and promote it, (3) understanding the effects of online hate on its victims, and (4) uncovering the motivations and gratifications for generating online hate (Walther, this volume). Although most of the chapters in this book focus on the fourth domain – the motivation and facilitation of hate through various social processes – the book would not be complete without an account of the other three, since it is the pervasiveness, nature, and effects of the phenomenon that make online hate the significant social problem that it is.

This chapter provides an overview of the first three foci. It begins by introducing various definitions and a taxonomy that classifies and frames the various forms of online hate that are the objects of contemporary public and scholarly concern. It then examines current estimates regarding the prevalence of online hate. It proceeds to an overview of how the various features and affordances found in social media platforms contribute to the

DOI: 10.4324/9781003472148-3

ease of creating and disseminating hate messages. The chapter also explores the effects of online hate on individual recipients and collective targets, as well as on observers who function alternatively as active responders or passive bystanders to hate within social media audiences. It then concludes with an examination of the remedies and solutions to online hate that have been proposed both online and offline.

Background and Definitions

There is no widely accepted definition of online hate, as it often highly depends on the specific perpetrators, targets, and contexts involved. However, many governing bodies have offered definitions to guide public discussion on online hate and hate speech. The United Nations (n.d.b) defines hate speech as

> any kind of communication in speech, writing or behaviour, that attacks or uses pejorative or discriminatory language with reference to a person or a group on the basis of who they are, in other words, based on their religion, ethnicity, nationality, race, colour, descent, gender or other identity factor.

Similarly, the United States Department of Justice (n.d.) notes that "hate" does not refer to basic disagreement, anger, or rage but requires specific bias against people or groups that reflect particular identity characteristics such as "race, color, religion, national origin, sexual orientation, gender, gender identity or disability."

Many of these definitions harken back to prior attempts to define hate speech offline, which is also notoriously difficult to do, especially against the backdrop of concerns about free speech in public discourse (see Paz et al., 2020; Siegel, 2020; Woods & Ruscher, 2021). Terminology abounds within the published research – online hate, cyberhate, toxicity, incivility, online aggression, extremism, and extreme speech are all used variably and (at times) interchangeably (see also Fox, 2023). At their core, many of these terms highlight that hate – both online and offline – is a form of communication that promotes denigration or harm against targets based on their stigmatized, identity-based characteristics. While some perpetrators are motivated by a deep-seated hatred or anger with a specific individual target, more often hate perpetrators are motivated by more general intergroup conflict and antipathy toward minority groups. Others simply revel in the joy and pleasure they get from causing chaos in targets' online (and offline) lives.

Though many scholars have wanted to understand, define, and document the differences of these various forms of online hate, such a task has been difficult to execute as the larger problem of online hate has continued to grow. To address this issue, this chapter offers a *relational taxonomy of online hate* that offers two particular dimensions: The first is the perpetrator-to-target *relationship* that can be *one-on-one, many-to-one,* and *group-level.* The second dimension is whether the hate messages are sent *privately* or if they are broadcast *publicly,* a difference that can radically change the function of hate messages with content that otherwise might appear identical. This is not the only way to parse online hate, and indeed many scholars have adopted different emphases (see for review Bliuc et al., 2018; Brown, 2018; Hassan et al., 2022; Siegel, 2020; Thomas et al., 2021; Waqas et al., 2019). However, this definitional taxonomy focuses on the perpetrator-to-target relationship and the nature of the audience, thus reflecting the *social nature* of online hate in which this book is grounded (see Walther, this volume).

A Relational/Broadcast Taxonomy of Online Hate

One-on-One Online Hate and Hate-Based Harassment

The first level offered in the current taxonomy constitutes *one-on-one* acts of online hate. Also known as *online harassment, cyberbullying,* or *cyberaggression* in the scholarly literature, one-on-one hate occurs when an individual perpetrator uses Internet communication technology to antagonize a selected individual target person through actions such as name-calling or insults, deliberate online shaming or embarrassment, threats, or (sexual) harassment – either in a single, one-time act, or repeated acts over a sustained period of time (Vogels, 2021).

In its *private* form, one-on-one online hate may involve a perpetrator sending a target unwanted, inappropriate, or threatening mediated messages. Jane (2020) notes the gender-based nature of one-on-one harassment, and how the "tenacity of misogyny" migrates to the online sphere (p. 2). Perpetrators may track their target's online behavior or hack into a target's social media accounts for personal information. In its *public* form, *one-on-one* hate messaging may involve bullying someone in a manner that others can observe, or spreading rumors or other private information about a specific target individual to others in public online spaces. A perpetrator may engage in excessive liking, tagging, or commenting on a target's social media posts or follow a target by joining the same social media groups. Generally, the same actions that can be done privately can be done publicly, with the public dimension adding embarrassment for individual targets and well-justified fear of damage to their reputation.

Critical to the one-on-one level of online hate is its *interpersonal* nature. Perpetrators and targets involved in one-on-one hate are often acquainted, having some kind of prior or existing relationship either online or offline, or both. Akin to *intimate partner violence* (Finkel & Eckhardt, 2013), much overlap exists between one-on-one offline and online hate and harassment.

For example, *cyberstalking* – defined as repeated unwanted online communication by a perpetrator intended to instigate stress, alarm, or fear in a specific target – is analogous to offline forms of stalking behaviors, through which perpetrators intend to create similar types of distress (Wilson et al., 2022), albeit privately. A public form of one-on-one hate is *image-based sexual harassment* – or nonconsensual sharing of intimate photographs – which may involve a perpetrator hacking and controlling, and then exchanging or posting, a target's private intimate images, in order to deliberately damage their reputation (see DeKeseredy, this volume). More recently, researchers have been discussing the potential uses of artificial intelligence technology by perpetrators to fabricate realistic-looking images and deep fake videos to exploit and harass their targets (Flynn et al., 2022). As Barth et al. (2023) note, the boundary between one-on-one and other levels of online hate is the perpetrator's intent to directly harm a known individual, as opposed to specific groups.

Many-to-One Online Hate

The second level is classified as *many-to-one* online hate, and although it is performed using the same kinds of technology as one-on-one hate, it differs in its relational scope. What may have begun as an interpersonal one-on-one act can transform into a larger scale attack in which several perpetrators "pile on" to engage in campaigns of many-to-one online hate. This form of online hate involves collective strategies and tactics by which an instigator signals enmity toward a specific person, and others follow suit. Thus, it is a social process of online hate and is the focus of this book. An infamous example of a coordinated many-to-one online hate act was 2014's Gamergate in which numerous perpetrators delivered a storm of insults, rape threats, and death threats to video game developer Zoe Quinn. From its origins in a series of angry blog posts written by Quinn's ex-boyfriend, it morphed into a larger, organized, many-to-one online hate campaign. As Dewey (2014) noted in her *Washington Post* article, "whatever Gamergate may have started as, it is now an Internet culture war." The events of Gamergate also introduced the term *doxxing* into the public vocabulary and consciousness, as the hateful practice of openly publishing a target's personal information (such as their residential address, place of work, phone number, etc.) online (Tiffany, 2022).

Notably because many-to-one online hate always involves a group of antagonists, many-to-one attacks have no form that is strictly private (unlike one-to-one hate messaging). However, the different perpetrators involved in many-to-one hate activity may nevertheless send their messages to a target using private channels (as doxxing may encourage) such as email, voicemail, or other means. Many-to-one hate may take place in more public spaces of social media such as comments or interactive threads, thereby adding a dimension of embarrassment, shaming, and potential isolation to the targets – although the terror of having many attackers reach a target through private channels cannot be overstated.

The coordinated nature of many-to-one hate is similar to Marwick's (2021) conceptual idea of *networked harassment* "in which an individual is harassed by a group of people networked through social media" (para 3). Marwick analyzes examples of "morally motivated" networked harassment in which an initial perpetrator targets an (out-group) member by publicly singling out the target's actions as an attack or violation of the perpetrator's rights or the social norms of their community. In framing their own message as a defensive attack against the target's bad behavior, perpetrators get to "portray themselves as defenders of enlightened public discourse and their targets as irrational and immoral" (Lewis et al., 2021, p. 735). Marwick and her colleagues go on to argue that these perpetrators' initial instigation can trigger moral outrage among other members of their in-group, thus justifying increasing online hate messages toward the initial target. She describes the case of Walter Palmer, a dentist and big-game hunter, who was the target of "worldwide harassment," after photos of a trophy lion he shot and killed in Zimbabwe were circulated on social media. Marwick (2021) points out that the anger and moral outrage sparked by this instance of big-game hunting was genuine, as was the "American arrogance, meaning that people who participated in the harassment believed they were in the right" (para. 9). Even though Palmer did nothing illegal, he still became the target of networked harassment and received several many-to-one hate messages – both publicly and privately, online and offline.

Another form of many-to-one online hate actions may or may not focus on any particular target. That is, while antagonists swarm and pile on in a collective and coordinated attack, their actions are not necessarily prompted by familiarity or relational history with a specific target or a target's supposed misdeeds. Rather, such events can be opportunistic, spontaneous acts of *mob-based hate*, extemporaneous undertakings in which groups of perpetrators find each other online and band together to produce an orchestrated many-to-one hate event. In many cases, they fit the mold of typical many-to-one attacks, such as *brigading* or *dogpiling* events, in which perpetrators swarm the comment feed of specific targets' online posts, attempting to embarrass or shame them. Such many-to-one forms of hateful overloading reflect organized efforts "wherein an attacker forces a target to triage hundreds of notifications or comments via amplification, or otherwise makes it technically infeasible for the target to participate online" (Thomas et al., 2021). This is also akin to *toxic commenting* streams in which perpetrators swarm an individual target's post with hateful comments and replies. This kind of many-to-one hate prompts targets to leave the ongoing discussions taking place in public Internet spaces, such as news websites (see Salminen et al., 2020).

Other extemporaneous, public attacks are more impersonal rather than personal. Rather than focus on any specific victim, these "crimes of opportunity" are primarily motivated to achieve disruption for the sake of disruption, resembling in purpose the act of trolling. (A troll "baits and provokes other group members, often with the result of drawing them into fruitless argument and diverting attention from the stated purposes of the group"; Herring et al., 2002, p. 371.) Recent examples include *Zoombombing*, when perpetrators hijack video conferences or classes and post hateful or obscene content in order to disrupt the conduct of the meeting. Zoombombing became particularly problematic during the COVID-19 pandemic when much of the global workforce moved to telework and used videoconferencing technology. Reports emerged of Zoombombers targeting K-12 and university online classrooms and remote religious services, taking control of screens to broadcast pornography, racial slurs, and insults (see Lee, 2022). A sign of its growing prevalence, in 2020, the U.S. Department of Justice was prompted to take the "weaponization of Zoom" more seriously and vowed to prosecute it as a crime at local, state, and federal levels (Statt, 2020; see also Stringhini & Blackburn, this volume).

Group-Level or Intergroup Online Hate

The final category of this typology describes the most diffuse *group-level* or *intergroup* form of online hate. Due to its nature, this kind of hate most fully involves social processes among perpetrators and is therefore almost always broadcast publicly. The intergroup level is where much of the politically motivated, extremist kinds of online hate content can be found and is also what much of the Internet-using public experiences more generally. At this level, perpetrators' goals are to demean, degrade, and insult, or to raise concerns over existential threats posed by members of some particular social group. Race, religion, gender, immigration, and other such social categories are the ultimate targets of this kind of hate.

There are, again, variants of intergroup online hate messages. Quite commonly, a scurrilous comment appears about the entire target group as a whole. In other cases, while it may appear as though a specific individual is the target of a hate message – a politician or some well-recognized public figure – there may be clues, or well-known linkages (factual or conspiratorial in nature), which associate the targeted person with a particular social group (see, e.g., https://www.ajc.org/translatehate/Soros). To attack the individual, who is a surrogate or prototype, is really to implicate the larger group with which the individual is associated. Because of its diffuse nature, many of the hate messages disseminated at the intergroup level appear in publicly accessible spaces online.

Although perpetrators may initially focus their attention on one particular group, researchers note that they often shift their focus to target additional

TABLE 3.1 A Relational/Broadcast Taxonomy of Online Hate

Broadcast Relational Patterns	Private	Public
One-on-One (often interpersonal, known target)	Targeted harassment; cyberstalking	Observable bullying; deep fake sexual harassment videos
Many-to-One (collective strategies toward known target, networked harassment, both personal and impersonal)	Doxxing	Gamergate; mob-based hate; overloading, dogpiling, toxic commenting, Zoombombing
Group or Intergroup (referencing groups, individual targets as surrogates for group)	–	Political, extremist, targeting social categories; often shift to target other/multiple groups

groups. For example, in its report on American White Supremacy, the ADL (2018) noted that while the alt-right is still grounded in antisemitic hate foundations, the "modern" White Supremacist resurgence taking place online is being dominated by young, white men who often attack many others, including Blacks, women, and LGBTQ+ groups. This "shifting" nature of hate targets suggests that at this intergroup level, degrading a specific identity-based group may not always be a galvanizing force for online hate; instead, it may be the underlying social processes provided by, and which reinforce, the act of hating itself that motivates and sustains perpetrators' behavior (Walther, this volume). Table 3.1 summarizes this typology.

Mapping the Online Hate Landscape: How Much, Who, and Where?

Many recent large-scale surveys have attempted to document the prevalence, the targets, and the venues of different kinds of online hate content that people report observing and experiencing. Although the specific forms or levels of online hate are not always clearly defined within the survey data or results, the general conclusion drawn from this body of work is that public exposure to online hate of all levels is increasing, with much of that exposure occurring on social media.

Prevalence: How Much?

Studies find very high rates of people having experienced online hate. However, like the variable definitions of online hate, researchers also lack consistency when defining what constitutes people "experiencing" online hate.

Experience sometimes refers to individuals' direct encounters as a specific target of one-on-one online hate or hate-based harassment, while, at other times, it is mere exposure to hateful content as an observer or passive bystander in social media spaces. Despite these discrepancies, the broader landscape of online hate underscores its seemingly ubiquitous nature. Survey data from Pew Research (Vogels, 2021) suggests that in the United States, 41% of Americans have "personally experienced some form of online harassment" – everything from forms of name-calling and deliberate embarrassment to (cyber)stalking and sustained harassment. The ADL's annual online hate and harassment survey found similar estimates in 2022, with 40% of their American sample reporting some kind of personal experience with online hate.

International survey results also emphasize online hate as a global problem: Reichelmann et al. (2021) asked respondents sampled from six countries about their exposure to hate content online: "In the past 3 months, have you seen hateful or degrading writings or speech online that attacked certain groups of people or individuals?" (p. 1102). They found Internet users from Finland reporting the greatest amount of online hate exposure (78.5%), followed by Spain (75.2%), the United States (73.2%), Poland (72%), the United Kingdom (65.6%), and France (64.8%). Overall, they conclude that the majority of their sample had "been exposed to hateful or degrading writings or speech online that attacked certain groups of people or individuals" (p. 1102) within the last three months.

These estimates, combined with public outcry of social media as a breeding ground for violent extremism, would lead us to believe that hate is prevalent and just "a click or two away" in any online space (Meyers & Thompson, 2022). Although the lack of consistent definitions makes it harder to definitively discern the specific kinds of online hate content, the public and scholarly consensus is that online hate is a pervasive, global, and increasing problem.

Who is Targeted?

Survey data also highlight how perpetrators of online hate target people based on a variety of identity-based characteristics – political beliefs, gender, sexuality, race/ethnicity/culture, nationality or national origin, religious beliefs, and disability status have all been documented. However, empirical trends indicate that younger individuals (i.e., 18 to 29) who spend more time online and identify as female, LBGTQ+, racial/ethnic minorities, or politically moderate-to-liberal are more likely to report being targets of online hate (Costello et al., 2017, 2019; Kenski et al., 2020; Obermaier & Schmuck, 2022).

Much evidence points to the pervasiveness of *gender-based online hate* that occurs at all three levels of the relational taxonomy of online hate. For example, in their Italian Hate Map project, Lingiardi et al.'s (2020) automated semantic content analysis of 2,659,879 Twitter tweets (as the platform X.com was then known) found that women were the most frequently insulted group – receiving 60.4% (roughly 71,000) of the hate tweets. Another survey by Amnesty International United Kingdom conducted in 2017, which included a sample of 504 women from the United Kingdom, the United States, New Zealand, Spain, Italy, Poland, Sweden, and Denmark, reported that "one in five women reported experiencing online hate-based harassment." More than a quarter of these cases (27%) were characterized as one-on-one harassment, with targets knowing the perpetrators; but 59% said that the perpetrator was a stranger, suggesting more anonymous forms of online hate. *Sexuality* or *sexual orientation* is also a frequent characteristic for group-level hate online, with recent estimates suggesting anywhere from 51% to 64% of LGBTQ+ individuals experiencing hate-based harassment (ADL, 2022; Vogels, 2021). A burgeoning area of scholarship further highlights the extreme level of hate that occurs against women and LGBTQ+ individuals in online gaming, an arena typically dominated by men (Ballard & Welch, 2017; Beres et al., 2021; Ortiz, 2019).

Race and *ethnicity* are also common factors in intergroup online hate. According to the UN, "70 percent or more of those targeted by hate crimes or hate speech in social media are minorities" (United Nations, n.d.a). Though online race-based hate is a global phenomenon, the specific racial-ethnic groups being targeted often change according to the region being examined. Unsurprisingly, most of the published studies of online racial hate have investigated the United States or Europe: In their comprehensive meta-analysis, Waqas et al. (2019) concluded that much of the published online racial hate scholarship reflects a "global dominance and higher share of Western institutions" (p. 16). This indicates that scholars know much about Westernized forms of online racial-ethnic hate and less about forms in other parts of the world. Yet, a more global focus is needed, especially because online race-based hate becomes more complex when it overlaps with *nationality*, *religion*, and *culture* (e.g., Udupa & Gerold, this volume). This creates intersectional contexts such as online Islamophobia or antisemitism that are difficult to parse out. Out of convenience, most researchers tend to simplify online hate against "all Muslims" or "all Jews" – even when targets have different racial-ethnic backgrounds, national origins, religions, or cultural traditions (see Sharif, 2018). Though more efficient, such definitional generalities often obscure the nuances in online race-based hate as a multifaceted communicative phenomenon.

Recent research also reflects increasing levels of *political online hate* that can coincide with other kinds of identity-based hate. In some instances, specific offline political events serve as the inception point for discordant interaction on popular social media spaces, which can then mutate into broader hateful exchanges of incivility and animosity. One example occurred during the 2016 Brexit referendum, a proposal for the United Kingdom to sever its relationship with the European Union. Evolvi's (2019) analysis of Twitter hashtags demonstrated how the offline 2016 Brexit referendum pushed right-wing populism and nationalistic identity to the forefront of online political discourse, as seen in many #Brexit tweets. Political disagreements about whether to "leave" or "remain" later evolved into intergroup insults and name-calling, with nationalistic groups further touting non-European migrants as a threat to British culture. This position then paved the way for derogatory, post-Brexit Islamophobic tweets that "framed Muslims as non-British foreigners that are 'different' from white British" (p. 392). The Brexit case exemplifies how offline political events can also fuel group-level online hate on social media.

In spring 2020, American social media users saw a sharp rise in anti-Asian online hate that coincided with the COVID-19 pandemic. Anger, fear, and frustration were high at the start of the pandemic when news outlets began reporting the origins of the coronavirus in Wuhan, China. At the time, prominent U.S. political leaders, including President Trump, blamed China (and Asian Americans by association) for causing the "kung flu" and the ensuing worldwide pandemic (Lee, 2020). As preventative health behaviors such as mask-wearing and social distancing became increasingly politicized, so did the amount of Sinophobic slurs seen on Twitter and 4chan (Tahmasbi et al., 2021). As members of the targeted group, Asian American social media users were generally more aware of the increasing anti-Asian online hate in 2020 compared to non-Asian Americans (Tong et al., 2022). Interestingly, this cycle – which began offline with the COVID-19 pandemic and led to increased online hate in social media – further suggests how offline events can reverberate online, and back again, indicating social processes across venues and time.

Lupu and colleagues (2023) investigated the relationships between the 2020 U.S. presidential election and online hate speech patterns on both mainstream (e.g., Facebook, Instagram) and less-moderated (e.g., Gab, Telegram, 4chan) social media platforms. They found that between November 3, 2020 (election day), and the ensuing announcement of Joe Biden as the winner by the Associated Press on November 7, a surprising spike in gender-based and LGBTQ+ online hate occurred. Although some of this online gender-based hate seemed to target Vice President-Elect Kamala Harris directly (suggesting deliberate acts of targeted many-to-one hate), Lupu et al. (2023) concluded that "the ensuing wave of associated online hate speech appears to be largely a case of users employing anti-LGBTQ+ slurs in a generalized manner to malign a wide range of political targets, such as candidates, parties, and voters" (p. 8) or the more anonymous form of many-to-many online hate. These findings further demonstrate the comingling of multiple forms of intergroup online hate with politics – in this case gender and sexual orientation.

Where Does Hate Happen Online?

Mainstream Social Media

The most recent surveys of U.S.-based samples indicate that the experience of online hate is mostly occurring on *mainstream social media*. Most individuals report that they don't seek out this content intentionally, but rather their exposure to hate content occurs accidentally. Of the 41% of respondents in the Pew Research (Vogels, 2021) sample who experienced online hate-based harassment, 75% of them reported that these incidents occurred on social media. The ADL's (2022) survey of American Internet users also found Facebook to be the most frequent social media platform for online hate (68%), followed by Instagram (26%) and Twitter (23%; see also Phadke and Mitra, this volume). Other oft-cited spaces where Americans encounter online hate include discussion forums, online gaming platforms, and romantic dating platforms. Internationally, online hate also occurs mostly in mainstream social media, with Facebook being the "most common location where hate materials were viewed" (Reichelmann et al., 2021, p. 1105).

This public focus on unintentional exposure to online hate in mainstream social media is also reflected in the published scholarship. Matamoros-Fernández and Farkas' (2021) review of 104 academic English-language studies of online race-based hate published between 2014 and 2018 revealed an emphasis on hate in mainstream social media, with the majority of studies examining Twitter (54.81%), followed by Facebook (34.62%) and YouTube (8.65%). They note that the "prominence of Twitter in the academic literature is likely tied to the relative historical openness of the platform's APIs" (application programming interfaces) (p. 211) and the fact that much of this data was freely available and could be collected without requiring informed consent.

Fringe Platforms and Alt-Tech Media

Tracking the nature of online hate circulated in mainstream social media (Facebook, Twitter/X, YouTube, Instagram, etc.) has resulted in important insights, but more research is needed into hate content exchanged on other, *fringe* social media platforms. Spaces like 4chan, 8chan, Gab, Gettr, and Telegram are sometimes called *fringe* because they are not frequented by most of the online public. Their near-zero level of content moderation makes them exceptional breeding grounds for the exchange of hateful and extremist content that is often banned within mainstream social media platforms. Recent work has attempted to examine the nature and spread of hate within fringe social media platforms. Rieger et al.'s (2021) content analysis estimated that as much as 24% of comments on such platforms contain explicit or implicit hate speech (p. 1). Hine et al. (2017) collected 8 million posts from the 4chan

/pol/ image board over a 2.5-month period. Using the *Hatebase* dictionary (hatebase.org) – "a crowdsourced list of more than 1,000 terms from around the world that indicate hate" – they found that 12% of the /pol/ posts contained hate speech terms (p. 97). They compared their 4chan /pol/ dataset to a corpus of 60 million Twitter tweets collected over a one-month period and found that the tweets contained "only" 2.2% of the same hate terminology (see also Stringhini & Blackburn, this volume).

Another popular fringe platform is Gab.com, a social media space that provides features similar to those of Twitter but without the dramatically looser terms of use or content moderation control. Indeed, it has embraced its place within the "alt-tech" movement: "At Gab, we believe . . . that users of social networks should be able to control their social media experience on their own terms, rather than the terms set down by Big Tech" (gab.com). Qualitative analyses of Gab posts indicate that much of its user-generated content contains far-right conspiracy theories and hate speech – primarily antisemitism, Islamophobia, anti-Black racism, and misogyny (Jasser et al., 2023). In their exploration of individual Gab user activities, Mathew et al. (2020) created "temporal hate vectors" that scored the "hatefulness of a user" during a single, month-long period. They then used these temporal snapshots to calculate the hate intensity among individual users and also at the larger network level. They concluded that not only is the overall amount of hate on Gab steadily increasing but also that "new users are becoming hateful at an increased and faster rate" (p. 1). Much of this content was being posted by especially hateful, core users – or *hate mongers* – who occupied a more central position within the network and disseminated more hateful content more frequently than "average hateful" and "non-hateful" Gab users (p. 15; see also Goel et al., 2023). Such analyses vividly demonstrate how much hate is ingrained in fringe social media platforms, and how it is circulated within groups, reinforcing the primary theme of this book.

Fringe platforms (like Gab and others) are characterized by a lack of content moderation, relative anonymity, ephemerality, and ease of multimedia message exchange. Because they are enigmatic and relatively unknown among most social media users, fringe platforms are often used to form what Massanari (2017) calls "toxic technocultures" or "leaderless, amorphous" cultures of hate that are "enabled and propagated through the sociotechnical networks" of spaces like Reddit, 4chan, and online gaming (p. 333). The specificity and often coded nature of the topics, meanings, and vocabulary exchanged among users of fringe platforms insulate them from the judgment of the general public, making them the perfect online environments for continued hate:

> [M]any of these spaces remain relatively (and purposefully) inaccessible to the average internet user, often requiring technological expertise to set up proxies (in the case of the darknet) or cultural expertise to understand the

myriad memes, in-jokes, and linguistic short-hand that serves the lingua franca of spaces like 4chan.

(p. 334)

Those who seek to join and participate in these fringe platforms must not only adopt the group's extremist views and identity, they must also have the required technological and terminological expertise.

Notably, scholars' use of terms like "fringe" or "alt-tech" to describe these platforms is relative and sometimes paints a misleading picture, portraying such usage as restricted to small sets of like-minded users (see also Rea et al., this volume). However, in June 2022, Telegram (2022) reported that it had "over 700 million monthly active users" making it one of the most heavily trafficked social media platforms. This is particularly problematic, given that recent estimates indicate that Telegram is an "actively growing environment for US-based hate speech and extremism with a range of ideologies present" (Walther & McCoy, 2021, p. 114; see also Udupa & Gerold, this volume). Similarly, 4chan reported that it receives 22 million unique visitors per month, with 11 million coming from the United States (4chan, n.d.). There is also evidence pointing to the increasing numbers of new users who are downloading these fringe social media apps to their phones internationally – Statista (2023) charted the growth in new Gettr users in 2022 and reported a 743% increase in the UK, 320% in Australia, and 266% in Brazil. Clearly, though such platforms may not be considered part of the mainstream social media ecosphere, they already have millions of users who function as a posting and receiving audience for hate messages through both intentional and accidental exposure.

Insular Extremist Sites and Forums

Finally, researchers have also examined the content that occurs in more insular social media spaces and websites that are founded, populated, and maintained by hate perpetrators and extremists themselves. As Bliuc et al. (2018) note, "group-based cyber-racism is generated by racist and white supremacist organisations, so it predominantly occurs on the websites of these groups in various forms" (p. 81). Prominent examples include Stormfront.org, Iron March, and Fascist Forge – online forums populated primarily (if not exclusively) by White Supremacists and right-wing extremists who deliberately seek out and exchange hateful content with like-minded others.

Such forums sometimes have rigorous application practices that screen for new members. Scrivens et al. (2021) describe the multistep process involved in gaining Fascist Forge membership in which candidates apply by stating their interests and goals in joining the forum. Site administrators then vet new candidates, admitting access only to those who are "committed to the extremist cause" (p. 4). In the public, mainstream social media arena, extremists and haters are a minority who often worry about violating the normative rules and policies of majority platforms (i.e., posting racial/homo-phobic/sexist slurs, circulating extremist images, inciting/calling for physical violence, etc.) or risk sanctions such as suspension or deplatforming. Inter-estingly, within Fascist Forge, content is also heavily moderated, but in these insular forums, administrators ensure that members' posts conform to the hateful extremist ideology, or else those users get kicked out of the forum. Clear content moderation practices exist in these insular forums; however, in a perverse twist, the content is screened for continued hateful sentiment that bolsters the collective extremist identity.

Though such insular forums are "fringe" in the sense that they are not spaces the general, Internet-using public might frequent, they are "main-stream" to perpetrators who know each as a place that invites, accepts, and nurtures the advocacy of violent extremism and hate-fueled content. As such, the membership of these insular spaces may be (relatively) few, but they account for an outsized proportion of race-based hate content online (see also Törnberg & Törnberg, this volume).

Virtual Reality (VR) and the Metaverse

Social VR platforms like Meta's Metaverse (sometimes also called multi-user immersive experiences) provide a three-dimensional, immersive envi-ronment where multiple users can meet and interact using head-mounted hardware. Research has indicated several advantages for users, such as enhanced self-expression and experience of identity through development of full-body avatars and the exchange of verbal and nonverbal behav-iors that can quickly promote close relationships with others (Freeman & Acena, 2021). However, there is also a darker side to social VR: Blackwell et al. (2019) interviewed 25 users and found that like any other online space, users were exposed to hate and harassment that ranged from *verbal* behaviors such as insults, to physical behaviors like unwanted touching among avatars, as well as *spatial* harassment – such as when "crashers" "flood" users' VR environment with unwanted sexual or violent content (Schulenberg et al., 2023).

Although VR users are free to construct their own avatars, identity-based characteristics are still important self-presentational features. Blackwell et al. (2019) found that among their sample of VR users, "certain types of people – namely, women, children, people of color, and people with strong accents – were much more likely to be harassed in VR than others, due to vocal cues and avatar appearance" (p. 1). In their interview study, Schulenberg et al. (2023) found that women who presented avatars with gendered characteris-tics experienced hate in VR that was akin to (but experienced more viscerally than) the hate encountered in online gaming spaces.

[T]he heightened sense of immersion and embodiment made all of our women participants feel significantly more harassed, anxious, and insecure when another user violates their personal physical space in social VR than when that same violation occurs in pre-existing online games and virtual worlds.

(pp. 9–10)

In some ways, the nature of one-on-one hate reported in social VR harkens back to the gender-based hate reported in text-based spaces like Lambda-MOO in the early days of the Internet (Dibbell, 1993). However, as recent studies suggest, the heightened sense of *presence* in VR seems to magnify the effects of one-on-one hate for many targets. Given its recent debut, there are few guidelines or policies being set by industry leaders like Meta (formerly Facebook), leaving users to grapple with the lack of social norms within such spaces: "It's kind of like the Wild West. There's no regulation, there's no moderation. People are just kinda doing their own thing" (Blackwell et al., 2019, p. 855). Relying on users to self-govern their own behavior seems problematic, given the potential for hate already being seen and reported within social VR interaction, though at present, few media companies seem interested in providing any guardrails. However, recent prompts from the Biden presidential administration on the issue of cybersecurity suggest that American social media companies are being forced to consider taking more specific actions to protect their users (Shear et al., 2023).

This review of the online hate landscape points to the nature of hate content that is being posted and exchanged in mainstream, fringe, and insular social media platforms, as well as within novel VR in the Metaverse. Such content raises the question of which features and affordances embedded in popular and fringe social media platforms facilitate easy creation and rapid dissemination of online hate.

The Features and Affordances that Contribute to Online Hate

There are many features unique to online social media platforms that make them an exceptional breeding ground for hateful communication. These include *system-based cues* and *paralinguistic digital affordances* native to online platforms. These cues and affordances not only provide information about *user influence* and *sociometric status*, they also contribute to the formation and furtherance of *collective group identity*. Perpetrators also take advantage of various kinds of *identifiability*: In some cases, they exploit *anonymity* and/or *pseudonymity* that shield them from offline sanctions for their hateful online expressions. In other cases, they manipulate their online *self-presentation* to create a *persistent, identifiable* presence and build both social and fiscal capital. Social media platforms also have features that enable users to organize and share content easily, while built-in *recommender algorithms* continue to feed users more deeply polarizing and hateful content in an effort to sustain their interest. These features all combine to make online platforms the ideal environment for easy and consistent dissemination of hate, and they pave the way for unique social dynamics that are often not found in offline interactions in such a direct and blatant way.

System-Based Cues and Paralinguistic Affordances: Sociometric Status, Influence, and Collective Identity Building

Among the most notable and unique features of social media platforms that shape online hate are the *system-based cues* and *paralinguistic digital affordances* embedded in their architecture. System-based cues are embedded automatically and cannot be changed or edited by its users (Walther & Jang, 2012). Prior work examining system-based cues in mainstream social media sites – like Facebook's friend count, Instagram's and Twitter's follower counts – has demonstrated that small cues provide important *sociometric*, or status-based, information about individuals' popularity and influence that can subsequently affect observers' judgments of their attractiveness and personality (Tong et al., 2008). Some platforms also provide what Hayes et al. (2016) call *paralinguistic digital affordances* (PDAs): "Cues in social media that facilitate communication and interaction without specific language associated with their messages" (pp. 172–173). Within mainstream social media sites, PDAs include cues such as Facebook's Like, Twitter's heart, and Reddit's upvoting and downvoting. Because such affordances are a unique product of the relationship between the technical feature provided by the system and users' perceptions (Treem & Leonardi, 2013), these lightweight PDAs can fulfill various communicative functions such as social support, relational closeness, or acknowledgment or interest in others' social media content (Hayes et al., 2016).

In the context of online hate, system-based and PDA cues can sometimes reveal basic information about a user's background – such as a flag that signals a poster's country of origin in 4chan's /pol/ (Hine et al., 2017). More often, however, they are used to signal status, influence, interest, and community within online hate forums. Examination of the function of Reddit votes as a PDA shows that (in aggregate) votes have the effect of promoting and spreading toxic content. When a particular post receives several upvotes, it signals increased user interest, which boosts that post's visibility and amplifies its presence on the site, whereas downvotes signal decreased user engagement and interest. The most sociometrically popular posts are featured on Reddit's front landing page (Gaudette et al., 2020).

In this way, such PDAs also serve as *vanity metrics*, which are the unique cues built into social media that can help audiences distinguish the "value" of a piece of content within the platform and subsequently the importance of the user who generated the valuable content (Rogers, 2018). Though their original intention was to measure user engagement on social media, vanity metrics can now serve a variety of purposes with respect to a user's social status and network influence. Ultimately, they have been co-opted as a way to place a literal numeric value on certain figures in virtual communities, including hate communities, which allows their *status* and *influence* to be tracked. Interestingly, Åkerlund (2021) notes that such metrics can also be especially useful for researchers trying to explore the relatively anonymous and seemingly leaderless nature of online hate groups.

PDAs can also bolster *community identity* and relational bonds among hate group members. Gaudette et al. (2020) analyzed how upvotes and downvotes functioned within the subreddit r/The_Donald – a board focused on former U.S. President, Donald Trump. Examining posts from 2017, they found that 11.6% of the 1,000 most highly upvoted comments in the subreddit contained Islamophobic and anti-immigration attitudes that instantiated a sense of "external threat" and promoted the nationalistic "America First" group mentality. Additionally, 13.4% of those comments rallied against the "Left" and often painted subreddit members as victims. The downvoting feature also provided a way to filter out content that detracted from the "us-against-them" attitude: "Reddit's downvoting feature functioned to ensure that members were not exposed to content that challenged their right-wing beliefs, which functioned as an echo chamber for hate and may have also functioned to correct the behavior of dissenting members" (p. 3503). From this detailed analysis, Gaudette et al. (2020) concluded that the Reddit vote feature served as a way for r/The_Donald subreddit users to strengthen the collective identity by sociometrically validating hateful, extremist attitudes with upvotes and sociometrically punishing nonconformist comments through downvotes (see Shmargad et al., this volume). This is another illustration of the social processes fostering online hate.

Even in the absence of system-based and PDA cues to officially track hate on varying platforms, researchers have found that members of online hate communities find ways to show their social support and interest in each other's posts in a form of pseudo-metrics via their comments, responses, or manual "sharing" of the content (Åkerlund, 2021; see also Walther, 2022). For instance, 4chan lacks specific PDA cues or vanity metrics to signal validation, common identity, or social support, so users must directly engage with each other's posts by commenting. As such, there is a unique form of *social learning* that seems to have emerged among the communities on platforms that lack PDA cues, with each developing its own unique sets of cultural norms, relational expectations, and social hierarchies around these metrics and the individual value placed upon these metrics by the members of each online hate community.

Anonymity, Pseudonymity, and Identifiability

Across social media, identity information varies. Some mainstream platforms like Facebook operate on a "real name" policy (i.e., profiles are expected to contain one's real first and last names, identity, and photograph), and others, like Twitter, allow users to choose a pseudonym or username that may or may not reflect their offline identity. Pseudonyms and usernames still offer some identifiable information that distinguishes individual users and tracks and records their activity on the platform. Other platforms such as Whisper or Secret offer even greater anonymity – usernames are assigned by the platform, and individuals may choose to change them at any time, making it harder to track activities of specific users.

Platforms that promote total anonymity give individuals an easier pathway to get involved in online hate – the lack of connection to one's outward-facing offline identity can embolden perpetrators to create and share extremely hateful or toxic content by reducing one's sense of personal responsibility (Brown, 2018). Even when operating with a pseudonym, the lack of connection to corporeal identity still lends itself to lower inhibitions (Suler, 2004) and decreased perceived social barriers, sanctions, and norms surrounding incivility and aggressive behavior (Rösner & Krämer, 2016). Theoretically, the *social identity model of deindividuation* (see Postmes et al., 2002) has long posited that the (pseudo)anonymous nature of online platforms can prime a sense of *deindividuation* – or a suppression of individual identity – and an increased salience of group-level identity. The cognitive experience of deindividuation has been shown to be correlated with propensity for online hate participation through the intervening mechanism of *moral disengagement* of the bullying behavior (i.e., vilifying a target of hate/maltreatment, disregarding consequences of the harassment, reconstruing the group's conduct, and obscuring their own personal agency) (Chan et al., 2022), with the simultaneous identification with a group with a norm of such behavior.

Similarly, some researchers contend that increased user identifiability can mitigate the extremity of online hate content. In their dataset of misogynistic tweets targeting Japanese female politicians on Twitter, Fuchs and Schäfer (2021) point out that "the language of abusive or insulting tweets was not as harsh as assumed on Twitter, if compared to what can be observed on 2channel" (p. 571). The authors suggest that perpetrators' fears of violating Twitter's conduct policies (Twitter, 2023) and the threat of account suspension resulted in relatively reduced nature of misogynistic tweets compared to the extremity of hate seen in 2chan. Note that this does not require specific individual identification; the pseudonym identifies the persistent user.

Interestingly, perpetrators rely on the duality of pseudonymity (and the privacy it offers) and the conspicuousness of public-facing online identity to create and circulate hate online. The duality of anonymity/identifiability depends on a perpetrator's goals: In some cases, anonymity and message encryption are required for individual exchange of hate content and coordination of and participation in hateful (potentially illegal) activities. In other cases, leaders of hate groups want to be identifiable, presenting themselves online to attract followers and court social influence. To build such status requires giving up full anonymity (to an extent) to create an outward-facing public identity using pseudonyms or avatars. In doing so, hate mongers can curate their identities, record their activities, archive their posts, and interact with members of their audience. Rogers (2020) describes this use of both private anonymity and public social identity as *private sociality* which reflects the chimera-like nature of identity among perpetrators of online hate. The ways that anonymity and identifiability can impact individuals' feelings and behavior clearly contribute to their propensity to consume and disseminate online hate.

Algorithmic Recommendation, Commenting, and Multimedia Hyperlinking/Content Sharing

Another factor involved in the circulation of online hate content is the algorithmic recommender systems found on many Internet platforms. In 1998, Amazon introduced item-based collaborative filtering that offered recommendations for its customers (Smith & Linden, 2017); in 2009, Facebook became one of the first mainstream social media companies to implement recommender algorithms when it introduced the Newsfeed that algorithmically curated each user's content and, doing so, encouraged its users to continue friending new people, while also avoiding the information overload associated with content from their growing networks (Smith et al., 2022). Other popular platforms such as YouTube and TikTok implemented their own recommender algorithms that provide content tailored to users' interests and preferences in an attempt to gain their attention and continued loyalty. These recommender systems have been portrayed as providing "radicalization by algorithm," which describes the process by which platforms like YouTube can "draw users into algorithmically induced encounters with more and more radical views" (Forestal, 2021, p. 306), particularly among those with politically conservative and alt-right perspectives. Akin to the idea of "filter bubbles" (Pariser, 2011), recommender algorithms feed content to users that aligns with their preexisting attitudes and reduces exposure to outside ideas, increasing polarization through so-called echo chambers.

However, as Munger and Phillips (2022) note, though cases of online radicalization through filter bubbles have been documented in the popular press, most "journalistic evidence is fraught with a bias toward sensationalism" (p. 192) that offers vivid description but lacks strong empirical trend evidence (see also Whittaker et al., 2021). Instead, they propose that the production and consumption of online hate content are motivated by the process of supply and demand and are further facilitated by particular affordances of social media. Focusing on YouTube, they argue that on the *supply* side, producers are often motivated to create hateful or extremist content to make money – the more substantial their audience, the greater their advertising revenue. The start-up cost for creating videos is relatively low, requiring minimal equipment and space. Second, on the *demand* side, YouTube videos offer a visual, multimedia experience that is easy for audiences to process – much simpler than reading text-based news – thus creating greater demand for easy-to-consume content. They also emphasize how affordances of YouTube amplify the supply and demand process. *PDAs* exist in the form of the YouTube Like that functions as a (private) way for users to indicate their preferences. These data are filtered by the recommender algorithm that suggests content for users made by the "same creator or milieu of content creators" (p. 192). Another affordance is *interactive commenting* through which users can not only discuss a particular video but also find a sense of community with others who share their extremist perspectives or hateful views.

Thus, recommender algorithms are not solely responsible for the problem of increasing polarization and radicalization of the online public. Personalization is often a two-way street involving a user who self-selects certain content and the system that then preselects content for the user based on their data. Whittaker et al. (2021) argue that few academics, critics, or political leaders note the nuance of this relationship, noting that past studies "have frequently posited a causative relationship between online echo chambers and radicalization – with little empirical evidence – and they are rarely clear as to whether they refer to users' own choices or the effects of algorithms" (p. 5). This combination of quick supply, easy consumption, increasing demand, PDAs, recommender algorithms, comment exchange, and online community demonstrates how platforms like YouTube can motivate and facilitate the production, consumption, and amplification of online hate.

This review summarizes how the flexible nature of various online cues and features afford not only the spread of hateful ideology but also the sharing of social and relational information that can strengthen bonds among members of larger hate groups. The hateful communication facilitated by these features and affordances also create harmful *effects* that spill over into targets' lives – both online and offline.

The Effects of Online Hate: Individuals, Bystanders, and Civic Life

Just as researchers have examined different patterns of online hate (e.g., one-on-one, many-to-one, and intergroup; public and private), similar attempts have been made to distinguish its effects on individual targets, audiences of social media bystanders, and larger consequences on civic and social life. We review each of these areas below and then expand on the potential solutions that have been proposed by targets of hate, advocates and activists, and social media platforms themselves, as ways to curb, control, and remedy the harms of online hate.

Individual Victims and Targets: Effects and Preferred Remedies

Researchers examining the deleterious effects of online hate have primarily focused on the effects reported by individual victims, what Woods and Ruscher (2021) call *consequential harms* "that occur as a *result* of hate speech" that "have historically received more empirical investigation" (p. 273). Commonly reported consequential harms toward victims' *mental* and *emotional* states include increases in anxiety, anger, depression, fear, stress, sadness, and shame (e.g., Keighley, 2022). Less attention has been paid to physical health outcomes, such as trouble sleeping and concentrating on everyday activities, though they do occur (ADL, 2022). Such consequential harms are so frequently reported that mental health professionals have described the effects of online hate as a public health crisis, most often experienced by members of particularly vulnerable communities (Cramer et al., 2020).

Researchers have also documented less obvious effects of online hate that reverberate in targets' offline lives. Interference in offline behaviors, such as increased *social isolation*, can occur when victims internalize the hate as a form of self-blame for being targeted in the first place (Hubbard, 2020). Increased *relational problems* with their family and friends can occur after direct experiences with online hate, or problems at *work* may increase. For many people, part of the job application process includes employers screening applicants' online presence using social media and Google search, and the wide-ranging effects of hate-based harassment on an individual's *reputation* may cost them new job offers or opportunities for career advancement (Jane, 2020). For example, Citron (2014) cites cases of female school teachers who have been fired after nude photos of them were posted on revenge porn sites as a form of image-based harassment.

Just as individual targets report substantial variation in the amount and severity of online hate effects, they also report desiring different *remedies* and *solutions* as a response to them. Schoenebeck et al. (2023) surveyed 650 Internet users and asked them to indicate what kind of remedy they most preferred in response to (hypothetically) receiving some form of online hate-based harassment. Participants were allowed to choose from six potential solutions; results indicated that *banning a perpetrator* from the social media platform where the harassment took place was most preferred, followed by *removing the hate content, public listing* (adding the perpetrator to an online public list of offenders), *payment* (paying the target or people who support the target), *requiring public apology*, and *flagging* the hate content as inappropriate (p. 5). Results also indicated that preferences varied as a function of the kind of hate the proposed solution was intended to remedy: Generally (and perhaps paradoxically), people reported lower preferences for any kind of remedy in response to those forms of hate-based harassment perceived to produce the greatest amounts of harm, including sharing sexual photos and doxxing.

Online Bystanders

Given the potential broadcast nature of online hate, while perpetrators may attack one specific victim or target a larger group with a hateful message, meme, or image, there is often a large public audience of *online bystanders* or *observers* who may see that content, as well. As noted above, many bystanders report inadvertently encountering – versus intentionally seeking out – instances of hate online, but even unintentional exposure can negatively impact bystanders' mental and emotional state (Bedrosova et al., 2023). As Benesch (2023) notes, the cumulative nature of repeated exposure to hate produces differential effects among bystanders. There is work examining *passive effects* on bystanders, such as withdrawing from online interaction (Barnidge et al., 2019) or becoming apathetic or desensitized to hate-fueled content (Schmid et al., 2022). In some cases, however, research points to *active responses*, with repeated exposures to online hate sometimes motivating bystanders to become *active perpetrators* of hate themselves (see Walther, this volume) or engage in defensive *counter-speech* or *social support* of targeted individuals and groups.

Passive Effects: Observation and Passive Response

Schmid et al. (2022) denoted the difference in observers' perceptions of hate in social media feeds, with *first-level* perceptions referring to basic recognition of online hate content and *second-level* perceptions referring to their "feelings, attitudes, and opinions regarding the content" (p. 4). From their qualitative interviews with 23 German social media users, they found that younger respondents were less sensitized to online hate content compared to older respondents, whose stronger first-level perceptual reaction was attributed to their "lack of familiarity with hate speech on social media" (p. 11). In some cases, respondents reported not perceiving the nuances of posts that contained more *indirect* hate, such as those using humor, or those that contained more specific memes, language, or symbols that had coded references or meanings that they did not know. These first-level perceptual patterns, in turn, affected second-level perceptions – those who deliberately chose to ignore or avoid hateful content, or could not discern the meanings, ended up not attending to nor having strong emotional responses to such posts.

Interestingly, such passive first- and second-level reactions to online hate among social media bystanders are a frequently reported trend, but pinpointing their causes is difficult. Researchers often cite different reasons for bystander inaction, including overall desensitization to hate in social media (Schmid et al., 2022), individual differences in bystanders' apathy versus empathy with targets of hate, a diffused sense of personal responsibility online, reduced feelings of self-efficacy to combat hate speech, or reluctance to defend victims of hate for fear of retribution by perpetrators (see Obermaier, 2022; Rudnicki et al., 2023). It is likely that all these factors contribute to bystanders' passive response to online hate, which in itself can help perpetuate the larger normative trends of verbal aggression, incivility, and hate present on many social media platforms (see Shmargad et al., this volume).

Bystanders' Active Responses to Online Hate

One potential effect that exposure to online hate can produce is active *counter-speech* or *counter-messages* in which bystanders attempt to refute hateful content and its influence on social media audiences. Bystanders may engage in counter-speech as individuals, or as part of a larger collective. For example, the Sweden-based group, #jagärhär ("I am here"), consists of "thousands of people who have made a regular practice of responding en masse to what they regard as hateful comments online" as a form of *collective counter-speech* (Buerger, 2020, p. 2). The counter-speech process begins when a member of the volunteer collective identifies online hate content on a social media platform such as Facebook. They begin their counterresponse by commenting under the initial post to either correct misinformation or criticize the hate. Other members of the collective then respond to those comments and use Facebook's PDAs to "like" each other's comments, thereby sociometrically pushing #jagärhär comments to the top. The #jagärhär collective now consists of approximately 74,000 volunteer members (70% women) primarily based in Sweden, a team of 15–20 moderators who organize the day-to-day counter-speech campaigns and the group's Facebook presence, and six administrators who oversee the collective's larger work (Buerger, 2020). As an organized whole, #jagärhär represents an impressive, if unique, coordinated bystander counter-speech response to online hate that has yet to be replicated.

It may be surprising to learn that the bystanders who engage in counter-speech do not usually intend to change the mind or behavior of perpetrators. Instead, the primary goals are to change the expectations and norms of *other* bystanders in the online audience and influence the aggressive rhetoric within the social media platforms (Buerger, 2020); that is, this approach invokes a social process. This is similar to results from offline bystander influence, which has found individual intervention in physical emergencies to be more likely when more bystanders are present in the situation (see for review Lytle et al., 2021; Nida, 2020). Some academics have also proposed *automated counter-speech* as a potential response to online hate in which AI-based social bots can be programmed to address perpetrators' hate posts with unique comments. Although some evidence suggests that automated counter-speech can persuade perpetrators to reduce their hateful language at least in the short term (e.g., Munger, 2017), there are both technical and ethical issues that must be addressed before it can be a widely implemented practice on social media. Technically, how might bots be programmed to detect instances of online hate that use language and imagery in coded, subtle ways? Ethical challenges regarding censorship and expression in political discourse might also arise, as Cypris et al. (2022) note: "If automated counterspeech turns out to be an effective 'silencer' of online discussions, authoritarian regimes could exploit this technique to shift, re-frame, or subdue user discourse that they deem 'undesirable'" (p. 7). While seemingly attractive, automated counter-speech remains a potential remedy rather than a current response to online hate.

Bystanders also respond to online hate through *reappropriation* or by *reclaiming* of the hateful hashtags, phrases, and memes coined by perpetrators to derogate targets. Cervone et al. (2021) summarize the philosophical debate over varying models of hateful language reappropriation. Some adopt a *polysemy* perspective that describes the need for multiple people to recognize a slur's new meaning for it to be fully reclaimed, whereas others offer an *echoic* perspective in which a slur can become separated from the hate it induces, while still retaining its meaning: "Thus, according to a polysemy perspective, reclamation only takes place if several people use the new meaning, whereas according to the echoic perspective, small acts of reclamation are possible and can eventually lead to polysemy" (p. 91). The process of echoic reappropriation is further spelled out by Galinsky et al.'s (2013) three-step model that begins with (1) individual's use of a slur for *self-labeling* – a tactic that not only prevents outsiders from using word for derogation but also imbues it with new positive connotations and meaning; (2) self-labeling then moves to the *collective* level in which other members of the targeted in-group begin to use the slur with its new, positive implications; and (3) in the final step, out-group members begin to *acknowledge the transition* of the slur's meaning from negative to positive.

Applying Galinsky et al.'s (2013) three-step process can help decipher the ways in which meanings of hateful hashtags, memes, and images can be reclaimed by members of targeted groups who want to "weaken" the "stigmatizing force" of such content (p. 2020). One illustrative example is the "Let's Go Brandon" meme, which was originally created as a right-wing coded slogan for "Fuck Joe Biden." In late summer of 2022, a small group of online Biden supporters reclaimed the meme, going so far as to create Biden's superhero online alter ego, #DarkBrandon. In the final step, #DarkBrandon was fully embraced as a positive figure and was even featured in Biden's 2024 U.S. presidential campaign. As such, Let's Go Brandon reflects how echoic reappropriation can give rise to reclaimed polysemic usage and meaning.

Though reclaiming hate memes seems like a potential path for bystanders to intervene in instances of viral online hate, in her analysis of the Dark Brandon meme, Romano (2023) eloquently raises the point that by the time hate-fueled language, images, and phrases have "memed their way into the mainstream," the

> average bystander is unlikely to know its original dark origins. It is doubtful the average internet user who picks up language like "simp," "Chads and Beckys," "cuck," "normie," "wrongthink," or "redpilled" really understands their deeply misogynistic and extremist origins or cares that much if they do. Most of the time, this lack of a watchful attitude, if it serves anyone except the garbage-eating deities of the internet, serves the aims of the trolls and the right wing.

Dark Brandon may have been a welcome addition to Biden's 2024 campaign; however, at other times, bystanders can run into trouble when reclaiming a hate meme, even if the motivation to do so is sincere: "Attempting to use the memes without full context can often spread confusion instead of bringing clarity and purpose" (Romano, 2023). In such cases, the act of reclaiming can sometimes result in bystanders further disseminating online hate memes, which inadvertently does more harm than good.

Like counter-speech campaigns, sometimes, bystanders' *social support response* to online hate can also be very well organized. Blackwell et al. (2017) interviewed members of the private Right To Be (righttobe.org) platform (formerly, HeartMob), that was launched in 2016 by Hollaback! – a nonprofit organization dedicated to "ending harassment in all its forms" – which describes it as a "safe space where you can share your harassment story, get support, and help others experiencing harassment." Individual targets share their stories of hate and hate-based harassment on the platform, and a team of vetted and trained bystanders then offer social support messages in response. Bystanders who participated in the Right To Be platform reported better understanding the problem of online hate in terms of its overall breadth, diversity, and frequency, as well as the severity of effects that hate-based harassment can have on individual targets. Offering support directly to targets was also a way for bystanders to gain a sense of agency toward combating online hate, which often feels like a vast, unsolvable problem (Blackwell et al., 2017).

The studies of collective counter-speech, reclaiming, and social support reviewed above offer interesting (if rare) glimpses into more organized, active responses to the harms that online hate can produce. Such campaigns require dedicated volunteer work, coordination, and sustained efforts that most average social media bystanders are unlikely to expend. Though some work simply points to the innate empathy of active bystanders, more recent research is looking into the particular *mechanisms* that drive them to take action against hate when they encounter it online. For example, understanding bystanders' *emotional reactions* to a specific hate post, or uncovering their *expectations* about the communicative exchange of hate on social media (Obermaier et al., 2021; Roden & Saleem, 2022; Schäfer et al., 2023; Tong & DeAndrea, 2023), may provide more insight into the motivations of those particular bystanders who offer smaller but consistent, defensive actions against online hate. Though research points to a myriad of responses to online hate among bystanders, the primary response among most tends to be one of deliberate passivity.

Big Tech Effects: Accountability, Methods of Moderation, and Platform Governance Practices

Accountability, Regulation, and Moderation

One particular effect of the ongoing problem of online hate, incivility, and aggression is increasing public concern that social media companies are not doing enough to address it and its associated harms. A recent Pew Research poll (Vogels, 2021) found that approximately 80% of Americans feel that Big Tech companies like Meta, Twitter, and Google "are doing an only fair to poor job" attending to the harassment and hate that occur on their platforms (and after Twitter became X in 2023, things are even worse; Barrie, 2023). Many individual users, as well as U.S. politicians, have called for greater accountability among social media companies that have been shielded by legal policies, mainly Section 230 of the United States' Communications Decency Act (CDA). Initially passed in 1996, Section 230 allows companies to moderate and govern their platforms, or not to, but it protects them from being liable for user-created content (which is itself protected by the First Amendment for free speech). Though Section 230 has enabled an open Internet and facilitated the growth of contemporary social media, many argue that it has also allowed online hate to flourish, creating a double-edged sword for modern-day communication freedoms (see for review, Wakabayashi, 2020).

One impetus for the CDA's development was to give companies the freedom to develop their own rules and processes for platform governance: Examples include Google's implementation of the European Union's General Data Protection Regulation or the Right to be Forgotten. Users can request, via webform, that content be "delisted" or removed from the search engine (Google, n.d.). A panel of reviewers manually examines the details and weighs "the rights of the individual and the public's interest in the content" before deciding whether to de-list the requested content. Other examples include Twitch's Safety Advisory Council formed in May 2020, designed to develop "new products and features to improve safety and moderation" (Twitch, n.d.). Such attempts, though novel, seem difficult for Big Tech companies to implement effectively to combat the amount of problematic hate content on their platforms.

At present, most mainstream social media companies rely on principles of *normative regulation* in which they establish terms and conditions of use that they then require users to abide by or risk various sanctions (Schoenebeck & Blackwell, 2021). But such terms are notoriously vague and difficult to enforce and require much content moderation, which is in itself hard to perform effectively and often comes at great cost to the human moderators responsible for implementing it (see Schöpke-Gonzalez et al., 2022; Spence et al., 2023).

Big Tech companies have proposed various moderation techniques that involve identifying and then deleting hate speech. Companies have embraced both human-based and automated detection methods, neither of which seem to have provided satisfying or effective ways to address the problem of curbing hateful online content. There are real inefficiencies and ethical issues with requiring human moderators to view questionable content and make judgments about its public harms; just as there are ongoing public, academic, and political debates about the transparency and overreach of artificial intelligence algorithms being developed by Big Tech companies for the purposes of *surveillance*, as well as the accuracy of these algorithms to correctly distinguish innocuous user-generated content from hate speech on social media (see commentary by Gillespie, 2020; Gillespie et al., 2020; Schoenebeck & Blackwell, 2021). Such debates highlight the intersections of the human and the technical, and the "gray area" of public opinion and individual judgments regarding offensive versus truly hateful content. However, there are clear-cut cases of users who routinely and deliberately disseminate hate on mainstream social media that Big Tech companies have been required to address, such as through deplatforming.

The Curious Case of Deplatforming

A common approach that social media companies rely on to deal with particularly problematic users includes *account suspension* and *deplatforming* – also known as *strategic network disruptions* – in which "identifiable 'core' members of a hate-based organization are removed from the platform all at once, eliminating the online leadership of the organization" (Thomas & Wahedi, 2023, p. 1). By deplatforming leaders, social media companies like Meta and Google hope to disrupt hate groups' structures and sense of collective identity, which should in turn affect the amount of hateful content that emerges from the groups' membership. This represents a sort of reversal of the social process of online hate.

Though theoretically, the idea of deplatforming seems a promising way to address with online hate, in practice, its effectiveness is a hotly debated topic in ongoing scholarship. Some researchers point to the positive "causal effects" of deplatforming hate group leaders on a platform's overall "health" as reducing the amount of production and circulation of hate content, decreased group engagement among remaining members, and the reduced likelihood of those remaining members reconstituting the group's organization and structure (Thomas & Wahedi, 2023). While this evidence suggests that deplatforming might help individual social media sites rid themselves of harmful content, other studies suggest that banned users simply migrate to other fringe platforms and are also motivated to spew even more toxic content as a result (e.g., Ribeiro et al., 2023). Other studies suggest that although banning or quarantining hateful content shared on platforms like Reddit might decrease hate activity initially, such efforts are ultimately responsible for a stronger "long-term increase in toxicity," especially among the core leaders of hate groups (Trujillo & Cresci, 2022).

Conclusions

The sprawling, multidisciplinary scope of online hate research published in recent years highlights the growing need for academic researchers to begin providing more detailed and deliberate organization of the various topical foci they investigate. The lack of conceptual definitions and organizational clarity can also lead to poor operationalization and measurement, inaccurate comparisons, or imprecise estimates of the prevalence and effects of each kind of online hate. This chapter offers a relational taxonomy as one heuristic framework to categorize and define the differences among *one-on-one/ hate-based harassment, many-to-one*, and *many-to-many* forms of online hate. The basis for each category is the relationship (or lack thereof) between perpetrators and targets and the channels used to disseminate hate messages, as a means of differentiating and classifying various acts of online hate.

Another advantage this taxonomy provides is the ability to delineate the *effects* that acts of online hate have at various levels – on individuals, targeted groups or group-level identities, social systems, and civic discourse. Notably, with this taxonomy, acts of online hate may begin at one level and then transition into others over time and involve use of private and public channels, such as Gamergate, or sometimes emerge simultaneously at different levels, such as the many-to-one attacks on Vice President Kamala Harris that also function as many-to-many intergroup (e.g., bipartisan) hatred. Examining and organizing the relational and communicative specifics of online hate might offer more nuance to current broad or general operational definitions often reflected in survey measurement. For example, researchers might be able to pinpoint differences in targets' "direct experience" with one-on-one/private online harassment versus repeated "exposure" to many-to-one/public intergroup messages to see which are more extreme or problematic. Cross-category comparisons become applicable as well: Are bystanders more affected by observing coordinated, many-to-one hate-based campaigns against a particular target (or set of targets) versus the (pseudo)anonymous, many-to-many, intergroup kinds of *ad hominem* hate that is so common on mainstream social media? Future work might also consider which affordances are most applicable in facilitating certain kinds of hate and effects at various levels as well as potential techniques that are used to combat those effects – among individual user and at larger group levels. Such comparisons can only be made if we can clearly differentiate among various kinds of online hate and their associated effects.

References

4chan. (n.d.). *Press.* https://www.4chan.org/press

ADL. (2022). *Online hate and harassment: The American experience 2022.* https://www.adl.org/resources/report/online-hate-and-harassment-american-experience-2022

Amnesty International UK. (2017, November 20). *More than a quarter of UK women experiencing online abuse and harassment receive threats of physical or sexual assault – new research.* https://www.amnesty.org.uk/press-releases/morequarter-uk-women-experiencing-online-abuse-and-harassment-receive-threats

Anti-Defamation League (2018, September 20). New hate and old: The changing face of American White supremacy. https://www.adl.org/resources/report/new-hate-and-old-changing-face-american-white-supremacy

Ballard, M. E., & Welch, K. M. (2017). Virtual warfare: Cyberbullying and cyber-victimization in MMOG play. *Games and Culture, 12*(5), 466–491. https://doi.org/10.1177/1555412015592473

Barnidge, M., Kim, B., Sherrill, L. A., Luknar, Ž., & Zhang, J. (2019). Perceived exposure to and avoidance of hate speech in various communication settings. *Telematics and Informatics, 44,* 101263. https://doi.org/10.1016/j.tele.2019.101263

Barrie, C. (2023, August 29). Did the Musk takeover increase contentious actors on Twitter? *Harvard Kennedy School Misinformation Review, 4*(4). https://doi.org/10.37016/mr-2020-122

Barth, N., Wagner, E., Raab, P., & Wiegärtner, B. (2023). Contextures of hate: Towards a systems theory of hate communication on social media platforms. *The Communication Review, 26*(3), 209–252. https://doi.org/10.1080/10714421.2023.2208513

Bedrosova, M., Mylek, V., Dedkova, L., & Velicu, A. (2023). Who is searching for cyberhate? Adolescents' characteristics associated with intentional or unintentional exposure to cyberhate. *Cyberpsychology, Behavior, and Social Networking, 26*(7), 462–471. https://doi.org/10.1089/cyber.2022.0201

Benesch, S. (2023). Dangerous speech. In C. Strippel, S. Paasch-Colberg, M. Emmer, & J. Trebbe (Eds.), *Challenges and perspectives of hate speech research* (pp. 185–197). Social Science Open Access Repository. https://doi.org/10.48541/dcr.v12.11

Beres, N. A., Frommel, J., Reid, E., Mandryk, R. L., & Klarkowski, M. (2021, May). Don't you know that you're toxic: Normalization of toxicity in online gaming. In *Proceedings of the 2021 CHI conference on human factors in computing systems* (pp. 1–15). ACM.

Blackwell, L., Dimond, J., Schoenebeck, S., & Lampe, C. (2017). Classification and its consequences for online harassment: Design insights from Heartmob. In K. Karahalios, G. Fitzpatrick, & A. Monroy-Hernández (Eds.), *Proceedings of the ACM on human-computer interaction: Vol. 1 (CSCW)* (pp. 1–19). ACM. https://doi.org/10.1145/3134659

Blackwell, L., Ellison, N., Elliott-Deflo, N., & Schwartz, R. (2019, March). Harassment in social VR: Implications for design. In *2019 IEEE conference on virtual reality and 3D user interfaces (VR)* (pp. 854–855). IEEE. https://doi.org/10.1109/VR.2019.8798165

Bliuc, A. M., Faulkner, N., Jakubowicz, A., & McGarty, C. (2018). Online networks of racial hate: A systematic review of 10 years of research on cyber-racism. *Computers in Human Behavior, 87*, 75–86. https://doi.org/10.1016/j.chb.2018.05.026

Brown, A. (2018). What is so special about online (as compared to offline) hate speech? *Ethnicities, 18*(3), 297–326. https://doi.org/10.1177/1468796817709846

Buerger, C. (2020, December 14). The anti-hate brigade: How a group of thousands responds collectively to online vitriol. *Dangerous Speech Project*. https://dangerousspeech.org/anti-hate-brigade/

Cervone, C., Augoustinos, M., & Maass, A. (2021). The language of derogation and hate: Functions, consequences, and reappropriation. *Journal of Language and Social Psychology, 40*(1), 80–101. https://doi.org/10.1177/0261927X20967394

Chan, T. K., Cheung, C. M., Benbasat, I., Xiao, B., & Lee, Z. W. (2022). Bystanders join in cyberbullying on social networking sites: The deindividuation and moral disengagement perspectives. *Information Systems Research*. https://doi.org/10.1287/isre.2022.1161

Citron, D. K. (2014, January 16). "Revenge porn" should be a crime in U.S. *CNN*. http://edition.cnn.com/2013/08/29/opinion/citron-revenge-porn

Costello, M., Hawdon, J., Bernatzky, C., & Mendes, K. (2019). Social group identity and perceptions of online hate. *Sociological Inquiry, 89*(3), 427–452. https://doi.org/10.1111/soin.12274

Costello, M., Hawdon, J., & Ratliff, T. N. (2017). Confronting online extremism: The effect of self-help, collective efficacy, and guardianship on being a target for hate speech. *Social Science Computer Review, 35*(5), 587–605. https://doi.org/10.1177/0894439316666272

Cramer, R. J., Fording, R. C., Gerstenfeld, P., Kehn, A., Marsden, J., Deitle, C., King, A., Smart, S., & Nobles, M. R. (2020, November 9). Hate-motivated behavior: Impacts, risk factors, and interventions. *Health Affairs Journal Health Policy Brief, 9*, 1–6.

Cypris, N. F., Engelmann, S., Sasse, J., Grossklags, J., & Baumert, A. (2022). Intervening against online hate speech: A case for automated counterspeech. *IEAI Research Brief*, 1–8.

DeKeseredy, W. S. (Chapter 4 this volume). Misogyny and woman abuse in the incelosphere: The role of online incel male peer support.

Dewey, C. (2014, October 14). The only guide to Gamergate you will ever need to read. *The Washington Post*. https://www.washingtonpost.com/news/the-intersect/wp/2014/10/14/the-only-guide-to-gamergate-you-will-ever-need-to-read/

Dibbell, J. (1993, December 21). A rape in cyberspace. *The Village Voice*. https://www.juliandibbell.com/texts/bungle_vv.html

Evolvi, G. (2019). # Islamexit: Inter-group antagonism on Twitter. *Information, Communication & Society, 22*(3), 386–401. https://doi.org/10.1080/1369118X.2017.1388427

Finkel, E. J., & Eckhardt, C. I. (2013). Intimate partner violence. In J. A. Simpson & L. Campbell (Eds.), *The Oxford handbook of close relationships* (pp. 452–474). Oxford University Press. https://doi.org/10.1093/oxfordhb/9780195398694. 001.0001

Flynn, A., Powell, A., Scott, A. J., & Cama, E. (2022). Deepfakes and digitally altered imagery abuse: A cross-country exploration of an emerging form of image-based sexual abuse. *The British Journal of Criminology, 62*(6), 1341–1358.

Forestal, J. (2021). Beyond gatekeeping: Propaganda, democracy, and the organization of digital publics. *The Journal of Politics, 83*(1), 306–320. https://doi.org/10.1086/709300

Fox, J. (2023). Online social aggression: Harassment and discrimination. In R. Nabi & J. G. Myrick (Eds.), *Emotions in the digital world* (pp. 193–214). Oxford University Press. https://doi.org/10.1093/oso/9780197520536.003.0011

Freeman, G., & Acena, D. (2021, June). Hugging from a distance: Building interpersonal relationships in social virtual reality. In *ACM international conference on interactive media experiences* (pp. 84–95). ACM. https://doi.org/10.1145/3452918.3458805

Fuchs, T., & Schäfer, F. (2021, October). Normalizing misogyny: Hate speech and verbal abuse of female politicians on Japanese Twitter. *Japan Forum, 33*(4), 553–579. https://doi.org/10.1080/09555803.2019.1687564

Galinsky, A. D., Wang, C. S., Whitson, J. A., Anicich, E. M., Hugenberg, K., & Bodenhausen, G. V. (2013). The reappropriation of stigmatizing labels: The reciprocal relationship between power and self-labeling. *Psychological Science, 24*(10), 2020–2029. https://doi.org/10.1177/0956797613482943

Gaudette, T., Scrivens, R., Davies, G., & Frank, R. (2020). Upvoting extremism: Collective identity formation and the extreme right on Reddit. *New Media & Society, 23*(12), 3491–3508. https://doi.org/10.1177/1461444820958123

Gillespie, T. (2020). Content moderation, AI, and the question of scale. *Big Data & Society, 7*(2), 2053951720943234.

Gillespie, T., Aufderheide, P., Carmi, E., Gerrard, Y., Gorwa, R., Matamoros-Fernández, A., Roberts, S. T., Sinnreich, A., & Myers West, S. (2020). Expanding the debate about content moderation: Scholarly research agendas for the coming policy debates. *Internet Policy Review, 9*(4). https://doi.org/10.14763/2020.4.1512

Goel, V., Sahnan, D., Dutta, S., Bandhakavi, A., & Chakraborty, T. (2023). Hatemongers ride on echo chambers to escalate hate speech diffusion. *PNAS Nexus, 2*(3), 1–10. https://doi.org/10.1093/pnasnexus/pgad041

Google. (n.d.). *Requests to delist content under European privacy law.* https://transparencyreport.google.com/eu-privacy/overview?hl=en

Hassan, G., Rabah, J., Madriaza, P., Brouillette-Alarie, S., Borokhovski, E., Pickup, D., Varela, W., Girard, M., Durocher-Corfa, L., & Danis, E. (2022). PROTOCOL: Hate online and in traditional media: A systematic review of the evidence for associations or impacts on individuals, audiences, and communities. *Campbell Systematic Reviews, 18*(2), e1245. https://doi.org/10.1002/cl2.1245

Hayes, R. A., Carr, C. T., & Wohn, D. Y. (2016). One click, many meanings: Interpreting paralinguistic digital affordances in social media. *Journal of Broadcasting & Electronic Media, 60*(1), 171–187. https://doi.org/10.1080/08838151.2015.1127248

Herring, S., Job-Sluder, K., Scheckler, R., & Barab, S. (2002). Searching for safety online: Managing "trolling" in a feminist forum. *The Information Society, 18*(5), 371–384. https://doi.org/10.1080/01972240290108186

Hine, G., Onaolapo, J., De Cristofaro, E., Kourtellis, N., Leontiadis, I., Samaras, R., Stringhini, G., & Blackburn, J. (2017, May). Kek, cucks, and god emperor trump: A measurement study of 4chan's politically incorrect forum and its effects on the web. *Proceedings of the International AAAI Conference on Web and Social Media, 11*(1), 92–101. AAAI. https://doi.org/10.1609/icwsm.v11i1.14893

Hubbard, L. (2020, June). Online hate crime report 2020. *Galop.* https://galop.org.uk/resource/online-hate-crime-report-2020/

Jane, E. A. (2020). Online abuse and harassment. In K. Ross, I. Bachmann, V. Cardo, S. Moorti, & C. M. Scarcelli (Eds.), *The international encyclopedia of gender, media, and communication* (Vol. 116). https://doi.org/10.1002/9781119429128.iegmc080

Jasser, G., McSwiney, J., Pertwee, E., & Zannettou, S. (2023). 'Welcome to# GabFam': Far-right virtual community on Gab. *New Media & Society, 25*(7), 1728–1745. https://doi.org/10.1177/14614448211024

Keighley, R. (2022). Hate hurts: Exploring the impact of online hate on LGBTQ+ young people. *Women & Criminal Justice, 32*(1–2), 29–48. https://doi.org/10.1080/08974454.2021.1988034

Kenski, K., Coe, K., & Rains, S. A. (2020). Perceptions of uncivil discourse online: An examination of types and predictors. *Communication Research, 47*(6), 795–814.

Lee, B. Y. (2020, June 24). Trump once again calls COVID-19 coronavirus the "kung flu". *Forbes.* https://www.forbes.com/sites/brucelee/2020/06/24/trump-once-again-calls-covid-19-coronavirus-the-kung-flu/?sh=49eec66a1f59

Lee, C. S. (2022). Analyzing Zoombombing as a new communication tool of cyber-hate in the COVID-19 era. *Online Information Review, 46*(1), 147–163. https://doi.org/10.1108/OIR-05-2020-0203

Lewis, R., Marwick, A. E., & Partin, W. C. (2021). "We dissect stupidity and respond to it": Response videos and networked harassment on YouTube. *American Behavioral Scientist, 65*(5), 735–756. https://doi.org/10.1177/0002764221989781

Lingiardi, V., Carone, N., Semeraro, G., Musto, C., D'Amico, M., & Brena, S. (2020). Mapping Twitter hate speech towards social and sexual minorities: A lexicon-based approach to semantic content analysis. *Behaviour & Information Technology, 39*(7), 711–721. https://doi.org/10.1080/0144929X.2019.1607903

Lupu, Y., Sear, R., Velásquez, N., Leahy, R., Restrepo, N. J., Goldberg, B., & Johnson, N. F. (2023). Offline events and online hate. *PLoS One, 18*(1), e0278511.

Lytle, R. D., Bratton, T. M., & Hudson, H. K. (2021). Bystander apathy and intervention in the era of social media. In J. Bailey, A. Flynn, & N. Henry (Eds.) *The emerald international handbook of technology-facilitated violence and abuse* (pp. 711–728). Emerald Publishing Limited. https://doi.org/10.1108/978-1-83982-848-520211052

Marwick, A. E. (2021). Morally motivated networked harassment as normative reinforcement. *Social Media + Society, 7*(2). https://doi.org/10.1177/20563051211021378

Massanari, A. (2017). #Gamergate and the fappening: How Reddit's algorithm, governance, and culture support toxic technocultures. *New Media & Society, 19*(3), 329–346. https://doi.org/10.1177/1461444815608807

Matamoros-Fernández, A., & Farkas, J. (2021). Racism, hate speech, and social media: A systematic review and critique. *Television & New Media, 22*(2), 205–224. https://doi.org/10.1177/1527476420982230

Mathew, B., Illendula, A., Saha, P., Sarkar, S., Goyal, P., & Mukherjee, A. (2020). Hate begets hate: A temporal study of hate speech. *Proceedings of the ACM on Human-Computer Interaction, 4*, Article 92, 1–24. ACM. https://doi.org/10.1145/3415163

Meyers, S. L., & Thompson, S. A. (2022, June 1). Racist and violent ideas jump from web's fringes to mainstream sites. *The New York Times.* https://www.nytimes.com/2022/06/01/technology/fringe-mainstream-social-media.html

Munger, K. (2017). Tweetment effects on the tweeted: Experimentally reducing racist harassment. *Political Behavior, 39*, 629–649. https://doi.org/10.1007/s11109-016-9373-5

Munger, K., & Phillips, J. (2022). Right-wing YouTube: A supply and demand perspective. *The International Journal of Press/Politics, 27*(1), 186–219. https://doi.org/10.1177/19401612209647

Nida, S. A. (2020). Bystander apathy. In I. Johnsrude (Ed.), *Oxford research encyclopedia of psychology*. Oxford University Press. https://doi.org/10.1093/acrefore/9780190236557.013.808

Obermaier, M. (2022). Youth on standby? Explaining adolescent and young adult bystanders' intervention against online hate speech. *New Media & Society*. Advance online publication. https://doi.org/10.1177/14614448221125417

Obermaier, M., & Schmuck, D. (2022). Youths as targets: Factors of online hate speech victimization among adolescents and young adults. *Journal of Computer-Mediated Communication*, 27(4), zmac012. https://doi.org/10.1093/jcmc/zmac012

Obermaier, M., Schmuck, D., & Saleem, M. (2021). I'll be there for you? Effects of Islamophobic online hate speech and counter speech on Muslim in-group bystanders' intention to intervene. *New Media & Society*, 25(9), 2339–2358. https://doi.org/10.1177/14614448211017527

Ortiz, S. M. (2019). "You can say I got desensitized to it": How men of color cope with everyday racism in online gaming. *Sociological Perspectives*, 62(4), 572–588. https://doi.org/10.1080/01639625.2020.1722337

Pariser, E. (2011). *The filter bubble: What the Internet is hiding from you*. Penguin Press.

Paz, M. A., Montero-Díaz, J., & Moreno-Delgado, A. (2020). Hate speech: A systematized review. *Sage Open*, 10(4). https://doi.org/10.1177/2158244020973022

Phadke, S., & Mitra, T. (Chapter 9 this volume). Inter-platform information sharing, roles, and information differences that exemplify social processes of online hate groups.

Postmes, T., Spears, R., & Lea, M. (2002). Intergroup differentiation in computer-mediated communication: Effects of depersonalization. *Group Dynamics: Theory, Research, and Practice*, 6(1), 3–16. https://doi.org/10.1037/1089-2699.6.1.3

Rea, S., Mathew, B., & Kraemer, J. (Chapter 8 this volume). 'Hate parties': Networked antisemitism from the fringes to YouTube.

Reichelmann, A., Hawdon, J., Costello, M., Ryan, J., Blaya, C., Llorent, V., Oksanen, A., Räsänen, P., & Zych, I. (2021). Hate knows no boundaries: Online hate in six nations. *Deviant Behavior*, 42(9), 1100–1111. https://doi.org/10.1080/01639625.2020.1722337

Ribeiro, M. H., Hosseinmardi, H., West, R., & Watts, D. J. (2023). Deplatforming did not decrease Parler users' activity on fringe social media. *PNAS Nexus*, 2(3), pgad035. https://doi.org/10.1093/pnasnexus/pgad035

Rice, R. E. (Chapter 12 this volume). Themes, challenges, and implications of social processes of online hate.

Rieger, D., Kümpel, A. S., Wich, M., Kiening, T., & Groh, G. (2021). Assessing the extent and types of hate speech in fringe communities: A case study of alt-right communities on 8chan, 4chan, and Reddit. *Social Media + Society*, 7(4). https://doi.org/10.1177/20563051211052906

Roden, J., & Saleem, M. (2022). White apathy and allyship in uncivil racial social media comments. *Mass Communication and Society*, 25(3), 383–406. https://doi.org/10.1080/15205436.2021.1955933

Rogers, R. (2018). Otherwise engaged: Social media from vanity metrics to critical analytics. *International Journal of Communication*, 12, 450–472. https://ijoc.org/index.php/ijoc/article/view/6407/2248

Rogers, R. (2020). Deplatforming: Following extreme Internet celebrities to Telegram and alternative social media. *European Journal of Communication*, 35(3), 213–229. https://doi.org/10.1177/0267323120922066

Romano, A. (2023, May 1). "The 'Dark Brandon' meme – and why the Biden campaign has embraced it – explained. *Vox*. https://www.vox.com/culture/23300286/biden-dark-brandon-meme-maga-why-confusing-explained

Rösner, L., & Krämer, N. C. (2016). Verbal venting in the social web: Effects of anonymity and group norms on aggressive language use in online comments. *Social Media + Society*, 2(3), https://doi.org/10.1177/2056305116664220

Rudnicki, K., Vandebosch, H., Voué, P., & Poels, K. (2023). Systematic review of determinants and consequences of bystander interventions in online hate and cyberbullying among adults. *Behaviour & Information Technology*, 42(5), 527–544. https://doi.org/10.1080/0144929X.2022.2027013

Salminen, J., Sengün, S., Corporan, J., Jung, S. G., & Jansen, B. J. (2020). Topic-driven toxicity: Exploring the relationship between online toxicity and news topics. *PLoS One*, 15(2), e0228723. https://doi.org/10.1371/journal.pone.0228723

Schäfer, S., Rebasso, I., Boyer, M. M., & Planitzer, A. M. (2023). Can we counteract hate? Effects of online hate speech and counter speech on the perception of social groups. *Communication Research*. Advance online publication. https://doi.org/10.1177/00936502231201091

Schmid, U. K., Kümpel, A. S., & Rieger, D. (2022). How social media users perceive different forms of online hate speech: A qualitative multi-method study. *New Media & Society*. https://doi.org/10.1177/14614448221091185

Schoenebeck, S., & Blackwell, L. (2021). Reimagining social media governance: Harm, accountability, and repair. *SSRN Electronic Journal*. https://doi.org/10.2139/ssrn.3895779

Schoenebeck, S., Lampe, C., & Triệu, P. (2023). Online harassment: Assessing harms and remedies. *Social Media + Society*, 9(1). https://doi.org/10.1177/2056305123115729

Schöpke-Gonzalez, A. M., Atreja, S., Shin, H. N., Ahmed, N., & Hemphill, L. (2022). Why do volunteer content moderators quit? Burnout, conflict, and harmful behaviors. *New Media & Society*. Advance online publication. https://doi.org/10.1177/14614448221138529

Schulenberg, K., Freeman, G., Li, L., & Barwulor, C. (2023). "Creepy towards my avatar body, creepy towards my body": How women experience and manage harassment risks in social virtual reality. In *Proceedings of the ACM on human computer interaction (PACM HCI), CSCW 23*. ACM. https://guof.people.clemson.edu/papers/cscw23women.pdf

Scrivens, R., Osuna, A. I., Chermak, S. M., Whitney, M. A., & Frank, R. (2021). Examining online indicators of extremism in violent right-wing extremist forums. *Studies in Conflict & Terrorism*, 35(6). https://doi.org/10.1080/10576 10X.2021.1913818

Sharif, M. Z. (2018). Islamophobia, health, and public health: A systematic literature review. *American Journal of Public Health*, 108(6), e1–e9. https://doi.org/10.2105/AJPH.2018.304402

Shear, M. D., Kang, C., & Sanger, D. E. (2023, July 21). Pressured by Biden, A.I. companies agree to guardrails on new tools. *The New York Times*. https://www.nytimes.com/2023/07/21/us/politics/ai-regulation-biden.html

Shmargad, Y., Coe, K., Kenski, K., Rains, S., & Bethard, S. (Chapter 10 this volume). Detecting anti-social norms in large-scale online discussions.

Siegel, A. A. (2020). Online hate speech. In N. Persily & J. A. Tucker (Eds.) *Social media and democracy: The state of the field, prospects for reform* (pp. 56–88). Oxford University Press.

Smith, B., & Linden, G. (2017). Two decades of recommender systems at Amazon.com. *IEEE Internet Computing*, 21(3), 12–18. https://10.1109/MIC.2017.72

Smith, J. J., Jayne, L., & Burke, R. (2022, September). Recommender systems and algorithmic hate. In J. Golbeck, F. M. Harper, V. Murdock, M. Ekstrand, B. Shapira, J. Basilico, K. Lundgaard, & E. Oldridge (Eds.), *Proceedings of the 16th ACM conference on recommender systems* (pp. 592–597). ACM. https://doi.org/10.1145/3523227.3551480

Spence, R., Harrison, A., Bradbury, P., Bleakley, P., Martellozzo, E., & DeMarco, J. (2023). Content moderators' strategies for coping with the stress of moderating content online. *Journal of Online Trust and Safety, 1*(5). https://doi.org/10.54501/jots.v1i5

Statista. (2023, April 17). *Number of Gettr app downloads worldwide from 3rd quarter 2021 to 4th quarter 2022, by region.* https://www.statista.com/statistics/1359898/gettr-number-of-worldwide-downloads-by-region/

Statt, N. (2020, April 3). 'Zoombombing' is a federal offense that could result in imprisonment, prosecutors warn. *The Verge.* https://www.theverge.com/2020/4/3/21207260/zoombombing-crime-zoom-video-conference-hacking-pranks-doj-fbi

Stringhini, G., & Blackburn, J. (Chapter 11 this volume). Understanding the phases and themes of coordinated online aggression attacks.

Suler, J. (2004). The online disinhibition effect. *Cyberpsychology, Behavior, & Social Networking, 7*(3), 321–326. https://doi.org/10.1089/1094931041291295

Tahmasbi, F., Schild, L., Ling, C., Blackburn, J., Stringhini, G., Zhang, Y., & Zannettou, S. (2021, April). "Go eat a bat, Chang!": On the emergence of Sinophobic behavior on web communities in the face of COVID-19. In *Proceedings of the web conference 2021* (pp. 1122–1133). ACM. https://doi.org/10.1145/3442381.3450024

Telegram. (2022, June 19). *700 million users and Telegram premium.* https://telegram.org/blog/700-million-and-premium

Thomas, D. R., & Wahedi, L. A. (2023). Disrupting hate: The effect of deplatforming hate organizations on their online audience. *Proceedings of the National Academy of Sciences, 120*(24), e2214080120. https://doi.org/10.1073/pnas.2214080120

Thomas, K., Akhawe, D., Bailey, M., Boneh, D., Bursztein, E., Consolvo, S., Dell, N., Durumeric, Z., Kelley, P. G., Kumar, D., McCoy, D., Meiklejohn, S., Ristenpart, T., & Stringhini, G. (2021, May). Sok: Hate, harassment, and the changing landscape of online abuse. In *2021 IEEE symposium on security and privacy (SP)* (pp. 247–267). IEEE.

Tiffany, K. (2022, April 22). Doxxing means whatever you want it to. *The Atlantic.* https://www.theatlantic.com/technology/archive/2022/04/doxxing-meaning-libs-of-tiktok/629643/

Tong, S. T. (Chapter 3 this volume). Foundations, definitions, and directions in online hate research.

Tong, S. T., & DeAndrea, D. C. (2023). The effects of observer expectations on judgments of anti-Asian hate tweets and online activism response. *Social Media + Society, 9*(1). https://doi.org/10.1177/2056305123115729

Tong, S. T., Stoycheff, E., & Mitra, R. (2022). Racism and resilience of pandemic proportions: Online harassment of Asian Americans during COVID-19. *Journal of Applied Communication Research, 50*(6), 595–612. https://doi.org/10.1080/00909882.2022.2141068

Tong, S. T., Van Der Heide, B., Langwell, L., & Walther, J. B. (2008). Too much of a good thing? The relationship between number of friends and interpersonal impressions on Facebook. *Journal of Computer-Mediated Communication, 13*(3), 531–549. https://doi.org/10.1111/j.1083-6101.2008.00409.x

Törnberg, A., & Törnberg, P. (Chapter 5 this volume). From echo chambers to digital campfires: The making of an online community of hate within Stormfront.

Treem, J. W., & Leonardi, P. M. (2013). Social media use in organizations: Exploring the affordances of visibility, editability, persistence, and association. *Annals of the International Communication Association, 36*(1), 143–189. https://doi.org/10.1080/23808985.2013.11679130

Trujillo, A., & Cresci, S. (2022). Make Reddit great again: Assessing community effects of moderation interventions on r/The_Donald. *Proceedings of the ACM on Human-Computer Interaction, 6*(CSCW2), Article 526. ACM. https://doi.org/10.1145/3555639

Twitch. (n.d.). *Safety Advisory Council*. https://safety.twitch.tv/s/article/Safety-Advisory-Council?language=en_US

Twitter. (2023, April). *Hateful conduct*. https://help.twitter.com/en/rules-and-policies/hateful-conduct-policy

Udupa, S., & Gerold, O. L. (Chapter 6 this volume). 'Deal' of the day: Sex, porn, and political hate on social media.

United Nations. (n.d.a) *Impact and prevention: Targets of online hate*. www.un.org/en/hate-speech/impact-and-prevention/targets-of-hate

United Nations. (n.d.b) *Understanding hate speech*. https://www.un.org/en/hate-speech/understanding-hate-speech/what-is-hate-speech

United States Department of Justice. (n.d.) *Learn about hate crimes*. www.justice.gov/hatecrimes/learn-about-hate-crimes/chart

Vogels, E. (2021, January 13). The state of online harassment. *Pew Research*. https://www.pewresearch.org/internet/2021/01/13/the-state-of-online-harassment/

Wakabayashi, D. (2020, May 28). Legal shield for social media is targeted by lawmakers. *The New York Times*. https://nytimes.com/2020/05/28/business/section-230-internet-speech.html

Walther, J. B. (2022). Social media and online hate. *Current Opinion in Psychology*, *45*, 101298. https://doi.org/10.1016/j.copsyc.2021.12.010

Walther, J. B. (Chapter 2 this volume). Making a case for a social processes approach to online hate.

Walther, J. B., & Jang, J.-W. (2012). Communication processes in participatory web sites. *Journal of Computer-Mediated Communication*, *18*(1), 2–15. https://doi.org/10.1111/j.1083-6101.2012.01592.x

Walther, S., & McCoy, A. (2021). US extremism on Telegram. *Perspectives on Terrorism*, *15*(2), 100–124. https://www.jstor.org/stable/e27007290

Waqas, A., Salminen, J., Jung, S. G., Almerekhi, H., & Jansen, B. J. (2019). Mapping online hate: A scientometric analysis on research trends and hotspots in research on online hate. *PLoS One*, *14*(9), e0222194. https://doi.org/10.1371/journal.pone.0222194

Whittaker, J., Looney, S., Reed, A., & Votta, F. (2021). Recommender systems and the amplification of extremist content. *Internet Policy Review*, *10*(2). https://doi.org/10.14763/2021.2.1565

Wilson, C., Sheridan, L., & Garratt-Reed, D. (2022). What is cyberstalking? A review of measurements. *Journal of Interpersonal Violence*, *37*(11–12), NP9763–NP9783. https://doi.org/10.1177/0886260520985489

Woods, F. A., & Ruscher, J. B. (2021). Viral sticks, virtual stones: Addressing anonymous hate speech online. *Patterns of Prejudice*, *55*(3), 265–289. https://doi.org/10.1080/0031322X.2021.1968586

Åkerlund, M. (2021). Influence without metrics: Analyzing the impact of far-right users in an online discussion forum. *Social Media + Society*, *7*(2). https://doi.org/10.1177/20563051211008831

4

MISOGYNY AND WOMAN ABUSE IN THE INCELOSPHERE

The Role of Online Incel Male Peer Support

Walter S. DeKeseredy

There is now a voluminous body of social scientific knowledge about what Levin and Nolan (2017) refer to as "the violence of hate,"[1] one that focuses primarily on face-to-face and online crimes against certain racial/ethnic and religious groups and members of the LGBTQ+ community. There is, however, as Bates (2020) puts it, "an extremism that nobody is talking about" and that is "men who hate women" (p. 2). She also reminds us that:

> We do not use the word "terrorism" when describing a crime of mass murder committed by a white man with the explicit intention of creating terror and spreading hatred against a specific demographic group – even though that is the definition of terrorism – if the demographic in question is women. . . . We do not call his online journey a "radicalization" or use the word "extremism" to label the online communities in which he immersed himself, though we would reach for those words in an instant when describing other, similar types of crimes, committed by other, different types of men. We do not examine what led him to commit those acts or how he became so full of hate.
>
> (p. 3)

There is a growing number of movements located in the digital world marked by extensive misogyny and male entitlement, as identified by various studies (Schwartz, 2021). One prime example is the *incel movement*. The hate spewed by incels predated the Internet, but this movement was splintered until the emergence of contemporary technology. The Internet now not only facilitates easy access to peaceful like-minded people, but it has also, to a

DOI: 10.4324/9781003472148-4

certain extent, created an environment that normalizes the hatred of women and racial/ethnic minority groups. Though the incel community is, as uncovered by Bates (2020) and others, "the most violent corner of the so-called manosphere," most people have never heard of incels; thus, much more political, scholarly, and media attention to the harms caused by them is crucial and important (p. 7).

The main objective of this chapter is to identify how *incel male peer support* contributes to in-person and digital variants of *woman abuse*. Male peer support refers to the attachments to male peers and the resources that these men provide that encourage and legitimate these gendered harms (DeKeseredy, 1988). Prior to covering empirical and theoretical social scientific work on the social processes associated with incel male peer support, it is first necessary to supply a brief history of the incel movement, also known as *the incelosphere* (Center for Countering Digital Hate, 2022).

What Are Incels?

The term *incel* was originally created in the 1990s by a Canadian woman who developed a website for lonely singles (DeKeseredy & Rennison, 2019; Yang & Gillis, 2018). It now means "involuntary celibate." Members of the incel movement are patriarchal men who assert that they cannot have sex with women but want to. An incel, according to Incels.Me,[2] is a "person who is not in a relationship nor has had sex in a significant amount of time, despite numerous attempts" (p. 1). Incels are also anti-feminist men who have sharp disdain for "Chads" and "Stacys." Chads are, as Incels. Me describes them, "sexually satisfied men, charismatic, tall, good looking, confident, muscular," and "Stacys" are stereotypically attractive women who reject incels' sexual advances (p. 1). Further, the incel movement consists of what Kimmel (2017) defines as a "new breed of angry white men" who are experiencing *aggrieved entitlement*:

> It is that sense that those benefits to which you believed yourself entitled have been snatched away from you by unseen forces larger and more powerful. You feel yourself to be the heir to a great promise, the American dream, which has turned into an impossible fantasy for the very people who were *supposed* to inherit it.
>
> (p. 18, emphasis in original)

Incels declare that: Inceldom has no relation with violence, misogyny, or illegal activities of any kind. Every once in a while, when a tragedy happens, the term incel is thrown around and we get an influx of guests. We do not advocate any illegal activity, nor do we allow it on the site.

(Incels.Me, 2018, p. 1)

Yet, as the Center for Countering Digital Hate (2022) uncovered, incels and other online misogynistic all-male groups "argue with each other, support each other, share ideas, promote each other's lexicon and values. In short, they are brothers-in-arms in a war against women" (p. 7). Also, countless online postings by incel members praise mass murderer Elliot Rodger, who is a hero and/or martyr in the incelosphere. For example, Alek Minassian, another mass murderer to be briefly discussed later in this section, ended a Facebook post before his 2018 rampage with the statement, "All hail the Supreme Gentleman Elliot Rodger" (CNN U.S., 2018, p. 1).

On May 23, 2014, in Isla Vista, California, the United States, Elliot Rodger murdered a total of 6 people (2 of whom were women) and injured 13 others before killing himself. Prior to shooting and killing the people outside a sorority house, he uploaded a video to YouTube titled "Elliot Rodger's Retribution,"[3] a misogynistic diatribe that includes these statements:

> Girls gave their affection and sex and love to other men, but never to me. I'm 22-years-old and still a virgin. I've never even kissed a girl. I've been through college for two and a half years, more than that actually, and I'm still a virgin. It's not fair. You girls have never been attracted to me. I don't know why you girls aren't attracted to me, but I will punish you all for it. It's an injustice, a crime, because I don't know what you don't see in me. I'm the perfect guy, and yet you throw yourselves at all these obnoxious men instead of me – the supreme gentlemen. I will punish all of you for it. If I can't have you girls, I will destroy you.
>
> You forced me to suffer all my life, and now I'll make you suffer. I've waited a long time for this. I'll give you exactly what you deserve, all of you. All you girls who rejected me and looked down upon me and, you know, treated me like scum while you give yourselves to other men. All of you men, for living a better life than me – all of you sexually active men, I hate you. I hate all of you and I can't wait to give you exactly what you deserve: utter annihilation.

Some of Rodger's words resemble those of many men who commit *intimate femicide* during or after the process of separation/divorce (DeKeseredy & Rennison, 2019): "If I can't have you, no one will" (Polk, 2003, p. 134). Intimate femicide is the killing of females by male partners with whom they have, have had, or want to have, a sexual and/or emotional relationship (Ellis & DeKeseredy, 1997).

Returning to Alek Minassian, in Toronto, Ontario, Canada, on April 23, 2018, he drove a rented van onto a curb on Young Street, south of Finch Avenue and deliberately ran down pedestrians, resulting in the worst mass murder thus far in Toronto's history (Yang & Gillis, 2018). His attack left 10 people dead (8 of whom were women) and 16 people injured. Since then, dozens more have been murdered by self-proclaimed incels around the world. Moreover, the Center for Countering Digital Hate's (2022) recent study of the incel forum found that its members post about rape every 29 minutes. The Center's study will also be referred to in subsequent sections of this chapter, but the study does not name the incel forum it examined to "avoid giving it publicity" (p. 6). The Center, however, claims that this forum is the largest one online.

The hatred of women is just one element of the incel ideology. Incels have strong connections to other extreme right-wing movements such as those promoting unbridled gun ownership, homophobia, racist discourses and practices, and policies and laws aimed at ending women's control over their reproductive health (DeKeseredy, 2022). Below are some of the most popular threads located on the incel forum, which was founded in 2017 by Diego Joaquin Galante (also known as "Sergeant Incel") (Nashrula, 2019) and studied by the Center for Countering Digital Hate (2022):

- American culture is centered around n*ggers.
- Society should return to tradition.
- I just want to go back to exploring new lands, killing enemies and raping countless foids.[4]
- With religion collapsing, foids celebrate the new age of globohomo, drag fags, pedos, and zoophiles.
- Earth needs an extinction event.
- I hate modern day.
- Women, like most western governments, want to uphold the current hierarchy, want you to have nothing, and want you to be happy with it.
- It's one of the Jews' tactics to control the world. And you can thank the Jews for destroying and altering this culture into a negative connotation of its former self.
- I think every virgin male should be granted a few guns, licenses, and unlimited van rentals paid for by the government.
- The future is masculinity – pure white masculinity. No weakness, no vulnerability, no femininity, no sex. Just pure, glorious strength and might as we conquer the cosmos and enslave it to us (cited in Jgin, 2023, p. 1).

What types of social media are used by incels and what do they post? Turning to the first question, the Center for Countering Digital Hate (2022) examined the number of links to websites from the incel forum between January 2021 and July 2022 and uncovered that links to YouTube were posted over 14,000 times, making it the most linked-to site on the platform. Reddit ranked second with over 5,000 links; links to other popular social media networks were also frequently uploaded, with 1,149 links to Twitter and 862 to TikTok, respectively. Incel communities are also on Facebook, 4chan, and on various sites run by incels themselves. Note, too, that the Center for Countering Digital Hate found that the United States accounted for the vast majority (43.8%) of web traffic to the incel forum, followed by the United Kingdom (7.5%) and Poland (4.2%). Moreover, the forum has 17,000 members and receives approximately 2.6 million visitors each month.

What do incels post? The best answers to date are also provided by the Center for Countering Digital Hate (2022), which found that the incel forum is a "self-proclaimed heterosexual male-only forum" that "prohibits women and the LGBTQ+ community and non-incels from attaining membership" (p. 12). As has been observed in several chapters of this book, while there are clearly "targets" of the hate that incels express online, the intended audience for such hate messages are not the targets they mention; it is other contributors to the hateful discussion (see, e.g., Walther, this volume). What is more,

- Over a fifth of the posts in the forum feature misogynist, racist, antisemitic or anti-LGBTQ+ language, with 16% of posts featuring misogynist slurs (p. 6).
- Forum threads are mainly centered around frustration and relationships, and the "black pill ideology," which revolves around the core belief that the ability to establish romantic relationships is determined by appearance and therefore genetics (p. 11).

Tranchese and Sugiura's (2021) linguistic analysis of the postings in the r/incels channel, or "Subreddit" within the Reddit social media platform, shows that there is also a strong connection between incel and mainstream pornography discourse. More specifically, these researchers found that in both discourses:

[M]uch of the denigration of women focuses on their sexuality. Their imagery and language present women as objects who deserve and enjoy sexual abuse and submission, and sex (particularly through the penis and semen) as a weapon to inflict these and express their hate. On r/incels the fact that hatred is the motivation behind the abuse is explicit. In pornography, this motive is often covert and consequently, easier to justify. . . . [T]he men in pornography are the embodiment of Chads. They have constant access to women despite hating them and treating them badly. While incels despise and envy Chads for this, for them these men (and their dominant sexuality) are the only way to obtain their revenge. What all these men have in common is the wish to see women suffer through sex, while drawing pleasure and satisfaction from it.

(p. 2728)

It should be mentioned in passing that violent porn is now mainstream. Routine features are painful anal penetration; brutal gang rape; and men slapping, pushing, gagging, choking, and pulling women's hair while they penetrate them orally, vaginally, and anally (Bridges et al., 2010; DeKeseredy et al., 2023; Fritz et al., 2020). Males constitute most of the perpetrators in porn videos, and the targets of their physical and verbal aggression are primarily female. What is more, female performers often show pleasure or respond neutrally to male aggression.

Theorizing the Incelosphere: The Contribution of Male Peer Support Theory

Male Peer Support and the Incelosphere

Although interdisciplinary research on incels is rapidly expanding, most of the work done so far is descriptive and atheoretical. Even so, some leading experts in the field (e.g., Thorburn et al., 2023) recognize the value of *male peer support theory*. The theory was originally developed in my prior research (see DeKeseredy, 1988) to explain why some men, due to their attachments to patriarchal and abusive male peers, abuse women in offline contexts. The social processes associated with male peer support have received much empirical scrutiny. Today, we have a wealth of rigorous qualitative and quantitative data supporting what Lee Bowker (1983) declared 40 years ago:

> This is not a subculture that is confined to a single class, religion, occupational grouping or race. It is spread throughout all parts of society. Men are socialized by other subculture members to accept common definitions of the situation, norms, values, and beliefs about male dominance and the necessity of keeping their wives in line. These violence-supporting social relations may occur at any time and in any place.
>
> (pp. 135–136)

Documented by a large sociological literature,[5] male peer pressure that legitimates the sexual objectification of women and the sexual, physical, and/ or psychological abuse of them is found in male collegial and professional contact sports (DeKeseredy, 2023; DeKeseredy et al., 2023), among African American men in Chicago (Wilson, 1996), among Puerto Rican drug dealers in East Harlem and poor African American boys in parts of St. Louis (Bourgois, 1995; Miller, 2008), on Canadian university/college campuses and their immediate surroundings (DeKeseredy & Schwartz, 1998), in rural Ohio and Kentucky (DeKeseredy, 2021; Websdale, 1998), and in rural New Zealand and rural South Africa (Campbell, 2000; Jewkes et al., 2006).

As uncovered by recent research on incels, sexual violence and harassment in the Metaverse, and on patriarchal men's rights groups (Center for Countering Digital Hate, 2022; DeKeseredy, 2022; SumOfUs, 2022), there is also strong evidence of the emergence of pro-abuse male peer support groups in cyberspace and many men who abuse women consume electronic forms of pornography with their male friends (DeKeseredy, 2020; DeKeseredy & Schwartz, 2016).

Research on male peer support processes inside the incelosphere is in its infancy, but based on the limited amount of empirical work done so far, we can conclude that there is a variety of sociological and social psychological processes by which male peers influence men to abuse women. Based on the writings of male peer support theorists DeKeseredy and Schwartz (2016), it appears that incels encourage, justify, and support violence against women as a means of repairing the damage done to their masculinity by Stacys and other women who fail to live up to their patriarchal standards (Manne, 2018). Incel male peer support influences men to "lash out" against women they cannot control (Bourgois, 1995), and their digital communication patterns are effective ways to do so. Consider that the Center for Countering Digital Hate (2022) found that incel forum members frequently post about rape, and 89% of posters are supportive of such violent discussions. As Tranchese and Sugiura (2021), discovered:

> What incels really hate – and what they blame feminists for – is women who refuse *them*, women who sleep with several men but say "no" to incels. It is these women who receive most online (sexualized) abuse (Lewis et al., 2017), arguably in an attempt to control them through silencing. This generates a paradoxical situation, in which derogatory terms that refer to "promiscuous" women are not being used for women who participate in sexual acts with numerous men, but for women who say "no."
>
> (p. 2723)

There are various types of male peer support in offline all-male patriarchal cohorts, but decades of research show that the most powerful form is *informational support*, which is guidance and advice that influence men to abuse women. Male peer support theory sees such informational support as a motivational factor, allowing men to develop pro-abuse attitudes and behaviors as a result of the encouragement and support of other males, if not the broader culture at large (Brubaker, 2019). However, in the case of the incel forum, the millions of visits to the forum greatly exceed the number of "conversations," which appear to be driven by a relatively smaller number of "powerusers." For instance, the Center for Countering Digital Hate (2002) found that since January, 2021, postings were driven mainly by a "dedicated core" of roughly 400 such users who made nearly three-quarters of all posts.

Online communities with members who never come into face-to-face contact with each other but who often exchange written, audio, and visual information with their peers are growing every day. Currently, 76% of Internet users take part in an online community (Troiano, 2022). The incel coalition is a prime example, and, as noted by the Center for Countering Digital Hate (2022), it "has developed its own intricate and extensive in-group language. Members extensively use specific terminology when interacting with each other and also employ it as a gatekeeping method that allows them to quickly identify who is welcome into the community" (p. 4). Such language exemplifies informational support.

It is not uncommon for patriarchal male peer support networks like the incel community to have a small number of *charismatic leaders* who embody *hegemonic masculine qualities* and offer the bulk of informational support (DeKeseredy, 2019; Joosse & Willey, 2020). Hegemonic masculinity is the dominant form of masculinity in the United States and in many, if not most, other countries (Connell, 1995; Katz, 2016), which is not surprising because most societies around the world are patriarchal (DeKeseredy, 2021; Renzetti, 2018). The basic components of hegemonic masculinity are: (1) Avoid all things feminine, (2) restrict emotions severely, (3) show toughness and aggression, (4) exhibit self-reliance, (5) strive for achievement and status, (6) exhibit nonrelational attitudes toward sexuality, and (7) engage in homophobia (Connell & Messerschmidt, 2005; DeKeseredy, 2017; Levant, 1995; Ptacek, 2023; Schwartz & DeKeseredy, 1997). Masculinities studies show that men are encouraged to live up to these ideals and are sanctioned for not doing so (DeKeseredy, 2019; West & Zimmerman, 1987). Furthermore, as masculinities theorist James Messerschmidt (1993) has argued, participating in the incel forum "is a resource, when other resources are unavailable, for accomplishing masculinity" (p. 85).

Not only do power users' peers publicly support the claim that sexual assault and other forms of abuse are legitimate means of *reasserting patriarchy* (Dragiewicz, 2008), they also serve as role models because some of them engage in lethal and nonlethal forms of violence against women who "they feel have wronged them" (Bates, 2020, p. 182). The precise number of incels who physically hurt women is thus far unclear, but what is known is that much of incel violence is digital and involves using *image-based sexual abuse* (sometimes referred to as *revenge porn*) against women they dislike, who left or broke off with them, or who try to stop their misogynist activities (DeKeseredy & Schwartz, 2016; Salter & Crofts, 2015).[6] For example, some studies reviewed by Henry et al. (2021) found that there are all-male forums that "specialize" in the sharing and trading of nonconsensual photos and/or videos taken of current or former female partners.

A more recent trend in image-based sexual abuse is, using artificial intelligence, posting *deepfake pornography*. There is a major demand for such porn as revealed by a growing number of online communities, forums, services, and websites (Ajder et al., 2019). Deepfaking entails replacing the face of one person with another one's to make it appear that a person is featured in a porn video when they are not (Henry et al., 2021; Okolie, 2023). Moreover, some deepfake tools are used to "spit out" constructed images depicting rape and child abuse because no one was hurt in the creation of such content, and thus it does not violate any laws (Hunter, 2023).

Incel communities, of course, are not the only online male peer support subcultures. Extensive research done by DeKeseredy (2022), Dragiewicz (2008, 2011, 2018), and others (e.g., Kimmel, 2017) show that some conservative men's and fathers' rights groups encourage men to hurt their ex-partners by portraying image-based sexual abuse and physical violence as acceptable solutions to their problems. One should reflect, too, on the overwhelming amount of male misogynistic social media responses to actor Johnny Depp's 2022 defamation trial against his ex-wife Amber Heard. There was a concerted anti-feminist effort to ferociously mobilize against Heard, and, as Scott (2022) observes, Depp's legal victory is also that of angry white men. "The rage of men whose grievances are inchoate and exhaustible found expression in a 58-year-old movie star's humiliation of his 36-year-old former wife" (p. 1).

Patriarchy and Misogyny Also Matter

Hence, of the limited theoretical work done so far on all-male social networks' digital abuse of women (e.g., DeKeseredy & Olsson, 2011; DeKeseredy & Schwartz, 2016), male peer support theory seems the most promising. The data gathered to date tell us much, but there are still many unanswered question and new avenues to explore. As well, it is always important to keep in mind that the incelosphere is a reflection of patriarchal offline environments. The organic growth of the Internet, including its hurtful elements, has globalized access to misogynistic hate discourses in converged online and offline environments. Incel messages can be distributed to millions of people around the world in seconds due to faster means of disseminating digital media, as the Internet facilitates access for those seeking communication with like-minded patriarchal men. Online communities with members who never come into face-to-face contact with each other but who often exchange written, audio, and visual information with their peers are growing every day. The incel coalition is a prime example.

Still, based on their study of the connections between incels and porn, Tranchese and Sugiura (2021) are right to direct us to the fact that while online incel communication processes reflect offline or "real-world" male peer support patterns and "enable the exponential replication of misogyny by inventing, spreading, and reproducing techniques to attack women (online and offline), online misogyny is not a product of the technology, but a result of the society that shaped it" (p. 2729). In fact, just as racism is deeply rooted in the legal system, so is misogyny. Feminist legal scholar Julie Suk (2023), for instance, shows:

> Misogyny is conventionally understood as woman-hatred, but it is much more, and much worse for women, than hatred. Misogyny is the set of [legal] practices that keep women down in order to keep everyone and everything else up. . . . Even in liberal constitutional democracies that celebrate the rule of law, enforce legal gender equality, criminalize violence against women, and prohibit sex discrimination in the workplace and schools, the state fails persistently to investigate, punish, eradicate, and prevent violence against women, from rape to femicide to workplace sexual harassment to campus sexual assault. The law enables men, and the society designed to fulfill their vision, to benefit from keeping women down, albeit in ways that are hidden from view.
>
> (pp. 2–3)

Patriarchy, too, is an "age-old structure" born long before the advent of the Internet (Gilligan & Snider, 2018), and men have been physically, sexually, psychologically, and economically abusing women for centuries (DeKeseredy & Donnermeyer, 2023; Dobash & Dobash, 1979). Miller (2017) reminds us:

> Patriarchy . . . as embedded in the Old and New Testaments in the Bible and in Roman legal precepts, has been a powerful organizing concept with which social order has been understood, maintained, enforced, contested, adjudicated and dreamt about over two millennia in Western history.
>
> (p. 3)

Men who hate women and the violence they use against women are not brand-new problems; the incelosphere exacerbates a long-standing condition. It is, then, in this current era, "patriarchy enhancing . . . and maintains or strengthens the given patriarchal order of a culture or society" (Applin et al., 2023, p. 1103).

What is to be Done about the Incelosphere?

Sex Robots?

There are a variety of courses that could be pursued to change the cultural and societal dynamics that promote the incel thinking and/or the online incelosphere or even approaches to redirect incels' frustration. Regarding the latter approach, one highly problematic option is to use another new technology – sex robots – which *New York Times* columnist Ross Douthat

(2018) views as solutions to misogyny and related violent crimes committed by incels. Actually, artificially intelligent robots are highly likely to intensify male sexual violence (DeKeseredy & Rennison, 2019). Take what happened to "Samantha," a sex robot displayed at the 2017 Arts Electronic Festival in Linz, Austria. She was so savagely attacked by a group of men and "badly soiled" that she had to be sent back to Barcelona for "repairs and cleaning after being left so filthy and broken by the never-ending male attention" (Barrie, 2017, p. 1). In other words, Samantha was gang raped. This behavior is labeled *streamlining* in South Africa. It is

> essentially a rape by two or more perpetrators. It is an unambiguously defiling and humiliating act, and is often a punishment, yet at the same time, it is an act that is often regarded by its perpetrators as rooted in a sense of entitlement.
>
> (Jewkes et al., 2006, p. 2950)

Sex robots are too new to allow for properly designed social scientific studies, but there are strong indicators that they eroticize non-consent (Norris, 2017). For example, U.S. robotics company True Companion sells a sex robot – "Roxy" – with programmable personalities, including "Frigid Farah," which allows it to resist men's sexual advances. According to Noel Sharkey, a professor of artificial intelligence at the University of Sheffield, the idea is that "robots would resist your sexual advances so that you could rape them" (cited in Shead, 2017, p. 1). To make matters worse, there are now child sex robots and sex dolls on the market, and some academics (e.g., Cheok & Levy, 2017) claim that they could provide men with legitimate outlets for their criminal sexual desires, thus reducing harm to women. This is especially troubling considering that incel communities promote and tolerate pedophilia. Truth be told, over a quarter of incel forum users have posted pedophilia keywords, and discussions of pedophilia show that 53% are supportive (Center for Countering Digital Hate, 2022).

Unsurprisingly, sex robots also promote the sexual objectification of women. They leave men

> with the impression that a good woman is just like their robotic sex toys; compliant, always ready to have sex and have a perfect, [in] their opinion, body. . . . It teaches them that if a woman does not act like their ideal, desirable sex toy that they are not to be treated as equals to robots. As a result, the robots will be treated more humanely than women will be.
>
> (Kezer, 2019, p. 1)

Again, more research is necessary, but it is fair to hypothesize that the negative consequences of using sex robots will greatly outweigh the positive ones. For example, millions of people have grown up viewing online porn, and large numbers of them now regard violent sex in which women are humiliated and defiled as normal (DeKeseredy et al., 2023; Foubert, 2022). It is terrifying to think that, as Kleeman (2017) surmises, "Similarly, the generation growing up when sex robots are commonplace might see brutally selfish sex as both desirable and achievable" (p. 1).

There are much more effective and safer ways of responding to online incel misogyny at the societal and cultural levels. The first step is to recognize it as a form of violent right-wing extremism, one that is strongly connected to other dangerous far-right organizations (Bates, 2020; DeKeseredy, 2022). The Canadian government has even gone so far as to categorize incel violence as terrorism, and law enforcement officials based in Canada and in the United States include incel activities in their threat assessments (New America, 2023).

The second and equally important step is to develop a coalition of broader progressive constituencies that prioritize gender and sexuality as well as race/ethnicity and social class in their efforts to curb hate crime. Reducing gun use and ownership, mass shootings, participation in racist and anti-immigration activities, and threats to women's access to the complete range of reproductive rights means using resistance initiatives that connect the incelosphere to other forms of right-wing extremism (DeKeseredy, 2022). This requires a multi-pronged approach, one that must involve a dedicated effort to develop "a new politics of sameness," a type of politics that recognizes that a diverse range of people, regardless of their gender, sexual identity, or race/ethnicity, are subordinated to the capitalist, patriarchal, and racist motives of neoliberalism (Winlow et al., 2019, p. 43).

Progressive coalitions called for here recognize that there is a strong association between membership in organizations seeking to reassert male supremacy and intimate violence against women and girls (Belew & Gutierrez, 2021; DeKeseredy & Rennison, 2019; Dhaliwal & Kelly, 2020; Dragiewicz, 2018). Violence against women, in fact, is the background for a host of other harms caused/advocated by alternative right coalitions and other major social problems that plague contemporary society (e.g., poverty) (DeKeseredy, 2022; DePrince, 2022). It is also a social issue that helps to energize institutional change and helps break down boundaries across organizations, government agencies, and social sectors. Violence against women as a social issue is a catalyst for discovering new ways of working together and helping one another, and it encourages people to see how we are all affected by woman abuse and how we directly or indirectly contribute to its perpetration through our values, attitudes, and behaviors (DeKeseredy & MacLeod, 1997).

Well-Meaning Men

Directly relevant to the role of patriarchal male (in particular, online incel) peer support examined in this chapter is work that is addressing the underlying and all-too-common attitude, "men who hate men who hate women" (Bates, 2020), also termed in some academic and activist circles as *feminist, pro-feminist,* or *anti-sexist men* (DeKeseredy et al., 2017; Messner et al., 2015). Such men are involved in the ongoing process of changing themselves, self-examination, and self-discovery (DeKeseredy et al., 2017), with the ultimate goal of shedding their "patriarchal baggage" (Thorne-Finch, 1992). Though constituting a relatively small but growing group, these men work individually and collectively to change other men. Depending on their time and energy, some feminist men work on the dual level of changing individual people and social institutions. Others have limited goals. Most limited of all are those who only privately support the principles of feminism and restrict their efforts to creating and maintaining egalitarian relationships. This separation of private and public attempts to eliminate patriarchy continues to be one of the most central challenges for feminist men (DeKeseredy & Schwartz, 2013).

Bates (2020) recommends, and rightfully so, that feminist men's work should be incorporated into mainstream education to prevent boys from becoming "incels." It is, indeed, time for more male teachers, administrators, and athletic coaches to "step up to the plate" and demonstrate some progressive leadership by offering programs on gender issues in their schools. They can also do things on a personal level (Katz, 2006), such as talking to male students and faculty in assemblies, classes, at sporting events, in faculty and school training, and in private conversations (DeKeseredy & Corsianos, 2016). It would also be useful for school staff to employ the following strategies informed by the work of Bates (2020), Messerschmidt (2012), Thorne-Finch (1992, pp. 236–237), and Warshaw (1988, pp. 161–164):

- Confront students, teachers, and athletic staff who speak about violence against women and misogynistic social media in an approving manner.
- Confront students and staff who perpetuate and legitimate rape myths.
- Take every opportunity to speak out against misogynistic social media and other symptoms of gender inequality.
- Create social media forums about the harms of misogyny and how men and boys can work together to curb patriarchal discourses and practices.
- Develop school curricula that make gender, healthy relationships, and sexuality a core subject.

Fathers can help play a vital role in preventing young boys from joining the incel movement and thus need to do some anti-sexist work at home because their masculinity ideology is a powerful determinant of their son's expressions of masculinity (Perales et al., 2023). It is unclear exactly how many North American men do this, but we can safely infer that most fathers are "well-meaning men" and outnumber abusive men. A well-meaning man is one

> who believes women should be respected. A well-meaning man would not assault a woman. A well-meaning man, on the surface, at least, believes in equality for women. A well-meaning man believes in women's rights. A well-meaning man honors the women in his life. A well-meaning man, for all practical purposes, is a nice guy, a good guy.
>
> (Porter, 2006, p. 1)

How many well-meaning men have long discussions with their sons about online misogyny, woman abuse, and sexism in general? The answer is probably "not many." This is problematic and must change because preventative or remedial programs designed to foster young men's healthy masculinities are most successful if they involve fathers (Perales et al., 2023). The adage "like father, like son" applies to this recommendation, and Katz's (2006) advice reinforces it:

> Clearly one of the most important roles a father – or a father figure – can play in his son's life is to teach by example. If men are always respectful toward women and never verbally or physically abuse them, their sons in all likelihood will learn to be similarly respectful. Nonetheless, every man who has a son should be constantly aware that how he treats women is not just between him and the women – there is a little set of eyes that is always watching him and picking up cues about how a man is supposed to act. If a man says demeaning and dismissive things about women, his son hears it. If he laughs at sexist jokes and makes objectifying comments about women's bodies as he watches TV, his son hears it.
>
> (p. 234)

Technology Approaches

Some technological work is also necessary in the struggle over digital misogyny, but it is beyond the scope of this chapter to specify all that is needed. Some potentially effective means worth mentioning and a few of those recommended by the Center for Countering Digital Hate (2022, pp. 42–44) include:

- Deplatforming incel YouTube channels.
- Deranking incelosphere sites in Google searches.
- Addressing digital harms to children that drive users to incelosphere communities.
- Creating online–offline referral mechanisms to offer support services and resources directly to at-risk individuals, offering reassurances on privacy.

• Infrastructure providers withdrawing their services from the incelosphere network.

There are many other strategies that could easily be proposed in this chapter and that are informed by a rich gendered understanding of online hate. And, it is likely that even more new approaches will be required as we encounter both new technologies and various societal changes that will affect and shape gender relations. Certainly, 35 years ago, we would have never thought of "sexting" becoming an integral part of peer culture. What is next? Many progressive scholars, practitioners, and activists are afraid to hear the answer, given the potential for major patriarchal harm to women (e.g., male violence) that has been mixed in with the tremendous changes for good provided by the Internet, smartphones, and other modern technology.

Conclusions

This chapter is not the first attempt to declare online misogyny like that perpetuated and legitimated by incels as a hate crime. Nonetheless, though there may be (and has been for a few decades) a strong international emphasis on naming face-to-face violence against women as a hate crime and as a violation of human rights, there is still much work to do, and, thus far, little has been done to eliminate and prevent the creation of cyber communities like those populated by incels. This is partially the fault of the social scientific research community, which has thus far done a minimal amount of empirical and theoretical work to raise awareness about the incelosphere. Hopefully, this chapter demonstrates the value of applying male peer support theory, a perspective that has received much empirical support over the past 35 years.

I would be remiss, though, if I did not state that a growing number of feminist scholars are helping to shed more light on the incelosphere and other misogynistic online communities. As well, the connections between Australian and U.S. experts in the field are especially strong and will contribute to new global perspectives on gendered hate in this digital era. For instance, both Australian and U.S. scholars draw attention to the value of male peer support theory in sociological efforts to understand the damage done by incels.[7] This is not surprising because male peer support for various types of woman abuse seems to be ubiquitous and definitely has a long history. Still, male peer support theorists have yet to answer the important question of how all-male patriarchal collectives like the incel movement form or come together.

As Thorburn et al. (2023) note, "Ultimately, there is much still unknown about the nature, reach and impacts of incel subcultures, yet their prevalence across the Anglosphere speaks to the pervasion of a masculine group identity grounded in hierarchy, misogyny and aggrieved entitlement" (p. 252). Both points are true, but the field will not advance unless rigorous research is done outside of the Global North and in non-English speaking communities, and the results are featured in widely read and cited academic periodicals. This work will often require translators, and, hopefully, leading book and journal publishers will recognize the importance of covering the costs of translational work. All the same, regardless of what new empirical and theoretical approaches are used to help develop a better understanding of incel subcultures in the Global North and Global South, we must keep this question at the forefront of our minds: "What is to be done about the incelosphere?"

Acknowledgments

I thank Joe Walther and Ronald Rice for their support and input.

Notes

1 This is the main title of their book, which is now in its fourth edition.
2 Incels.Me was deplatformed on October 15, 2018, although it has been succeeded by the site INCELS.IS. Some of the content from the original Incels.Me site can be found through the internet archive, https://web.archive.org/web/20180611074529/https://incels.me/; for more information see https://blog.nameshield.com/blog/2019/01/10/the-shutting-down-of-incels-me-the-involuntary-single-website/
3 See https://www.nydailynews.com/news/national/elliot-rodger-retribution-santa-barbara-shooter-sick-words-article-1.1804761.
4 This term is short for "female humanoids" or "females" (Jgin, 2023).
5 See DeKeseredy (2019, 2023) and DeKeseredy and Schwartz (2013) for in-depth reviews of the extant empirical and theoretical literature on the connection between male peer support and woman abuse.
6 Image-based sexual abuse websites and blogs first appeared on the internet in 2000 and started to gain U.S. national attention in 2010 following Hunter Moore's creating of *IsAnyoneUp.com* (Lamphere & Pikciunas, 2016).
7 See, for example, DeKeseredy and Rennison (2019) and Thorburn et al. (2023).

References

Ajder, H., Patrini, G., Cavalli, F., & Cullen, L. (2019). *The state of deepfakes: Landscapes, threats, and impact*. Deeptrace.

Applin, S., Simpson, J. M., & Curtis, A. (2023). Men have gender and women are people: A structural approach to gender and violence. *Violence Against Women*, 29(5), 1097–1118. https://doi.org/10.1177/10778012221104844

Barrie, J. (2017, September 28). Sex robot display model molested so much it breaks before anyone can actually use it: Sex doll Samantha was left filthy and in need of repairs after being mounted by excitable men. *Mirror*. https://www.mirror.co.uk/news/weird-news/expensive-sex-doll-molested-much-11251239

Bates, L. (2020). *Men who hate women: The extremism nobody is talking about*. Simon & Schuster.

Belew, K., & Gutierrez, R. A. (Eds.). (2021). *A field guide to white supremacy*. University of California Press.

Bourgois, P. (1995). *In search of respect: Selling crack in el barrio*. Cambridge University Press.

Bowker, L. H. (1983). *Beating wife-beating*. Lexington Books.

Bridges, A. J., Wosnitzer, R., Scharrer, E., Sun, C., & Liberman, R. (2010). Aggression and sexual behavior in best-selling pornography videos: A content analysis update. *Violence Against Women, 16*(10), 1065–1085. https://doi.org/10.1177/1077801210382866

Brubaker, S. J. (2019). *Theorizing gender violence*. Cognella.

Campbell, H. (2000). The glass phallus: Pub(lic) masculinity and drinking in rural New Zealand. *Rural Sociology, 65*(4), 562–581. https://doi.org/10.1111/j.1549-0831.2000.tb00044.x

Center for Countering Digital Hate. (2022). *The incelosphere: Exposing pathways into incel communities and the harms they pose to women and children*. Center for Countering Digital Hate. https://counterhate.com/research/incelosphere/

Cheok, A. D., & Levy, D. (Eds.). (2017). *Love and sex with robots*. Springer.

CNN U.S. (2018, April 25). The Toronto suspect apparently posted about an "incel rebellion." Here's what that means. https://www.cnn.com/2018/04/25/us/incel-rebellion-alek-minassian-toronto-attack-trnd/index.html

Connell, R. W. (1995). *Masculinities*. University of California Press.

Connell, R. W., & Messerschmidt, J. W. (2005). Hegemonic masculinity: Rethinking the concept. *Gender & Society, 19*(6), 829–859. https://doi.org/10.1177/0891243205278639

DeKeseredy, W. S. (1988). Woman abuse in dating relationships: The relevance of social support theory. *Journal of Family Violence, 3*(1), 1–13. https://doi.org/10.1007/bf00994662

DeKeseredy, W. S. (2017). Masculinities, aggression, and violence. In P. Sturmey (Ed.), *The Wiley handbook of violence and aggression* (pp. 1–12). John Wiley & Sons. https://doi.org/10.1002/9781119057574.whbva024

DeKeseredy, W. S. (2019). But why this man? Challenging hegemonic masculinity in an age of repression. In W. S. DeKeseredy & E. Currie (Eds.), *Progressive justice in an age of repression: Strategies for challenging the rise of the right* (pp. 11–25). Routledge.

DeKeseredy, W. S. (2020). *Understanding the harms of pornography: The contributions of social scientific knowledge*. Culture Reframed.

DeKeseredy, W. S. (2021). *Woman abuse in rural places*. Routledge.

DeKeseredy, W. S. (2022). Men's rights, gun ownership, racism, and the assault on women's reproductive health rights: Hidden connections. *Dignity: A Journal of Analysis of Exploitation and Violence, 7*(3). https://digitalcommons.uri.edu/cgi/viewcontent.cgi?article=1347&context=dignity

DeKeseredy, W. S. (2023). *Secret connections: Male collegial and professional contact sports, pornography, and violence against women*. Culture Reframed.

DeKeseredy, W. S., & Corsianos, M. (2016). *Violence against women in pornography*. Routledge.

DeKeseredy, W. S., Cowan, S., & Schwartz, M. D. (2023). *Skating on thin ice: Professional hockey, rape culture, and violence against women*. Aevo UTP.

DeKeseredy, W. S., & Donnermeyer, J. F. (2023). A new theory of globablization, natural resource extraction and violence against women: Toward solving the linkage problem. *Critical Criminology, 31*, 61–81. https://doi.org/10.1007/s10612-022-09668-3

DeKeseredy, W. S., Dragiewicz, M., & Schwartz, M. D. (2017). *Abusive endings: Separation and divorce violence against women*. University of California Press.

DeKeseredy, W. S., & MacLeod, L. (1997). *Woman abuse: A sociological story*. Harcourt Brace.

DeKeseredy, W. S., & Olsson, P. (2011). Adult pornography, male peer support, and violence against women: The contribution of the "dark side" of the internet. In

M. Vargas Martin, M. A. Garcia-Ruiz, & A. Edwards (Eds.), *Technology for facilitating humanity and combating social deviations: Interdisciplinary perspectives* (pp. 34–50). IGI Global.

DeKeseredy, W. S., & Rennison, C. M. (2019). Key issues in the rape and sexual assault of women. In W. S. DeKeseredy, C. M. Rennison, & A. K. Hall-Sanchez (Eds.), *The Routledge international handbook of violence studies* (pp. 403–418). Routledge.

DeKeseredy, W. S., & Schwartz, M. D. (1998). *Woman abuse on campus: Results from the Canadian national survey.* Sage.

DeKeseredy, W. S., & Schwartz, M. D. (2013). *Male peer support & violence against women: The history & verification of a theory.* Northeastern University Press.

DeKeseredy, W. S., & Schwartz, M. D. (2016). Thinking sociologically about image-based sexual abuse: The contribution of male peer support theory. *Sexualization, Media, & Society, 2*(4). https://doi.org/10.1177/2374623816684692

DePrince, A. P. (2022). *Every 90 seconds: Our common cause ending violence against women.* Oxford University Press.

Dhaliwal, S., & Kelly, L. (2020). *Literature review: The links between radicalization and violence against women and girls.* London Metropolitan University.

Dobash, R. E., & Dobash, R. P. (1979). *Violence against wives: A case against the patriarchy.* Free Press.

Douthat, R. (2018, May 2). The redistribution of sex. *The New York Times.* https://www.nytimes.com/2018/05/02/opinion/incels-sex-robots-redistribution.html

Dragiewicz, M. (2008). Patriarchy reasserted: Fathers' rights and anti-VAWA activism. *Feminist Criminology, 3*(2), 121–144. https://doi.org/10.1177/1557085108316731

Dragiewicz, M. (2011). *Equality with a vengeance: Men's rights groups, battered women, and antifeminist backlash.* Northeastern University Press.

Dragiewicz, M. (2018). Antifeminism and backlash: A critical criminological imperative. In W. S. DeKeseredy & M. Dragiewicz (Eds.), *Routledge handbook of critical criminology* (2nd ed., pp. 334–347). Routledge.

Ellis, D., & DeKeseredy, W. S. (1997). Rethinking estrangement, interventions, and intimate femicide. *Violence Against Women, 3*(6), 590–609. https://doi.org/10.1177/1077801297003006003

Foubert, J. D. (2022). *Protecting your children from internet pornography: Understanding the science, risks, and ways to protect your kids.* Northfield Publishing.

Fritz, N., Malic, V., Paul, B., & Zhou, Y. (2020). A descriptive analysis of the types, targets, and relative frequency of aggression in mainstream pornography. *Archives of Sexual Behavior, 49*(8), 3041–3053. https://doi.org/10.1007/s10508-020-01773-0

Gilligan, C., & Snider, N. (2018). *Why does patriarchy persist?* Polity Press.

Henry, N., McGlynn, C., Flynn, A., Johnson, K., Powell, A., & Scott, A. J. (2021). *Image-based sexual abuse: A study on the causes and consequences of non-consensual nude or sexual imagery.* Routledge.

Hunter, T. (2023, February 13). AI porn is easy to make now. For women, that's a nightmare. *The Washington Post.* https://www.washingtonpost.com/technology/2023/02/13/ai-porn-deepfakes-women-consent/

Incels.Me. (2018, October 11). https://web.archive.org/web/20180611074529/https://incels.me/

Jewkes, R., Dunkle, K., Koss, M. P., Levin, J. B., Nduna, M., Jama, N., & Sikweyiya, Y. (2006). Rape perpetration by young rural South African men: Prevalence, patterns, and risk factors. *Social Science and Medicine, 63*(11), 2949–2961. https://doi.org/10.1016/j.socscimed.2006.07.027

Jgin, K. (2023, March 14). The problem with incels no one seems to talk about. *The Noosphere.* https://medium.com/the-noösphere/the-problem-with-incels-no-one-seems-to-talk-about-fb03bd2dd135

Joosse, P., & Willey, R. (2020). Gender and charismatic power. *Theory and Society*, 49(4), 533–561. https://doi.org/10.1007/s11186-020-09392-3

Katz, J. (2006). *The macho paradox: Why some men hurt women and how all men can help*. Sourcebooks, Inc.

Katz, J. (2016). *Man enough? Donald Trump, Hillary Clinton and the politics of presidential masculinity*. Interlink Books.

Kezer, T. (2019, April 26). The dangers of sex robots. *Her Campus*. https://www.hercampus.com/school/alaska/dangers-sex-robots/

Kimmel, M. (2017). *Angry white men: American masculinity at the end of an era*. Nation Books.

Kleeman, J. (2017, September 25). Should we ban sex robots while we have the chance? *The Guardian*. https://www.theguardian.com/commentisfree/2017/sep/25/ban-sex-robots-dolls-market

Lamphere, R. D., & Pikciunas, K. T. (2016). Sexting, sextortion, and other internet sexual offenses. In J. N. Navarro, S. Clevenger, & C. D. Marcum (Eds.), *The intersection between intimate partner abuse, technology, and cybercrime: Examining the virtual enemy* (pp. 141–165). Carolina Academic Press.

Levant, R. (1995). Male violence against female partners: Roots in male socialization and development. In C. D. Spielberger, I. G. Sarason, J. M. T. Brebner, E. Greenglass, P. Laungani, & A. M. O'Roark (Eds.), *Stress and emotion: Anxiety, anger, and curiosity* (Vol. 15, pp. 91–100). Taylor & Francis.

Levin, J., & Nolan, J. (2017). *The violence of hate: Understanding harmful forms of bias and bigotry* (4th ed.). Roman & Littlefield.

Lewis, R., Rowe, M., & Wiper, C. (2017). Online abuse of feminists as an emerging form of violence against women and girls. *British Journal of Criminology*, 57(6), 1462–1481. https://doi.org/10.1093/bjc/azw073

Manne, K. (2018). *Down girl: The logic of misogyny*. Oxford University Press.

Messerschmidt, J. W. (1993). *Masculinities and crime*. Roman & Littlefield.

Messerschmidt, J. W. (2012). *Gender, heterosexuality, and youth violence: The struggle for recognition*. Rowman & Littlefield.

Messner, M. A., Greenberg, M. A., & Peretz, T. (2015). *Some men: Feminist allies & the movement to end violence against women*. Oxford University Press.

Miller, J. (2008). *Getting played: African-American girls, urban inequality, and gendered violence*. Oxford University Press.

Miller, P. (2017). *Patriarchy*. Routledge.

Nashrula, T. (2019, June 6). Incels are running an online suicide forum that was blamed for a young woman's death. *BuzzFeed.News*. https://www.buzzfeednews.com/article/tasneemnashrulla/incels-suicide-forum-woman-killed-herself

New America. (2023). *Misogynist incels and male supremacism*. https://www.newamerica.org/political-reform/reports/misogynist-incels-and-male-supremacism/recommendations/

Norris, S. (2017, September 28). The damage to Samantha the sex robot shows male aggression being normalized: These problematic dolls invite abusive treatment. *NewStatesman*. https://www.newstatesman.com/politics/2017/09/damage-samantha-sex-robot-shows-male-aggression-being-normalised

Okolie, C. (2023). Artificial intelligence-altered videos (deepfakes), image-based sexual abuse, and data privacy concerns. *Journal of International Women's Studies*, 25(4), 1–16. https://vc.bridgew.edu/cgi/viewcontent.cgi?article=3079&context=jiws

Perales, F., Kuskoff, E., Flood, M., & King, T. (2023). Like father, like son: Empirical insights into the intergenerational continuity of masculinity ideology. *Sex Roles*, 88(9–10), 399–412. https://doi.org/10.1007/s11199-023-01364-y

Polk, K. (2003). Masculinities, femininities, and homicide: Competing explanations for male violence. In M. D. Schwartz & S. E. Hatty (Eds.), *Controversies in critical criminology* (pp. 133–146). Anderson.

Porter, T. (2006). *Breaking out of the "man box", a call to men: The next generation of manhood*. Skyhorse Publishing.

Ptacek, J. (2023). *Feeling trapped: Social class and violence against women*. University of California Press.

Renzetti, C. M. (2018). Feminist perspectives. In W. S. DeKeseredy & M. Dragiewicz (Eds.), *Routledge handbook of critical criminology* (2nd ed., pp. 74–82). Routledge.

Salter, M., & Crofts, T. (2015). Responding to revenge porn: Challenges to online legal impunity. In L. Comella & S. Tarrant (Eds.), *New views on pornography: Sexuality, politics, and the law* (pp. 223–253). Praeger.

Schwartz, M. D. (2021). Masculinities, sport, and violence against women: The contribution of male peer support theory. *Violence Against Women, 27*(5), 688–707. https://doi.org/10.1177/1077801220958493

Schwartz, M. D., & DeKeseredy, W. S. (1997). *Sexual assault on the college campus: The role of male peer support*. Sage.

Scott, A. O. (2022, June 2). The actual malice of the Johnny Depp trial. *The New York Times*. https://www.nytimes.com/2022/06/02/arts/depp-heard-trial-malice.html

Shead, S. (2017, July 5). A new report showed all the different ways that sex robots could be used in society. *Businessinsider.com*. https://www.businessinsider.com/our-future-with-sex-robots-noel-sharkey-report-2017-7

Suk, J. C. (2023). *After misogyny: How the law fails women and what to do about it*. University of California Press.

SumOfUs. (2022). *Metaverse: Another cesspool of toxic content*. SumOfUs.

Thorburn, J., Powell, A., & Chambers, P. (2023). A world alone: Masculinities, humiliation, and aggrieved entitlement on an incel forum. *The British Journal of Criminology, 63*(1), 238–254. https://doi.org/10.1093/bjc/azac020

Thorne-Finch, R. (1992). *Ending the silence: The origins and treatment of violence against women*. University of Toronto Press.

Tranchese, A., & Sugiura, L. (2021). "I don't hate all women, just those stuck-up bitches": How incels and mainstream pornography speak the same extreme language of misogyny. *Violence Against Women, 27*(14), 2709–2734. https://doi.org/10.1177/1077801221996453

Troiano, G. (2022, June 2). 40 statistics you should know about online communities in 2022. *Amity*. https://www.amity.co/blog/40-statistics-you-should-know-about-online-communities

Walther, J. B. (Chapter 2 this volume). Making a case for a social processes approach to online hate.

Warshaw, R. (1988). *I never called it rape*. Harper & Row.

Websdale, N. (1998). *Rural woman battering and the justice system: An ethnography*. Sage.

West, C., & Zimmerman, D. H. (1987). Doing gender. *Gender & Society, 1*(2), 125–151. https://doi.org/10.1177/0891243287001002002

Wilson, W. J. (1996). *When work disappears: The world of the new urban poor*. Knopf.

Winlow, S., Hall, S., & Treadwell, J. (2019). Why the left must change: Right-wing populism in context. In W. S. DeKeseredy & E. Currie (Eds.), *Progressive justice in an age of repression: Strategies for challenging the rise of the right* (pp. 26–41). Routledge.

Yang, J., & Gillis, W. (2018, April 28). Shadowy online subculture in spotlight after Toronto van attack. *Toronto Star*. https://www.thestar.com/news/gta/2018/04/28/shadowy-online-subculture-in-spotlight-after-toronto-van-attack.html?rf

5

FROM ECHO CHAMBERS TO DIGITAL CAMPFIRES

The Making of an Online Community of Hate in Stormfront

Anton Törnberg and Petter Törnberg

Social media has emerged as a dominant mode of communication in contemporary society, eliciting concerns regarding its influence on political life. Social media platforms appear to encourage a more radical, conflictual, and hateful form of politics and discourse, as fringe online spaces become home to cesspools of hateful discourses and extremist movements. Although there is mounting evidence that links social media with these polarized forms of politics, the underlying causal mechanisms remain elusive. Specifically, how does social media fuel political extremism and the rise of online hate?

For years, a leading explanation has centered on the "echo chamber" theory, positing a feedback loop between isolation with like-minded individuals and more extreme politics. Captured in their echo chamber, individuals do not encounter opposing views, causing them to diverge toward more extreme opinions – they fall into online "rabbit-holes" and emerge as "lone-wolf" terrorists. Through its emphasis on deliberation, the echo chamber notion implicitly builds on an assumption of politics as existing primarily in the realm of individual consumption of arguments and opinions, while leaving its more social dimensions to the side.

In this chapter, we propose a new perspective on how fringe online spaces contribute to the rise of political extremism and online hate. Using our findings from previous empirical and interpretive research, we draw on Émile Durkheim's work, which sought to identify the social mechanisms that bind communities together. We see online interactions in these spaces not as rational deliberation but as a form of "rituals" that bind a community together around the opposition to an out-group. We thus propose a shift

DOI: 10.4324/9781003472148-5

from understanding online extremism and hate through the lens of rational and critical discussions, to emphasizing underlying social and emotional processes.

As a case, we focus on what has been described as the most extreme space of online hate, Stormfront.org. Established in the mid-1990s, Stormfront is a White Supremacist and neo-Nazi online community and forum. It stands out as one of the earliest and most significant websites promoting far-right ideologies, racial supremacy, and hate speech on the Internet.

The community is built around participatory technology, with members engaging in user-generated message postings organized into numerous topics, or "subforums." Overall, the forum is teeming with hate-related posts, primarily concerning race and ethnicity, often using derogatory speech, describing Jews as "parasites" and Black people as "inferior life forms." Holocaust denial, misogynistic remarks, and various antisemitic conspiracy theories – claiming Jews control the world's financial system and the media – are prevalent. Some users openly glorify, endorse, or promote violence against the groups they target.

In contrast to mainstream sites like X (previously Twitter) or Facebook, Stormfront is explicitly dedicated to White Nationalists. Consequently, the messages expressing hatred toward different races, religions, and immigrants are not framed as if they are intended for the targeted groups to see; rather, they are composed about those groups, meant for consumption by fellow White Nationalists (see Walther, this volume).

We have acquired a longitudinal database of Stormfront comments containing 10,172,069 posts by 354,574 users, spanning over 20 years of discussions. This unique dataset enables us to examine the intricate social processes that shape the emergence and propagation of online hate.

Building on the Durkheimian perspective, we argue for understanding isolated online hate communities such as Stormfront as constituting a type of "digital campfires." Within these spaces, participating members engage in discussions, drawing on shared experiences and interests to cultivate a sense of community and shared identity. Through recurrent interaction rituals, they elaborate a collective worldview, while simultaneously fostering a hyperpersonal sense of intimacy within an unseen collective. These are grassroots, collective processes, often rife with conflict and fragility, and they materialize through interaction and discussion.

This chapter draws on three empirical research papers by the authors, focusing on three interrelated dimensions of online community formation – identity, worldview, and affect – to elaborate a new theoretical framework for the mechanisms through which far-right extremism emerges on online media. By synthesizing these previous studies and complementing them with additional primary sources, the chapter provides a *more social* theoretical foundation for understanding online hate.

Social Media and the Rise of the Politics of Hate

The rise of social media has transformed political life. Recent years have seen the rise and mainstreaming of forms of politics that center around opposition to out-groups, such as the other political party or minorities (Chua, 2019; Mason, 2018). The literature on affective polarization suggests that this form of polarization should not be understood as merely diverging opinions but rather as a reinforcement of a sense of in-group based on political affiliation (Iyengar et al., 2019; Törnberg, 2022). While a vast body of literature has established a link between social media and political polarization, emerging findings increasingly indicate that this polarization is asymmetrical: It is primarily driven by the radicalization of the far right (e.g., González-Bailón et al., 2023; Soares et al., 2019). Social media appears to have transformed the far right, catapulting a previously fringe form of hate-driven politics into the political mainstream.

In this context, online hate can be viewed as a manifestation of out-group derogation, fueled by a desire for social validation and affirmation from like-minded peers (Walther, 2022). Such behaviors thus aim to foster a sense of belonging and to solidify friendships online, with the detriment to victims emerging as a secondary consequence of this approval-seeking behavior. Far-right groups focus on building and nurturing their group identity, in part through attacking others. Hate messaging is pivotal in this process as it bolsters feelings and in-group cohesion through negative expressions and feelings toward an out-group. In this sense, group identity appears as the underlying bond of the nexus between racism, hate, and political worldviews.

Online hate movements cannot be understood as a strictly discursive phenomenon, however. Research has identified a close relationship between online hate and offline violence. Offline trigger events, such as protests and elections, are often followed by spikes in types of online hate activity that bear seemingly little connections to the underlying event itself (Lupu et al., 2023). Similarly, online activity can fuel offline violence, such as the January 6th attack on the U.S. Capitol. Both experimental evidence and observational studies have furthermore demonstrated that passive and, particularly, active exposure to radical content online increases both willingness to use radical violence in the name of a cause or ideology and actual involvement in such violence (Hassan et al., 2018; Wolfowicz et al., 2022). For example, Müller and Schwarz (2021) have established a causal relationship between social media usage and hate crimes in their study on violent crimes against refugees in Germany, with anti-refugee sentiments on Facebook serving as predictors of crimes against refugees. Similar patterns have been observed in a study on Twitter, showing that a one standard deviation – higher exposure to Twitter – is associated with a 32% larger increase in hate crimes within the 2016 presidential campaign period (Müller & Schwarz, 2023).

In sum, this suggests understanding the role of social media at the nexus of political polarization, online hate, and violent extremism (see also Karell et al., 2023). Extremism has been transformed by the growing role of social media, leading to a shift from formal organizations to informal, networked bottom-up activities. We can point to two ways in which extremism has been transformed by social media.

First, digitalization has led to more porous and ill-defined boundaries of movements, as the previous importance of face-to-face encounters, physical gatherings such as street protests and white power concerts, and certain subcultural attire and artifacts symbolizing belonging is now diminishing. The most critical means of distinguishing insiders from outsiders now resides in the discursive realm: Specific words, themes, stories, ideas, or images function as emblems and evidence of group membership (see e.g., Burston, this volume).

Second, digitalization has driven the decentralization of extremist movements, resulting in a lack of explicit and clear leadership. In formal movements, ideology and framing processes were primarily driven by movement leadership, who defined and diagnosed the problem, provided potential solutions, and suggested courses of action (Benford, 1997; Benford & Snow, 2000). Frames and ideologies were typically constructed and disseminated in a top-down process. However, we now see the emergence of a more fragmentary and decentralized type of radicalization, driven by social media users themselves. Traditional frames tended to be relatively consistent and integrated packages, polished to avoid contradictions, and strategically designed both to garner the support of politicians and to attract sympathizers. In stark contrast, the construction of ideology and movement framing are now fragmented processes by and for movement actors. A typical example is the right-wing QAnon conspiracy that emerged mainly from discussions on 4chan and later spread to mainstream media platforms and even into the U.S. Congress (Amarasingam & Argentino, 2020).

One effect of this decentralization of extremist organization is, in part, that the far right has become more unpredictable and, in many ways, more dangerous. Scholars have described the emergence of what has been referred "stochastic terrorism" in which the timing and specific targets of these attacks are probable but unpredictable (Hamm & Spaaij, 2017; Miller-Idriss, 2022; Rae et al., this volume; Tsesis, 2017). The absence of formal organizations means that radical actors may be inspired to commit violent actions rather than channel their energy into more long-term strategic work, such as organization-building or collective manifestations. Data on far-right attacks in Europe from 1990 to 2021 supports this notion, showing that the majority of fatal attacks during this period were carried out by lone actors. In contrast, nonfatal attacks were predominantly executed by autonomous cells, informal groups, organized groups, and affiliated members (Ravndal, 2016, 2018).

Mechanisms of Radicalization: Echo Chambers

While it is now broadly agreed among scholars that social media is associated with the rise of a new hate-driven form of politics, the reason for the link between social media and political extremism remains poorly understood. Within media and communication studies, notions such as "echo chambers" and "filter bubbles" have become dominant explanations for online radicalization (Pariser, 2011; Sunstein, 2002, 2007). The most influential version of the echo chamber hypothesis suggests that these spaces isolate individuals from opposing viewpoints, resulting in a divergence of issue positions. Since the work of Habermas (1989), public sphere theorists have long argued that the coming together of individuals with diverse ideas and perspectives is central to democracy, as it enables the formation of a public through rational deliberation. However, when such deliberation takes place in ideologically homogeneous spaces, the result is divergence toward political extremism (McPherson et al., 2001), as individuals are "self-radicalized" through repeated exposure to one-sided content, resulting in extreme political views that potentially lead them to even greater polarization (Sunstein, 2007). The related notion of "filter bubbles" suggest that these effects are further reinforced by algorithmic personalization that automatically selects content based on viewers' preferences, while hiding opposing views and perspectives.

The concept of echo chambers builds on two main assumptions. The first is the notion that opinions and political views stem from rational understanding and interpretation of information and knowledge, presented in arguments. Accordingly, radicalization is thus cast as chiefly a question of opinions and issue positions and social media as chiefly a space for debate and the consumption of a curated subset of arguments and (mis)information. Although the processes occurring inside echo chambers may appear anything but "rational," this perspective treats politics to be intrinsic to individuals. The echo chambers approach is thus *receiver-oriented*, that is, its activation depends only on reading what others post. It is passive in the sense that it is not about posting nor about interacting – that is, not a social process. Second, social media are presumed to further spur radicalization and polarization by facilitating and accelerating isolation and keeping ideological groups separate from each other.

However, accumulating empirical evidence suggests that neither of these assumptions holds. First, substantial empirical evidence demonstrates that while political information often circulates within specific channels and groups, groups also communicate with each other, allowing arguments and worldviews to permeate various environments (Bail, 2022; Dubois & Blank, 2018; Jungherr et al., 2020). For instance, Brundidge (2010) found that Internet usage actually contributes to an increased heterogeneity of political discussion networks through inadvertent exposure. This increased exposure originates from the Internet's capacity to facilitate access to political differences, even when the individuals do not actively seek them. Wojcieszak and Mutz (2009) also found that an exposure to diverse networks and political views frequently occurs unintentionally in spaces where political and nonpolitical discussions coexist.

This is also true for online extremist groups. Our previous studies have shown that far-right groups extensively link to mainstream media platforms and news sites, as well as to sites belonging to opposing groups (Törnberg & Nissen, 2022; see also Phadke & Mitra, this volume). Examining Twitter debates, our previous work has also found that user network clusters are characterized not by isolation, but by substantial negative interaction across the political divide (Keuchenius et al., 2021). Similarly, Bright et al. (2022) demonstrate in their study of Stormfront that engaging with oppositional views is in fact a core practice among its users. In fact, these posts tend to stimulate discussion within and encourage users to remain active on the site. We have observed similar results in far-right Facebook groups, where users extensively engage with both confirming and contradicting arguments: They distort, decontextualize, reinterpret, and ridicule these arguments in a process that might be more aptly described as "trench warfare" rather than "echo chamber" (Karlsen et al., 2017; Törnberg & Wahlström, 2018). This suggests that these environments are not isolated, and that social media, in many cases, actually reinforce interaction, but not agreement, between groups and individuals. Thus, many "echoes" within these echo chambers are not core beliefs being restated but, rather, the sound of opposing viewpoints being undermined and marginalized.

However, there is limited evidence to support the claim that exposing individuals to opposing viewpoints results in more moderate and informed citizens. On the contrary, it may even reinforce their preexisting views (Bail et al., 2018; Hemmingsen & Castro, 2017; Schmitt et al., 2018). Empirical studies on counter-radicalization reveal that strategies based on increasing interaction between opposing groups can actually fuel conflicts and intensify radicalization among those who already harbor extreme views (Bélanger et al., 2020; Lewandowsky et al., 2012). For instance, in a study on Twitter users, Bail and colleagues (2018) exposed 1,200 users to content from the opposite political spectrum over a one-month period. The results showed that Republicans who followed a Democratic bot for this period expressed markedly more conservative views than before. In fact, the more attention they paid to the content, the stronger the effect. Many participants in the study described the experience of stepping outside their echo chamber and encountering opposing ideas and arguments as an attack upon their identity. Similar results have been observed in other de-radicalization strategies such as "debunking" or "counter-messaging," which aim to correct factual inaccuracies. For example, studies have shown that attempting to refute or quash rumors that vaccines cause autism may make those who believe in these rumors even more opposed to inoculating their children (Berinsky, 2017; Nyhan et al., 2014). Overall, stepping outside one's echo chamber seems not to contribute to a better competition of ideas but rather a vicious competition of identities, sharpening the contrast between "us" and "them" (Törnberg, 2022).

If it is not the echo chamber mechanism of a feedback loop between isolation and diverging opinions, which drives polarization and radicalization, then what is? Why do social media – and fringe digital spaces in particular – seem to fuel a hate-driven form of politics?

The Case of Stormfront: White Pride, Worldwide

To examine the role of fringe digital spaces in online radicalization, we center our discussion on the case of Stormfront. Stormfront emerged as a community for White Nationalists in the mid-1990s. By the early 2000s, the forum was described in an article in *USA Today* as "the most visited white supremacist site on the net" (McKelvey, 2001). Among these users were prominent White Supremacists, such as Thom Robb; the founder of National States Rights Party, Ed Fields; and former KKK leader, David Duke. The community is distinguished by its remarkable longevity: While the Internet went through waves of transformation – the Dot-Com boom of the early 2000, Web 2.0, Facebook, Instagram, and TikTok – Stormfront persisted.

Stormfront has been described as a bastion and breeding ground for violent extremism and racially motivated hate. Over the years, members of the site have been linked to over 100 terrorist attacks, including the 2011 Norway attacks and the 2015 Charleston church shootings (Beirich, 2014). Stormfront members themselves describe the forum as an "online refuge" (de Koster & Houtman, 2008), a place where they connect and actively engage with others who share their racist and White Supremacist beliefs (Bowman-Grieve, 2009; Hartzell, 2020). The forum is marked by both radical views and relative opinion homogeneity. Levin (2002) sees the website as the earliest "web-based hate entity" that inspired many similar forums on the far right. About 14% of posts on the forum can be classified as explicit hate posts (Berglind et al., 2019), and recent longitudinal studies on Stormfront have also revealed patterns suggesting that, over time, members increasingly adopt more radical stances in their anti-Black and antisemitic narratives (Scrivens et al., 2020; Törnberg & Törnberg, 2022). While anyone can read the Stormfront message boards, one must apply for and be granted membership in order to post in most sub-forums. The architecture of the site itself not only presents listings of conversational threads within topics, but it also displays the linked, hierarchically threaded replies within those threads, indicating the dialogic nature of Stormfront participation.

This chapter will elaborate a new perspective to explain how online media are linked to extremist radicalization. This perspective draws on Durkheim's research on the development of community through ritual activity and on previous empirical studies of our own that examine in detail the Stormfront community (Törnberg & Törnberg, 2021, 2022, 2023). For these studies, we developed custom-made web crawlers in order to create a dataset comprising 10,172,069 posts and 354,574 members, spanning 20 years of discussions on Stormfront. This dataset offers a powerful view into the political lives of individual members and a way to explore empirically what takes place within these fringe communities. We used a combination of computational and interpretive methods to examine how individuals are affected by participating in the community.

Durkheim and the Social Function of Campfires

As discussed above, the existing literature on echo chambers has implicitly treated online communities as spaces of rational debate and the deliberation over arguments – becoming poisoned by the fact that the arguments presented stem from a narrow band of the political spectrum. Our work on Stormfront, over time, however, brought us to seek a different theoretical foundation, building on Émile Durkheim's study of communities, through which he sought to understand the social activities that bind communities and societies together.

In his work examining aboriginal communities in Australia, Durkheim (1912/1915) observed that most of the community's time was dedicated to routine activities involving a small group, such as food gathering and childcare. However, the rare occasions where the entire tribe assembled for shared *rituals* were considered sacred. These rituals, characterized by synchronized movements and chanting, induced trance-like states of *collective efferves-cence*, imbuing participants with emotional energy and a sense of intersubjectivity. The community's focus on common objects, such as religious symbols and artifacts, flags and banners, or tribal artifacts, fostered shared feelings, unifying the group as a whole, a *community*, rather than just an aggregation of individuals. In our work with Stormfront, we began seeing online spaces such as Stormfront as the digital manifestations of the campfires around which aboriginals congregated, as described in Durkheim's research over a century ago.

While the exchange of messages online may seem somewhat more mundane, the notion of a *ritual* in many ways captures the role and effects of these online interactions. For the users on Stormfront, the content of the messages seems to carry less relevance than the *act of interacting*. The threads of discussion appear like drawn-out collective moments of shared energy and emotion. Such a broadening of the notion of ritual is consistent with other scholars who have built on the work of Durkheim. Collins (2004), for instance, expanded and reinterpreted Durkheim's findings to apply to our understanding of contemporary society. Linking together Durkheim with the micro-sociology of Erving Goffman, Collins used the notion of rituals to examine how groups today establish social membership and intersubjectivity – that is, a shared sense of "we." The expanded notion of rituals pointed to the centrality of moments of shared attention and emotion that come to imbue objects with a sense of group belonging. Recent work has extended Collins's theoretical framework, arguing that these rituals can also occur in mediated environments (DiMaggio et al., 2018; Johannessen, 2023; Wahlström & Törnberg, 2021; Wästerfors et al., 2023). According to these studies, Collins' basic criterion of an interaction ritual is present online – a gathering with shared focus under a dominant definition of the situation and a tendency to defend boundaries. As seen in other research, while mediated interaction rituals lack full bodily presence, they arguably make up for it through increased frequency (Walther & Burgoon, 1992), especially in our age of "deep mediatization" (Couldry & Hepp, 2018), where mediated interaction is ubiquitous.

The Durkheimian perspective on online communities suggests that the exchange of arguments in these online discussions should not be primarily viewed as the rational exchange that it may superficially appear, but as content that serves the role of symbolic markers of identity and belonging. They aim not to rationally persuade but aim instead to highlight similarities and differences, to distinguish an "us," separated from a "them." What takes place on social media is as much or more in the realm of identity, ritual, symbolisms, and belonging as it is in the realm of argumentation, opinion, and rationality.

In examining Stormfront through this Durkheimian lens, the community's discourse appears as a continuous chain of interaction rituals, which gradually weaves a web of symbolically imbued narratives that link the individuals together in a community. This narrative web is more than told – they are viscerally felt, as part of the collective identity and self-understanding of the participants.

The Durkheimian notion of a ritual thus links together three dimensions of community life – *identity, narratives*, and *emotions* – in a single process. In our empirical work, we came to structure the research according to these three dimensions, in order to support this theoretical foundation for understanding online extremist communities. We will therefore structure the subsequent discussion according to these dimensions.

Identity: Language as Process and Product

The Durkheimian perspective puts *identity* at center stage: Rituals create a sense of group solidarity, strengthening the collective identity by the gradual articulation of a common cultural system. As individual participants develop a stronger sense of solidarity and intersubjectivity, they come to also assume the thoughts, morals, and behaviors internal to their group, viewing themselves less as individuals and more as part of the community. The ritual, embodied in reciprocal and complementary messaging, transforms a group of individuals into a community, a shared sense of "we." The construction of a social and collective identity in digital spaces is thus entangled with the construction of an internal discourse and culture: A community is made up of stories, and these stories intertwine its members with the community (Schwartz et al., 2011).

This linkage between social identity and community speaks to a long tradition within psychology and sociology, according to which identity is constructed precisely through discursive activities – it is negotiated among speaking subjects (Polkinghorne, 1988; Sarbin, 1986). These and other scholars place language in a central role in structuring our identities and our relationship to our social groups. Central to socialization is the acquisition of a shared system of discourse, which provides the illusion of coherent and bounded identity by situating the individual in the social. Language *contains* the social, and its structure is the structure of the social. This suggests a broad notion of stories, as the cultural web that situates people in their social worlds.

Measuring Identity Formation on Stormfront

The suggestion of a link between discourse and identity raises the possibility that we can study the formation of collective identities through the flow and shifts in linguistic patterns. The terms and words used by members on a community provide a link to examining how they are affected by engaging in the interaction rituals, and how their understanding of themselves is transformed.

To study community formation through language, we examined how members' terminology changed as they engaged with the community (Törnberg & Törnberg, 2022). We organized each member's messages, with the earliest message labeled as "Message 1" and subsequent messages numbered in order. This allowed us to observe how their word choices shifted over time, reflecting the influence of engaging in continuous online interaction rituals on individual participants.

We first examined the overall similarity between the language used by new members and the community overall. To do so, we constructed a language model that represents the forum's overall language, based on a random sample of 20,000 messages. To measure the distance between two corpora, we used "bag-of-words" representations, that is, we captured the frequency of each word used in each corpus and used cosine similarity to measure the distance in terms of word frequency (Joachims, 2002). In essence, this mathematical method helps us understand how related or distinct two collections

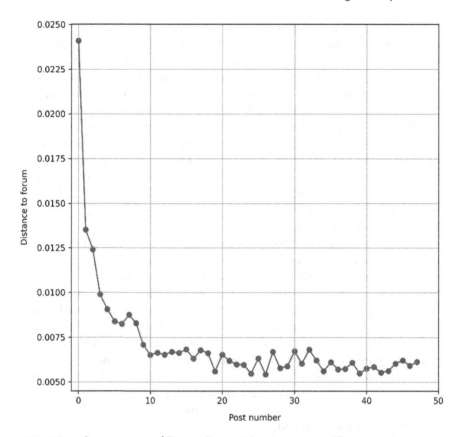

FIGURE 5.1   Convergence of Forum Posters' Language over Time

Note: This figure shows the cosine distance between members' posts, in posting order, with the overall community language, over time. As the figure shows, new members quickly converge on the forum discourse.

of text are from each other by measuring the "distance" in terms of the words they use.

Figure 5.1 shows the cosine distance between the words used by new members and those written by the community as a whole, as a function of how many posts they have contributed. As we wanted to follow the same members over a longer time to see how their language use evolved, we focused on members who had sent at least 50 posts, since this selection effectively captures active long-term members. The results are striking. The new members began far from the language of the forum as a whole, but new members relatively quickly converged as they engaged with the community. After about 20 posts, almost complete convergence had taken place. This suggests that members quickly absorb the defining discourse of the community.

We then turned more closely to the content of these linguistic shifts by using inductive computational methods to compare the language of new versus long-term members. These analyses point to two concurrent changes.

First, the members picked up different slangs and vernacular that are particular to the community. For instance, while new members may speak of "the government," insiders instead use "zog" – short for "Zionist Occupied Government" – a reference to a common White Supremacist belief that the U.S. government is controlled by Jews. The language of this acronym reflects the ideology and beliefs of the community. The use of these internal terms in their postings served to demarcate insiders from outsiders. The language changed from mainstream terms to community-specific vernacular and themes, which functioned as markers of community belonging, embracing the White Supremacist ideology of the forums.

Second, the language of the members also shifted in more subtle ways, revealing a change in self-understanding in relation to the community. There was a shift toward the use of pronouns and "indexical" statements – such as "you," "me," "here," and "this" – which both scholars of discourse analysis and ethnomethodologists point to as being important means through which identity and interpersonal relations are expressed (Fairclough, 1989), reflecting how the posters view themselves and their relationship with their audience. The word "I," for instance, suggests a sense of individuality, whereas the use of "we" suggests that writers view themselves as representing something larger than individuals or mere aggregations. A clear example of this is that new users wrote of "I," but, over time, they often used "wn" – short for "white nationalists" – instead.

Making of an Imagined Community of Hate

The example above reveals how engaging with online communities transforms the self-understanding of the participants. Their discussions matter less for their content than for their role in defining a shared identity – the content acts not as rational arguments but as symbols for community becoming. Narratives, internal jargon, and discussion topics are cultural capital that help define the boundaries of the community. Individuals acquire the language of a community and absorb its symbols, in ways that also transform their political identities.

Interaction rituals both use and produce discursive symbols: an internal culture that defines the community. These symbols simultaneously form the linguistic capital and emblems of group membership (Collins, 2004). The language that is shared and understood within the community provides barriers to outsiders; although anyone can read Stormfront postings, only those who are "in the know" can participate meaningfully. This function can be seen in how meme culture tends to exhibit complex layers of intertextual references and abstract and ironic styles, constantly in flux and innovation, requiring both literacy and dedication to decode and stay up-to-date with the latest trends (Knobel & Lankshear, 2007; Shifman, 2013; see also Walther, this volume). This challenge is precisely the point (Phillips & Milner, 2017): Language functions to create a subcultural definition of cultural capital that stands in opposition to mainstream culture. The subcultures thus define forms of distinction through a linguistic market, conferring cultural capital and authority on those who master the language (Bourdieu, 1991). Subcultural literacy separates insiders from outsiders through deliberate semantic disorientation of those who are unfamiliar with the subcultural logic and the values of the community that are reified through secret linguistic codes.

The turn to a Durkheimian perspective on online communities therefore highlights the role of identity in online extremism, in distinction to the more automatic and mechanical view assumed by the echo chamber approach. The discussions on Stormfront seek not to convey rational arguments but to activate and trigger markers of social identities – denigrating the out-group and rallying the in-group. They seek not to convince but rather to highlight similarities and differences: To identify an "us" and to separate out a "them." They operate in the realm of identity, not of rationality.

Worldviews: Spaces for Interpreting Reality

The discussions on Stormfront are not only important as expressions of community belonging and shared identity: They are also important in themselves, as ways of understanding the world. The stories they share define how the members of the community identify problems and suggest solutions. Reality itself is always filtered through the narratives that they share. This means that participants do not respond to "objective" threats or advocate realistic solutions; rather, threats and advocacies pass through a process of social construction and attribution (Snow, 2004). Reality does constrain these inventions, and the stories must be explained with some degree of internal consistency. Ultimately, however, people do not seek accurate stories but stories that work for them in the social world. No one wants to be the villain of their own story. People seek stories in which they play the hero – or if that is not available, at least the victim.

Measuring how Stormfront Makes Sense of the World

To study these processes of sense and meaning-making on Stormfront, we examined the processes through which the community came to build a narrative around two events that were especially important for the community: The U.S. presidential elections of Barack Obama in 2008, and of Donald

Trump in 2016. We used close readings of Stormfront forum postings to generate qualitatively based identification of narrative themes within the corpus. We also subjected the text to computer-based natural language processing and analyzed changes in the numbers of members in the platform as well as related search engine records. These methods, together, showed how Stormfront members created a collective understanding of these events and how they responded to them intellectually and emotionally.

The 2008 election of Obama was a decisive moment for Stormfront, spurring an unprecedented increase in user activity on the forum. The day after the election alone saw the single highest number of new members in the history of the forum (2,581 new users on November 5, 2008). In line with this, Google Trends shows a dramatic increase in Google searches for "Stormfront forum" in November 2008, for which the most activity occurred on the day of the election. Similarly, the number of postings within Stormfront skyrocketed in the days around the election.

When investigating the content of the posts in the immediate aftermath of the election, a dominant narrative emerged framing Obama as a threat to the country, a national disaster that would lead to chaos. Many users expressed frustration, desperation, and hopelessness. As one member concisely put it, "This country is finished. This empire, this civilization, this culture. . . . I don't honestly believe there are nearly enough people who are, or ever will be willing to fight for its survival." Many members seemed to fear that chaos would ensue, and that "negro rule" would drive American cities to become "crime-ridden, bankrupt slums." Along these lines, the election was described as a catalyst that would embolden the Black population in the United States, representing the start of "white slavery" that would ultimately lead to the end of the white race. (For instance, word frequency analysis showed that the usage of the terms "slave" and "slavery" increased by 50% during the days surrounding the election, compared to the average during the two prior weeks.)

However, only a few days after the election, a competing narrative emerged in the Stormfront community, reconstructing Obama's election as a unique opportunity for the white people. The underlying idea in this narrative was that "worse-is-better"– that the threat of Obama's presidency would serve as a *wake-up call* or an *eye-opener* for white people, increasing racial awareness and contributing to racial polarization, thereby serving as a potential catalyst for radical change. As one user expressed this,

> I think we should see this as more of an opportunity to change the world in which we live for the better. Maybe this is a new chance to recruit and spread our message faster and further than ever before. Remember, things will get much worse before they begin to get better and Obama might speed this process for us.

This discursive shift in the community sparked a self-critical discussion among members to reconsider support for established strategies and methods within White Supremacist movements. Many subsequent discussions thus circulated around whether people should "fight within the system" or "fight the system" in which most users expressed skepticism toward the idea and feasibility of achieving radical political change through the system. One user summarized, "We cannot win by the ballot box." While few members believed that a political revolution would be realistic at the time, it was more common to advocate for creating autonomous, model, separatist communities, a "Stormfront on the streets."

In contrast, the 2016 election of Trump sparked significantly less dramatic changes in users' activity on Stormfront, with few newly registered users and only minor increases in posting activity. The discussions during the first days after the election were characterized by optimism and anticipation, with many triumphant and celebratory posts, typically framing the election as a victory for the white race. For instance:

> It will be a major deterrent and a symbol that they [immigrants] are not as welcome as they thought they once were. The illegals will roam streets and be reported and arrested. The wall will inspire patriotism in several Whites. This election has been a turnaround for us.

Some members remained more skeptical about Trump, emphasizing that he could not be trusted. More generally, however, we observed a general discursive shift in the community, moving from the worse-is-better narrative that dominated discourse after Obama's election to a better-is-better narrative, one that framed Trump's election as a positive opportunity and source of momentum. Simultaneously, we observed a related shift in political advocacy, from promoting extra-parliamentary methods that dominated discussions after Obama to an increasing belief in the possibilities of achieving radical change through the established political system. A majority of the members now argued that Trump's presidency served to legitimize White Supremacist movements and to open (discursive) space within the established political system to air ideas that were previously banned and stigmatized. As one member expressed this: "We should be peaceful and solve our problems through the 'system,' abiding by all the laws, and setting examples such that we become role models for everyone to emulate."

This shift in perspective was accompanied with decreasing skepticism toward the government and other established political institutions. Our word-embedding analysis of the representation of out-groups on Stormfront illustrated that "Blacks," "minorities," and "Jews" were consistently the most frequently recurring oppositional categories on the forum. However, "Illegals" and "invaders" became more salient as an out-group following the election of Trump, and, more intriguing, terms such as "government," "zog," and "police" decreased in significance as out-groups, indicating that members may have become less skeptical toward the government and established political institutions. Trump was seen as an entrance for people like them to political power, and members started to reformulate the optimal goals in relation to the government by defining their roles and functions as to "influence Trump," to "push him to the right," and – commonly – to be "fire to his feet."

A Tribal Epistemology

The analysis above illustrates how communities collectively construct an understanding of political events. It is evident that the discursive creation of opportunity was a consistent driver of the framing process, aimed at identifying an optimistic interpretation. Participants thus bend, reformulate, recontextualize, and narrativize events to make them appear beneficial. This can be referred to as a type of "tribal epistemology." Contrary to the echo chamber thesis, political communities do not primarily develop their worldviews through rational deliberation and critical reasoning (Roberts, 2017). Instead, their perception of the world is influenced by their specific interests and wishes – what they *want to be true*. Communities do not choose their positions based on rational evaluation of evidence, arguments, and counterarguments; rather, they choose positions that support their tribe's values and goals. Their reasoning and comprehension of the world are inseparable from their identity and sense of community (Funkhouser, 2022).

This perspective also provides an explanation for the observed link between online communities and the rise of misinformation. These spaces allow for the growth of conspiracies that are detached from reality, as members strongly desire something to be true in order to maintain their connection with their community. Truth is only perceived through the white-tinted lens of identity, as information is assessed not based on common standards of evidence applied to commonly accepted facts but on its alignment with the requirements of ones' community (see also, e.g., Kahan, 2013). The ways of knowing become defined by ones' identity and belonging, reducing what they know to merely another expression of who they are. "Good for our side" and "true" begin to blur into one.

Spaces for Verbalizing and Transforming Emotions

Exchanging messages in Stormfront thus socially facilitates the construction of a shared worldview among members. Since these messages are tightly entangled with the identities and self-understanding of the members, they are not merely descriptions of the world but are also deeply emotionally charged. Their stories are not only narrated but – as reflected in their language – are also viscerally *felt*. As Durkheim emphasizes, rituals are highly emotional experiences. Participants in rituals perceive them as pleasurable, filling them with what Durkheim refers to as *collective effervescence:* A positive feeling of emotional energy that encourages participants to remain in the community, often manifested as confidence, warmth, and enthusiasm.

Capturing Emotional Processes among White Supremacists

In exploring these emotional dimensions of online rituals, we revisited the Stormfront postings that followed the 2008 election of Barack Obama, using sentiment analysis and close reading (Törnberg & Törnberg, 2023). As previously noted, the election sparked an unprecedented surge in the entry of new members to Stormfront. For many of these members, the election was experienced as deeply unsettling – a threat against something unspoken at the very core of who they understood themselves as white Americans. When comparing the reactions to the election by these newly registered members to those of long-term members of Stormfront, we discovered a surprising pattern.

Long-term members reflected a relatively well-established sense of collective identity. This sub-corpus was distinguished by the extensive use of "we," often found in word collocations such as "We whites," "We nationalists," "We fighting," "We act," and "We want." Moreover, this group has a narrative in place in which Jews were portrayed as the master enemy, with top-ranked word pairs such as "Jews their," "Jewish media," "Jewish influence," "Jews us," and "Jews control." Consistent with this narrative, these members perceived the election as a regrettable yet anticipated event, a foreseeable consequence of the "prevailing Jewish order." As one user expressed,

> Are we losing sight of the fact that Obama is just a figurehead puppet? Do you really think that Obama controls anything? International jewry is the greatest threat, hands down. Obama is an impotent house negro, nothing more.

These members' messages presented long-established grievances, and the election did not challenge their identities or compel them to reevaluate fundamental beliefs. If anything, Obama's election enabled long-term members to (re-)enforce their worldviews, solidify their solidarity, and intensify their sense of "we-ness." This narrative focusing on Jews, along with the members' social and discursive integration within the community, seems to have functioned as a shock-absorber, shielding them from the adverse effects of the traumatic event. It provided meaning and coherence, narrating a story of what happened, who is culpable, and what needs to be done.

The postings by newly registered members, in contrast, suggest that they were severely affected by the election. These individuals lacked the means to cope with the election's outcome; more specifically, their established worldview, which relied on viewing Blacks as belonging to a subordinated race, was upended when a Black man was elected president, resulting in trauma. When examining keywords characterizing their sub-corpus, the single most frequent word collocation is "I White," followed by "I American," "I People," "I nationalist," "I race," and "I country." The absence of "we" suggests that they are less inclined to identify themselves as part of a clearly defined in-group; instead, they describe themselves as individuals belonging to broader and more abstract categories or ethnic groups.

Comparative sentiment analysis showed that these new members expressed significantly more intense negative emotions, compared to the long-term members. Words indicating shame, disgust, and nausea were particularly prevalent in this sub-corpus, with expressions like: "Last night made me sick to my stomach," "I'm heartsick and saddened," "I vomit in my mouth a bit," and "I want to puke." Many of these reports of strong visceral, bodily reactions were related to the members' observations that a person from an allegedly "inferior" race won the election and the possibility of white people being "subordinated to Blacks."

> The national disgrace! To elect a representative of a sub-human black race that is so hostile and hateful to the white people; that is the ENEMY of the white people; that is despicable and disgusting; that is so inferior to the white people; that is so destructive to the society; that never belonged among the white people. Shame on you!

Many new members thus grappled with the contradiction that a person from an alleged "inferior" race could hold the same position of power as a series of "dignified" white presidents before him, framing the election result as a threat to the white race and expressing fears of becoming a minority and being discriminated against. As we have seen, while long-term members resolved this apparent contradiction by focusing on Jews as the primary target and out-group (thus viewing Obama as merely a "Jewish puppet"), new members identified Black people as the main concern and the most prominent out-group. In fact, there are no highly ranked words or word pairs relating to Jews in the sub-corpus of new members' postings. Consequently, the election posed a fundamental challenge to these new members who based their identity and self-value on social comparison with other races and the devaluation of Black people.

The election was repeatedly and explicitly described as a turning point for new forum members, influencing their decision to register and actively post messages for one another within the Stormfront community. Many expressed a need to "take action" and "do something" in response to the event, while also seeking comfort, moral support, and a means of making sense of their distress. For instance: "I have been reading for some time, but this was the final tipping point, I felt compelled to register and post" and "over the years my concerns has grown this was a tipping point." The election thus served as a trigger or a "moral shock" (Snow & Soule, 2010; Warren, 2010) that propelled these individuals to join Stormfront in order to process their trauma, as well as to seek moral and social support and belonging.

Upon joining the community, new members engaged in developing new narratives to provide coherence and meaning to the situation. They achieved this by sharing personalized stories of past injustices, alleged offenses, assaults, and violence purportedly committed by Black people against white people, which served to ignite a sense of moral outrage. These stories often featured an idealized victim, such as a young woman or daughter, who had allegedly been assaulted. For instance:

> Last night made me so sick to my stomach. One of my female friends was robbed of all her things. I saw black teens harassing white cops, saying they aren't **** [sic] and don't matter. I think I vomited in my mouth.

By sharing these stories, the new members of the community collectively cultivated anger and outrage toward outsiders. In their discussions, they identified concrete and specific adversaries, shifting attention from the specific "disaster" of the election and the resulting feelings of grief and despair to focus instead on the corruption and dangerous nature of their enemies. In this way, the indignities of daily life are transformed into a shared grievance with a focused target of collective action.

Importantly, the social and interactive processes of formulating these new narratives, in which members come together and synchronize their thoughts and actions, can itself be a powerful tool for healing and strengthening collective identity and in-group solidarity. These collective gatherings – or community rituals – involve both *shared* and *reciprocal emotions* (Jasper, 2008).

Shared emotions refer to the collective emotional experiences that arise from a common cause or event, such as a shared trauma or a victory. These emotions reflect how the group collectively nurtures anger toward outsiders, such as outrage over government policies. This process is particularly evident in some of these narratives: While the stories depict concrete and actual events that involve Black people, they simultaneously emphasize that violence and immoral acts are inherent in the very nature of Black people. In this manner, members connect broader sociocultural forces with human agents who are appropriate targets of collective action. Through this type of cognitive reframing, the members thus transform passive emotions, such as dread, hopelessness, fear, resignation, shame, and disgust, into active emotions, such as moral indignation and outrage, which provide better foundations both for their demands of as well as for their collective identity. While resignation can dampen the perceived opportunity for change, emotions like anger, indignation, and pride are commonly associated with political agency (Jasper, 2011). In contrast, the established, long-term members do not need this: Their grievances are firmly established – they are already angry.

Reciprocal emotions include emotions individuals experience in response to others' emotions within a group or social context. When one person expresses anger or sadness about an issue, others may reciprocate these emotions, leading to a shared emotional experience that bolsters social bonds and strengthens group cohesion. On Stormfront, this can be seen in the expressions of social bonding and support among members. Members have thanked each other for receiving support and being welcomed to the forum. Many claimed that their reason for joining the forum was to find moral and social support and a protected space to discuss with like-minded people. As one user put it: "I came here to converse and find solidarity with fellow White Nationalists." Through these posts and the ensuing discussions, members forged personal bonds of friendship and loyalty, and enhanced feelings of trust and solidarity, as expressed in these two posts: "I'd just like to thank everyone for responding to my posts and for the most part being respectful"; "Very happy to have joined SF, glad to have joined this site, the election has fired up my desire to reach out to other whites." Participating in these positively toned interactions reinforces a common identity and bolsters personal and collective self-esteem – similar to De Koster and Houtman's (2008) emphasis on Stormfront messages as sources of sociability, resulting in communal solidarity among members. Both the notions of shared and reciprocal emotions underscore the significance of emotional exchanges in shaping social interactions and collective action.

Online Therapy for White Supremacists

Our analysis reveals that Stormfront serves not only as a refuge for the far-right to express conventionally distasteful opinions and ideas (de Koster & Houtman, 2008) but also as an "emotional refuge" (Reddy, 2001), providing space and legitimacy to their emotional experiences. This speaks to Ganesh's (2018, pp. 33–34) suggestion that, for the far right, what unites communities online are "forms of intimacy, sense, and feeling that are maligned or considered unacceptable in mainstream society."

The 2008 election of Obama drove a large number of individuals to join the community, driven by an unarticulated sense of confusion, discomfort, and anxiety. A Black president seemed to question not only something at the very core of their identity as white Americans but also something to which they had never put words – a feeling that felt forbidden to utter in mainstream society. Stormfront offered a space to meet others who had the same experience and offered a new narrative – *White Supremacy* – to explain *why* it felt wrong and to legitimize their experience. The White Supremacy that is part of American history and culture – and still rooted in its collective uncon-scious – was thus put proudly forth, not as a shameful legacy of slavery, but as a proud badge of honor. Thus, while one may believe that communities such as Stormfront merely draw a collection of already radicalized extrem-ists, our analysis shows that it does not merely gather them but also trans-forms them as it brings them into an extremist community.

Both the trauma narratives themselves and the participation in the collec-tive processes that generate them impart meaning and coherence to feelings of pain, fear, and confusion. By supporting and encouraging each other (recip-rocal emotions) and collectively diagnosing and describing shared injustices and grievances (shared emotions), members on Stormfront created a sense of unity and solidarity, reinforcing their collective identity and commitment to a common goal. Through social rituals of online interaction, their feelings of shame, despair, depression, and disgust are thus transformed into solidarity in the community. They felt one with the community. The vague sense of dif-ference was replaced by an articulated belief in the superiority of the white race. They were the heroes of their stories once again. In this experience of emotional communion, individuals forged a sense of social belonging and shared beliefs. Pain turned into anger, thence hatred.

Stormfront functioned as a form of online therapy group for White Suprem-acists, where members vented, articulated, and collectively made sense of their emotional reactions, thereby shaping an emotionally energized collec-tive with a focused target of collective action. Spaces like Stormfront can thus enable counterreactions and backlashes to events perceived as threatening to their community or identity, leading to emotionally charged mobilizations. These rituals of narrative construction are collective, bottom-up processes involving many members, rather than being strategically shaped by indi-vidual leaders, as is often described in social movement literature (see e.g. Oliver & Johnston, 2000).

Conclusion: From Echo Chambers to Digital Campfires

The concept of the echo chamber emerged as a response to the suggestion that social media would usher in a new era of democratization by serving as new critical-rational public sphere. While the echo chamber thesis posited that the Internet might enable us to avoid engaging with political opponents, it never interrogated the underlying assumption that political life ultimately is constituted solely in rational debate. Throughout the many characteriza-tions of the nature of digital media participation, this rationalist assumption has been a widely accepted presupposition: Whether delivered by algorithms, sociometric choices, or both, politics primarily concerns opinions, and these opinions are in turn the product of rational arguments and information. These tenets have been the unchallenged foundations of analyses, focusing on the potential existence of online echo chambers.

In this chapter, we have laid the groundwork for an alternative paradigm for understanding online extremism and hate messages. Politics is not merely about opinions, we have argued, but exists in the social realm, encompassing identity, emotion, and discourse. Similarly, online interaction is not exclusively focused on the rational and individual consumption of information; it is a *social process* of mutual influence and co-creation. As an alternative to the rationalist paradigm, this chapter has proposed a Durkheimian interpretation of digital media, viewing online interaction as a form of ritual. This casts online communities like Stormfront as a tribe gathered around a campfire, creating a shared narrative of belonging and identity through their stories and emotional exchanges. The content of the messages functions as a symbolic marker of identity rather than rational facts. As in Aboriginal chanting, the words are no more important than the rhythm, the feeling, and the sense of shared activity that the words convey.

While the echo chamber hypothesis of radicalization emphasizes the impact of reading and consuming others' posts, the perspective introduced in this chapter underscores participation – actively conversing, posting, and sharing experiences – as the primary driver of radicalization. Simply consuming content related to a subject, whether through newspapers, television, or social media, can cultivate interest and shape opinions on it, but it does not foster a sense of community. On the other hand, active participation and dialogue online resonate at a deeper, emotional level, nurturing the emergence of shared identity through the articulation of a view of the world.

On Stormfront, the community is centered around a shared activity and mood defined by the unified hatred of Jews – a totem that unites the community. On this foundation, an entire worldview is erected, simultaneously representing the shared identity of the members and distinguishing insiders from outsiders. Blacks are subhuman. Jews are engaged in a conspiracy to enslave and replace white people. To the extent that such views are linked to ostensibly rational arguments, the latter are *expressions*, not causes, of the community belonging.

By considering the interactions within fringe extremist spaces as rituals rather than rational deliberations, we can better understand the emotional dynamics that drive individuals to participate in extremist communities and the social processes through which these communities maintain their cohesion and vitality. This approach also allows us to identify the ways in which online spaces can amplify and reinforce the narratives and symbols that underpin extremist ideologies, thus promoting their dissemination and persistence.

References

Amarasingam, A., & Argentino, M. A. (2020). The QAnon conspiracy theory: A security threat in the making. *CTC Sentinel, 13*(7), 37–44.

Bail, C. (2022). *Breaking the social media prism: How to make our platforms less polarizing*. Princeton University Press.

Bail, C. A., Argyle, L. P., Brown, T. W., Bumpus, J. P., Chen, H., Hunzaker, M. F., Lee, J., Mann, M., Merhout, F., & Volfovsky, A. (2018). Exposure to opposing views on social media can increase political polarization. *Proceedings of the National Academy of Sciences, 115*(37), 9216–9221. https://doi.org/10.1073/pnas.1804840115

Beirich, H. (2014, May 24). *White homicide worldwide: Stormfront, the leading white supremacist web forum has another distinction – murder capital of the internet*. Southern Poverty Law Center Intelligence Report. https://www.splcenter.org/fighting-hate/intelligence-report/2014/white-homicide-worldwide

Bélanger, J. J., Nisa, C. F., Schumpe, B. M., Gurmu, T., Williams, M. J., & Putra, I. E. (2020). Do counter-narratives reduce support for ISIS? Yes, but not for their target audience. *Frontiers in Psychology, 11*, 1059. https://doi.org/10.3389/fpsyg.2020.01059

Benford, R. D. (1997). An insider's critique of the social movement framing perspective. *Sociological Inquiry, 67*(4), 409–430. https://doi.org/10.1111/j.1475-682x.1997.tb00445.x

Benford, R. D., & Snow, D. A. (2000). Framing processes and social movements: An overview and assessment. *Annual Review of Sociology, 26*(1), 611–639. https://doi.org/10.1146/annurev.soc.26.1.611

Berglind, T., Pelzer, B., & Kaati, L. (2019, August). Levels of hate in online environments. In *Proceedings of the 2019 IEEE/ACM international conference on advances in social networks analysis and mining* (pp. 842–847). https://doi.org/10.1145/3341161.3343521

Berinsky, A. J. (2017). Rumors and health care reform: Experiments in political misinformation. *British Journal of Political Science, 47*(2), 241–262. https://doi.org/10.1017/s0007123415000186

Bourdieu, P. (1991). *Language and symbolic power*. Harvard University Press.

Bowman-Grieve, L. (2009). Exploring "Stormfront": A virtual community of the radical right. *Studies in Conflict and Terrorism, 32*(11), 989–1007. https://doi.org/10.1080/10576100903259951

Bright, J., Marchal, N., Ganesh, B., & Rudinac, S. (2022). How do individuals in a radical echo chamber react to opposing views? Evidence from a content analysis of stormfront. *Human Communication Research, 48*(1), 116–145. https://doi.org/10.1093/hcr/hqab020

Brundidge, J. (2010). Encountering "difference" in the contemporary public sphere: The contribution of the Internet to the heterogeneity of political discussion networks. *Journal of Communication, 60*(4), 680–700. https://doi.org/10.1111/j.1460-2466.2010.01509.x

Burston, A. (Chapter 2 this volume). Digitally mediated spillover as a catalyst of radicalization: How digital hate movements shape conservative youth activism.

Chua, A. (2019). *Political tribes: Group instinct and the fate of nations*. Penguin.

Collins, R. (2004). *Interaction ritual chains*. Princeton University Press.

Couldry, N., & Hepp, A. (2018). *The mediated construction of reality*. John Wiley & Sons.

de Koster, W., & Houtman, D. (2008). 'STORMFRONT IS LIKE A SECOND HOME TO ME' On virtual community formation by right-wing extremists. *Information, Communication & Society, 11*(8), 1155–1176. https://doi.org/10.1080/13691180802266665

DiMaggio, P., Bernier, C., Heckscher, C., & Mimno, D. (2018). Interaction ritual threads: Does IRC theory apply online? In E. B. Weininger, A. Lareau, & O. Lizardo (Eds.), *Ritual, emotion, violence* (pp. 99–142). Routledge.

Dubois, E., & Blank, G. (2018). The echo chamber is overstated: The moderating effect of political interest and diverse media. *Information, Communication & Society, 21*(5), 729–745. https://doi.org/10.1080/1369118x.2018.1428656

Durkheim, E. (1915). *The elementary forms of the religious life.* Free Press. (Les Formes élémentarires de la vie religieuse: le systéme totémeque en Australie, Paris: Alcan). (Original work published 1912)

Fairclough, N. (1989). *Language and power.* Longman.

Funkhouser, E. (2022). A tribal mind: Beliefs that signal group identity or commitment. *Mind & Language, 37*(3), 444–464. https://doi.org/10.1111/mila.12326

Ganesh, B. (2018). The ungovernability of digital hate culture. *Journal of International Affairs, 71*(2), 30–49. https://www.jstor.org/stable/26552328

González-Bailón, S., Lazer, D., Barberá, P., Zhang, M., Allcott, H., Brown, T., Crespo-Tenorio, A., Freelon, D., Gentzkow, M., Guess, A. M., Iyengar, S., Kim, Y. M., Malhotra, N., Moehler, D., Nyhan, B., Pan, J., Rivera, C. V., Settle, J., Thorson, E., . . . & Tucker, J. A. (2023). Asymmetric ideological segregation in exposure to political news on Facebook. *Science, 381*(6656), 392–398. https://doi.org/10.1126/science.ade7138

Habermas, J. (1989). *The structural transformation of the public sphere: An inquiry into a category of bourgeois society.* Polity.

Hamm, M. S., & Spaaij, R. (2017). *The age of lone wolf terrorism.* Columbia University Press.

Hartzell, S. L. (2020). Whiteness feels good here: Interrogating white nationalist rhetoric on stormfront. *Communication and Critical/Cultural Studies, 17*(2), 129–148. https://doi.org/10.1080/14791420.2020.1745858

Hassan, G., Brouillette-Alarie, S., Alava, S., Frau-Meigs, D., Lavoie, L., Fetiu, A., Varela, W., Borokhovski, E., Venkatesh, V., & Rousseau, C. (2018). Exposure to extremist online content could lead to violent radicalization: A systematic review of empirical evidence. *International Journal of Developmental Science, 12*(1–2), 71–88. https://doi.org/10.3233/dev-170233

Hemmingsen, A.-S., & Castro, K. I. (2017). *The trouble with counter-narratives.* Danish Institute for International Studies Report. http://pure.diis.dk/ws/files/784884/DIIS_RP_2017_1.pdf

Iyengar, S., Lelkes, Y., Levendusky, M., Malhotra, N., & Westwood, S. J. (2019). The origins and consequences of affective polarization in the United States. *Annual Review of Political Science, 22*, 129–146. https://doi.org/10.1146/annurev-polisci-051117-073034

Jasper, J. (2008). *The art of moral protest: Culture, biography, and creativity in social movements.* University of Chicago Press.

Jasper, J. (2011). Emotions and social movements: Twenty years of theory and research. *Annual Review of Sociology, 37*, 285–303. https://doi.org/10.1146/annurev-soc-081309-150015

Joachims, T. (2002). *Learning to classify text using support vector machines* (Vol. 668). Springer Science & Business Media.

Johannessen, L. E. (2023, June). Interaction rituals and technology: A review essay. *Poetics, 98.* https://doi.org/10.1016/j.poetic.2023.101765

Jungherr, A., Rivero, G., & Gayo-Avello, D. (2020). *Retooling politics: How digital media are shaping democracy.* Cambridge University Press.

Kahan, D. M. (2013). Ideology, motivated reasoning, and cognitive reflection. *Judgment and Decision Making, 8*(4), 407–424. https://doi.org/10.1017/s1930297500005271

Karell, D., Linke, A., Holland, E., & Hendrickson, E. (2023). "Born for a storm": Hard-right social media and civil unrest. *American Sociological Review, 88*(2), 322–349. https://doi.org/10.1177/00031224231156190

Karlsen, R., Steen-Johnsen, K., Wollebæk, D., & Enjol ras, B. (2017). Echo chamber and trench warfare dynamics in online debates. *European Journal of Communication, 32*(3), 257–273. https://doi.org/10.1177/0267323117695734

Keuchenius, A., Törnberg, P., & Uitermark, J. (2021). Why it is important to consider negative ties when studying polarized debates: A signed network analysis of a Dutch cultural controversy on Twitter. *PLoS One, 16*(8), e0256696. https://doi.org/10.1371/journal.pone.0256696

Knobel, M., & Lankshear, C. (2007). Online memes, affinities, and cultural production. In M. Knobel & C. Lankshear (Eds.), *A new literacies sampler* (pp. 199–227). Peter Lang.

Levin, B. (2002). Cyberhate: A legal and historical analysis of extremists' use of computer networks in America. *American Behavioral Scientist, 45*(6), 958–988.

Lewandowsky, S., Ecker, U. K., Seifert, C. M., Schwarz, N., & Cook, J. (2012). Misinformation and its correction: Continued influence and successful debiasing. *Psychological Science in the Public Interest, 13*(3), 106–131. https://doi.org/10.1177/1529100612451018

Lupu, Y., Sear, R., Velásquez, N., Leahy, R., Restrepo, N. J., Goldberg, B., & Johnson, N. F. (2023). Offline events and online hate. *PLoS One, 18*(1). https://doi.org/10.1371/journal.pone.0278511

Mason, L. (2018). *Uncivil agreement: How politics became our identity*. University of Chicago Press.

McKelvey, T. (2001, October 31). Father and son team on hate site. *USA Today.com.* https://www.usatoday.com/life/2001-07-16-kid-hatesites.htm

McPherson, M., Smith-Lovin, L., & Cook, J. M. (2001). Birds of a feather: Homophily in social networks. *Annual Review of Sociology, 27*(1), 415–444. https://doi.org/10.1146/annurev.soc.27.1.415

Miller-Idriss, C. (2022). *Hate in the homeland: The new global far right*. Princeton University Press.

Müller, K., & Schwarz, C. (2021). Fanning the flames of hate: Social media and hate crime. *Journal of the European Economic Association, 19*(4), 2131–2167. https://doi.org/10.1093/jeea/jvaa045

Müller, K., & Schwarz, C. (2023). From hashtag to hate crime: Twitter and anti-minority sentiment. *American Economic Journal: Applied Economics, 15*(3), 270–312. https://doi.org/10.1257/app.20210211

Nyhan, B., Reifler, J., Richey, S., & Freed, G. L. (2014). Effective messages in vaccine promotion: A randomized trial. *Pediatrics, 133*(4), e835-e842. https://doi.org/10.1542/peds.2013-2365

Oliver, P., & Johnston, H. (2000). What a good idea! Frames and ideologies in social movements research. *Mobilization: An International Journal, 5*(1), 37–54. https://doi.org/10.17813/maiq.5.1.g54k222086346251

Pariser, E. (2011). *The filter bubble: What the Internet is hiding from you*. Penguin.

Phadke, S., & Mitra, T. (Chapter 9 this volume). Inter-platform information sharing, roles, and information differences that exemplify social processes of online hate groups.

Phillips, W., & Milner, R. M. (2017). Decoding memes: Barthes' punctum, feminist standpoint theory, and the political significance of #yesallwomen. In S. Harrington (Ed.), *Entertainment values: How do we assess entertainment and why does it matter?* (pp. 195–211). Palgrave.

Polkinghorne, D. E. (1988). *Narrative knowing and the human sciences*. SUNY Press.

Ravndal, J. A. (2016). Right-wing terrorism and violence in Western Europe: Introducing the RTV dataset. *Perspectives on Terrorism, 10*(3), 2–15. www.sv.uio.no/c-rex/english/groups/rtv-dataset/

Ravndal, J. A. (2018). Right-wing terrorism and militancy in the Nordic countries: A comparative case study. *Terrorism & Political Violence, 30*(5), 772–792. https://doi.org/10.1080/09546553.2018.1445888

Rea, S., Mathew, B., & Kraemer, J. (Chapter 8 this volume). 'Hate parties': Networked antisemitism from the fringes to YouTube.

Reddy, R. W. (2001). *The navigation of feeling: A framework for the history of emotions*. Cambridge University Press.

Roberts, D. (2017, May 19). Donald Trump and the rise of tribal epistemology. *Vox Media*. https://www.vox.com/policy-and-politics/2017/3/22/14762030/donald-trump-tribal-epistemology

Sarbin, T. R. (1986). Narrative psychology: The storied nature of human conduct. In T. R. Sarbin (Ed.), *Narrative psychology: The storied nature of human conduct* (pp. 3–21). Praeger.

Schmitt, J. B., Rieger, D., Rutkowski, O., & Ernst, J. (2018). Counter-messages as prevention or promotion of extremism?! The potential role of YouTube: Recommendation algorithms. *Journal of Communication, 68*(4), 780–808. https://doi.org/10.1093/joc/jqy029

Schwartz, S. J., Luyckx, K., & Vignoles, V. L. (Eds.). (2011). *Handbook of identity theory and research*. Springer.

Scrivens, R., Davies, G., & Frank, R. (2020). Measuring the evolution of radical right-wing posting behaviors online. *Deviant Behavior, 41*(2), 216–232.

Shifman, L. (2013). Memes in a digital world: Reconciling with a conceptual troublemaker. *Journal of Computer-Mediated Communication, 18*(3), 362–377. https://doi.org/10.1111/jcc4.12013

Snow, D. (2004). Framing processes, ideology, and discursive fields. In D. Snow, S. A. Soule, & H. Kriesi (Eds.), *The Blackwell companion to social movements* (pp. 380–412). John Wiley & Sons.

Snow, D., & Soule, S. (2010). *A primer on social movements*. W. W. Norton.

Soares, F. B., Recuero, R., & Zago, G. (2019). Asymmetric polarization on Twitter and the 2018 Brazilian presidential elections. In *Proceedings of the 10th international conference on social media and society* (pp. 67–76). https://doi.org/10.1145/3328529.3328546

Sunstein, C. (2002). *Republic.com*. Princeton University Press.

Sunstein, C. (2007). *Republic.com 2.0*. Princeton University Press.

Törnberg, A., & Nissen, A. (2022). Mobilizing against Islam on social media: Hyperlink networking among European far-right extra-parliamentary Facebook groups. *Information, Communication & Society*, 1–19. https://doi.org/10.1080/1369118X.2022.2118546

Törnberg, A., & Törnberg, P. (2021). "Wake-up call for the white race": How Stormfront framed the elections of Obama and Trump. *Mobilization: An International Quarterly, 26*(3), 285–302. https://doi.org/10.17813/1086-671x-26-3-285

Törnberg, A., & Törnberg, P. (2023). White supremacists anonymous: How digital media emotionally energize far-right movements. *Journal of Information Technology & Politics (Online First)*. https://doi.org/10.1080/19331681.2023.2262459

Törnberg, A., & Wahlström, M. (2018). Unveiling the radical right online: Exploring framing and identity in an online anti-immigrant discussion group. *Sociologisk forskning, 55*(2–3), 267–292. https://doi.org/10.37062/sf.55.18193

Törnberg, P. (2022). How digital media drive affective polarization through partisan sorting. *Proceedings of the National Academy of Sciences, 119*(42), e2207159119. https://doi.org/10.1073/pnas.2207159119

Törnberg, P., & Törnberg, A. (2022). Inside a white power echo chamber: Why fringe digital spaces are polarizing politics. *New Media & Society*. https://doi.org/10.1177/14614448221122915

Tsesis, A. (2017). Terrorist speech on social media. *Vanderbilt Law Review, 70*(2), 651–708.

Wahlström, M., & Törnberg, A. (2021). Social media mechanisms for right-wing political violence in the 21st century: Discursive opportunities, group dynamics, and co-ordination. *Terrorism and Political Violence, 33*(4), 766–787. https://doi.org/10.1080/09546553.2019.1586676

Walther, J. B. (2022). Social media and online hate. *Current Opinion in Psychology*, *45*, 101298. https://doi.org/10.1016/j.copsyc.2021.12.010

Walther, J. B. (Chapter 2 this volume). Making a case for a social processes approach to online hate.

Walther, J. B., & Burgoon, J. K. (1992). Relational communication in computer-mediated interaction. *Human Communication Research*, *19*(1), 50–88. https://doi.org/10.1111/j.1468-2958.1992.tb00295.x

Warren, M. R. (2010). *Fire in the heart: How white activists embrace racial justice*. Oxford University Press.

Wästerfors, D., Burcar Alm, V., & Hannerz, E. (2023). The bumpy paths of online sleuthing: Exploring the interactional accomplishment of familiarity, evidence, and authority in online crime discussions. *New Media & Society*. https://doi.org/10.1177/14614448221149909

Wojcieszak, M. E., & Mutz, D. C. (2009). Online groups and political discourse: Do online discussion spaces facilitate exposure to political disagreement? *Journal of Communication*, *59*(1), 40–56. https://doi.org/10.1111/j.1460-2466.2008.01403.x

Wolfowicz, M., Hasisi, B., & Weisburd, D. (2022). What are the effects of different elements of media on radicalization outcomes? A systematic review. *Campbell Systematic Reviews*, *18*(2), e1244. https://doi.org/10.1002/cl2.1244

6

"DEAL" OF THE DAY

Sex, Porn, and Political Hate on Social Media

Sahana Udupa and Oeendrila Lahiri Gerold

I had no idea about Sulli deals. And then finally I saw this random girl . . . when I clicked on "find your sulli", [an image of] a girl popped up. I had no idea. I was still trying to understand. The second time I clicked it, a friend of mine popped up. That's when I realized *ke yeh toh kuch galat he* [something is wrong]. Then the third or fourth time when I checked, it was my picture [out] there! Aaargh, I was disgusted, like what the hell!

– Naziya

[A]nd when my brother opened Twitter, he saw that there was a post where I was being sold. It was written, "enjoy, brother, enjoy this Sulli for 30 cents" and some man was tagged. My brother was furious that we were being sold like prostitutes. And when I say "prostitute," I don't say it in a derogatory way. . . . It's just that we were seen as just a piece of meat. They didn't take our consent; they were just selling us like cows or buffaloes . . . and for sexual trade! It was very bad . . . my brother got mad."

– Nadiya

Naziya and Nadiya were recounting the horrific experiences of being "auctioned" online, two years after this incident erupted as a scandal in India in 2021, stirring a nationwide media debate. The scandal revolved around a chain of events triggered by a "live event" on a YouTube channel, when a male right-wing 'celebrity' hosted what he described as an "Eid Special." The event paraded nonconsensually sourced images of Pakistani women, inviting the followers of the channel to survey the women's sexual worth and "quench their lust with their eyes" ["*aaj apni tharak bhari ankho se ladkiya tarenge*," in Hindi].

DOI: 10.4324/9781003472148-6

After the stream ended, numerous Twitter accounts proceeded to "auction" Indian Muslim women, employing the same tactics by displaying non-consensually obtained images and videos that were profiled as though they were "items on auction" and encouraging users to browse and rate them. Prominent handles behind the auctions on Twitter were traced to the creator of the first live event on YouTube and another Indian youth studying computer science at the time (Goyal, 2021; Taskin, 2022). Both were in their twenties.

In a short span of time, the obscure online activity had snowballed. In July 2021, the media reported existence of a web application with the name "Sulli Deals" on GitHub, an open-source software repository, which conducted similar online auctions of minority Muslim women derisively labeled as "Sulli" (Goyal, 2021).[1] The app had been created almost a month earlier, and a Twitter handle with the same name and other allied handles shared screenshots of the "deals of the day" and linked the GitHub page in their "bio" to promote the content (Zubair et al., 2021). The handles invited users to the landing page of the app "Sulli Deals," where a randomly selected photograph of a Muslim woman was showcased as "Sulli of the day" (Fazili, 2022). Images were sourced from the web of over 90 Muslim women without their consent. Users could browse the application for the entire "collection" of Muslim women. A slew of police complaints and law enforcement actions ensued.

Law and order actions and media exposures notwithstanding, the auction practice continued to persist. In January 2022, yet another "auction" app appeared on GitHub, listing over a 100 Indian Muslim women. It described itself as "Bulli Bai," another derogatory term for Muslim women. The police claimed that the creator of the app had copied and edited the code repository and graphics features of Sulli Deals to create the new Bulli Bai version of the auction app. Some of the key Twitter handles that promoted this new app had appeared in police complaints related to the 2021 Sulli Deals, indicating a close web of actors who seemed relentless despite disciplinary actions (Ojha, 2022; Shekhar, 2022).

Soon after, the Delhi Commission for Women, a statutory body for protecting women's rights, filed a complaint with the Delhi police drawing attention to the "obscene comments against Muslim women" on yet another platform, Clubhouse, which is branded as a social audio app (Bhalla, 2022). Taking *suo moto* (a court taking action of its own accord) cognizance of the snippet of such sexually offensive Clubhouse conversations made public on Twitter, the police arrested three young men aged between 19 and 22 years. The fourth accused was the creator of the original YouTube auction, who was absconding at the time. The accused men had participated and moderated discussions in two Clubhouse rooms titled "Muslim gals are more beautiful than Hindu gals" and "Girls don't have the privilege to marry upper caste boys." A related First Information Report (FIR) was filed in relation to a complaint that a Hindu woman had lodged, providing details around how she had been "auctioned" on the two Clubhouse rooms.

Secondary and Evolutionary Developments

As these activities rippled across various platforms, setting off a series of interconnected actions with a shared repertoire, a distinct digital practice began to crystallize. Thick with sexual degradation and "pornification" (Sarracino & Scott, 2008), "online auctions" sought to perform a politics of masculine majoritarianism by peddling objectified female bodies of the minority religious community as online artifacts, without the knowledge or consent of the women. The crass dehumanizing act invited strong criticism, including the attention of the UN (*The Hindu*, 2022), while also spotlighting an amalgam of murky practices that had been brewing on online channels among niche communities of extreme ideological tactics writ in an "extended adolescence of video games, porn and pranks" (Nagle, 2016, p. 71).

Following fragmented law and order measures and YouTube's decision to ban the channels that featured this content, the creators sought alternative online avenues. A leading figure reassembled his loyal audience on Telegram, an encrypted messaging application known for its lax content regulation (Semenzin & Bainotti, 2020). Utilizing the platform's functionalities such as creating public or private groups with as many as 200,000 members, and public channels for broadcasting content (Khaund et al., 2021), auction actors launched both chat groups and channels. The newly created avenues, some of which were still active as of this writing, feature an archive of banned videos, new video creations, and interactive messaging and largely contains anti-Muslim content alongside graphic and explicit sexual "humor." Sex and sexuality are indeed the running themes in the videos and chats. Muslim men are portrayed as having an uncontrolled appetite for bestiality, with no desire or ability to sexually gratify their many wives. In turn, Muslim women are portrayed as stuck in loveless marriages, often being forced to have sex with their fathers-in-law or brothers-in-law or enjoy "halala" (sexually suggestive in-group idiom with alleged scriptural reference). The Muslim woman is portrayed as young, with or without hijab; she is sexual and sexually vocal and seeks sexual gratification repeatedly. A semi-clad and hijab-adorned picture of Mia Khalifa – the Lebanese porn actress who is a vocal Muslim and liberal activist on social media with 4.8 million followers on Twitter – is often used in the videos to refer to porn, virgins, and other references to sex, and so is another Indian porn star, Sunny Leone. The content is dotted with parodic Islamophobic *shayaris* (short verses in Urdu/Hindi with lyrical and semantic flourish) and occasional career tips for the youth in addition to sexual material. The news covered in the groups relays political ideologies of Indian

Hindu nationalism, training its criticism against Muslim Pakistan as well as religious minorities, liberal media, and those seen as "moderate" Hindu nationalist leaders in India.

The Focus of this Study

In this chapter, we navigate this corpus of volatile and provocative content and activities, to explore new social dynamics of hateful cultures emerging at the intersection of gender, religion, and platform affordances. We combine the analysis of Telegram posts and extracts from online auctions with ethnographic interviews among women political actors who were affected by the auctions in several ways and journalists who investigated the episode. The goal is to better understand how online actors who espouse extreme forms of religious majoritarian ideologies distinguish themselves from other "moderates"; exhibit their masculine politics vis-à-vis the Muslim male "rivals" through a rather contrived way of sexualizing Muslim women; and participate in homosocial networks in which porn, sexual innuendo, political messages, and career advice comingle. Although direct interactions between the authors and the message perpetrators were not possible because of difficulties in accessing that elusive group, we aim to gain a grasp of their manners, motivations, and gratifications by navigating the corpus of content they leave behind online, alongside an analysis of how targeted women and journalists who reported the incident recount describe and assess the dynamics of these "auctions" and related online activities.

Taking a social dynamics and media practice approach to digitally mediated forms of life and relatedness (Couldry, 2012; Geismar & Knox, 2021; Walther, this volume) and informed by speech act theory which posits content and conduct as co-constitutive (Butler, 1997), we advance three analytical points around online hate dynamics that take a specifically gendered dimension. First, we dispute what the "cute cat theory of Internet censorship" (to be described further, later in the chapter) considers as a neat separation between the seemingly apolitical activity of porn and online political activism (Zuckerman, 2008) and argue instead that digital sexual violence gets enmeshed with political aggression via the consumption of porn. Here, we engage with philosopher Rae Langton's (2012) arguments around structural affinities between pornography and hate speech. Second, we suggest that such grave practices are shaped by digital environments which are consumed and articulated as "fun" through the specific affordances and playful interactional frames of online media (Udupa, 2019). Finally, these overlapping practices are embedded within a longer history of postcolonial politics of religious majoritarianism and recent manifestations of global Islamophobia (Hansen, 1999; van der Veer, 1994). In particular, we show how pornified abuse of Muslim women ironically complements the Hindu nationalist narratives around "moral restraint" and its conservative politics focused on regulating the sexuality of Hindu women (Sinha & Fernandes, 2014).

For digital hate scholarship, the social interactional dynamics captured in this study reveal the ways in which exclusionary ideologies with long histories perpetuate through niche groups of supporters as they draw strength from the viscerality of sharing, playing, and mashing up objects floating in the Internet world, charging some of them with widely consumed tropes of sex and porn.

The content we analyze, cite, and show is extremely offensive and presenting them here bears the risks of amplifying the voices of online actors who circulate such content. However, by limiting the cited online texts to the defined objectives of content and ethnographic analyses carried out here, we seek to not only follow the data minimization principle but also evince the possibility of advancing a critical conversation around them.

Porn, Politics, and Misogyny

Pornographic and sexual content in online political discourses has drawn the attention of various recent studies of digital communication. While feminists remain divided around questions of sex work and pornography – reflecting the tension between exploitative and agentic views of porn among contesting feminist traditions (Patu & Schrupp, 2017) – a significant branch of recent scholarship has linked pornography with online misogyny and massive troves of anti-feminist, anti-women, and transphobic content in social media networks (Mantilla, 2015; Massanari, 2015; Tranchese & Sugiura, 2021).

As studies attest, such practices are not contained within the silos of Internet communities. They have seeped into and increasingly frame mainstream political cultures. Segarra and Anderson (2019) define this as a "pornified political culture." Using the example of the 2015 Spanish elections, they argue that pornification of politics extends beyond the United States and is now a global phenomenon "endemic to twenty first century democratic cultures shaped by the 24-hour news cycle, the reach of social media, the ubiquitous objectification of women, sophisticated image-editing technology, and political norms that are persistently patriarchal" (p. 205). They draw on Nussbaum's (1999) concept of "fungability" to describe "pornified political culture" as political processes in which women are divested of their uniqueness, suggested to be violable, and are treated as interchangeable objects.

Although sexualized abuse arguably permeates and shapes different ideological groups within diverse local and national contexts, studies of the alt-right and far-right in the West have highlighted that online anti-feminist discourses prominently figure in right-wing radicalization processes (Keskinen, 2013; Walton, 2012). Fuchs (2018) considers resurgent nationalism in contemporary Europe as an articulation of racisms, misogyny, sexisms, and xenophobia. Socially conservative sections within these groups express the desire to preserve patriarchal and heteronormative families by allocating traditional gender roles and reducing women "to sexuality, biology and housework" (Fuchs, 2018, p. 240). Such utopias around heteronormative traditional families have found a renewed emphasis within newer movements such as QAnon – a pro-Trump conspiracy movement with a large number of women supporters advocating for notions of femininity "centered on motherhood and maternal duty" (Bracewell, 2021, p. 1; Forberg, 2022).

The conservative "happy family" trope has reappeared at the same time when online worlds have seen a veritable expansion of explicit anti-women subcultures – loosely defined as the "Manosphere" – ranging from "reactionary and alt-right YouTubers who rage against the apparent current moral decline due to the sexual revolution and feminism" and MGTOWs (Men Going Their Own Way) who advocate a "male lifestyle without women" to "NoFap members who abstain from pornography and masturbation but hold equally problematic views of women and feminism" (Johanssen, 2022, p. 4) and groups "obsessed with rape statistics and false rape claims" (Hawley, 2017, p. 62).

While the Manosphere's contradictory strands pull the communities in different directions, posing conceptual quagmires to researchers, what emerges is the common thread of sexualization of women that runs through these varied groups, as sex figures in deeply conflicting forms of anxiety, withdrawal, desire, fantasy, and morality. Psychoanalytical perspectives, to cite one stream of scholarship, have highlighted the contradictory impulses of fantasy, victimhood, and sexual anxiety of male perpetrators of the Manosphere (Johanssen, 2022). Hinting that such seemingly contradictory impulses are subsumed within a discourse that is already bounded and sexualized, studies have rightly drawn a comparison with pornography, arguing that

> both pornography and incels [involuntary celibates; Dekeseredy, this volume] are different manifestations of the same misogyny ... both ... share discourses that reflect a broader societal misogyny in which sex is punitive and strictly connected with women's submission.
>
> (Tranchese & Sugiura, 2021, pp. 2709–2710)

All these leave us with a picture of sexualized anti-women discourses and alt-right discourses developing closely and almost inseparably in the transatlantic context. Johannsen describes this relation as "borrowing": "The Manosphere ... explicitly borrows from or makes use of alt-right discourses, ideas, images, and terminology" (Johanssen, 2022, p. 8). While Manosphere members "borrow" alt-right tropes, the reverse, as we demonstrate in this chapter, is equally true. Right-wing political ideological groups that are racist, anti-minority, and anti-immigrant *rely* on a particular form of misogyny – sexualized and pornographic visual-textual practices – to sustain their practices, while what comes first and what follows is a chicken and egg question. It is in this context that the sexualized objectification of Indian Muslim women as items in an auction via social media takes on numerous layers of meaning.

Sexual Politics of the Hindu Right

The auctioning of Muslim women particularly reflects the ideology of Hindu nationalism, which frames the politics of the current ruling regime in India and has had a Janus-faced moral position on sexuality. Hindu national-ism's advocacy for a Hindu-first India and repression of minority religions (Hansen, 1999; van der Veer, 1994) have shaped the schism around sexuality in ways that follow and replicate the religious divide (between majority Hin-dus and minority Muslims). Hindu nationalists have articulated patriotism in relation to conceptions of *maryada* [honor], which partly unfolds through a conservative politics focused exclusively on regulating sexuality and cel-ebrating the heteronormative "happy family" seen as coextensive with the national community (Udupa, 2018). However, the gendered conception of *maryada* maps out in diametrically opposite ways for the Hindu and Muslim women.[2]

Studies have shown that sexual violence has been a part of interreligious conflicts and riots in India, especially in the late colonial period and years fol-lowing its formal political independence in 1947 (Agarwal, 1995; Das, 2007; Sarkar, 2021). Examining gendered communal conflicts in India, Megha Kumar (2022) emphasizes the importance of the interaction of an elite ide-ology (Hindu nationalism) and the unique economic, social, and political dynamics at work within different conflict situations, tracing some of the motivations behind sexual violence to the founding texts of the ideologues of the Hindu nationalist movement. The founding members of Rashtriya Swayam Sevak Sangh (RSS), the nodal Hindu nationalist organization estab-lished in 1925, articulated sexual violence against "enemy women" within a historical narrative of India's misery under a violent Muslim rule (Kumar, 2022). An image of sexually depraved yet physically powerful Muslim men was pitted against virtuous but weak Hindu men. Muslim women were condemned as complicit in the sexual and material exploitation of Muslim men. In contrast, Hindu women were portrayed as honorable who would rather commit suicide than fall prey to the lascivious marauding Muslims. Paola Bachetta (2004) similarly informs that the core and marginal informa-tional materials of RSS, which had an effective marketing machinery even as early as the 1990s, construed "Muslim women as objects of potential and realized communal and sexual appropriation" (p. 98) vis-a-vis an idealized patriotic Hindu male and the alleged anti-national sexually violent Muslim male. Representations of Muslim women in the Hindu nationalist discourse, Bachetta states, draw on a long tradition of colonial and fascist discursive practices of gendered sexualized "othering." However, instead of an assumed biological inferiority, Indian Muslim women, she argues, are viewed as "lost property" for the Hindus because of religious conversion that "took away" women who were Hindus from their "original" religious community while their status in Islam is assumed to be of tradeable sexual objects. Such ideological justifications for cultivating an aggressive male sexuality have served to exempt sexual degradation of Muslim women from moral reproach within the Hindu nationalist thought.

Against this historically fraught sexual politics of religious majoritarian nationalism which has sought to "divide Muslims along gender lines, and to use Muslim women to denigrate Muslim men" (Bachetta, 2004, p. 123), including through seemingly emancipatory legislations around banning the hijab and the tripal *talaq* (Piedalue et al., 2021), a broader culture of sexualized imagery and sexualization has swept mainstream politics in recent years. In an ethnographic conversation with the authors, Kavita Krishnan, a left-progressive feminist and staunch opponent of Hindu right politics, tells us:

> One set [of people] will keep reacting by calling you a terrorist and a terrorist supporter, and these will always be sexualized because they will say you are the *hoor* who will be gifted to Muslim terrorists when they go to heaven. So [they chide us that] you want to sleep with Muslims, they ask you how did you like the taste of this guy's . . . take this, that . . . all that kind of thing. So there's a whole sexualization of that political angle.

Sexist and sexualized attacks of the kind Krishnan describes have become not only more common but also more sweeping, since women who come from the Hindu communities are also targeted by Hindu nationalists for their feminist and critical views about nationalist politics (Amnesty International India, 2020). This enlarging of the ambit – of who is considered as rightful targets for sexist and sexually violent attacks – has upset, if not completely upturned, the schism in sexual politics along the religious divide. Simultaneously, it has accentuated the contradictions of a conservative politics of the "save the family" discourse of the Hindu right and the disruptive energies of sexualized epithets that drive the ideology.

We suggest that digital mediation is squarely at the center of this churning. As affordable Internet media and social media platforms have expanded, India has become the second-largest country in terms of Internet users (700 million in 2022; Farooqui, 2023). If thousands of newly minted nationalistic ideologues are drawn into a recursive loop of digital influence strategies of the right-wing party – blurring the boundaries between organic and manufactured traction – a bottom-up swelling of nationalist affect on digital platforms has also led to a diversification of strategies, actors, and affects that compose this ideological space.

A significant rupture exists along an emic divide between "trads" (staunch traditionalists) who have sought to revive practices deemed as "properly" Hindu, versus "raitas" ("moderates") who are blamed by the opposing camp for going soft on Hindutva (Hindu nationalism). Trads have taken up some of the most regressive tropes of gender, including the dehumanizing tradition of Sati – the alleged voluntary and divinely sanctified sacrifice of a widow by ending her life on the burning pyre of the deceased husband – which is now considered illegal. Much of their activities heavily hinge on digital work, as these tech-savvy actors charge up a panoply of digitally native tactics to assemble and articulate nationalist views and combat and counter those seen as hostile. In the next two sections, we examine digital activities (online auctions and Telegram chats) of a particular community of such niche extreme actors – the self-defined trads – to ask whether and how they renew and revamp key ideological tenets of exclusionary nationalism foremost by centering the Muslim female body and ramping up gendered discourses with the vocabularies and visualities of Internet porn.

Online Auctions

The online auction scandal in 2021, with which we began this chapter, first came to public knowledge when journalists and members of Article-14, a legal advocacy group, reported about a "tool" called "Sulli Deals" on GitHub (Jafri & Aafaq, 2021). Fashioning itself as an "auction" tool, Sulli Deals showcased images of Muslim women largely sourced from Twitter without their consent or knowledge, inviting users to "take their pick" from the stock of "Sullis" as the "deal of the day." These pictures and more information about the auctions were shared on Twitter and other social media platforms, inviting more users to haggle their "deal of the day." Typically, users would select the image, "rate" the woman in the image, and "auction" her off to each other. Even before the tool appeared on GitHub, similar "deals" were offered on some accounts of Twitter. Several Twitter accounts with apparent pseudo names – some with Muslim-sounding names and others sounding Sikh – with a follower count ranging from 600 to 65,000 were actively promoting the auctions (Jafri & Aafaq, 2021). The deals were also "broadcast" live on YouTube. "I saw it live on YouTube," said Nazia Ahmad, our interlocutor in Delhi; "They were talking like, '2 *rupees ki #&**, *khud ki paisa* [a #&* of 2 Indian rupees worth]'. *'iska yeh, iska wo'* [she's for him, she's for the other]. I cannot even say the word they were using. I saw them, I saw them being auctioned like that" (see Figure 6.1).

FIGURE 6.1 A Tweet on Sulli Deal

Source: Retrieved June 30, 2023, from https://twitter.com/ALeelwala/status/1393076401826
271239

Once images of "auctioned" women appeared on the screens, a typical interaction unfolded as follows:

User 1: *Like thoko bhaiyo* [shower with likes, brothers]
User 2: *Link do bhai* [give me the link, bro]
User 3: *Edi inki nahi mili to unsubscribe kar denge molana* [If indeed I don't get to take them, then I'll unsubscribe, maulana]
User 4: *Band karo yeh chutiyapaa Kameeno* [Stop this f***ery, scoundrels]
User 5: *Video utube se nikal Gaya toh firse upload karna warna unsubcribe karenge n private bhi mat karna* [If the video disappears from YouTube, then please upload again, otherwise we'll unsubscribe and don't even make it private]
User 6: *Bhai inko bakri ki review karo tab khus hoke one hand dumble karenge* [Brother, do reviews of goats and only then they'll be happy to exercise their one hand]

Soon after the incidents came to the attention of the media, journalists reported that a 23-year-old resident in a Northern Indian technology city, who maintained multiple accounts on Twitter and YouTube, was the central figure running the technical set up for the first of such auctions in May, 2021, and, thus, he was an influencer for the large social media following he commanded. Before facing suspension, the YouTube channels "Liberal Doge" and "Secular Doge" that he ran had a combined viewership of 200,000 (Goyal, 2021). The key protagonist of the videos on these channels was a caricaturized Muslim male in the image of a Cheems dog from the global memes world but with a Muslim skull cap (Figure 6.2). Auctions were arguably the most insulting of what these channels produced. As Liberal Doge's posts created a stir, an auction "app" (Bulli Bai app) was subsequently created by a group of youths in November 2021, and soon attracted more attention (Garg, 2022).

The new controversy dragged opposing political parties into the fray, raising the political stakes of this obscure online practice that had now spanned different platforms (see Table 6.1). The arrested youth were software engineering students from different cities of India, and, according to our journalist interlocutor, who published detailed stories on the episode, the parents of the teenagers were unaware of what their children were up to. "They are from very simple middle class family," said the journalist, hinting that one might appreciate their teenage vulnerabilities without casting too harsh a light on them as masterminds of an elaborate criminal conspiracy. "They were really young chaps," he continued; "They did not get the bail in the beginning but after spending some months in the jail, they were released on bail." A feminist politician who spoke to us added, "These 18-year-old, 19-year-old, 20-year-old youngsters who are behind the auctions are earning a buck as well as getting a kick out of doing this kind of thing."

FIGURE 6.2   Meme Shared in the Chat Group

TABLE 6.1   Activities Related to Auctions and Pornified Content on Different Platforms

Twitter	YouTube	GitHub	Clubhouse	Telegram
Amplification and promotion of auctions on other platforms	Live broadcast of an "auction" of Pakistani women	Creation of applications to "auction" Muslim women	Audio discussions around Muslim women and their sexual worth	Chat groups created for circulating political, communal, and misogynistic content
Trolling and auctioning exclusively on Twitter	Misogynistic and Islamophobic content creation and hosting	Hosting of such applications	Auctions of both Hindu and Muslim women	Channels were deleted; YouTube videos are archived and made accessible. Other new channels created at different intervals

"Auction" as a form of online activity is not merely persistent individual heckling that typifies "trolling" (Hardaker, 2010). As the conversation thread and Figure 6.1 illustrate, prankster perpetrators of Sulli/Bulli Deals offered it instead as an activity where users can collaboratively "rate" the images, ask for more images, and express a sense of "procuring" the women depicted in them. The activity bears a similarity with pornography in that they both work on the assumption that women could be rated, sold, and "consumed" in a sexualized way. However, it sits oddly with generous readings of "traditional" pornography as "in a sense, a substitute for a sexual partner" and harmless fiction (Burgess, 1970, p. 8). With nonconsensually sourced images of real women thrown into a male virtual marketplace, the online auction recreates pornographic conditions that depict and endorse women's degradation (Brownmiller, 1975). Even more, with its interactive features, the "auction" transforms the seemingly solitary activity of porn consumption into group aggression laced with sexual innuendo and shaming and the pleasures of "rating" and "bidding" for "items" tagged with real pictures of actual women. Thus, the exemplification of hate becomes a highly social process.

Social Organization

As Nur Akhtar, who was one of the Muslim women "auctioned" online, recounted to us:

> It was not like any other. It wasn't even like a rape threat or whatever that you face online. It was more real, it was more real than mere trolling. It wasn't just saying something and moving on, because there was this element of auctioning . . . a whole activity around you where there are people now commenting on you and talking about you, objectifying you.

This "whole activity," as Nur says, suggests that what emerge in auctions are not just individual and isolated strings of comments to a pornified image but a "porn event," a social interaction episode.

Clusters of users who congregated at the auctions were also simultaneously talking to one another and building up more cheerleaders. One of the women who were "auctioned" told us:

> Before the auctions, I had probably taken it [online harassment] for granted. I thought its okay, *chaar panch log he jo troll karte byathte he types* [it's just about four, five people trolling and suchlike]. After the auctions, I realized they are very well connected, they talk to each other, they have all these DM [direct messaging] groups in which they are discussing, and they are constantly finding people, making lists of people whom they want to attack.

Group Participation

The online uproar that erupted following the arrests of the auctions' creators is a vivid illustration of group camaraderie and tactical noise of supporters. While feminists and liberal progressive voices welcomed the originators' arrests and rallied against the grossly degrading online activity, right-wing patrons of the auction sites posted angry comments. Coining the hashtag "#IamWithLiberalDoge" and claiming that it was trending on Twitter, supporters urged fellow users to "make sure to tweet as much as you can. They are fighting alone, we must support them" (Goyal, 2021). "They have entertained us a lot," reminded another supporter, adding "it's our payback time." Some of them were reeling with anger: "Is freedom of speech for Muslims and leftists?" asked a user; "Why can't someone from HINDU community express himself #IamWithLiberalDoge" [original capitalization].

It was thus of little surprise that following the bans on YouTube and Twitter, some of auction masterminds migrated to Telegram, one of the least regulated platforms, carrying with them the loyal tribe of gleeful hate mongers and the entire bank of deleted content to curate elsewhere. The next section turns to assess content that has been archived on a public Telegram channel run by these actors and samples of conversations among them in a Telegram chat group.

Telegram Chat Worlds

For this analysis, following an initial search on Telegram for the keywords "Liberal Doge," "Secular Doge," and "Sulli Deals," three sites were selected for closer exploration: "Liberal Doge All Videos" (LDAV, a public channel with archived videos), "Secular Doge" (a music, discography public channel), and "Secular Doge Chats" (SDC, a public chat group). The sampled content gathered during observations of group activities between May and June 2022 contains videos, audio clips, chat texts, and still images. LDAV had 59 videos, out of which 2 were forwarded videos and the rest were "restored" from the YouTube channel after it was banned following the live auctions in May 2021. Although the creator of this channel appears to have many more videos scattered around social media channels, this corpus of videos presents an interesting sample of banned videos that are now archived and available using Telegram's unique affordances of encrypted and group messaging functionalities, as well as its radical free speech approach to regulation (Rogers, 2020). Aside from the 57 videos archived in this channel, 13 new videos that the channel owner created and shared on the chat group (SDC) were included in the sample of videos for annotation and analysis. Using the feature of Telegram exports of historical data, we also obtained 149 voice/audio clips from the chat group. The material from the chat group contains images (.png files), stickers (Telegram's own stickers and those created by users), video

TABLE 6.2 Corpus Description

Data type	Location	Total number of items found	Annotated items
Video	Telegram Channel + Chat Group	72	70 (97.2%)
Voice/audio	Telegram Chat group	149	51 (34.2%)
Still images	Telegram Chat Group	811*	129 (15%)

* Excluding duplicates and thumbnails

files (short and embedded videos), other files (shared on the group, including pdfs), and text messages in html files.

For the final annotation, all 70 of "original" videos created by the channel owner were selected for analysis (see Table 6.2). From the large chat data from SDC, only posts with explicit or indirect reference to sex/sexuality, porn, women, and gendered violence were selected. With this selection, a total of 811 images in the chat group were reduced to 129 images for final annotation. Textual data in the chats helped to interpret the meanings of videos, still images, and audio files in the chat group and make sense of the contexts of sharing, but it was not included for coding.

We built two annotation schemes based on bottom-up coding and labels derived from previous work on Hindu nationalism, listing key themes in the corpus. The first list contained gender-based labels: (1) Porn, (2) Muslim femininity and female sexuality, (3) Muslim masculinity and male sexuality, (4) homophobic, (5) morphing, (6) sexually explicit "humor," (7) calls for violence, (8) allegations of sexualizing Hindu deities and motifs, and (9) threats to Hindu masculinity and safety of Hindu women. The second list had "general" themes: (10) Islamophobia, (11) extreme Islamophobia, (12) Hindu nationalism and patriotism, (13) anger against liberal/secular/left politics, and (14) derogatory speech against religions other than Islam (a detailed description of the labels is available from the first author).

Prominent Themes

Table 6.3 shows the most frequently occurring themes in the dataset across videos, voice, and images. It might be noted that coding here is based on its obviousness in the elements analyzed and not its contextual presence. As we gleaned from observations of group discourses during the two-month period, subtle calls for violence are running themes and constitute the ideological framing of the posts. The dataset contains no direct calls for violence, revealing that indirect expressions are employed to signal the desire for sexual and political aggression.

TABLE 6.3 Frequency of Themes

Code	Theme	Occurrences
3	Muslim male sexuality	77
10	Islamophobia	76
12	Hindu nationalism	41
9	Threats to Hindu masculinity	37
11	Extreme Islamophobia	33
1	Porn	32
2	Muslim female sexuality	30
13	Anger against liberal/secular/left politics	24
6	Sexually explicit humor	22
14	Derogatory speech against other religions	10
4	Homophobia	8
8	Allegations of sexualizing Hindu deities	6
5	Morphing	3
7	Direct call for violence	0

Islamophobic and anti-Muslim minority speech constitutes a major part of the content. Masculinity and sexualized speech form core components within the discourse. Doge's videos draw on historical stereotypes of Muslim men as sexually and politically aggressive, and he expands their scope by claiming that Muslim men's hypermasculinity extends to animalistic tendencies including bestiality. Stereotypes of Muslim women are also regurgitated – they are over-sexualized as well as shown to be oppressed. In the chat group, for instance, a user started an "anonymous poll" with the question, *"Mulli ki ch**t kaise hoti hai?"* [What does the vagina of a Muslim girl look like? "Mulli" is an offensive term for Muslim women.] The question was followed by a list of options with sexually explicit descriptions on which users could vote.

Subthemes of love-jihad, *"Hindu khatre mein hain"* [Hindus are under threat], notions of "violent Islam," and allegations that the ruling Hindu nationalist party (BJP) is too "soft" are prominent subthemes. Other subthemes include anti-caste politics and criticism of affirmative action (reservation for oppressed castes) and anger against the "liberals." In videos as well as chats, the language used is often abusive, lewd, and xenophobic. Ironically, the tone is also almost always "humorous" and playful. Further analysis will reveal how diverse themes appear in relation to one another and how full conversational spaces emerge within the Telegram group. To address this lacuna in our content analysis, we conducted conversation analysis of an extract from the chat group, offering a glimpse of how a "typical" exchange unfolds in the group.

Conversation Analysis

- 15 June 2022: Starts like any other day for the group, but sadder. The discussion is sparked by news reports on the grim realities facing young jobseekers from rural areas who had come to the expensive capital city of New Delhi, aspiring to find government and bureaucratic jobs. Members discuss how government jobs are mismanaged and scarce, pushing the youth to commit suicides over failed careers.

- Soon, "CK," a group admin, enters the conversation and launches a diatribe against a group member whom he accuses of blaming the youth for their fate. The messages to which CK replies are deleted already and therefore one cannot gauge the provocation. CK's abuses are packed with Islamophobic, sexist, and sexual punches, attacking Muslim women in particular.

- "Green Bag" intervenes and clarifies that CK has mistaken his target to be a Muslim, when in fact he is a Hindu. He urges CK to calm down saying he is also about to start "raid training" on the group.

- CK clarifies that he was provoked by the person's irreverence toward the deceased and continues to use sexual gifs and to hurl insults against the antagonist's mother, now combining graphic sexual violence against Muslim women with stereotypes around terrorism. A meme with a possibly masturbating body with Leonardo DiCaprio's face pops up in the midst.

- Green Bag suggests that CK and his opponent join forces in violating a "mulli" as a means to foster harmony between themselves. He then suggests that a second phone number, preferably a fake American one, will help dodge Telegram's bans.

- Meanwhile, CK posts a meme that depicts a nude Mia Khalifa, a porn actress and activist of Lebanese origin, with the Pakistani flag painted on her. She is being penetrated by a muscular faceless man painted in the Indian flag. The still image used in the meme comes from one of Khalifa's movies, depicting her contorted face conveying in that moment seeming shock and unease.

- The topic shifts. CK's next message is to Grain Bag asking why their telephone call is not connecting. Grain Bag replies to "Olla Ubar," another active participant in the group, asking him to use the shared fake number to make a sham ID, posing as a Muslim girl.

- CK chips in to suggest "*nudes bhi bhejna*" [send nude pics] and asks Grain Bag to call again.

- Grain Bag says he shall deliver [nude pics] and continues to elaborate on his idea to infiltrate Muslim groups with fake ids. The idea is to act like an ex-Muslim, doxx them, and destroy their online presence. The matter of youth suicides is thus laid to rest for the day.

The mind-numbing mix of themes in the thread – beginning with the sober story of youth suicide to a swift descent to sexualized abusive message to violating a "Mulli" for group solidarity to a wacky cry for nude pics – all ostensibly for the noble cause of the nation – reveals how masculine rage and revenge fantasies around a sexualized female Muslim body animate and hold up the groups. In a vital sense, these groups represent and tap an expanding uptake for porn in India, which has peaked since the advent of smartphones and affordable data plans (Aulakh & Sengupta, 2017; Singh, 2020). According to Porn Hub, India is one of the top consumers of porn ("Pornhub's Third Largest Customer Base Comes from India," 2018) and registered the greatest visits during the pandemic (Kannan, 2020). In addition, India now boasts of amateur local porn productions as well as subscription-based mobile apps for porn (Jaiswal, 2021).

Set in this context of digitally delivered porn riding on cheap data and smartphones, the striking visuality of sexualization and occasional self-references to incels among the "Doges" might be tempting enough to conclude that they are like incels who "dehumanize, yet desire, women" (Johanssen, 2022, p. 4). However, the affective charge of religious nationalism that animates and binds the social interactions among the members – and the group energies around the political ideology which they draw on and fuel – suggest that the confusing concoction of political, pornographic, and sexual matters within such communities holds some new lessons for digital hate scholarship. The next section raises some of these.

Online "Basic Misogyny" to Porn Fun

In his succinct and widely cited "cute cat theory of Internet censorship," Ethan Zuckerman (2008) considers the Internet's immense potentiality for social movements as arising from its architecture that poses a deep dilemma for dictators inclined to control what flows through these channels. Authoritarian will to control the Internet confronts a double bind. If regimes do not censor, all manner of speech, including resistance, will flood the public space. If they censor the Internet, they raise the risk of blanket banning the content, including content that has nothing to do with politics. Censoring the net risks politicizing publics who were until then unconcerned or unaware of what was going on. Worse still, it could antagonize them since they now cannot search the Internet for cute cat pictures and – this is perhaps even more important – pornography. Furthermore, the Internet's open architecture allows for features that expand and improve regardless of the purpose to which they are put. He argues, "Sufficiently usable read/write platforms will attract porn and activists. If there's no porn, the tool doesn't work. If there are no activists, it doesn't work well." While much of this analysis holds true for the risks of censorship, the argument, although not intended, makes a sweeping distinction between porn and political activism, to the extent of suggesting that they represent two different social processes altogether or at the very least, two separate domains of online activities. The analysis presented in the preceding sections reveals how online porn and political activity are not only intertwined but co-constitute one another.

Rooted in the pragmatics tradition, Langton (2012) offers some important clarifications. Bringing hate speech and pornography into the same analytical frame, she highlights how hate speech and pornography "work" as speech acts in "a perlocutionary, causal sense, and an illocutionary, constitutive sense" (p. 76). Extending speech act theory with the argument on "presupposition accommodation," Langton concludes that hate speech and pornography

> work more subtly. . . . They implicitly presuppose certain facts and norms. . . . Consumers then change their factual and normative beliefs by taking on board the common ground . . . or the conversational score . . . that is presupposed in the pornographic [or hateful] conversation.
>
> (p. 83)

The pragmatic model offers an "adequate story about how belief change can be achieved," she points out, but what about "feelings and desire" (p. 85)? Here, Langton ventures to take a leap:

> [T]he phenomenon of accommodation might extend beyond belief – beyond conversational score, and common ground, as originally conceived – to include accommodation of other attitudes, including desire and hatred . . . just as a hearer's belief can spring into being, after the speaker presupposes that belief, so too a hearer's desire can spring into being, after the speaker presupposes the hearer's desire; and so too a hearer's hatred can spring into being, after the speaker presupposes that hatred.
>
> (p. 86)

In so doing, Langton puts emotion in an explanatory model that was originally conceived to explain processes that apply reason to achieve belief. What this formal analysis in the pragmatic model lacks – which makes the argument seem like a leap – can be addressed with a social interactional model and a media practice approach linked to it. The social interactional frame of "fun" as a "meta-practice of extreme speech" (Udupa, 2019) offers ways to account for how Doge and his followers are not merely reproducing religious majoritarian nationalism as a cognitive script – a belief – but renewing it through the affective charge of participation, drawing support from one another, scheming "raids" on opponents, and applauding the "hard work" of fellow members, all while consuming and beseeching porn. Fun as a meta-practice of online extreme speech unfolds in four interconnected ways:

- "being 'funny' as a tactical way to enter and rise to prominence within online debates and, by extension, the broader public domain

- deriving fun from the sheer freshness of colloquialism in political debates, which stands in contrast to the serious tone of political deliberation and official centricity, and by mainstreaming the witty political campaign styles as an everyday form of political communication
- fun as satisfaction of achieving a goal by working with one's own resources and in finding tangible results such as hashtag trending, virality, and perceived "real world" changes
- as group identification and collective (if at times anonymous) celebration of aggression"

(Udupa, 2019, p. 3144)

While pornified hate groups share all these features, male homosociality – "performance of manhood as staged in front of, and granted, by other men" – is a distinctively pronounced feature (Semenzin & Bainotti, 2020, p. 3). The sexualized nature of conversations builds on an appetite for porn, as ring leaders of the movement articulate disinhibition and open embrace, in distinction to a more conservative view of feeling secretive or even embarrassed about porn consumption. Homosociality can itself have disinhibiting effects as there is a performative aspect to such group gatherings with validating impacts, but what is significant, as the thematic mix in the chat groups illustrates, is that right-wing nationalist groups of Doge's kind indicate they need no further justification than the frame of the nation itself. Put differently, there is not just an "elective affinity" or "family resemblance" (Brubaker, 2017) between right-wing discourses and misogyny, but right-wing political cultures thrive on sexualized and pornified anti-women cultures as digitally savvy teenagers become their torchbearers.

In the Indian context, for right-wing nationalism, which today relies on extensive networks of digital propaganda and an army of seemingly spontaneous "volunteers," gendered abuse is a crucial tactic, strategy, and sensibility. As gendered abuse expands within different political groups in their online campaigns and confrontations, it has become not only more common, as our interlocutors vouch and reports confirm (Amnesty International India, 2020; Gurumurthy & Dasarathy, 2022), but it has also become more variegated. Trolling, slut-shaming, infantilizing, and *ad hominem* attacks that make up what one of our interlocutors described rather piquantly as "basic misogyny" are today digitally "enhanced" with the easy creation and devious circulation of "dick pics," pornified images, and auctions, brewed as such within the caldrons of Internet fun and in service of nationalist majoritarianism.[3] While the content and manner of engagement around porn fun are not uncontested even among right-wing ideologues, they are absorbed within the vastly diversified digital antics, as one other activity that helps the purpose.

Acknowledgments

This project has been supported by generous funding from the Bavarian Research Institute for Digital Transformation (BIDT Project: Understanding, Detecting and Mitigating Against Politically Active Women, 2022–25).

Notes

1 "Sulli" and "Bulli" are derivatives of "Mulli," a slang word for Muslim women. These are considered as "Islamophobic slurs" which originate from the derogatory use of the word "Mulla" which refers to a Muslim male (Salim, 2022).
2 Politics around queer publics is also shifting within and beyond Hindu right ideological groups. This requires a separate discussion, which is beyond the scope of this chapter. The discussion here also leaves out questions of sexuality in relation to Christians, Sikhs, and other religious minorities.
3 Rape and death threats against women constitute another type of misogyny, which is recognized as a serious issue in contemporary digital politics (Gurumurthy & Dasarathy, 2022; Iyer et al., 2020; Kenya ICT Action Network, 2020).

References

Agarwal, P. (1995). Surat, Savarkar, and Draupadi: Legitimizing rape as a political weapon. In T. Sarkar & U. Butalia (Eds.), *Women and the Hindu right: A collection of essays* (pp. 29–57). Women for Kali.

Amnesty International India. (2020). *Troll patrol: Exposing online abuse faced by women politicians in India.* Indians for Amnesty International Trust.

Aulakh, G., & Sengupta, D. (2017, June 2). Plunging mobile data costs present a dirty picture. *The Economic Times.* https://economictimes.indiatimes.com/article show/58967964.cms?utm_source=contentofinterest&utm_medium=text&utm_ campaign=cppst

Bachetta, P. (2004). *Gender in the Hindu nation: RSS women as ideologues.* Women Unlimited.

Bhalla, G. (2022, January 19). Obscene comments made against Muslim women on Clubhouse App now, Delhi police file FIR. *IndiaTimes.* https://www.indiatimes. com/news/india/obscene-comments-muslim-women-clubhouse-559731.html

Bracewell, L. (2021). Gender, populism, and the QAnon conspiracy movement. *Frontiers in Sociology, 5.* https://doi.org/10.3389/fsoc.2020.615727

Brownmiller, S. (1975). *Against our will: Men, women and rape.* Bantam.

Brubaker, R. (2017). Why populism? *Theory Society, 46,* 357–385.

Burgess, A. (1970). What is pornography? In D. A. Hughes (Ed.), *Perspectives on pornography.* St. Martin's Press. Cited in Langton, R. (2012). Beyond belief: Pragmatics in hate speech and pornography. In I. Maitra & M. K. McGowan (Eds.), *Speech and harm: Controversies over free speech* (pp. 72–93). Oxford University Press.

Butler, J. (1997). *Excitable speech: A Politics of the performative.* Routledge.

Couldry, N. (2012). *Media, society, world: Social theory and digital media practice.* Polity.

Das, V. (2007). *Life and words: Violence and the descent into the ordinary.* University of California Press.

DeKeseredy, W. S. (Chapter 4 this volume). Misogyny and woman abuse in the incelosphere: The role of incel male peer support.

Farooqui, J. (2023, March 17). Report says over 700 million active internet users in India as of December 2022. *The Economic Times.* https://economictimes.indiatimes.com/

tech/technology/report-says-over-700-million-active-internet-users-in-india-as-of-december-2022/articleshow/98673654.cms

Fazili, S. (2022, January 2). Months after Sulli deals, Bulli Bai app puts Muslim women on "Auction." *BOOM*. https://www.boomlive.in/explainers/muslim-women-online-auction-github-sulli-deals-bulli-bai-16236

Forberg, P. L. (2022). From the fringe to the fore: An algorithmic ethnography of the far-fight conspiracy theory group QAnon. *Journal of Contemporary Ethnography*, *51*(3), 291–317. https://doi.org/10.1177/08912416211040560

Fuchs, C. (2018). *Digital demagogue: Authoritarian capitalism in the age of Trump and Twitter*. Pluto Press. https://doi.org/10.2307/j.ctt21215dw

Garg, A. (2022, October 1). What is Bulli Bai app, what is its link to Sulli deals, and how GitHub is involved: Story in 10 points. *India Today*. https://www.indiatoday.in/technology/features/story/what-is-bulli-bai-app-what-is-its-link-to-sulli-deals-and-how-github-is-involved-story-in-10-points-1898365-2022-01-10

Geismar, H., & Knox, H. (Eds.). (2021). *Digital anthropology* (2nd ed.). Routledge. https://doi.org/10.4324/9781003087885

Goyal, P. (2021, May 15). Ritesh Jha aka 'Liberal Doge': The man behind the livestream spewing hate against Pakistani women. *Newslaundry*. https://www.newslaundry.com/2021/05/15/ritesh-jha-aka-liberal-doge-the-man-behind-the-livestream-spewing-hate-against-pakistani-women

Gurumurthy, A., & Dasarathy, A. 2022. *A study on abuse and misogynistic trolling on Twitter directed at Indian women in public-political life*. https://itforchange.net/a-study-of-abuse-and-misogynistic-trolling-on-twitter-directed-at-indian-women-public-political

Hansen, T. B. (1999). *The saffron wave: Democracy and Hindu nationalism in modern India*. Princeton University Press.

Hardaker, C. (2010). Trolling in asynchronous computer-mediated communication: From user discussions to academic definitions. *Journal of Politeness Research*, 6(2), 215–242. https://doi.org/10.1515/jplr.2010.011

Hawley, G. (2017). *Making sense of the Alt-Right*. Columbia University Press.

The Hindu. (2022, January 12). 'Sulli deals', form of hate speech in India, must be condemned: UN official. https://www.thehindu.com/news/international/sulli-deals-form-of-hate-speech-in-india-must-be-condemned-un-official/article38247094.ece

Iyer, N., Nyamwire, B., & Nabulega, S. (2020). *Alternate realities, alternate Internets: African feminist research for a feminist internet*. https://ogbv.pollicy.org/report.pdf

Jafri, A., & Aafaq, Z. (2021, May 21). Unchecked Tsunami of online sexual violence by Hindu right against India's Muslim women. *Article-14*. https://www.article-14.com/post/unchecked-tsunami-of-online-sexual-violence-by-hindu-right-against-india-s-muslim-women

Jaiswal, P. B. (2021). Indians scoured the internet for porn during the pandemic. *The Week*. https://www.theweek.in/theweek/cover/2021/08/26/indians-scoured-the-internet-for-porn-during-the-pandemic.html

Johanssen, J. (2022). *Fantasy, online misogyny and the Manosphere: Male bodies of dis/inhibition*. Routledge.

Kannan, S. (2020, April 11). Pornography gets a pandemic boost, India reports 95 per cent rise in viewing. *India Today*. https://www.indiatoday.in/news-analysis/story/pornography-gets-a-pandemic-boost-india-reports-95-per-cent-rise-in-viewing-1665940-2020-04-11

Kenya ICT Action Network. (2020). *Trends of online violence against women in politics during the COVID19 pandemic in Kenya*. Retrieved March 2, 2021, from https://africaninternetrights.org/sites/default/files/Trends-of-Online-Violence-against-Women-in-Politics-During-the-COVID19-pandemic-in-Kenya.pdf

Keskinen, S. (2013). Antifeminism and white identity politics: Political antagonisms in radical right-wing populist and anti-immigration rhetoric in Finland. *Nordic Journal of Migration Research*, 3(4), 225–232. https://doi.org/10.2478/njmr-2013-0015

Khaund, T., Hussain, M. N., Shaik, M., & Agarwal, N. (2021). Telegram: Data collection, opportunities and challenges. In J. A. Lossio-Ventura, J. C. Valverde-Rebaza, E. Díaz, & H. Alatrista-Salas (Eds.), *Information management and big data* (pp. 513–526). Springer. https://doi.org/10.1007/978-3-030-76228-5_37

Kumar, M. (2022). *Communalism and sexual violence in India: The politics of gender, ethnicity and conflict*. Bloomsbury Academic India.

Langton, R. (2012). Beyond belief: Pragmatics in hate speech and pornography. In I. Maitra & M. K. McGowan (Eds.), *Speech and harm: Controversies over free speech* (pp. 72–93). Oxford University Press.

Mantilla, K. (2015). *Gendertrolling: How misogyny went viral*. ABC-CLIO, LLC.

Massanari, A. (2015). #Gamergate and the fappening: How Reddit's algorithm, governance, and culture support toxic technocultures. *New Media and Society*, 19(3), 329–346. https://doi.org/10.1177/1461444815608807

Nagle, A. (2016, March). The new man of 4chan. *The Baffler*, 30, 64–76. https://thebaffler.com/salvos/new-man-4chan-nagle

Nussbaum, M. C. (1999). *Sex and social justice*. Oxford University Press.

Ojha, A. (2022, January 8). Bulli Bai app creator Niraj Bishnoi a repeat offender: Here's how Delhi cops nabbed him. *India Today*. https://www.indiatoday.in/india/story/bulli-bai-app-creator-neeraj-bishnoi-delhi-police-1897033-2022-01-07

Patu, & Schrupp, A. (2017). *A brief history of feminism*. The MIT Press.

Piedalue, A., Gilbertson, A., & Raturi, M. (2021). A majoritarian view of 'gender justice' in contemporary India: Examining media coverage of 'triple Talaq' and 'love Jihad.' *South Asia: Journal of South Asian Studies*, 44(4), 739–755. https://doi.org/10.1080/00856401.2021.1951477

Rogers, R. (2020). Deplatforming: Following extreme internet celebrities to Telegram and alternative social media. *European Journal of Communication*, 35(3), 213–229. https://doi.org/10.1177/0267323120922066

Salim, M. (2022, January 16). 'Bulli Bai', 'Sulli deals': On being put up for 'auction' as an Indian Muslim woman. *The Wire*. https://thewire.in/communalism/indian-muslim-woman-auction-bulli-bai

Sarkar, T. (2021). *Hindu nationalism in India*. C Hurst and Company Pub Limited.

Sarracino, C., & Scott, K. M. (2008). *The porning of America: The rise of porn culture, what it means, and where we go from here*. Beacon Press.

Segarra, I. M., & Anderson, K. V. (2019). Political pornification gone global: Teresa Rodríguez as fungible object in the 2015 Spanish regional elections. *Quarterly Journal of Speech*, 105(2), 204–228. https://doi.org/10.1080/00335630.2019.1595102

Semenzin, S., & Bainotti, L. (2020). The use of Telegram for non-consensual dissemination of intimate images: Gendered affordances and the construction of masculinities. *Social Media + Society*, 6(4), 1–12. https://doi.org/10.1177/2056305120984453

Shekhar, R. (2022, January 7). Bulli Bai app case: How BTech student from Assam lost his way. *The Times of India*. https://timesofindia.indiatimes.com/city/delhi/virtual-harassment-how-student-lost-his-way/articleshow/88742860.cms

Singh, R. (2020, January 2). Are Indians obsessed with sex? Report says India leads global porn consumption on smartphones. *India.Com*. https://www.india.com/viral/india-leads-global-porn-consumption-on-smartphones-at-89-says-report-3896539/

Sinha, M., & Fernandes, L. (2014). Gendered nationalism: From women to gender and back again? In L. Fernandes (Ed.), *Routledge handbook on gender in South Asia* (pp. 13–27). Routledge.

Taskin, B. (2022, January 7). Bulli Bai "mastermind" part of Sulli deals too, made Muslim alias to mislead: Delhi police. *The Print*. https://theprint.in/india/bulli-bai-mastermind-part-of-sulli-deals-too-made-muslim-alias-to-mislead-delhi-police/798116/

The Times of India. (2018, December 27). *Pornhub's third largest customer base comes from India*. https://timesofindia.indiatimes.com/home/news/pornhubs-third-largest-customer-base-comes-from-india/articleshow/67268431.cms#:~:text=As%20per%20a%20report%2C%2035,Indians%20aged%20between%2018%2D34

Tranchese, A., & Sugiura, L. (2021). "I don't hate all women, just those stuck-up bitches": How incels and mainstream pornography speak the same extreme language of misogyny. *Violence Against Women, 27*(14), 2709–2734. https://doi.org/10.1177/1077801221996453

Udupa, S. (2018). Gaali cultures: The politics of abusive exchange on social media. *New Media & Society, 20*(4), 1506–1522. https://doi.org/10.1177/1461444817698776

Udupa, S. (2019). Nationalism in the digital age: Fun as a metapractice of extreme speech. *International Journal of Communication, 13*, 3143–3163. https://doi.org/10.5282/ubm/epub.69633

van der Veer, P. (1994). *Religious nationalism: Hindus and Muslims in India*. University of California Press.

Walther, J. B. (Chapter 2 this volume) Making a case for a social processes approach to online hate.

Walton, S. J. (2012). Anti-feminism and misogyny in Breivik's "Manifesto". *NORA-Nordic Journal of Feminist and Gender Research, 20*(1), 4–11.

Zubair, M., Sinha, P., & Chaudhuri, P. (2021, November 15). Sulli deals: Organised attempt to blame a Muslim youth for the app. *Alt News*. https://www.altnews.in/sulli-deals-organised-attempt-to-blame-a-muslim-youth-for-the-app/

Zuckerman, E. (2008, March 9). *The cute cat theory of digital activism*. WorldChanging. https://web.archive.org/web/20120630231006/https://www.worldchanging.com/archives/007877.html

7

DIGITALLY MEDIATED SPILLOVER AS A CATALYST OF RADICALIZATION

How Digital Hate Movements Shape Conservative Youth Activism

Adam Burston

Between 2017 and 2023, American universities reported more than 1,000 incidents of white supremacist recruitment materials on college campuses (ADL, 2019, 2023), thousands of hate crimes (Bauman, 2018), and myriad instances of right-wing extremist mobilization (Iannelli, 2018; Quintana, 2018; SPLC, 2018). While the perpetrators behind extremist recruitment and hate crimes are rarely identified, right-wing extremist mobilization has been linked to rogue chapters of conservative youth organizations. These rogue chapters have espoused such extreme ideology that they were de-chartered by their parent organization and denounced by the Republican Party (Alonso, 2022; ND GOP, 2022; Polletta, 2019). Campus-based extremism carried out by conservative youth organizations is alarming because these organizations function as a bellwether of the Republican Party. Participation often leads to a political career (Binder & Kidder, 2022). James O'Ryan Allsup (SPLC, 2022a), Kyle Bristol (SPLC, 2022b), and Crystal Clanton (Raymond, 2022) are examples of extremists who used participation in a conservative student organization to attain positions of power within the Republican Party. Extremism on college campuses represents a social problem and a potential national security threat. Yet, it is understudied.

This chapter provides an explanation for campus-based radicalization. It emerged from a four-year, multisite ethnography of College Conservatives for Freedom and Liberty, a national conservative youth organization with chapters in major universities across the United States. At each of the field sites, I witnessed a phenomenon I call *digitally mediated spillover*. Digitally mediated spillover occurs when activists who participated in a digital social movement enter a new movement, bringing their ideology and culture, tactical repertoires, and social networks.

DOI: 10.4324/9781003472148-7

Digitally mediated spillover began when right-wing extremists who had formerly participated in digital movements during high school began their university career and joined moderate conservative youth groups. In the chapters where moderates remained a majority and retained leadership positions, digitally mediated spillover was highly disruptive but did not result in radicalization. However, at one of the field sites, right-wing extremists obtained leadership positions and radicalized a sufficient number of moderate activists to become the majority. There were three phases of digitally mediated spillover that ultimately yielded extremism. First, extremists altered the collective identity at W-CCFL by exposing their peers to extremist cyberculture. Second, extremists rendered their peers ideologically extreme and transformed the Group Chat into a "radical milieu," a social network in which sympathetic members of the public offer moral support to extremists. Third, W-CCFL activists became tactically extreme, and this led to organizational implosion.

Defining Key Terms

It is important to define key constructs for interdisciplinary audiences. *Extremism* and *radicalization* are terms that are highly contested across the social sciences (McCauley & Moskalenko, 2017). Ideological extremism entails sympathizing with and advocating for ideologies and practices that disturb a target (e.g., targeted online harassment, sharing racist conspiracy theories online), whereas behavioral extremism describes a willingness to organize or enact physical violence against perceived enemies or innocent civilians (e.g., hate crime, terrorism). Common elements of ideological and behavioral extremism include a shared disdain for democracy, pluralistic society, and the rule of law (Lowe, 2017). Thus, for the purposes of this chapter, I define radicalization as the process in which a moderate social movement becomes ideologically or behaviorally extreme.

A *social movement* is a social network that enacts "collective efforts, of some duration and organization, using noninstitutionalized methods to bring about social change" (Flacks, 2005, p. 5). Historically, successful social movements have been dense, relatively closed social networks with strong ties among members and organizations at their center (e.g., community centers, nonprofit organizations). However, social media platforms have given rise to "connective action" or social movements comprising loosely connected social networks with weak ties among members (Kasimov, 2023). Social movements based on connective action are less effective at coordinating offline protests and lobbying for policy reform, but more effective at disseminating movement ideology to the public (Malthaner & Waldmann, 2014).

Social movement spillover is a phenomenon in which the "the ideas, tactics, style, participants, and organizations of one social movement spill over its boundaries to effect other social movements" (Meyer & Whittier, 1994, p. 277). Originally, spillover was formulated to describe Second Wave Feminists joining and altering the trajectory of the Nuclear Freeze Movement in the 1980s. Feminists left an indelible mark on that movement by infusing anti-nuclear ideology with feminist logics, teaching feminist protest tactics to Nuclear Freeze activists, and providing personnel and organizations to the fledgling movement.

My designation "digitally mediated" refers to social processes that are altered by digital *cultures*. Digitally mediated social processes occur when ideologies, social norms, and behaviors that originated in a particular online context shape social processes in a new online or offline context. Digitally mediated social processes are often but not always transacted through computer-mediated communication. Examples of digitally mediated social processes range from participation in Internet raids in which members of one digital community infiltrate another as a prank or cyber-attack, offline conventions in which fans of a web-based comic series meet to discuss their shared passion, to QAnon protests in which offline mobilization is governed by a community of web-based conspiracy theorists. This chapter examines digitally mediated *spillover* to explain the social processes through which extremist social movements transmit the culture of cyberhate into new online and offline spaces. Put differently, digitally mediated spillover illustrates that the social processes of online hate are transmissible.

Pathways to Radicalization

In response to the recent wave of right-wing extremism, a body of interdisciplinary scholarship has emerged to explain the influence of social media technologies in radicalization. This research mostly addresses the influence of "echo chambers," or ideologically homogenous social networks online, and filter bubbles in which algorithms assign certain users ideologically homogenous and polarizing content (for review, see Zhuravskaya et al., 2020). Despite the strengths of this research, its approach to online radicalization is too narrowly focused on the "how," not the "why," of radicalization. Sociological insights about the macrostructural trends and interactional dynamics that produce the radicalization prove useful.

Right-wing extremist social movements emerge in response to macrostructural threats that undermine their political, cultural, and economic power (for review, see Simi et al., 2024). In response to these threats, right-wing extremist movements form hidden spaces of hate and radical milieus. A hidden space of hate is a closed social network where activists cultivate collective identity and plan protest activity while avoiding outside interference from law enforcement and enemies (Simi & Futrell, 2015). Whether digital or physical, hidden spaces of hate are instrumental to right-wing movements, given the time and resources required to transform members of the general public into committed extremists (Atran, 2021; Simi & Futrell, 2015). Movement leaders create hidden spaces of hate to foment feelings of isolation, despair, and anger as well as a collective identity that supplants activists' individual identity (Atran, 2021). A radical milieu is a large social network comprising extremists and sympathetic members of the general public, who encourage one another to adopt extremist ideology and employ violent or antisocial tactics. Radical milieus are the social environments that produce ideological and behavioral extremism (Malthaner & Waldmann, 2014).

Taken together, scholarship on pathways into radicalization suggests that the recent wave of right-wing extremism is due to a combination of macrostructural trends that threatened white and male dominance, thereby incentivizing the formation of hidden spaces of hate for movement expansion and radical milieus for increased dialogue with the general public. The algorithms, features, and affordances of social media technology accelerated nationwide radicalization by conveying extremist ideology to segments of the population that did not seek it out voluntarily (Zhuravskaya et al., 2020).

However, despite the explanatory power of scholarship cited above, it does not account for the mass radicalization of conservative student movements. Conservative student organizations have a preexisting commitment to the electoral process and social pluralism. They are not hidden spaces of hate, and their preexisting ideological commitments should – in theory – make members more resistant to extremist ideological appeals. Some social scientists offer a different explanation for this radicalization, although it is highly problematic. A recent body of scholarship explains the recent surge of right-wing extremism on college campuses with a theory of "entryism," which argues that right-wing extremist organizations like the Proud Boys and the American Identity Movement (formerly Identity Evropa) send members to college campuses to infiltrate and coopt conservative student organizations in the hopes of sending right-wing extremists into Congress (ADL, 2019; Miller-Idriss, 2020). The concept of entryism emerged in case studies of successful infiltration attempts as well as in internal documents from extremist organizations. Although entryism provides a partial explanation for right-wing extremism in universities, it is inadequate. First, despite their outsized political influence, right-wing extremist organizations have insufficient personnel and funding to stage a national conspiracy. Moreover, the fractious nature of right-wing extremist movements often impedes their execution of complex plans (Simi & Windisch, 2020). For instance, Patriot Front, the organization responsible for the majority of reported white supremacist recruitment flyers on college campuses between 2017 and 2019, is now defunct (ADL, 2019). Second, the radicalization of conservative youth organizations has occurred in locations where there are no known extremist organizations that recruit on university campuses. Third, entryism assumes that a few infiltrators can fundamentally alter organizations that have a preexisting ideological commitment to moderate conservatism and civic engagement. Other literature suggests that group radicalization is a time-consuming process that requires majority consensus (Atran, 2021; Simi & Futrell, 2015). Thus, infiltrating and radicalizing student organization *en masse* are beyond the capabilities of contemporary hate organizations.

In light of the shortcomings of current explanations for radicalization on college campuses, this study sought, and developed, an alternative explanation. This alternative is the process of digital mediated spillover. This new notion was informed by a grounded theory analysis and interpretation of the results of a multisite ethnography of a right-leaning college conservative movement student organization, the procedures and research methods of which are described as follows.

Method

Field Sites

Data for this study come from a multisite ethnography of a conservative social movement, College Conservatives for Freedom and Liberty (hereafter CCFL). CCFL is one of several organizations for politically conservative college and high school students who wish to participate in activism and electoral politics. CCFL's primary goals are spreading conservative values on university campuses and achieving electoral victories for Republican and Libertarian candidates. Every CCFL chapter meets weekly or biweekly and relies on digital chat platforms, like GroupMe and Facebook Messenger, to keep members connected between organizational meetings. I entered the field in January 2018 and concluded my study in December 2021.

My initial goal in doing a multisite ethnography was to capture important variations in regional and local political culture. In order to understand these variations, I studied a CCFL chapter in three U.S. census regions[1]: The West, the Northeast, and the South. In each census region, I studied a flagship public university located in a mid-size city. I selected public universities because they recruit heavily from the local population, enabling me to better understand the influence of local culture on activism. I assigned each university and CCFL chapter a pseudonym based on their census region. West Coast University (hereafter W-CCFL)[2] is situated in a progressive city in a state that is considered a bulwark of Democratic party votership. East Coast University (hereafter E-CCFL) is located on the border of the Midwest and East Coast and attracts students from both census regions. East Coast University is located in a purple state that is hotly contested by Democrats and Republicans during election season. Southern University (hereafter S-CCFL) is located in a majority Republican city in a state that has a nationwide reputation as a bastion of Republican votership and conservative culture.

The ethnographic research involved a mixture of 34 behavioral observations, 64 interviews,[3] and a review of organizational documents and social media activity at each field site.[4] At Western University (January 2017 to March 2018), I conducted 21 instances of observation and 24 interviews; at Eastern University, I conducted 8 instances of observation and 22 interviews; at Southern University, I conducted 5 instances of observation and 15 interviews. During interviews, I offered informants a research laptop and asked them to show me how they use social media in their activism. Informants at W-CCFL, the most extreme field site and the primary focus of this chapter, refused to show me their social media activity, having sworn an oath of secrecy to leadership. At this field site, I had to rely on my informants' descriptions of their social media behavior. Table 7.1 summarizes basic demographics of the informants.

During the chapters' organizational meetings, activists met face to face for 60 to 90 minutes. Because the majority of organizational meetings consisted of debates and strategy sessions, I was able to take highly detailed records of dialogue which appear more like transcripts or meeting notes than typical ethnographic fieldnotes from dynamic settings. During fundraisers and campaigning events, my fieldnotes were more focused on behavior than dialogue. At each field site, I began by introducing myself to the president and asking their permission to describe my research project to the members. In my announcement, I gave members the opportunity to opt out of being included in my fieldnotes. I did not audio record meetings due to a prohibition by my university's Institutional Review Board for the protection of human research participants. Below, interview and fieldnote excerpts with direct quotations are presented in double quotation marks (" "), while paraphrased statements are in single quotation marks (' ').

Coding and Analysis

My concept of digitally mediated spillover was developed using grounded theory analysis (Corbin & Strauss, 2008; Saldaña, 2013). I used Atlas.Ti to apply codes to the data. In a preliminary round of "process coding," I labeled each sentence with gerunds to capture social action (Saldaña, 2013). Examples of axial codes include "encountering extremism online" and "enforcing group hierarchy." Subsequently, I completed "axial coding" in which I removed redundant codes and grouped thematically similar codes under a common heading. For instance, "memeing," "making fun of peers," and similar codes were unified under the code: "Strategic humor." I completed the analysis by synthesizing the axial codes to develop my model of digitally mediated spillover.

TABLE 7.1 Informant Data

Pseudonym	Age	Race	Religion	Annual Parental Income Range ($)	Political Ideology at Time of Interview	Radicalization Source
W-CCFL						
Antonio	22	White	Agnostic	50,000–69,999	Moderate	Digital Movement
Atticus	21	White	Christian	200,000–249,999	Moderate	NA
Bruce	22	White	Agnostic	100,000–149,999	Extremist	Digital Movement
Caleb	20	White	Christian	74,000–99,999	Extremist	Digital Movement
Chloe	–	Black	Christian	–	Progressive	NA
Daphne	21	White	Christian	50,000–74,999	Moderate	NA
David	–	Hispanic	Christian	–	Extremist	Digital Movement
Dustin	24	White	Christian	250,000–299,999	Moderate	NA
Eddy	19	Hispanic	Christian	25,000–50,000	Extremist	CCFL
Garrett	29	White	Christian	25,000–50,000	Moderate	NA
James	21	White	Christian	200,000–249,999	Extremist	Digital Movement
Joe	22	White	Agnostic	–	Moderate	NA
Josh	19	White	Atheist	150,000–199,999	Moderate	NA
Justin	20	White	Atheist	150,000–199,999	Extremist	CCFL
Martin	18	White	Christian	200,000–250,000	Extremist	CCFL
Michael	20	Hispanic	Christian	25,000–49,999	Extremist	Digital Movement
Sahil	20	South Asian	Agnostic	300,000+	Extremist	CCFL
Scott	21	White	Agnostic	–	Extremist	Digital Movement
Sebastian	24	Male	Christian	50,000–75,000	Extremist	CCFL
Sheila	19	White	Christian	75,000–99,999	Moderate	NA
Shoshana	18	White	Jewish	300,000+	Moderate	NA
Summer	21	Hispanic	Christian	75,000–99,999	Moderate	NA
Taylor	26	White	Christian	100,000–149,999	Moderate	CCFL

(Continued)

TABLE 7.1 (Continued)

Pseudonym	Age	Race	Religion	Annual Parental Income Range ($)	Political Ideology at Time of Interview	Radicalization Source
E-CCFL						
Aaron	21	White	Christian	100,000–149,000	Moderate	NA
Alek	19	White	Christian	100,000–149,000	Moderate	NA
Alfred	20	White	Christian	75,000–99,999	Moderate	NA
Asher	20	White	Jewish	300,000+	Moderate	NA
Connor	19	White	Christian	150,000–199,999	Moderate	NA
Haim	20	White	Jewish	300,000+	Moderate	Digital Movement
Isaac	21	White	Jewish	75,000–99,999	Moderate	NA
Jason	23	White	Christian	200,000–249,999	Moderate	NA
Jon	21	White	Christian	–	Moderate	NA
Mario	20	White	Christian	300,000+	Moderate	NA
Mary	19	Black	Christian	75,000–99,999	Moderate	NA
Pam	19	White	Christian	25,000–49,999	Moderate	NA
Patrick	20	White	Christian	75,000–99,999	Moderate	Digital Movement
Paul	20	White	Christian	300,000+	Moderate	NA
Rich	20	White	Christian	300,000+	Moderate	NA
Robert	22	White	Atheist	100,000	Moderate	Digital Movement
Smith	19	White	Christian	100,000–149,999	Moderate	NA
Thomas	20	White	Christian	100,000–149,999	Moderate	Digital Movement
Timothy	20	White	Christian	100,000–149,999	Moderate	Digital Movement
Tyler	20	White	Christian	75,000–99,999	Moderate	NA
Vimay	18	South Asian	Christian	100,000–149,000	Moderate	NA

(Continued)

TABLE 7.1 (Continued)

Pseudonym	Age	Race	Religion	Annual Parental Income Range ($)	Political Ideology at Time of Interview	Radicalization Source
S-CCFL						
Barry	20	White	Christian	50,000–74,999	Moderate	NA
Bethany	–	White	Christian	–	Moderate	NA
Charles	23	White	Christian	150,000–199,999	Moderate	NA
Connor	18	White	Christian	300,000+	Moderate	NA
Davis	20	White	Christian	150,000–199,999	Moderate	NA
Elijah	22	Black	Christian	50,000–74,999	Moderate	NA
George	–	White	Christian	300,000+	Moderate	NA
Isabelle	19	White	Christian	200,000–249,999	Moderate	NA
Jacobo	22	Hispanic	Christian	25,000–49,000	Moderate	NA
Jake	–	White	Christian	200,000–249,999	Moderate	NA
Joseph	22	White	Christian	300,000+	Moderate	NA
Locke	21	Hispanic	Deist	150,000–199,999	Moderate	NA
Tony	19	Asian	Christian	300,000+	Moderate	NA
William	19	White	Christian	25,000–49,999	Moderate	NA

Note: This table contains demographic information for interviewees at each of the three field sites. In total, there were 12 extremists at W-CCFL. Seven were radicalized in digital social movements, and six were radicalized during their time at CCFL.

Findings

Computer-mediated communication has enabled a new form of social movement that operates primarily or exclusively online (Kasimov, 2023). This new type of social movement enables a new type of spillover – digitally mediated spillover. Digitally mediated spillover occurs when activists who participated in a digital social movement enter a new movement, bringing their ideology and culture, tactical repertoires, and social networks. Thus far, instances of digitally mediated spillover have garnered too little social scientific attention save for a few high-profile instances such as the Unite the Right Rally (2017) and the January 6th insurrection (2021) in which activists belonging to digital hate movements coordinated lethal, offline protests. This study demonstrates that spillover from extremist digital movements into offline communities may actually be a common occurrence.

The following sections outline my theory of digitally mediated spillover. First, I explain why digitally mediated spillover is a unique product of 21st century activism and a common occurrence on college campuses. I explain that preexisting organizational dynamics at W-CCFL rendered it vulnerable to digitally mediated spillover and radicalization. Lastly, I explain that digitally mediated spillover facilitated radicalization in three phases. First, activists at W-CCFL developed an extremist collective identity. Second, as formerly moderate activists at W-CCFL began spending more time in extremist digital spaces, they became ideologically extreme and transformed their Facebook Messenger chat into a radical milieu. Third, W-CCFL became a tactically extremist organization and adopted antisocial, nondemocratic tactics before imploding.

Digitally Mediated Spillover on College Campuses

Digitally mediated spillover occurred at each field site when former participants of the Manosphere and the Alt-Right joined CCFL. The Manosphere is a loose coalition of digital, male supremacist movements containing Gamergate, the redpill, and others, while the Alt-Right is a loose coalition of digital, white supremacist and ethnonationalist movements. In total, 11 of my informants were extremists in high school, during which time they immersed themselves in cyberhate, shared extremist memes, and participated in online collective action such as harassment campaigns, disinformation campaigns, and helping Donald Trump gain popularity with "meme magic." I refer to these individuals as "agents of spillover." It is notable that *none* of these agents of spillover was raised in ideologically extreme households. All of them became extremists online in one of two ways: Via social media and via online multiplayer video games.

The first and primary sites of online radicalization were social media platforms with large user bases and lax content moderation policies, like 4chan,

Reddit, and YouTube. Aaron, an extremist new member of E-CCFL, discovered right-wing cyberculture while exploring 4chan's /lit (literature) forum. He showed me the literature forum, and he mentioned that it is common for /lit's members to post pictures of their bookshelves:

Aaron: This is pretty normal, they'll post pictures of their book stacks. This guy seems to be a little edgy.
Researcher: Oh, okay, sure. What do you mean edgy?
Aaron: He could just be a little extreme is what I'm trying to get at, he has *Mein Kampf* on his shelf.
Researcher: Oh, and *How the West Won*. Okay, *Protocols of Zion*.

By pursuing his passion for literature on 4chan, Aaron was continuously exposed to extremist ideology, which he shared with members of E-CCFL, a moderate social movement organization.

Similarly, Antonio, an activist at W-CCFL, participated in the Gamergate movement. He described how his frustration with feminist critiques of the video game industry led him to join the male supremacist movement in high school:

Antonio: It wasn't until my senior year when Gamergate broke out and I've always been a big-game nerd. . . . And then there was this big thing of people starting to say like, "Games are promoting toxic masculinity. Games promote this evil image. They're not inclusive enough for women" . . . I was alone, I was an only child. My parents didn't care about video games. I wasn't talking to people so . . . Of course, the Internet's there . . . and you start finding a community of people who are like, "Yeah, this is awful. What are they [feminists] doing to video games?"

Like Antonio, after prolonged participation in online right-wing movements, other individuals who would become agents of spillover began to believe that left-wing social movements posed an existential threat to American society.

The second site of online radicalization was multiplayer video games. These game platforms were ideal for recruitment into extremist movements because of their chat functionality that enables players to communicate via instant messages and over audio chat without scrutiny from content moderators. For instance, James, a white supremacist at W-CCFL, explained that he discovered the Alt-Right after going through a breakup in high school. Seeking to relieve his loneliness, he recruited people on 4chan's /pol/ board (a hub of Alt-Right activism) to play video games with him.

James: I've never mentioned this, but I met a lot of different alt-righters by playing Minecraft. This is really deep lore, because I went through a really bad breakup in high school. And then I played a shit-ton of Minecraft. . . . I formed a town, and I recruited off of the "pol board." All of these right-wingers playing Minecraft and taking things way too seriously. Because it's so funny how the modern alt-right comes from so many different avenues.

James' new, white supremacist friends encouraged him to migrate from 4chan to websites exclusively dedicated to white supremacist movements. By the time James entered university, he was a committed white supremacist who sought to teach his fellow students about the biological superiority of White Christians over Black people and Jews.

Robert, an activist at E-CCFL, developed a deep fascination with fascism after accidentally joining a transnational, Alt-Right group chat in high school.

[At War] is actually like a war game. And we got it, because myself, my brothers, my cousins – we live far apart. And we went to a wedding my freshman year of high school and we were like, "hey wouldn't it be good if we found an online game to play together?" . . . but there's a forum on it . . . [with a thread] called "off topic forum." Certainly, I knew about the alt-right before the media did . . . you can read like paragraphs of them connecting Jewish businessmen from Germany and the Ottoman Empire and Armenia.

Although Robert was not a committed extremist upon entering university, his fascination with fascism persisted. Upon joining E-CCFL, he created a private group chat on GroupMe in which he introduced his peers to pro-fascist content.

Digitally mediated spillover began when extremists like Antonio, Aaron, James, and Robert applied to their respective CCFL chapters after participating in extremist digital social movements in high school. CCFL chapters welcomed these activists into their midst with open arms. Although most agents of spillover were no longer active members of extremist digital movements upon joining CCFL, they remained "lurkers" who frequently browsed extremist online platforms. Thus, they were able to share with their new friends the latest memes, jargon, and ideological developments from extremist digital movements. Agents of spillover exposed their peers to the ideologies and tactics from extremist digital movements in their chapters' digital group chats and in face-to-face organizational meetings.

I witnessed digitally mediated spillover occur in CCFL chapters throughout the United States. Contrary to entryism, which assumes that extremists are deliberate and insidious infiltrators, the primary reason why extremists entered CCFL was a genuine desire for like-minded peers. Extremists entered CCLF the same way other freshman would: By contacting recruiters at the school-wide club fairs and on social media. Whereas entryism argues that extremists strategically share their ideology with the intention of radicalizing others, agents of spillover began to spread extremist ideology at CCFL by honestly sharing their perspectives and trying to help with organizational activities.

Susceptibility to Spillover and Radicalization

The remainder of this chapter will focus on W-CCFL, the field site situated in West Coast University. Agents of spillover came to radicalize W-CCFL because of two factors that differentiated them from their peers at other field sites. First, a comparatively large number of them were accepted to East Coast University and happened to join W-CCFL at the same time, making them a sizeable minority. Second, the moderate incumbent leaders at W-CCFL were incompetent and, by numerous accounts, too cowardly to mobilize in pursuit of CCFL's objectives: Spreading conservative culture on campus and campaigning for Republican and Libertarian candidates.

This cowardice was not without cause. Following the 2016 U.S. presidential election, W-CCFL activists were being constantly targeted and harassed by vengeful progressive activists who were enraged by Trump's victory. Sheila, a moderate member of W-CCFL, recalls being tagged in a Facebook post with a picture of W-CCFL captioned: "These are the conservatives on campus. They don't deserve to feel safe."[5] Similarly, Daphne was tagged in Facebook posts by progressive activists who encouraged others to shun her on- and offline because of her political beliefs. Worst of all, progressive activists routinely blocked W-CCFL activists' efforts to secure funding, even though this violated university policy.

Hardened by combative digital activism, agents of spillover were disgusted by the passivity of CCFL leadership. They had already experienced heated debates on 4chan, coordinated the pro-Trump meme campaigns that helped him ascend to office, and staged raids of progressive online communities that filled them with extremist memes and iconography. Agents of spillover believed that the pugnacious ideology and tactics they learned online would translate well offline.

David, a former participant in the Gamergate and redpill movements, assumed an informal leadership position. He convinced other agents of spillover to join him and coordinated a counter offensive. He explained:

David: One of my gripes with the [former] board was that they didn't really care about activism; they were afraid of offending people and they were afraid of seeming controversial. And I would say the majority of the club agreed with that sentiment. . . . I was advocating "we should do more activism, we should be more controversial. Who cares what they think about us? They're always gonna hate us."

With the help of other extremists, David led his fellow activists to the student union to demand funding for the club. At the student union, David's peers watched with admiration as he faced dozens of angry progressives. Many hurled insults, and one threatened him with physical assault.[6]

Whereas previous leaders saw misfortune in progressives' attacks against their club, David saw opportunity. Taking inspiration from "Ben Shapiro Owns the Libs" videos on YouTube, he decided to turn his liberal opposition into a viral laughingstock. He instructed his fellow CCFL members to remain calm as they endured harassment from liberal counter-protestors. He captured the contentious interaction on video and uploaded the footage to YouTube where viewers watched angry liberals harassing stoic W-CCFL activists. David ensured that his video garnered attention across the spectrum of right-wing politics, from conventional conservative news outlets to extremist corners of the Internet. The ensuing public outrage forced West Coast University to give W-CCFL funding, and it drove up recruitment. After this hard-won victory, everyone in W-CCFL begged David to run for an elected position. He ran uncontested for the presidency and filled his executive board with other agents of spillover. In the following sections, I explain how David's presidency and W-CCFL's newfound trust in extremists yielded three phases of radicalization.

Phase 1: Immersion in Extremist, Digital Culture Leads to an Edgy Collective Identity

Radicalization began slowly at W-CCFL. Agents of spillover began to slowly expose their moderate peers to jargon and memes that originated in extremist segments of the Internet. This occurred both offline in organizational meetings and online in their Facebook Messenger group chat. While it is commonly understood that ideology and jargon can translate from online to offline contexts, memes are commonly understood as an exclusively digital phenomenon because they usually comprise a photo, video, or gif, with a text catchphrase. However, the W-CCFL informants explained that when a meme becomes ubiquitous, the imagery or idea behind the meme can be invoked simply by reciting its catchphrase. Examples of meme catchphrases include the phrases "2–1" (the idea that the second amendment upholds the first amendment) and "no dox" (a phrase indicating that the speaker is about to share an extremist perspective and does not want to be "doxed" or exposed to the public as an extremist). By acclimating moderates to extremist memes, agents of spillover were also acclimating them to the underlying ideologies within the memes: White supremacy, ethnonationalism, and male supremacy. At this stage, moderates did not fully understand the extreme nature of the content they were being exposed to. For instance, Sheila casually mentioned that in group chats, her peers joked "about the future for white children or something like that." This is a direct reference to the white supremacist creed, *The Fourteen Words*: "We must secure the existence of our people and a future for white children" (Simi & Futrell, 2015, p. 22).

By design, extremist memes did not alienate moderates. In extremist digital cultures, the individuals who post memes have plausible deniability (i.e., it's just a joke) when their peers are shocked and offended and receive acclaim when their peers find the meme humorous (Milner, 2013; Windisch & Simi, 2023). In offline spaces where memes are divorced from their digital context of origin, they still serve this purpose. This is illustrated in an exchange in which Sebastian, a former member of the redpill movement, argues that Catholic education should replace American public education. He was supported by James, a white supremacist, and Silva, a Nazi sympathizer. These extremists disarmed moderates' shock with memes and hyperbolic rhetoric, staples of extremist digital culture.

Sebastian: Maybe I'm too *black pilled* on this issue, but we need to turn schools over to the Catholic church. I'm protestant, so I would normally advocate for protestant education, but the protestant church is too fragmented; there are too many heretics. If we can't bring Christian morals back into public schools, we are doomed. Also, we're forgetting that people can go to hell! Why aren't we worried about the moral salvation of American children? We are an Anglo-protestant nation, Christian morality in schools is the American way.

Jude: Um, excuse me? Does separation of church and state mean anything to you? Our founding fathers wanted a separation of church and state. Parents should teach morals at home. School should be where you learn that 2 plus 2 is four and how to read.

Sebastian: I agree that they believed in the separation of church and state, but I think that there's a high wall between church and state and we need to lower it. Obviously, the state would be run by non-godly authorities, but students would have a good Catholic education. Look we're a Judeo-Christian nation.

Silva: Judeo?

Sebastian: Okay, just Christian.

James: *Based*!

[Club laughs]

In the above interaction, "black pilled" is a redpill meme/designation indicating that one's hopes for a male supremacist future have been dashed, resulting in nihilism or a desire for violence (Preston et al., 2021). "Based" is cyberjargon, usually posted in response to memes, to indicate approval of an underlying idea. The use of such extreme language (e.g., heretics, doomed) is a rhetorical strategy to cast doubt on the seriousness of the point being raised (Milner, 2013). Whereas moderates heard this statement and assumed Sebastian was being playfully hyperbolic, extremists understood he was expressing his true beliefs. Shoshana, a moderate Jewish member of W-CCFL, reflected on this interaction and explained that she found it funny:

Shoshana: Last week, one of the guys was like we should have a . . . mandatory Catholic school system. And then they talked about it, but then after, I was just like, "What about the Jews?" blah, blah, blah. But I mean, that's a joke. I mean he probably doesn't think so, but to everyone else it was a joke.

The plausible deniability afforded by memes was so strong that a misogynist, white supremacist, and Nazi sympathizer could belong to same organization as a Jewish woman without raising her suspicions.

As moderates became more accustomed to extremists' humor, extremists increased the vitriol of their jokes. Numerous informants explained that their humor was racist, sexist, and often joked about acts of brutality and mass casualty violence. Michael, a former member of The redpill, simply described the humor as "kill all of group x." Formerly moderate men began participating in this humor, because it was enjoyable to break the stifling, progressive norm of political correctness at West Coast University. The thrill of sharing hate content was exhilarating to these men, because the potential discovery of such extreme content within their Messenger posts could have serious ramifications (e.g., expulsion from school). Men in W-CCFL began referring to posting memes with terms like "bonding" and "brotherhood." In contrast, many moderate women were shocked and offended by the denigrating content about women. Some of these offended women (e.g., Daphne, Chloe) demanded that the men change their posting behavior whereas others (Sheila, Taylor) tried to acclimate themselves to misogynist humor. Fights between extremists and aggrieved moderate women reached a fever pitch when Antonio, an extremist, found an innovative solution: He created a separate Facebook group chat for moderate women so that extremists could continue posting misogynist content.

Eventually, extremist digital content altered the culture of W-CCFL. Specifically, immersion in cyberhate began to alter W-CCFL's collective identity or their "shared definition of a group that derives from members' common interests, experiences, and solidarity" (Taylor & Whittier, 1992, p. 105). Across the nation, most CCFL activists refer to themselves as "conservative," reflecting their commitment to moderate conservatism. At W-CCFL, activists began referring to themselves as "edgy" or "edgy memelords," a designation that signifies cultural competence in cyberhate. Informants described what is entailed in being edgy:

Sahil (extremist):   What is edgy? I guess the easiest way to coin it is nonpolitically correct. . . . If a liberal saw it . . . They'd be like "What the fuck is that? That's racist and xenophobic!"

Sheila (moderate):   What's edgy? . . . The same stuff, I could post on my normal timeline, and people would be like, "Whoa, that's not cool." Like, "How dare you joke about that? It's too soon," kind of stuff. . . . And then there's context. So, if you post an anti-Semitic meme on a Jewish group's Facebook page, that's pretty awful. But if you post it in your private shitposting group, it's received a lot better.

Given that collective identity determines a social movement's goals and the tactics deemed appropriate to achieve them, the widespread adoption of an edgy identity marked a significant step in W-CCFL's radicalization.

Their edgy collective identity led moderates and new members of W-CCFL to try and impress their peers by making increasingly offensive jokes on- and offline. Mimicking dynamics common in extremist digital forums, moderates felt frustrated when their attempts at edgy humor fell flat, because they felt like outsiders.

Sheila: I could literally say some of the worst shit in our shitposting [chat] groups, and it's not that edgy. They would call me out on it for not being that edgy. . . . They just don't wanna admit the fact that a woman can meme just as hard as them.

Another aspect of edginess is that when someone is offended by extremist memes, they are subject to ridicule. Pressure on moderates to share extremist memes and the looming threat of ridicule incentivized moderates to hide any residual discomfort they had with extremist humor. Pressure to ramp up extremism transformed W-CCFL's Facebook Messenger chat into a hidden space of hate, a closed social network that produces radicalization (Simi & Futrell, 2015).

Phase 2: Ideological Extremism and Integration into a Radical Milieu

Under the guise of edginess, extremist activists began to strategically disseminate their ideologies from the Manosphere and the Alt-Right. For instance, Max, a male supremacist, tried to popularize the idea that women should not be allowed to vote, while James, a white supremacist, wanted his peers to acknowledge the biological superiority of white Christians. James, one of the extremists, used the guise of edginess to paste memes directly from 4chan, Reddit, and hate websites into W-CCFL's Facebook Messenger chat:

James: Already, these people [moderates] share Alt-Right memes, talking points. Even about IQ [differences between racial groups]. Even if they disagree with what we're saying, the fact that they're even engaging is a sign of our influence.

As former moderates became increasingly interested in extremist ideology, agents of spillover advanced radicalization by introducing their peers to extremist social networks.

While some extremists encouraged their peers to visit 4chan and Reddit, others began inviting extremists from the online Manosphere and the Alt-Right directly into W-CCFL's Facebook Messenger chat. W-CCFL's group chat ballooned in size from several dozen members and alumni to more than 1,000 members at its peak. This drastic expansion of W-CCFL's social network introduced former moderates into a radical milieu, an open social network that brought CCFL activists into contact with extremist activists from other digital movements (Malthaner & Waldmann, 2014).

The rapidly evolving culture on W-CCFL's group chats was disconcerting to the remaining moderates, now a minority, who were not used to interacting with denizens of 4chan, Reddit, and cyberhate. For instance, a lot of the extremists who joined W-CCFL's group chat used fake names and fake profile pictures because they knew it would be catastrophic for their social lives and careers if the hate content they posted was linked to their identity. Daphne explained, "If you have to have a fake account to feel comfortable posting this, then maybe you just shouldn't be posting it. Because it's just not a good thing to be posting, you know?" Daphne and other moderates longed for a return to the days when the chat was merely an extension of W-CCFL. Other W-CCFL activists began anonymizing their digital presence for fear that they would be unemployable if the group chat was exposed. The content in the group chat became so extreme that on numerous occasions, it was "perma-Zucked," or permanently banned by Facebook's content moderators for violating their hate speech policies. Like most extremist digital communities, W-CCFL quickly reestablished their social media network on another platform after bans (Johnson et al., 2019).

As W-CCFL's online social network continued to expand, they began to make contact with high-profile extremists. Chloe, a Black, female, moderate, was enraged to learn that David was Facebook friends with George Zimmerman, an outspoken white supremacist who stalked and killed Trayvon Martin, an unarmed Black teenager, in 2012. In 2018, W-CCFL activists made digital contact with a prominent redpill activist and invited him to speak at their next meeting. This redpill blogger went by his screenname, GayLubeOil.

Even some extremists were shocked when GayLubeOil spoke about his Reddit posts advocating for physically disciplining women, "treating women like children," and celebrating the sexual prowess of Nazis. GayLubeOil's speech signified another milestone in digitally mediated spillover and radicalization at W-CCFL. By leveraging the ideologies and social networks from digital hate activism, extremists expanded the organization's social network to include high-profile extremists. All that remained to complete radicalization was for W-CCFL to adopt extreme and antisocial tactics.

Phase 3: Tactical Extremism and Organizational Implosion

After an extensive immersion in extremist digital communities, many W-CCFL members soured on democracy. They embraced the supremacist belief that an enfranchised, pluralistic electorate would plunge the nation into its "degeneracy." Even in Trump's America, W-CCFL activists no longer believed that the democratic process could bring about their desired future. W-CCFL activists adopted a new tactical repertoire which they described as "winning the culture war." In theory, this was a noble campaign to change the hearts and minds of young Americans. In practice, this involved antisocial and anti-democratic tactics.

First, W-CCFL activists transitioned from being consumers of cyberhate to disseminators. In order to increase the number of American youth who sympathized with their cause, W-CCFL activists posted extremist content on popular social media platforms like 4chan, Reddit, and Facebook. Bruce, a white supremacist and antisemite, boasted about his ability to spread hate ideology on Facebook where his meme pages had cumulatively garnered hundreds of thousands of members and millions of likes.

As W-CCFL radicalized, members felt that even the most right-wing Republicans were too moderate. These accusations even applied to their former idol, Donald Trump:

James (extremist): The Republican Establishment doesn't give a fuck about advancing a conservative agenda –

Atticus (moderate): Trump is the establishment! He's president.

Max (extremist): That doesn't mean anything!

James (extremist): Absolutely right, it doesn't mean anything. The Republican establishment doesn't care anymore. They've won. They have nothing more to gain, so they kowtow to the left. They're fucking worthless.

Offline, W-CCFL's relationships with Republican and Libertarian politicians suffered.

Roughly half of W-CCFL activists adopted an authoritarian ideology. One group of authoritarians believed that voting should be reserved for a privileged segment of the population. For instance, Martin suggested the United States should implement rigorous IQ tests to determine voter eligibility:

> It's not like I want to take away voting rights from Black people, Women, Asians, or whatever. . . . But to be honest, I have a hot take. If it *did* disproportionately affect Black people because of mental deficiencies, maybe that's okay.

Other activists like David believed that the United States should reconvene the House Un-American Activities Committee (HUAC) to prevent socialists, communists, and progressives from holding public office. A second group of authoritarians wanted to abolish voting entirely. For instance, Caleb wanted Mussolini-style fascism; Silva wanted Nazi-inspired "nationalist socialism;" James supported a white supremacist regime; and Eddy wanted an authoritarian surveillance state in which leaders "rule through fear."

As is the case with many extremist movements, W-CCFL activists felt they had no direct pathway to create their desired totalitarian state (Simi & Windisch, 2020). Instead, they settled for a tactical repertoire based on trolling their enemies and "gaslighting the Dems." Trolling occurs when an antagonistic individual or group makes a target or another individual or group exhibit distress, then documents this distress, and posts the documentation on social media. W-CCFL activists held strategy sessions where they debated how best to adapt this digital strategy for offline use to "rustle some jimmies" [meme speak for causing anger] and "freak out the feminists." W-CCFL activists laughed and cheered as they recalled previous success and imagined future victories trolling undocumented immigrants and feminists. They also began entering classes taught by progressive professors and speaking engagements featuring progressive intellectuals in order to ask questions designed to enrage, befuddle, and publicly humiliate their targets. Subsequently, W-CCFL activists enjoyed posting these interactions on social media, eliciting a wave of support.

Although many W-CCFL activists no longer believed in the electoral system, they continued to campaign for Republican and Libertarian candidates. This is because they had a vested interest in "gaslighting the Dems" or intentionally making stops at Democratic households to share heavily skewed if not entirely false information about Democratic candidates. This included exaggerated rumors about Democratic taxes on fossil fuels, to conspiracy theories suggesting that Democrats had a racist hidden agenda. In meetings, extremists justified this tactic by explaining that, "a Democrat that stays home is like a vote for the Republican party!"

After repeatedly adapting digital ideologies and tactics for offline use, W-CCFL leaders grew careless and released a public statement on their website replete with memes and references to extremist digital movements. This statement condemned local politicians for failure to act against "transgenderism" and "degeneracy." This criticism of local politicians was met with outrage from their political sponsors and parent organization. Local politicians severed ties with W-CCFL, replacing them with a different conservative youth organization. W-CCFL was also de-chartered from its parent organization.

Some of the remaining moderates grew enraged that extremists had rendered W-CCFL financially and politically impotent. They began "doxxing" extremists and leaking excerpts of the group chat to university administrators and the student newspaper in the hopes of getting their former allies expelled. Fearing for their careers, extremists in W-CCFL deleted their group chat and other digital evidence of their extremism. In doing so, they effectively disbanded their online community and deleted the digital platforms that enabled them to fight the culture war. Like many extremist organizations, W-CCFL imploded (Simi & Futrell, 2015; Simi & Windisch, 2020).

Conclusion

This chapter introduces the concept of *digitally mediated spillover*. This concept advances our understanding of both the social processes of online hate and social movement dynamics, namely the nationwide radicalization and extremism of formerly moderate conservative youth groups. Digitally mediated spillover advances theory about the social processes of online hate by demonstrating that these social processes are easily translated to new on- and offline contexts. To radicalize their peers, agents of spillover imported digital cultures, ideologies, and tactics from the Alt-Right and the Manosphere to a Facebook Messenger chat and offline CCFL meetings.

Skeptics may claim that there is nothing innately digital about the culture, ideologies, and tactics utilized by agents of spillover. After all, what differentiates the redpill ideology from other manifestations of virulent sexism, memes from traditional forms of humor, and trolling from harassment? While each of these digital phenomena bear a strong resemblance to their offline counterparts, they also contain referents to extremist digital movements. Redpill ideology trains men to seek community in digital forums; memes cannot be understood without exposure to the original, digital content; and trolling is not finished until evidence has been posted online. These referents to digital culture acclimate activists to digital extremist cultures and incentivize them to participate more deeply. Acculturation to online extremism incentivized W-CCFL activists to invite extremists into their Facebook Messenger chat and flock to extremist digital movements on 4chan and Reddit. Thus, in addition to adapting online social processes and practices *from* digital culture for offline applications, digitally mediated spillover also encourages individuals to seek out and participate *in* digital culture.

Just as 20th-century feminism left an indelible mark on the nuclear freeze movement, the Manosphere and the Alt-Right have left an indelible mark on many chapters of conservative youth movements throughout America. Caleb, an extremist, attended a CCFL convention for every major chapter located in the West Coast. He saw multiple activists carrying flags for "Kekistan," a fictitious nation which symbolizes membership in the Alt-Right. This indicates that extremists have indoctrinated future generations of Republican and Libertarian leadership. Scholars and policy experts who wish to understand and prevent further campus-based radicalization must gain a deeper understanding of digitally mediated spillover and the diffuse social processes by which extremist digital movements shape offline life.

Notes

1 https://www2.census.gov/geo/pdfs/maps-data/maps/reference/us_regdiv.pdf
2 Not to be confused with the actual West Coast University, a for-profit graduate institution (https://westcoastuniversity.edu/).
3 Three of my interviews were follow-up interviews.
4 My ability to collect data at each site was mediated by a variety of factors such as balancing coursework and teaching, limited and sporadic grant funding, the frequency of meetings at each field site, and COVID-19.
5 Although CCFL activists did not show me their own social media posts, they had no qualms about showing me antisocial tactics employed by their progressive opponents.
6 Video coverage shows progressive antagonists insulting and threatening W-CCFL activists.

References

ADL. (2019). *White supremacists increase college campus recruiting efforts for third straight year*. Anti-Defamation League. https://www.adl.org/resources/press-release/white-supremacists-increase-college-campus-recruiting-efforts-third

ADL. (2023). *White supremacist propaganda incidents reach all-time high in 2022*. Anti-Defamation League. https://www.adl.org/resources/press-release/white-supremacist-propaganda-incidents-reach-all-time-high-2022

Alonso, J. (2022, October 14). College GOP President resigns over hateful Instagram posts. *Inside Higher Ed*. https://www.insidehighered.com/quicktakes/2022/10/14/college-gop-president-resigns-over-hateful-instagram-posts

Atran, S. (2021). Psychology of transnational terrorism and extreme political conflict. *Annual Review of Psychology, 72*(1), 471–501. https://doi.org/10.1146/annurev-psych-010419-050800

Bauman, D. (2018). After 2016 election, campus hate crimes seemed to jump. Here's what the data tell us. *The Chronicle of Higher Education*. https://www.chronicle.com/article/After-2016-Election-Campus/242577

Binder, A. J., & Kidder, J. L. (2022). *The channels of student activism: How the left and right are winning (and losing) in campus politics today*. University of Chicago Press.

Corbin, J. M., & Strauss, A. (2008). *Basics of qualitative research: Techniques and procedures for developing grounded theory*. SAGE Publications.

Flacks, R. (2005). The question of relevance in social movement studies. In D. Croteau, W. Hoynes, & C. Ryan (Eds.), *Rhyming hope and history: Activists, academics, and social movement scholarship* (pp. 3–20). University of Minnesota Press.

Iannelli, J. (2018, October 16). Chats show FIU turning point USA members sharing racist memes and rape jokes. *Miami New Times*. https://www.miaminewtimes.com/news/turning-point-usa-fiu-chapter-shares-racist-sexist-pepe-memes-10827433

Johnson, N. F., Leahy, R., Restrepo, N. J., Velasquez, N., Zheng, M., Manrique, P., Devkota, P., & Wuchty, S. (2019). Hidden resilience and adaptive dynamics of the global online hate ecology. *Nature*, 573(7773), 261–265. https://doi.org/10.1038/s41586-019-1494-7

Kasimov, A. (2023). Decentralized hate: Sustained connective action in online far-right community. *Social Movement Studies*, 1–19. https://doi.org/10.1080/14742837.2023.2204427

Lowe, D. (2017). Prevent strategies: The problems associated in defining extremism: The case of the United Kingdom. *Studies in Conflict & Terrorism*, 40(11), 917–933. https://doi.org/10.1080/1057610X.2016.1253941

Malthaner, S., & Waldmann, P. (2014). The radical milieu: Conceptualizing the supportive social environment of terrorist groups. *Studies in Conflict & Terrorism*, 37(12), 979–998. https://doi.org/10.1080/1057610X.2014.962441

McCauley, C., & Moskalenko, S. (2017). Understanding political radicalization: The two-pyramids model. *American Psychologist*, 72(3), 205–216. https://doi.org/10.1037/amp0000062

Meyer, D. S., & Whittier, N. (1994). Social movement spillover. *Social Problems*, 41(2), 277–298. https://doi.org/10.2307/3096934

Miller-Idriss, C. (2020). *Hate in the homeland: The new global far right*. Princeton University Press.

Milner, R. M. (2013). FCJ-156 Hacking the social: Internet memes, identity antagonism, and the logic of lulz. *The Fibreculture Journal*, 22 2013: Trolls and The Negative Space of the Internet. https://twentytwo.fibreculturejournal.org/fcj-156-hacking-the-social-Internet-memes-identity-antagonism-and-the-logic-of-lulz/

ND GOP. (2022). *NDGOP response to offensive statements by a group of young Republicans*. North Dakota Republican Party. https://ndgop.org/ndgop-response-to-offensive-statements-by-a-group-of-young-republicans/

Polletta, M. (2019). Conservative group at ASU apologizes for racist, anti-Semitic postings online. *The Arizona Republic*. https://www.azcentral.com/story/news/politics/arizona/2019/03/25/college-republicans-united-arizona-state-university-apology-racist-materials/3271365002/

Preston, K., Halpin, M., & Maguire, F. (2021). The black pill: New technology and the male supremacy of involuntarily celibate men. *Men and Masculinities*. https://doi.org/10.1177/1097184X211017954

Quintana, C. (2018, October 21). 'Degenerate and murderous': California campus Republicans' platform attacks college culture. *The Chronicle of Higher Education*, 65(9). https://www.chronicle.com/article/degenerate-and-murderous-california-campus-republicans-platform-attacks-college-culture/

Raymond, N. (2022, July 11). U.S. judicial panel orders probe into hiring of clerk accused of racism. *Reuters*. https://www.reuters.com/legal/government/us-judicial-panel-orders-probe-into-hiring-clerk-accused-racism-2022-07-08/

Saldaña, J. (2013). *The coding manual for qualitative researchers* (2nd ed.). SAGE.

Simi, P., & Futrell, R. (2015). *American Swastika: Inside the white power movement's hidden spaces of hate*. Rowman & Littlefield.

Simi, P., Futrell, R., & Burston, A. (2024). How threat mobilizes the resurgence and persistence of US white supremacist activism: The 1980s to the present. *Annual Review of Sociology*.

Simi, P., & Windisch, S. (2020). Why radicalization fails: Barriers to mass casualty terrorism. *Terrorism and Political Violence*, 32(4), 831–850. https://doi.org/10.1080/09546553.2017.1409212

SPLC. (2018). *Turning point USA's blooming romance with the alt-right (Hate Watch)*. Southern Poverty Law Center. https://www.splcenter.org/hatewatch/2018/02/16/turning-point-usas-blooming-romance-alt-right

SPLC. (2022a). *James Orien Allsup (extremist files)*. Southern Poverty Law Center. https://www.splcenter.org/fighting-hate/extremist-files/individual/james-orien-allsup

SPLC. (2022b). *Kyle Bristow (extremist files)*. Southern Poverty Law Center. https://www.splcenter.org/fighting-hate/extremist-files/individual/kyle-bristow

Taylor, V., & Whittier, N. (1992). Collective identity in social movement communities: Lesbian feminist mobilization. In A. D. Morris & C. M. Mueller (Eds.), *Frontiers in social movement theory* (pp. 104–130). Yale University Press.

Windisch, S., & Simi, P. (2023). More than a joke: White Supremacist humor as a daily form of resistance. *Deviant Behavior, 44*, 381–397. https://doi.org/10.1080/01639625.2022.2048216

Zhuravskaya, E., Petrova, M., & Enikolopov, R. (2020). Political effects of the Internet and social media. *Annual Review of Economics, 12*(1), 415–438. https://doi.org/10.1146/annurev-economics-081919-050239

8

"HATE PARTIES"

Networked Antisemitism from the Fringes to YouTube

Stephen C. Rea, Binny Mathew, and Jordan Kraemer

Hate is a widespread, pernicious feature of contemporary life online that spreads via the interweaving of hateful ideologies, the influencers who promote them, and the digital tools influencers use for communicating with their followers – and that those same followers use to communicate amongst themselves. Understanding online hate as a social process entails accounting for how these elements interact and reinforce each other in facilitating the formation of virtual communities organized around shared values and practices, much as more positive virtual communities do as well. For instance, online social spaces have become indispensable resources for activism and democratic social movements from the Arab Spring (Gerbaudo, 2012) to Black Lives Matter (Freelon et al., 2016). Yet hate groups have also weaponized these tools to their own ends; Daniels (2018) characterizes white nationalists in particular as "innovation opportunists" (p. 63) who have long been at the bleeding edge of digital technology adoption. No online social space – online games, virtual worlds, social media, livestreaming, messaging apps, etc. – is immune to hate, and none is a purely closed system that can prevent its spread from one space to another.

Previous research has focused on online hate purveyors' presumed instrumental goals, that is, how they deploy hateful messaging in order to terrorize targets or otherwise disrupt out-group activities. Such research presumes that online hate messages, when instigated by groups rather than "lone wolves," are transmitted unidirectionally in two complementary ways: They are produced on one platform and deployed on another (Hine et al., 2017; Velasquez et al., 2020), and they travel linearly from instigators through other aggressors toward targets (e.g., Marwick, 2021). In this chapter, we present research that complicates the received wisdom about online hate's unidirectionality,

DOI: 10.4324/9781003472148-8

as well as its instrumentality. Purveyors of online hate maintain presences in multiple online social spaces and often fall into call-and-response patterns between influencers and rank-and-file followers that extend conversations across platforms. Moreover, the correspondence between their activities on different platforms is not solely dedicated to harassment and disruption but also includes celebrating and amplifying would-be "fellow travelers."

We came to this research while working with the Anti-Defamation League's (ADL) Center for Technology and Society (CTS), which advocates for targets of online hate and harassment and recommends policy and technological interventions aimed at mitigating the harms that result from these kinds of activities. In this original study, we investigated how sharing links to You-Tube videos on so-called "alt-tech" platforms (Donovan et al., 2019) such as Gab, Telegram, and 4chan in turn affected comment activity on YouTube. We identified a distinct, unanticipated circularity in hate messengers' reciprocal switching among multiple platforms that appeared strategic, networked, and at times self-reflexive. In dozens of cases, we found a significant increase in antisemitic comments on the YouTube videos in the period directly after their links had been shared on other platforms. The comments were not written to victimize the YouTube creator, nor were they even addressed to the creator. Rather, the messages were written for one another. While other recent research suggests that social media hate perpetrators are often the implicit audience for their hate postings (Walther, this volume), our analyses suggest that other hate promoters are the explicit audience, and in fact, the intended participants in an interactive conversation.

The types of videos whose links were shared were not by Jewish creators, or Judaism-related, as would typically be expected in the literature on online hate (e.g., Hine et al., 2017; Stringhini & Blackburn, this volume). The commenters did not target YouTube creators for harassment, as researchers have documented in cases of online "hate raids" (Mariconti et al., 2019; Meisner, 2023; Saaed et al., 2023). Rather, commenters appeared to form bonds and reinforce conspiratorial, hateful worldviews common to their communities beyond YouTube while seeking to amplify content they perceived to confirm their antisemitic beliefs. The comment sections for these videos became, in effect, host to what we call "hate parties": Threads of hateful rhetoric that are not significantly different from content found in the darkest corners of the Internet. Crucially, the majority of such comments expressed approval of the YouTube channels and their content; hence the party-like characteristic. The videos that attracted the greatest volume of antisemitic comments were produced by professional influencers, some of whom were explicit promoters of online hate and others who were more mainstream figures whose content overlapped with topics of interest in online hate communities. Our research suggests that online hate purveyors often post messages across platforms for their own consumption rather than to harass targets, an example of the main thesis of this book – that is, that social processes are central to understanding how hate propagates online.

Additionally, hate messengers appear to exploit known differences in content moderation policies and practices on platforms like YouTube by strategically offloading elements of conversations across media systems – and explicitly articulating those strategies for their peers. To mitigate hate parties' harms, social media platforms like YouTube will need to consider cross-platform constellations of user behaviors and thread-level phenomena rather than strictly local, within-platform messaging and individual posts isolated from their surrounding contexts.

Virtual Communities and Online Hate

In their critical analysis of Silicon Valley's sociocultural antecedents, Barbrook and Cameron (1996) argue that the social Internet emerged from a "heterogeneous orthodoxy" (p. 44) combining New Left utopianism with a libertarian emphasis on personal freedoms. From these strange ideological bedfellows sprang the first "virtual communities," such as Stewart Brand's Whole Earth 'Lectronic Link (WELL), an online bulletin-board system (BBS) organized around a counterculture magazine and product catalog (Rheingold, 2000; Turner, 2005). Electronic Frontier Foundation co-founder John Perry Barlow's "A Declaration of the Independence of Cyberspace" (1996) offered a concise articulation of Silicon Valley's heterogeneous orthodoxy and its vision of virtual communities as digital utopias: "We [citizens of cyberspace] believe that from ethics, enlightened self-interest, and the commonweal, our governance will emerge" (para. 10).

From today's vantage point, Barlow's declaration appears either woefully naive or a dream deferred, depending on one's appetite for cynicism. Some spaces within contemporary social media platforms may represent the kind of digital utopia Barlow imagined, but most are also apparatuses of surveillance capitalism (Zuboff, 2019) or the targets of state censorship (Zittrain et al., 2017). And in many ways, the libertarian ethos that Barlow and his contemporaries espoused has – albeit unintentionally – helped facilitate online hate's propagation through virtual communities.

Online hate has been a feature of virtual communities since their inception. In fact, one could argue that hate communities were the *original* networked virtual communities. In January 1985, one month before Stewart Brand launched The WELL, ADL published a report about far-right extremist organizations Aryan Nations and Liberty Bell Publishing using BBSes to network with other neo-Nazis and white supremacists in North America (ADL, 1985).[1] BBSes afforded groups like the Aryan Nations the ability to bypass national embargoes on imported hate literature – such as that existing in Canada and much of Western Europe – and circulate their materials in places that had previously been unreachable. While digital telecommunications afforded more expansive dissemination than previous communication technologies such as pamphlets or leafleting (see Perry, 2000), BBS communities were still relatively contained at the time by the cost of access and difficulty of discovery; users could typically only find a BBS via word of mouth or by seeking out existing topics of interest. Moreover, hate BBS operators limited access to member – and enemy – lists only to paying subscribers who had been vetted, likely due to fears of infiltration and surveillance by law enforcement agencies, not to mention the opportunity for collecting revenue.

The advent of the public Internet in the 1990s proved to be an even greater boon for hate groups. In 1995, Ku Klux Klan Grand Wizard and American Nazi Party member Don Black created Stormfront, the first and oldest dedicated hate website. Stormfront grew out of a BBS but was able to reach a much wider audience as a public website in no small part because it was indexed by search engines. By 1999, more than 2,000 white supremacy websites were online, a clear indication of the opportunities that hate groups like Black's saw in the Internet for recruitment, mobilization, and spreading propaganda. As Black told an interviewer in the early 2000s, "the Net has certainly provided our movement, and other movements like ours with only limited resources, with the ability for the first time to compete with what we consider to be a very biased and controlled news media" (quoted in Swain & Nieli, 2003, p. 155). To this day, Stormfront functions as a clearinghouse of sorts for online hate resources by helping visitors to its site navigate to less prominent sites (Swain & Nieli, 2003; see also Törnberg & Törnberg, this volume).

The social networking services that emerged in the early 2000s represented the next great innovation in virtual communities, as well as a new era for online hate. User-generated content had always been a feature of hate BBSes and web forums like Stormfront's, but social media platforms like Facebook, YouTube, and Twitter built their entire operations around users and their creations in ways that previous online services had not. Whereas the likes of Liberty Bell and Stormfront had catered directly to extremists and their niche interests, social media platforms' sophisticated data harvesting and algorithmic recommendation systems made it possible for online hate purveyors to reach even wider audiences. Instead of relying on users to seek out hate content intentionally or to be referred via others in their offline social networks, social media serve up hate to anyone whose combination of search history, friend connections, and topic interest signals trigger a platform's recommender. This is not to say that algorithmic recommenders are wholly responsible for supercharging online hate and thereby perpetuating the "modern myth" (Lim, 2020, p. 186) that algorithms *determine* ever narrower aspects of daily life. Rather, following Daniels (2018), online hate in the age of social media must be understood as a sociotechnical phenomenon rooted in long organizational histories that complement how social media's advertising-driven business model privileges content that attracts the most engagement and boosts its visibility (Shaffer, 2017).

Social media also helped empower less-established hate purveyors by making it possible for independent influencers to build audiences without the help of communications infrastructures from groups like the Ku Klux Klan or the American Nazi Party. As a subset of the influencer economy and phenomenon of the social media celebrity (Abidin, 2018; Marwick, 2013), many contemporary hate messengers have leveraged social media platforms' affordances to attract followers without having to tie themselves directly to more conventional hate group "brands." Nor do they have to rely on their actual-world identities: Pseudonymous influencers like Bronze Age Pervert (Gray, 2023) or GhostEzra (Gilbert, 2021) have successfully amassed followings based entirely on their online handles and the hateful or hate-adjacent content that they post. Online hate in the age of social media need not be tied to any single group or personality, either. Simple online image boards like 4chan and 8kun facilitate the kind of "leaderless resistance" that Aryan Nations founder Louis Beam saw as an advantage in moving white supremacy online (SPLC, n.d.), occupying a similar role as discussion forums like Stormfront's, but for loose collectivities of anonymous Internet users who are plugged into current digital culture trends (Hagen & Tuters, 2021). All of these factors have shifted the relationship between leaders and followers and professionals and amateurs in social processes of online hate, as we explore in what follows.

Contemporary social media are varied and numerous, affording users different degrees of privacy, customization, modes of expression, and monetization opportunities. Social media taxonomies are also plentiful (e.g., El Ouirdi et al., 2014; Koukaras et al., 2020; Zuckerman, 2023), though no consensus exists for how best to categorize different platforms and services. For our purposes, we draw an analytical distinction between YouTube and platforms such as 4chan, Gab, Gettr, and Telegram based on content moderation. While YouTube's and other "mainstream" social media platforms' content moderation policies and enforcement have not been entirely effective at quarantining hate or mitigating its spread, they are nonetheless far more robust than the services we refer to here as "fringe" – and others have called "alt-tech" (see Bär et al., 2023) – that are promoted directly to hard-right audiences. Despite its flaws, the mainstream/fringe distinction is relevant for our analysis for two reasons. First, it helps capture the emic values that online hate messengers assign to different social spaces: It is common to see influential hate messengers on the fringes refer to mainstream platforms as "the battlefield" where they expect to encounter resistance from other users and the platforms' moderation teams, and must be strategic about the content they post so as to avoid penalties. By contrast, they typically address their followers on the fringes as like-minded allies who share their hateful worldviews. Second, mainstream platforms' more stringent content moderation policies signal to advertisers that their services are "safe," which in turn helps those platforms build and maintain scale. Even if their participation risks suspension or expulsion, hate messengers recognize the importance of being active on mainstream platforms because of the audience reach that they afford, made possible in large part by those platforms' relationships with advertisers. Mainstream platforms' dependence on advertisers also makes them, in theory, more amenable to removing hateful content, thereby making our findings all the more troubling.

As our data show, mainstream platforms' content moderation policies have not relegated online hate to virtual communities on the fringes of social media. Rather, the fringes are intimately connected to the mainstream not only as sites on which to deploy attacks but more importantly as platforms where they can connect with other and with sympathetic users via hate parties, and together promote their hateful messages to audiences that otherwise may not encounter them.

Research Methods

Initially, we set out to identify examples of cross-platform hate and harassment targeting YouTube videos. Our goal was to show how individuals and groups operating on mainstream and fringe social media platforms exploit differences in content moderation and to apply our insights toward suggestions for improving safety mechanisms on YouTube. We used the Social Media Analysis Toolkit (SMAT) – an open-source platform designed to facilitate research on trends in online hate – to collect message postings on fringe platforms (and collateral data) that had shared links to YouTube videos. Using the SMAT API, we queried for posts or messages containing links to YouTube. We restricted our search to one month (December 24, 2022 to January 24, 2023) but did not selectively sample videos or channels based on political affiliation or ideology. In early February 2023, we collected data from the following "fringe" platforms: 4chan, 8kun, Bitchute, Gab, Gettr, LBRY, MeWe, Minds, Parler, Poal, Rumble, Truth Social, Wimkin, and Win.[2] The final dataset consisted of over 153,000 messages with at least one YouTube link. We extracted the YouTube links from the messages, resulting in nearly 86,000 unique links to YouTube videos. Since collecting the comments and their replies for each video would be a daunting task, we decided to analyze activity only for links that appeared on at least 3 of the 14 fringe platforms (1840 total videos). For each of the selected videos, we used the YouTube data API to collect all of the comments and their replies. Our final dataset consisted of 3,257,299 comments and 1,481,544 replies to these comments.

We then used ADL's in-house antisemitism classifier, the Online Hate Index (OHI), to assign each YouTube comment a score regarding the likelihood of it being antisemitic.[3] The OHI is a machine learning-based model that uses natural language processing and human annotation to evaluate social media content. It was trained on a dataset of over 80,000 social media items annotated by ADL volunteers with topic expertise in antisemitism. Scores range from 0.0, not at all likely to have the antisemitic qualities the classifier is looking for, to 1.0, high probability that the content is antisemitic. After scoring the YouTube comments and replies, we separated out all of the antisemitism scores above a threshold of 0.9. We found 7,969 total comments on 805 YouTube videos – representing 44% of the total video dataset – that scored above 0.9 for antisemitism using the OHI, an average of nearly ten comments per video (with a median of 4). By applying this high threshold, however, we likely underestimated the prevalence of antisemitism in the comments. In fact, upon manual review, several comments that were clearly antisemitic in their intent and contributed to the hate party phenomenon we have identified in this study fell below the 0.9 threshold; for example, "[Star of David emoji] Zelensky [menorah emoji] doing shady business? Call me not even remotely surprised" has clear antisemitic dog whistles – insinuating that Ukrainian President Volodymyr Zelensky's alleged corruption is due to his Jewish heritage – yet scored only 0.019475 on the OHI, possibly because the classifier is not well trained to interpret emojis and other symbols.

Twenty-five videos had 50 or more antisemitic comments that scored above the 0.9 threshold, accumulating 2,844 total comments and average of almost 57 per video (with a median of 77). In other words, 36% of all the highly antisemitic comments in our dataset appeared on just 3% of the videos, with comments scoring above 0.9 on the OHI (and just 1.3% of all videos whose links were shared to at least three fringe platforms). This figure indicates that while antisemitic comments were widespread on YouTube, they clustered around particular videos and channels. We then performed manual, qualitative analysis of these 25 videos and their comments.

With these data in hand, we tried to ascertain the extent to which sharing YouTube video links on fringe platforms affected comment activity on those specific videos. We cross-referenced the times when comments were left on the YouTube videos with times when the links had been shared on fringe platforms, in order to assess probable causal relationships between sharing links and posting hateful comments (see Davis, 1979 on the validity of this method). For a selection of videos that received a higher percentage of antisemitic comments than the others (between 0.7% and 16% of all comments left on the videos at the time of data collection), we manually reviewed the fringe platform posts that had shared links to the videos and the commentary and replies – if any – that those posts received. Some videos experienced a spike in antisemitic comments that was nearly simultaneous with their posting date on YouTube, while others had waves of spikes weeks and months after their initial posting. We speculate that these differences were due to a combination of the relative popularity of the YouTube video channels and the degree to which the videos' authors – the channel operators – shared the links to their own fringe social media accounts. Popular creators who are known to make borderline antisemitic content may be more likely to attract "organic" antisemitism on YouTube, while accounts that share links to the fringes at the same time as they post their videos make identifying causal relationships more difficult. Without access to YouTube's referrer URL data or the commenters' IP addresses, we cannot prove absolutely that these comments were written by the same individuals who saw the link postings on fringe platforms. However, the temporal correlation between link sharing and commenting demonstrated a strong relationship. So, too, were the associations between the content of the comments across platforms, using nearly identical language and references in many instances in both the comments on YouTube and on the fringe posts where the links were shared.

Party over Here

In 526 cases – 65% of the 805 total videos with the highest-scoring antisemitic comments – we found that YouTube videos experienced a nearly 18% increase in the share of antisemitic comments in the first 48 hours after they had been shared on a fringe platform, a pattern that would appear to support previous studies about hate raids being coordinated from the fringes. However, we did not find any examples of explicit coordination or directions being issued to followers; even in cases where a fringe platform user encouraged their followers to watch the video and share it with others, they did not call for flooding the comments sections on YouTube. For instance, a 4chan thread discussing one of the channels analyzed in the following sections praised the channel's operator and told others, "We also need to protect him whatever the costs for whenever he does get a bigger audience."[4]

The findings that the videos that attracted hateful comments were, themselves, similarly or somewhat hateful, and that videos were congenial to hate comments rather than being the targets of hate themselves, complicate the currently accepted wisdom about online hate and its social processes. Rather than being examples of hate moving purposefully and unidirectionally from the fringes to the mainstream as forms of harassment in hate raids, the cases we observed could be more accurately characterized as broader discussions taking place simultaneously and interactively in different online social spaces, like groups of people clustered together in conversation in different parts of a room at the same party – hence our term, hate parties. The lack of any clear direction or coordination can be explained in large part by the differences between hate *raids* and hate *parties* regarding their respective goals. While the purpose of a hate *raid* is to disrupt and harass a specific target or targets, we want to suggest that hate *parties* are not motivated by antagonism; their goal is to share and promote hateful world views on mainstream platforms like YouTube that afford the possibility of reaching a relatively large audience of like-minded individuals, connecting with others online who share similar perspectives, a deeply social process.

The users who participated in these hate party conversations often had sophisticated understandings of the informal "rules" governing their engagement. They articulated certain expectations regarding content moderation on different platforms that they and others could exploit in order to extend conversations into mainstream spaces and "keep the party going," so to speak, without having their content removed. According to its hate speech policy, YouTube will remove content, including comments, that "promot[es] violence or hatred against individuals or groups" based on protected attributes including ethnicity, race, and religion. This policy covers content that dehumanizes individuals, uses slurs and stereotypes to incite or promote hatred, and forwards conspiracy theories about individuals or groups being "evil, corrupt, or malicious" (YouTube, 2019). The descriptions in this policy can, in theory, be interpreted quite broadly, but in practice, YouTube's moderators apply them narrowly. As such, ambiguous and borderline content often escapes detection and remains on the platform. Users are adept at using slang, symbols, or deliberate misspellings to avoid automated detection and to toe the line of acceptability. Fringe platforms, on the other hand, have branded themselves as "free speech alternatives" where content moderation is more relaxed or nonexistent. For example, Gab claims that it will "ensure that all content moderation decisions and enforcement of these terms of service does not punish user for exercising their God-given right to speak freely" (Gab, 2023); Gettr prohibits "content that endorses violence against, or promotes segregation of, individuals or groups" based on protected class characteristics, but "discussions and comments of sensitive topics relating to these characteristics" are allowed (Gettr, n.d.); and 4chan has some global rules prohibiting activities that violate local and U.S. laws, but enforcement is inconsistent at best. Each 4chan board has its own rules as well, such as the "Politically Incorrect" or "/pol/" board where anything is permitted except attacking other users or posting pornography (4chan, n.d.).

In the following, we analyze three YouTube channels and their operators that stood out in our data as different ideal types of hate party hosts and describe how they are situated in broader social processes of online hate: (1) "Redpill" opportunities, that is, more mainstream voices that followers on the fringes designate as potential gateways to hate; (2) channels and operators whose hateful subtext is clear for audiences who are primed to hear it, but whose content does not violate any of YouTube's rules; and (3) more extreme creators who push the boundaries of acceptable content on YouTube.

Redpills

The term "redpill" is inspired by the 1999 action sci-fi blockbuster movie *The Matrix*, in which the redpill allows the film's protagonist to see that he has been living in an elaborate simulated reality. Many extremists describe becoming aware of media and political institutions' supposed lies as "being redpilled." They also express the need to redpill others, that is, help them see the world from a different – and in this case, more conspiratorial – perspective.[5] Users on the fringes look to mainstream sources for possible redpill opportunities: Influential figures with large followings who can function as gateways to more extreme talking points.

English comedian Russell Brand is one example of a potential redpill. On his YouTube channel, which had over 6.56 million subscribers as of August 2023, Brand gives his takes on current events and pitches himself as an anti-establishment "free thinker," often from a left-leaning perspective.[6] Since the COVID-19 pandemic, his videos have increasingly embraced conspiracy theories that merge with far-right talking points and have garnered Brand respect on the fringes (see Merlan, 2022). As one 4chan user commented, "russell brand is the new gateway redpill now, [Tucker] carlson is old hat. even my mom watches that cockney faggot spout shit you would have only heard on 4chan a few years back."

On January 12, 2023, Brand posted a video to his YouTube channel titled "IT'S STARTING" about an agreement between Ukrainian president Volodymyr Zelensky and the investment company BlackRock to coordinate efforts rebuilding Ukraine (Brand, 2023). In the video, Brand insinuated that the agreement – and the United States' support of Ukraine in its war with Russia war more broadly – was all part of a plan for powerful financial interests like BlackRock to profit from the conflict. By August 1, 2023, the video had received more than two million views and 13,011 comments. While none of Brand's commentary was explicitly antisemitic, 290 comments received a high antisemitism score from the OHI (2.2% of all comments at that time).

Several commenters picked up on Brand's emphasis on conspiratorial business opportunities, and the fact that both Zelensky and BlackRock CEO Larry Fink are Jewish, to repeat well-worn antisemitic tropes about Jews controlling global finance. However, most comments were careful to use coded language and signals that other antisemites would recognize but that would avoid YouTube's content moderation rules. For example, "Everything Russel talked about here is JU owned and controlled. End ZOG in Washington!" uses "JU" in place of "Jew" and the acronym ZOG, which stands for "Zionist-occupied government," is commonly used by antisemites on- and offline. While this comment could be interpreted as violating YouTube's prohibition against conspiracy theories based on protected attributes, it can only be identified as such if one has the requisite contextual knowledge. Another user wrote, "(((BlackRock)))? (((Zelensky)))? If only there was some kind of connection . . . [thinking face emoji]," using the triple parentheses symbol to identify someone or something as Jewish (Smith & Fleishman, 2016). This comment, too, was ambiguous enough to avoid removal by YouTube.

Brand posted the same video to his Rumble account, a YouTube competitor with less stringent content moderation. The video received far less engagement on Rumble than on YouTube (only 30,800 views and 188 total comments), but some commenters were more overt in their antisemitism. One wrote, "2 more thieving Jews," while another opined, "BlackRock C.E.O. Larry Flink? Jewish by any chance? Or is that antisemitic to point out Jewish elites and Israel are responsible for wars?" Another commenter, however, was more hesitant, writing, "All gews," before adding as a threaded reply, "I can't I have to stay incognito. sry Russ [kissing face emoji]." Notably, one of the YouTube commenters had left a similar reply – "All bloody Gews" – demonstrating the shared lexicon in this loose community.

Comments responding to Brand's same videos appeared on fringe platforms such as Gab, Gettr, Twitter, and Truth Social as well, with links to the respective videos. This inter-platform cross talk was so prevalent that it suggested that the comments arising on these various platforms, anchored by a common referent (the video), are part of a continuous conversation going on among several social media platforms. The participants in these conversations traverse the different platforms with considerable facility in order to exploit respective variations in content moderation practices within the social media ecosystem, about which they are clearly cognizant, as reflected in their comments. For instance, some of the posts revealed users' awareness of the different restrictions on hate speech on alternative platforms. In a secondary thread on Gab, one user noted with regard to YouTube, "I suggest people dont say whatthey think inn the comments. Russell seems to be leading everyone to reveal their thoughts on a highly monitoored medium."

While some social media users identified antisemitic subtext in Russell Brand's video about BlackRock and Ukraine, it would be unfair to say that Brand intended for his words to be interpreted that way (he has elsewhere denied accusations of antisemitism; Brand, 2014). In fact, the absence of intentional subtext in Brand's videos is among the reasons that extremists describe him as a redpill: His content should, theoretically, appeal to "normies" while seeding talking points, including antisemitism, that they might encounter again in more extreme content.

Focus on the Subtext

Beyond figures like Brand are influencers whose far-right bona fides are more obvious, but who do not fully commit to overtly extremist positions lest they lose their accounts on mainstream platforms. Mark Dice is one such YouTuber. A far-right conspiracy theorist, Dice joined YouTube in 2007 and boasts that his was "the first conservative YouTube channel to reach 1 million sub-scribers" (Dice, n.d.). On his channel, Dice covers political and pop culture news and adds his own commentary and analysis. As of August 2023, his channel had over 1.86 million subscribers.

One of Dice's videos, titled "The Truth About Steven Crowder's $50 MILLION DOLLAR Feud with Ben Shapiro's Daily Wire," was posted on January 19, 2023. By August 1, 2023, it had received 433,345 views and 13,151 comments, including 347 that scored highly on the OHI (2.6% of the total). In the video, Dice commented on a high-profile dispute[7] over a term sheet offer between two of the most popular conservative YouTubers: comedian-turned-pundit Steven Crowder and Ben Shapiro, cofounder of the hardline conservative news and opinion outlet *The Daily Wire*. Shapiro's Orthodox Jewish heritage is a core part of his public identity. In Dice's video commentary, he described Shapiro as being "in bed with Big Tech" because he spends millions of dollars on Facebook advertising annually and had a "secret dinner" with Meta CEO Mark Zuckerberg, who, Dice noted, is also Jewish.

The video's antisemitic subtext was clearest, however, in Dice's reference to "cultural Marxism" as a threat to American society and his use of the phrase "dual loyalty" to describe Crowder's relationship with leaders of American conservatism. Both of these phrases are common antisemitic dog whistles, the former part of a conspiracy theory about Jewish control of entertainment media (Braune, 2019), and the latter an accusation often made of Jewish Americans who express support for Israel (Elman, 2022). Dice argued that YouTubers like himself would be unable to criticize Israel if they signed a contract with a major conservative media outlet, thereby insinuating Jewish influence over the topics conservative media covers (Dice, 2023).

None of the ambiguous language that Dice used in his video would likely be considered hate speech by YouTube regulations. But many of the video's commenters picked up on the subtext implicit in Dice's targeting of conserva-tive Jewish individuals and his references to antisemitic tropes. Commenters, too, used strategic language and symbols to communicate antisemitic rheto-ric covertly. For instance, one commenter wrote, "Crowder is right, (((()))) took control of conservatism," using the triple parentheses as a metonym for Jews. Another wrote, "Shapiro. Rubin. Connect the dot goy," using the Yiddish/modern Hebrew word for non-Jew that is popular among far-right antisemites (Friedman, 2017). Others were less hesitant, leaving comments that would appear to violate YouTube's prohibitions against promoting con-spiracy theories about a group based on protected attributes, but without explicitly inciting violence. To wit, one commenter wrote, "Who the hell trusts Shapiro? He's a Zionist puppet in a big big world ruled by his kosher uncles."

Nine comments included some variation of the phrase "name the Jew," a rallying cry of sorts (ADL, 2018) that online antisemites often use as a measuring stick to evaluate how far an influencer like Dice is willing to go; if they "won't name the Jew," they are either still compromised by Jewish media censorship or not yet "awakened" to the antisemitic worldview in its totality. One commenter picked up on Dice's "cultural Marxism" dog whistle and wrote, "And who are these cultural Marxists? What ethnic group is pushing the cultural Marxism? If you won't name the Jew you are subservient to them." Most comments in this vein lamented what they saw as Dice's failure to adequately name the Jew, but one voiced their approval: "Jews out-jewing each other . . . nothing new, the only one I trust is mark dice because he calls out the Jew. . . . Alway remember kids, 'if they don't name the Jew, their message isn't true.'"

The discussion in the YouTube comments about whether or not Dice was willing to name the Jew closely mirrored conversations taking place more or less simultaneously on fringe platforms where the video's link had been shared. Dice posted the link to his own Gab account, where nearly one-quarter of the replies to his post were antisemitic. Four sequential replies all chided Dice for not explicitly naming the Jew, including one that posted an antisemitic infographic created by the hate group the Goyim Defense League (see Figure 8.1).

In addition to its discussion on Gab, it was a topic on 4chan's /pol/ board. There, one commenter drew a distinction between Dice and Crowder on this issue, writing, "Mark Dice called out the kikes. Crowder doesn't [.] crowder is not the 'right.'" Another in the same thread disagreed: "Show me one video where [Dice] names the Jew. I will wait. Protip: You can't." The /pol/ board has hosted similar discussions about Dice and his subtextual antisemitism in other threads that were unrelated to the video about Crowder and Shapiro. In one thread titled simply "Mark Dice," the original poster asked, "How is this guy still kicking? He names the Jew in almost every video now," to which another user replied, "Saying 'a certain group of people' is not naming them." Whether 4chan users lauded Dice for his antisemitic tropes or criticized him for not going far enough, several noted his savvy in avoiding being suspended by YouTube; as one commenter put it, "Looks like he's studied how to sidestep the censorship."

These comments and others like them are strong indications of the affirming cross-platform dynamics in which certain figures serve as gathering points. Nearly identical conversations (save for the slurs) unfold in the comments sections on YouTube videos and in reply threads on fringe platforms where links to those videos are shared.

Saying the Quiet Part Out Loud

For many antisemites on the fringes, YouTubers like Russell Brand and Mark Dice are useful for redpilling or as fellow travelers who attract like-minded

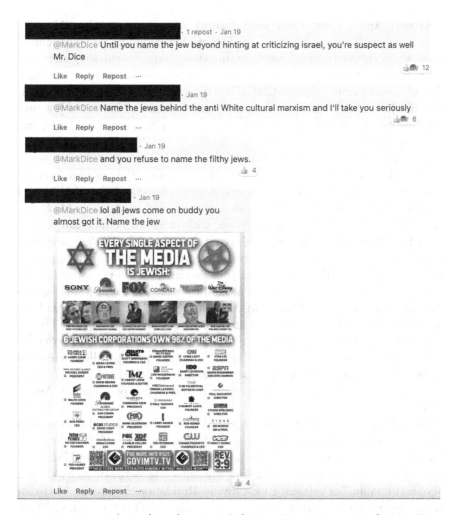

FIGURE 8.1 Screenshot of Replies to a Gab Post Discussing a Mark Dice You-
Tube Video

Note: Taken by the authors, September 11, 2023.

communities with their content. But they are still seen as relative outsiders,
either because they are not actually antisemitic themselves (Brand) or not
antisemitic enough (Dice). A third, rarer category of YouTuber includes those
who produce channels with multiple videos that contain overtly antisemitic
content but have thus far avoided suspension. The videos in these channels
"say the quiet part out loud," that is, turn what is subtext in videos like
Dice's into explicit verbiage. For this reason, they are also more obviously
integrated with antisemitic cross-platform conversations.

Leather Apron Club is one such channel. Its creator goes by "Alex" in interviews with other far-right YouTubers. He produces pseudoscientific essay-style videos from a distinctly anti-democratic worldview, including a series on "Jewish overrepresentation" in media. A comment on a 4chan thread about Leather Apron Club's YouTube channel on January 2, 2023, stated, "Just found this guy today, underrated channel. Names the Jew and calls out the controlled opposition such as [Jordan] Peterson, Alex Jones, and [Lex] Fridman."

The first video in Leather Apron Club's Jewish overrepresentation series addressed the idea that Jewish people hold many influential positions because of they supposedly have high IQ scores. Alex's video claimed to debunk this notion. In this October 24, 2022 video, he reviewed academic publications about IQ scores and how they correlate with racial and ethnic categories.[8] Alex asked his audience to question, even if they accept the IQ data, does that mean that it is "good" for Jews to be overrepresented in positions of power, especially in the media? Alex also insinuated that Jews do not have the best interests of American society in mind and that Jews are an outsider group that has usurped political power in the United States. He concluded with an argument that could reasonably be interpreted as promotion of hatred based on a conspiracy theory about alleged Jewish malice, and therefore in violation of YouTube's hate speech policy: "We should no longer allow ourselves to be browbeaten by this false sense of inferiority, nor should we be made to accept what is obviously an astroturfed media landscape" (Leather Apron Club, 2022).

As of August 1, 2023, the video had been viewed over 200,000 times and received 5,859 comments, 711 (12%) of which scored above 0.9 on the OHI. As with the Brand and Dice videos, many commenters used coded language and implicit references to communicate antisemitic sentiments, such as "Synagogue of satan," a reference to a line in Revelation 3:9 in the Christian Bible that antisemites often quote to one another; "OY VEY THE GOYIM KNOWS!!!" another phrase common among online antisemites for communicating beliefs about a secretive Jewish cabal controlling power from behind the scenes (ADL, n.d.); and "[Jordan] Peterson is a j3w shill," using the number "3" in place of "e" to avoid detection.

There were also a handful of comments that took issue with the claims about Jewish IQ in the video from a perspective embedded in a broader, more esoteric antisemitic conversation. While Alex expressed skepticism that Jews actually have higher average IQs than other groups in his video, a different faction of antisemites and white supremacists are committed to that belief because it helps explain their antisemitic conspiracy theories about Jewish control of business, media, and politics (see Welton, 2023, responding directly to Leather Apron Club's video in an antisemitic, white supremacist online publication). For example, one commenter wrote:

Jew IQ didn't get debunked. Anymore than IQ did or Asian IQ did. It's 3% racially of the US population but yes. They seem to have lots of $$$ like, 30% of US wealth compared to 3% of the population. But Asians don't overrepresent anywhere near that much of the wealth holdings? Note I don't say that their high IQ is why the wealth holdings exist.;)

The same contours of this conversation were evident on the fringe platforms where the link to Leather Apron Club's video was shared. For instance, in a 4chan /pol/ thread praising the video, one dissenter commented, "fact is, Jews actually aren't smarter than Europeans," to which another replied, "Then what is your theory on why they are overrepresentated in powerful and influential positions?" Another commenter in the same thread asked, "If Jews aren't smarter then why are they so successful?" which received this reply: "Because they groom their kids to have PTSD from an imaginary prosecution and set them up with both nepotism and a highly competitive mindset." In a Telegram channel linking to the video and another far-right YouTube video criticizing Leather Apron Club, a user wrote:

> Jewish high IQ is an objective fact. . . . That alone explains a huge (though not all) amount of Jewish power and influence. . . . [All this] is supported by other figures such as [former evolutionary psychology professor] Kevin MacDonald and [professor and YouTuber] Edward Dutton.

Similar discussions unfolded on Gab, where the Leather Apron Club video's link was shared 42 times.[9] In one thread, users defended the validity of the high Jewish IQ claim by referencing similar arguments made by Jared Taylor, the white supremacist founder of American Renaissance. One commenter skirted the alleged factuality of the IQ question entirely, writing, "Jew's IQ is not the issue; high or low – No it is their consuming hatred for the White Race that is germane to White Survival under the Tyranny of the Jew." Notably, YouTube commenters referenced both MacDonald and Taylor as well in their criticisms of Alex's argument, further demonstrating the shared conversation across platforms of the Leather Apron Club hate party.

More so than the other types of video in our analysis, channels like Leather Apron Club attract antisemitic comment spikes on YouTube not because of organized hate raids or as organic reactions from antisemites to their content, but rather because their channels are recognized on the fringes and in the mainstream as social spaces where antisemitism is welcome. Since it was first posted, the "High Jewish IQ Debunked" video has received multiple waves of antisemitic engagement in the comments, almost always accompanied by its link being posted yet again to a fringe platform. To wit, it has been shared on Gab at least 30 different times and on 4chan at least 208 times at the time of this writing (August 13, 2023). The video's staying power speaks to its status, and Leather Apron Club's, as touchstones for online hate; by contrast, Brand's and Dice's video links were shared within the first few days of their release, but never subsequently.

Keeping the Party Going

Some fringe platform commenters speculated that Leather Apron Club could not possibly remain on YouTube for much longer; as one 4chan user put it, "This dude is keyed as hell. Enjoying him before schlomo kicks him to [YouTube competitor] bitchute." In an interview with fellow far-right YouTuber Keith Woods on cozy.tv – a livestreaming platform created by white supremacist Nick Fuentes – Leather Apron Club's Alex explained that YouTube is necessary for pushing his extremist messaging out to a wider audience, but that this means being careful about how he packages his videos to avoid their removal or YouTube suspending his account.[10] His comments and the commentary from the fringes about his channel reveal two important insights about the social media ecosystem and social processes of hate: Hate purveyors are acutely aware of content moderation differences and work to exploit them, and they value their ability to remain on mainstream platforms. Their relationship to YouTube and how they approach it strategically also help to explain the hate party phenomenon, why partygoers participate, and what – if anything – can be done to mitigate its harms.

Why Do They Come, and Why Do They Stay?

There is a clear throughline from Don Black's comments about the importance he saw in bringing Stormfront to the public Internet to contemporary online hate on the fringes and its relationship to mainstream social media like YouTube. Outside observers may question why antisemites, white supremacists, and others would want to be active on platforms where they face the possibility of suspension when there are plenty of viable fringe alternatives where they can network. While we can only speculate as to individual motivations, a few key possibilities bear mentioning.

First, fringe social media users, from garden variety conspiracy theorists to the true extremists, often talk of the need to be on the "digital battlefield" where they can "redpill normies" and potentially recruit new followers to their causes (Hannah, 2023; Munn, 2023). To wit, in his interview with Keith Woods, Alex of Leather Apron Club agreed with Woods' assessment that YouTube is "obviously bad" regarding alleged censorship, but added, "There's no better platform to be on than YouTube. We need to get [our message] out there in order to bring in new followers, as it were" (Woods, 2023). Some hate messengers may also believe that their presence in the mainstream can help "push open the Overton window," that is, expand the range of politically acceptable positions to include more and more extreme ideas (Marwick & Lewis, 2017). In other words, their ability to normalize hateful worldviews and influence policy depends upon their continued access to communication platforms with the largest audiences, rather than broadcasting to a relatively narrow group of users on the fringes.[11]

Second, from the channel operators' perspective, YouTube affords opportunities for making money that other platforms do not or cannot. While financial incentives were beyond the scope of this particular study, all three of the channels we analyzed here were able to collect revenue from their presence on YouTube in a variety of ways. The first and most obvious way was via the platform's monetization system, the YouTube Partner Program. While we cannot say for certain that Brand, Dice, and Leather Apron Club applied to be YouTube Partners, all three met the basic eligibility requirements – at least 1,000 subscribers and 4,000 public watch hours in the last 12 months – and a look at the page source code revealed that monetization was enabled for both their channels and the individual videos we analyzed in this piece.[12] All three also collected modest sums on each of the videos we looked at with "Super Thanks," a feature that allows viewers to donate directly to the channel operator when they leave a comment. And all three shared links in the video descriptions to websites where viewers could purchase their merchandise or donate to their crowdfunding accounts (e.g., Patreon, SubscribeStar, and Buy Me a Coffee). Brand, Dice, Leather Apron Club, and others have a clear financial interest in remaining on YouTube, and while we can only speculate, their followers and supporters may also want to be active in the mainstream to lend material support to the influencers they see as being instrumental in advancing their ideological and political causes. By contrast, fringe sites like Gab and 4chan do not enable monetization.

Finally, some hate partiers may derive pleasure from spreading hate "out in the open" and pushing the boundaries of what mainstream platforms allow. As in hate raids and other forms of malicious trolling – where the goal is to disrupt the target's normal life or "do it for the lulz," that is, to revel in the target's suffering or protestations (Phillips, 2015) – there is a libidinal dimension to hate parties (Matheson, 2022; see also Hook, 2017). But while the pleasures of trolling or sadistic cruelty come in large part from observing targets' reactions – for example, "triggering the libs" (Aspray, 2019) – the pleasure of participating in a hate party may be more complex, akin to what Udupa (2019) calls "fun as a metapractice" in extreme speech communities. For hate partiers, there appears to be some joy in seeing and being seen in a loose community of others who share their worldview and in knowing that they are doing or saying something they expect would get them banned. To wit, a Gab user highlighted and celebrated the hate party phenomenon in a YouTube comment section on another of Mark Dice's videos (see Figure 8.2). Future research could address *jouissance*[13] in social processes of online hate and how it manifests, such as in hate parties.

FIGURE 8.2   Screenshot of a Gab Post Celebrating the Antisemitic Comments on a Mark Dice YouTube Video

Note: Taken by the authors, September 11, 2023.

What Can Be Done?

In a sense, hate parties are the contemporary equivalent of hate BBSes like Aryan Nations and Liberty Bell Publishing: Virtual mini-communities where users can connect over shared hateful worldviews and forge social bonds. Two key differences, however, make YouTube hate parties more concerning. First, they are embedded in larger, looser communities that span multiple platforms and are somewhat ephemeral, coalescing around certain pieces of content or specific events but without any formal or stable membership. These communities' multi-locality and ephemerality make it more difficult to fully appreciate the scope and impact of hate parties, which serve as digital artifacts of their existence. Second, hate parties are examples of how broader online hate communities exploit the reach that mainstream platforms afford, which is magnitudes greater than anything they could hope to achieve on the fringes. Whereas hate BBSes had to rely on word of mouth to build their audiences, and hate websites like Stormfront are dependent on their own platforms and being indexed by search engines for their reach, YouTube hate parties and the channels that make space for them have the world's second-largest social media platform and its sophisticated recommendation algorithms at their disposal.

The hate party phenomenon exposes the limits of YouTube's content moderation policies specifically and of social media platforms more generally. Platforms typically detail content moderation approaches in their terms of service or community guidelines, all of which currently treat offenders individually and look for clear evidence of intention before taking action against any potentially violative behavior. No platform considers an account's indirect impacts and influence or the networked characteristics of online hate and harassment, not to mention how such harms unfold across different platforms. One could say that they do not take social processes of online hate into account. And although platforms can detect spikes in inbound traffic from fringe sites via referrer URL data, they have no power over where and when links to content on their sites are shared.

Researchers at ADL have called such indirect and networked activity "stochastic" hate and harassment (2022, 2023a, 2023b; see also Abdul Rahman (forthcoming)), a riff on the concept of "stochastic terrorism" (Amman & Meloy, 2021). YouTube hate parties are prime examples of stochastic hate: Unlike hate raids, they are not explicitly coordinated, and none of the channel operators implore their viewers to take action or engage hatefully with their content. Moreover, the influential accounts whose content attracts hate parties do not, in most cases, violate any content moderation rules. Even Leather Apron Club, arguably the most antisemitic of the three channels we analyzed for this chapter, produces content that is borderline at worst and which YouTube has determined does not break its hate speech policy. Yet when accounting for the surrounding context, it is clear that channels and video pages are facilitating social spaces for hate to flourish.

If the content is not violative, and no one is being targeted for harassment, what, then, is harmful about hate parties? We contend that the implicit normalization of hate they represent is itself harmful and is one of the unexamined consequences of narrowly considered content moderation. Adding to that sense of normalization is the fact that hate party videos are monetized and recommended to viewers by YouTube's algorithm; as one user posted on Y Combinator's Hacker News forum, they were unaware of Leather Apron Club or its content until the "High Jewish IQ Debunked" video appeared in their "Up Next" recommendations (Hacker News, 2023). In other words, it is not just that the YouTube platform has questionable content but also that it actively promotes such content and empowers hate purveyors to profit from it. Additionally, hate parties may work as tools for radicalization, though more research is needed to test this hypothesis. So long as they leverage their understanding of content moderation rules to avoid removal, hate partiers and the accounts that host them can continue to insert fringe talking points into the mainstream and, potentially, lead viewers from the mainstream further into the fringes.

Notes

1 Extremism researcher Chip Berlet estimates that the Liberty Bell BBS first went online in March 1984 (2001, p. 2).
2 These platforms represent the fringe platforms that we had access to via SMAT's API and data scraping tools, and on which users primarily post in English. They are not an exhaustive list of fringe platforms.
3 Since our primary interest for an advocacy research project we were working on at ADL was documenting and measuring online antisemitism, this motivated our decision to use the OHI and to narrow the focus of our analysis. Future research could use the same methods and different classifiers to identify similar patterns in anti-Black, anti-LGBTQ+, or other forms of hate that coalesce into hate parties.
4 Unless otherwise noted, all direct quotes from social media comments and posts are presented verbatim and retain spelling and grammar errors.
5 Redpilling is often a gradual process, as Rebecca Lewis details here in the case of white nationalists specifically:

> White nationalists often describe [redpilling] as a stepwise process. For example, in one possible pathway, they may start by rejecting the mainstream media and "PC culture"; then embrace anti-feminist ideas; then embrace scientific racism of the idea that racial oppression is not real; and then finally, the idea that Jewish people wield positions of influence and harbor malicious intents against white people. (They often refer to these processes as addressing the "woman question," the "race question," and the "Jewish question," or alternatively as "getting redpilled" on any of these individual issues.)
> *(2018, p. 35)*

6 In September 2022, Brand announced that he would be moving his daily livestream from YouTube to its fringe video hosting competitor Rumble, accusing YouTube of "censorship" after one of his videos that violated YouTube's policies on medical misinformation was removed. However, Rumble does not afford Brand the same reach as YouTube: his Rumble channel has only 1.34 million subscribers, and his videos receive fewer views (just 136,000 views for a conspiratorial video about the Centers for Disease Control and COVID-19 vaccine mandates posted on August 4, 2023, compared to 852,000 views for the same video posted the same day on YouTube).
7 See Ramirez (2023) for a more detailed explanation of the dispute.
8 White Nationalists in particular fixate on IQ scores as evidence in support of their so-called "race realist" arguments that posit fundamental biological differences in the human species according to race (see Panofsky et al., 2021).
9 In fact, one commenter wrote, "Be sure to get on gab there is a lot of people that would love to know about the Jews," further demonstrating hate parties' cross-platform dynamics.
10 His approach appears to be working for now. ADL's online incident response center reported Leather Apron Club's video using our status in YouTube's Trusted Partner Program, which provides faster escalation paths for reports of violative content. YouTube replied,

> We have determined that the video does not violate our Hate Speech policy and will remain live on the platform. While this channel may contain controversial or inflammatory views on topics related to stereotypes that incite or promote

hatred based on protected group status, we did not identify content violating our Hate Speech policies.

11 Though beyond the purview of this chapter, there is also a strain within fringe hate and conspiracy theory groups that frames the digital battlefield in eschatological terms, that is, as the site of a spiritual struggle between the forces of good and evil that portends Biblical end times (Hannah, 2021; Macklin, 2018). For adherents to this worldview, their participation on mainstream platforms assumes a religious valence to which they may feel "called" to fulfill a purpose greater than themselves.

12 Notably, YouTube does not run ads before or during any of the three videos.

13 We are indebted to Brock (2020) for the application of *jouissance* to virtual communities and cybercultures. However, it is important to note the incommensurability of culture-specific affect between the communities Brock writes about and online hate purveyors.

References

4chan. (n.d.). *Rules: /pol/ – politically incorrect*. 4chan Community Support LLC. https://4chan.org/rules#pol/

Abdul Rahman, E. (forthcoming). The anatomy of indirect swarming. In K. Barker & O. Jurasz (Eds.), *Routledge handbook of social media, law and society*. Routledge.

Abidin, C. (2018). *Internet celebrity: Understanding fame online*. Emerald Publishing, Ltd.

Amman, M., & Meloy, J. R. (2021). Stochastic terrorism: A linguistic and psychological analysis. *Perspectives on Terrorism, 15*(5), 2–13.

Anti-Defamation League (ADL). (1985). *Computerized networks of hate: An ADL fact finding report*. ADL.

Anti-Defamation League (ADL). (2018, August 23). *Patrick Little's "name the Jew" tour spreads anti-semitic hate nationwide*. ADL. https://www.adl.org/resources/blog/patrick-littles-name-jew-tour-spreads-anti-semitic-hate-nationwide/

Anti-Defamation League (ADL). (2022, December 15). *The reality of how harassment spreads on Twitter*. ADL. https://www.adl.org/resources/blog/reality-how-harassment-spreads-twitter/

Anti-Defamation League (ADL). (2023a, May 24). *Threads of hate: How Twitter's content moderation misses the mark*. ADL. https://www.adl.org/resources/blog/threads-hate-how-twitters-content-moderation-misses-mark/

Anti-Defamation League (ADL). (2023b, September 14). *Hate parties: Sharing links on fringe platforms drives antisemitic comments on YouTube*. ADL. https://www.adl.org/resources/report/hate-parties-sharing-links-fringe-platforms-drives-antisemitic-comments-youtube/

Anti-Defamation League (ADL). (n.d.). *The goyim know/shut it down*. ADL. www.adl.org/resources/hate-symbol/goyim-knowshut-it-down/

Aspray, B. (2019). On trolling as comedic method. *Journal of Cinema and Media Studies, 58*(3), 154–160. https://doi.org/10.1353/cj.2019.0030

Bär, D., Pröllochs, N., & Feuerriegel, S. (2023). *New threats to society from free-speech social media platforms*. arXiv. https://doi.org/10.48550/arXiv.2302.01229

Barbrook, R., & Cameron, A. (1996). The Californian ideology. *Science as Culture, 6*(1), 44–72. https://doi.org/10.1080/09505439609526455

Barlow, J. P. (1996, February 8). *A declaration of the independence of cyberspace*. Electronic Frontier Foundation. https://www.eff.org/cyberspace-independence/

Berlet, C. (2001, April 28). *When hate went online* [Paper presentation]. Northeast Sociological Association, Spring Conference, Fairfield, CT, United States.

Brand, R. (2014, August 20). Why I oppose anti-semitism. *Huffington Post*. https://www.huffingtonpost.co.uk/russell-brand/why-i-oppose-anti-semitism_b_5694864.html

Brand, R. (2023, January 12). *It's starting* [Video]. YouTube. www.youtube.com/watch?v=4v_aC1ZTlOg&ab_channel=RussellBrand/

Braune, J. (2019). Who's afraid of the Frankfurt School? "Cultural Marxism" as an antisemitic conspiracy theory. *Journal of Social Justice, 9*(1), 1–25.

Brock, A. (2020). *Distributed blackness: African American cybercultures.* NYU Press.

Daniels, J. (2018). The algorithmic rise of the "alt-right". *Contexts, 17*(1), 60–65. https://doi.org/10.1177/1536504218766547

Davis, J. A. (1979). *The logic of causal order.* Sage.

Dice, M. (2023, January 19). *The truth about Steven Crowder's $50 million dollar feud with Ben Shapiro's daily wire* [Video]. YouTube. https://www.youtube.com/watch?v=_t5cHVMEqbE/

Dice, M. (n.d.). *Description.* YouTube. https://www.youtube.com/@markdice/about/

Donovan, J., Lewis, B., & Friedberg, B. (2019). Parallel ports: Sociotechnical change from the alt-right to alt-tech. In M. Fielitz & N. Thurston (Eds.), *Post-digital cultures of the far right: Online actions and offline consequences in Europe and the US* (pp. 49–65). Transcript-open.de. https://doi.org/10.14361/9783839446706-004

El Ouirdi, M., El Ouirdi, A., Segers, J., & Henderickx, E. (2014). Social media conceptualization and taxonomy: A Lasswellian framework. *Journal of Creative Communications, 9*(2), 107–126. https://doi.org/10.1177/0973258614528608

Elman, R. A. (2022). The mainstreaming of American antisemitism: The defeat of an ideal. *Journal of Contemporary Antisemitism, 5*(1), 105–120. https://doi.org/10.26613/jca/5.1.104

Freelon, D., McIlwain, C. D., & Clark, M. D. (2016). *Beyond the hashtags: #Ferguson, #Blacklivesmatter, and the online struggle for offline justice.* Social Science Research Network. https://doi.org/10.2139/ssrn.2747066

Friedman, D. (2017, August 25). Why I won't stop using the term 'goy'. *The Forward.* https://forward.com/life/381035/why-i-wont-stop-using-the-term-goy/

Gab. (2023). *Website terms of service.* Gab AI Inc. https://gab.com/about/tos/

Gerbaudo, P. (2012). *Tweets and the streets: Social media and contemporary activism.* Pluto Press.

Gettr. (n.d.). *Hateful behavior.* GETTR USA, Inc. https://gettr.com/communityguidelines#hateful-behavior/

Gilbert, D. (2021, August 20). One of QAnon's most antisemitic influencers is actually a 39-year-old Baptist from Florida. *Vice.* https://www.vice.com/en/article/93yvmv/qanon-ghostezra-is-robert-randall-smart/

Gray, R. (2023, July 16). How bronze age pervert built an online following and injected anti-democracy, pro-men ideas into the GOP. *Politico.* https://www.politico.com/news/magazine/2023/07/16/bronze-age-pervert-masculinity-00105427

Hacker News. (2023, January 20). Dear YouTube AI, I am not a Nazi. *Y Combinator.* https://news.ycombinator.com/item?id=34452863

Hagen, S., & Tuters, M. (2021). The internet hate machine: On the weird collectivity of anonymous far-right groups. In M. Devries, J. Bessant, & R. Watts (Eds.), *Rise of the far-right: Technologies of recruitment and mobilization* (pp. 171–192). Rowman & Littlefield.

Hannah, M. N. (2021). A conspiracy of data: QAnon, social media, and information visualization. *Social Media + Society, 7*(3). https://doi.org/10.1177/20563051211036064

Hannah, M. N. (2023). Information literacy in the age of internet conspiracism. *Journal of Information Literacy, 17*(1), 204–220. https://doi.org/10.11645/17.1.3277

Hine, G. E., Onaolapo, J., De Cristofaro, E., Kourtellis, N., Leontiadis, I., Samaras, R., Stringhini, G., & Blackburn, J. (2017). Kek, cucks, and god emperor Trump: A measurement study of 4chan's politically incorrect forum and its effects on the web. *Proceedings of the International AAAI Conference on Web and Social Media, 11*(1), 92–101. https://doi.org/10.1609/icwsm.v11i1.14893

Hook, D. (2017). What is "enjoyment as a political factor"? *Political Psychology*, 38(4), 605–620. https://doi.org/10.1111/pops.12417

Koukaras, P., Tjortjis, C., & Rousidis, D. (2020). Social media types: Introducing a data driven taxonomy. *Computing*, 102(1), 295–340. https://doi.org/10.1007/s00607-019-00739-y

Leather Apron Club. (2022, October 24). *High Jewish IQ debunked – Joe Rogan follow-up* [Video]. YouTube. https://www.youtube.com/watch?v=stLCurXu0fc/

Lewis, R. (2018). Alternative influence: Broadcasting the reactionary right on YouTube. Analysis & Policy Observatory. https://apo.org.au/node/193281

Lim, M. (2020). Algorithmic enclaves: Affective politics and algorithms in the neo-liberal social media landscape. In M. Boler & E. Davis (Eds.), *Affective politics of digital media: Propaganda by other means* (pp. 186–203). Routledge.

Macklin, G. (2018). 'Only bullets will stop us!' – the banning of National Action in Britain. *Perspectives on Terrorism*, 12(6), 104–122.

Mariconti, E., Suarez-Tangil, G., Blackburn, J., De Cristofaro, E., Kourtellis, N., Leontiadis, I., Serrano, J. L., & Stringhini, G. (2019). "You know what to do": Proactive detection of YouTube videos targeted by coordinated hate attacks. *Proceedings of the ACM on Human-Computer Interaction*, 3(CSCW), 1–21. ACM. https://doi.org/10.1145/3359309

Marwick, A. E. (2013). *Status update: Celebrity, publicity, and branding in the social media age*. Yale University Press.

Marwick, A. E. (2021). Morally motivated networked harassment as normative reinforcement. *Social Media + Society*, 7(2). https://doi.org/10.1177/20563051211021378

Marwick, A. E., & Lewis, R. (2017, May 15). Media manipulation and disinformation online. *Data & Society*. https://datasociety.net/library/media-manipulation-and-disinfo-online/

Matheson, C. L. (2022). Liberal tears and the rogue's yarn of sadistic conservatism. *Rhetoric Society Quarterly*, 52(4), 341–355. https://doi.org/10.1080/02773945.2022.2061587

Meisner, C. (2023). Networked responses to networked harassment? Creators' coordinated management of "hate raids" on Twitch. *Social Media + Society*, 9(2). https://doi.org/10.1177/20563051231179696

Merlan, A. (2022, September 12). Russell Brand tries to promote ivermectin, gets instantly fact-checked by his own followers. *Motherboard/Vice*. https://www.vice.com/en/article/z34zd9/russell-brand-ivermectin/

Munn, L. (2023). *Red pilled – The allure of digital hate*. Bielefeld University Press.

Panofsky, A., Dasgupta, K., & Iturriaga, N. (2021). How white nationalists mobilize genetics: From genetic ancestry and human biodiversity to counterscience and metapolitics. *American Journal of Physical Anthropology*, 175(2), 387–398. https://doi.org/10.1002/ajpa.24150

Perry, B. (2000). "Button-down terror": The metamorphosis of the hate movement. *Sociological Focus*, 33(2), 113–131. https://doi.org/10.1080/00380237.2000.10571161

Phillips, W. (2015). *This is why we can't have nice things: Mapping the relationship between online trolling and mainstream culture*. MIT Press.

Ramirez, N. M. (2023, January 19). Far-right blowhard calls $50 million Daily Wire offer a 'slave contract'. *Rolling Stone*. https://www.rollingstone.com/politics/politics-news/steven-crowder-feuds-daily-wire-50-million-offer-1234664277/

Rheingold, H. (2000). *The virtual community: Homesteading on the electronic frontier* (Rev. ed.). MIT Press.

Saaed, M. H., Papadamou, K., Blackburn, J., De Cristofaro, E., & Stringhini, G. (2023). *TUBERAIDER: Attributing coordinated hate attacks on YouTube videos to their source communities*. arXiv. https://doi.org/10.48550/arXiv.2308.05247

Shaffer, K. (2017, April 24). The business of hate media. *Data for Democracy/ Medium*. https://medium.com/data-for-democracy/the-business-of-hate-media-47603a5de5f4/

Smith, A., & Fleishman, C. (2016, June 1). (((Echoes))), exposed: The secret symbol neo-Nazis use to target Jews online. *Mic*. https://www.mic.com/articles/144228/echoes-exposed-the-secret-symbol-neo-nazis-use-to-target-jews-online/

Southern Poverty Law Center (SPLC). (n.d.). *Louis beam*. SPLC. https://www.splcenter.org/fighting-hate/extremist-files/individual/louis-beam/

Stringhini, G., & Blackburn, J. (Chapter 11 this volume). Understanding the phases and themes of coordinated online aggression attacks.

Swain, C. M., & Nieli, R. (Eds.). (2003). *Contemporary voices of white nationalism in America*. Cambridge University Press.

Törnberg, A., & Törnberg, P. (Chapter 5 this volume). From echo chambers to digital campfires: The making of an online community of hate in Stormfront.

Turner, F. (2005). Where the counterculture met the new economy: The WELL and the origins of virtual community. *Technology and Culture, 46*(3), 485–512.

Udupa, S. (2019). Nationalism in the digital age: Fun as a metapractice of extreme speech. *International Journal of Communication, 13*(2019), 3143–3163. https://doi.org/10.5282/ubm/epub.69633

Velasquez, N., Leahy, R., Restrepo, N. J., Lupu, Y., Sear, R., Gabriel, N., Jha, O., Goldberg, B., & Johnson, N. F. (2020). *Hate multiverse spreads malicious COVID-19 content online beyond individual platform control*. arXiv. https://doi.org/10.48550/arXiv.2004.00673

Walther, J. B. (Chapter 2 this volume). Making a case for a social processes approach to online hate.

Welton, L. (2023, January 28). Yes Leather Apron Club, Jews DO have higher average IQ. And they are more ethnocentric. *The Unz Review*. https://www.unz.com/article/yes-leather-apron-club-jews-do-have-higher-average-iq-and-they-are-more-ethnocentric/

Woods, K. (2023, January 24). *Leather Apron Club on effective messaging* [Video]. YouTube. https://www.youtube.com/watch?v=sHOqSKMNHao/

YouTube. (2019). Hate speech policy. *YouTube Help*. https://support.google.com/youtube/answer/2801939?sjid=17062414790824244739-NA/

Zittrain, J., Faris, R., Noman, H., Clark, J., Tilton, C., & Morrison-Westphal, R. (2017). *The shifting landscape of global internet censorship*. Berkman Klein Center for Internet and Society. https://hls.harvard.edu/bibliography/the-shifting-landscape-of-global-internet-censorship/

Zuboff, S. (2019). *The age of surveillance capitalism: The fight for a human future at the new frontier of power*. PublicAffairs.

Zuckerman, E. (2023, February 19). A social network taxonomy. *New_ Public/Substack*. https://newpublic.substack.com/p/a-social-network-taxonomy/

9

INFORMATION SHARING AND CONTENT FRAMING ACROSS MULTIPLE PLATFORMS AND FUNCTIONAL ROLES THAT EXEMPLIFY SOCIAL PROCESSES OF ONLINE HATE GROUPS

Shruti Phadke and Tanushree Mitra

Since their earliest days, information and communication technologies have served as attractive conduits for hate groups' operations (Gerstenfeld et al., 2003; Levin, 2002). The rise of social media has opened additional avenues for hate groups to profess extreme ideologies, champion their causes, recruit members, and spread hateful content. According to the Southern Poverty Law Center (SPLC), the number of active, offline hate groups has increased over the last few years (Beirich & Buchanan, 2018). Prior work investigating hate groups' online activities has primarily focused on examining individual websites run by recognized hate groups (Chau & Xu, 2007; Schafer, 2002; Zhou et al., 2005). However, more recent research finds that the web-based outposts of hate online do not operate in isolation: Nearly 72% of hate group websites contain links to other extremist blogs and sites that are primarily used to sell extremist products online (Schafer, 2002). Research on link sharing across extremist blogs has reported that information communities exist across various hate ideologies (Zhou et al., 2005). Even more concerning is that hate groups' online presence has progressed from being limited to a dedicated website (a single platform) to multiple social media platforms. The ecosystem of online hate movements is complex, involving thousands of online accounts on numerous social media.

Most of the chapters in this book focus on how casual, unaffiliated, or informally organized hate messages operate on particular sites (such as Stormfront.org; Törnberg & Törnberg, this volume) or hop from one social media site (where attacks are planned) to another (where attacks are executed; e.g., Rae et al., this volume; Stringhini & Blackburn, this volume). This chapter, instead, examines how existing, recognized hate groups that are rooted in offline organizations use social media, and what practices they

DOI: 10.4324/9781003472148-9

deploy to strategically intertwine social media, websites, blogs, and news media to spread their messages.

This chapter summarizes our research that investigated how extremist organizations exploit social media.[1] The approaches, methods, and results relied on research that scrutinized three months' of postings on the public Twitter and Facebook page profiles of 72 SPLC-designated U.S.-based hate groups, spanning five hate ideologies (e.g., white supremacy, anti-LGBTQ+) and five URL content types (e.g., information domains, recruitment websites). The research examined the strategies of framing and information sharing employed by hate groups based in the United States, both within and across online platforms such as Facebook and Twitter (now renamed "X"). The research uncovered the different approaches that hate groups take when utilizing different social media platforms. Collectively, these findings suggest that hate groups are tailoring their content and information-sharing practices to address certain differences in the relative diversity (or homogeneity) of the audiences on these platforms.

Inter-Platform Content Framing and Information Sharing by Online Hate Groups

The first set of research draws upon the scholarship of Social Movement Organizations (SMO; Zald & Ash, 1966). Although hate messaging online is often considered to reflect some kind of social movement (see the explanation in Burston, this volume), despite the parallels between hate groups and SMOs, research has not yet positioned hate group operations within the SMO perspective. Doing so, however, provides a useful approach, bringing to bear background on collective action framing and information sharing by SMOs. Our research addresses these research questions: (RQ1) How do hate groups frame content across platforms? (RQ2) How do hate groups share information across platforms? And (RQ3) how do the framing and information-sharing efforts differ across multiple ideologies of hate across platforms?

For instance, Facebook appeared to serve as a platform for radicalizing like-minded followers, while Twitter was employed for maintaining a positive self-image and a broader educational outreach to diverse audiences. A deeper analysis of the information-sharing network on Twitter revealed a higher proportion of news sources. Notably, some of these sources have been classified as mainstream with a right-leaning bias, according to fact-checking organizations. Given their mainstream status, these sources may be considered more suitable for a general audience compared to the extreme blogs or websites often associated with hate groups. In essence, hate groups appeared to be leveraging the broadcasting capabilities of both Facebook and Twitter while adapting their content framing and information-sharing strategies based on the diversity of their Twitter audience and the relative homogeneity of their Facebook following.

Hate Groups and Online Information Sharing

This research investigated hate group information-sharing activities across two popular social media platforms – Twitter and Facebook. The empirical study comprised five phases: (1) Developing a framing annotation scheme, (2) identifying and mapping hate groups and their ideologies across platforms, (3) identifying content framing across platforms, (4) analyzing URL domains shared across platforms, and (5) describing communication within disparate ideologies. The next sections describe how this work analyzes content framing by hate groups through the lens of social movement and collective action framing theories.

Hate Groups as Social Movement Organizations

Social Movement Organizations (SMOs) are purpose-driven organizations with societal reconstruction agendas (McCarthy & Moskalenko, 2003). An SMO is activated when changes in a society are misaligned with an organization's goals (Zald & Ash, 1966). Thus, in the case of hate groups, when society witnesses increased racial, sexual, or religious diversity, hate groups tend to be more active and aggressive in their efforts to target the respective marginalized communities or minorities (Zald & Ash, 1966). SMOs use social media for various purposes, such as knowledge sharing, recruitment, collective action, and political advocacy (Auger, 2013; Bozarth & Budak, 2017; Guo & Saxton, 2014; Obar et al., 2012). Hate groups, like any other SMO, are increasingly shifting their information dissemination operations to online communication channels and social media platforms (Donovan, 2019; Johnson et al., 2019; O'Callaghan et al., 2013).

Like other approaches to intergroup conflict, in the case of online extremism, participants in hate groups relate as "in-groups" – a population internal to the extremist social movement – and their targets as "out-groups" (Costello et al., 2019; Hewstone et al., 2002). Returning to the SMO perspective, organizations need to "frame" their communication to legitimatize their actions, inspire potential recruits, negotiate a shared understanding of the problematic societal condition that needs change, offer alternative arrangements to promote change, and finally, urge others to act so as to effect that change (Benford & Snow, 2000).

Collective Action Frames and Hate Group Communication

The SMO perspective is further informed by the collective action framing scholarship. Framing refers to portraying an issue from one particular perspective, emphasizing certain aspects while de-emphasizing competing perspectives, in order to influence people's interpretation of the issue (Boydstun et al., 2014; Entman, 1993; Goffman, 1974). One type of framing uses *collective action frames*, a widely used sociological approach that identifies framing approaches adopted by social movements, including *diagnostic* (which states the social movement's problem), *prognostic* (which offers a solution), and *motivational* (which serves as a call to action) *frames* (Benford & Snow, 2000; Snow & Benford, 1988).

Developing a Framing Annotation Scheme

The first research question aims to discover how hate groups utilize collective action frames (Snow & Benford, 1988) to *diagnose* the problems, offer *(prognostic) solutions*, and provide *motivations* for action. We employed a multistage annotation scheme development process (described in detail by Phadke & Mitra, 2020; see prior work by Phadke et al., 2018). Specifically, a small sample of the dataset of tweets generated by online hate groups was annotated through theory-guided inductive and deductive coding, which resulted in 23 coding categories spread across the three collective action frames. Through multiple rounds of coding and discussions, this framework was consolidated into 13 categories (see Table 9.1, with examples).

Identifying and Mapping Hate Groups and Their Ideologies across Platforms

This phase began by using the hate group list published by SPLC on their *Hate Map* web page (SPLC, 2019a), which enumerates the names of 367 hate groups (e.g., VDare, Patriot Front, Strormfront, Oath Keepers) along with their ideologies. We manually identified and verified the social media accounts of each. The majority of the hate groups had a public Facebook page as well as a Twitter handle – a total of 75 organizations representing 5 extremist ideologies with accounts. The official social media handles of other groups were not found on Facebook or Twitter. The research gathered public Twitter tweets and posts from the public Facebook profile pages of these accounts, between March 31, 2019, and July 1, 2019, accumulating three months of hate group activities. The dataset comprised 16,963 tweets and 14,642 Facebook messages across 72 accounts.

After consulting with an expert sociologist, we grouped some of the ideologies described by the SPLC (2019b) directory into five broader categories or groups based on the overlap in their beliefs: *White Supremacy, Religious Supremacy, anti-Muslim, anti-LGBT group*, and *anti-Immigration*.

How active were the 72 hate groups on Facebook and Twitter? Hate groups contributed significantly more tweets than Facebook posts, but hate group members produced significantly more Facebook *Likes* compared to Twitter followers' hearts postings. There was no significant difference between the two platforms in terms of the overall distribution of messages per organization, or the levels of posting activity within individual ideologies.

TABLE 9.1 Frame Annotation Scheme

Diagnostic

Oppression: In-group complains about being oppressed through violent or repressive action, infringement on their rights or resources, or through indictment or sanctions

Ex: "Forced to abandon biblical principles"

Failure: In-group assesses that the government, the system, or other agencies such as media have failed to protect them from the problems caused by the out-group

Ex: "Government placing Americans in danger"

Immorality: In-group indicates that the out-group demonstrates immorality though unethical, immoral, or uncivil behavior or values dissonance.

Ex: "Islam teaches and Muslims practice deception"

Inferiority: In-group believes that the out-group is inherently inferior to them based on the political influence, genetics, or the collective failure of the out-group

Ex: "Anti-border liberals are of inferior intellect than pro-enforcement Americans"

Prognostic

Violence: In-group promotes violent actions toward the out-group

Ex: "Choose to be a dangerous man for Christ, wear your cross-hat"

Hatred: In-group advocates' protests, criticism, or the show of disdain toward the out-group

Ex: "Don't take feminism or the women who support it seriously. She thinks being an obnoxious bitch with a chip on her shoulder is empowerment"

Discrimination: In-group promotes avoidance, segregation, or disassociation toward the out-group

Ex: "Separation of the races is the only perfect preventive of amalgamation"

Policy: In-group suggests formal or hypothetical legislation and promotes political party candidates or other legal measures that would negatively affect the out-group

Ex: "1. Mandatory E-Verify for all the workers hired, 2. No federal funding for jurisdictions/entities blocking ICE"

Membership: In-group demands active association, participation in events or funds toward solving the problem

Ex: "Join us at DC rally in support and solidarity"

Motivation

Fear: In-group emphasizes on severity and urgency of the problem by mentioning existential or infringement threats

Ex: " There is no way mumps is not being spread outside ICE facilities"

Efficacy: In-group emphasizes the effectiveness of the action or the solution proposed at the individual or organizational level

Ex: "Major pro-family victory!!! Washington MassResistance strategically helped to stop terrible comprehensive sex ed bill"

Moral: In-group discusses the moral responsibility of the audience for taking the action suggested

Ex: "Survival of people. That is the mission that matters the most"

Status: In-group discusses increased privilege, social class, or benefit from being associated with the in-group or by following the solution provided

Ex: "Our people are destined to have a prosperous future, but only by bearing fruits worthy of repentance"

RQ1: Identifying Content Framing across Platforms

In order to address the question of how hate groups frame content across platforms, sub-samples of the social media postings were annotated with respect to their collective action frames. The annotations applied to 1,440 Facebook posts and 1,440 tweets (approximately 10% of the total), comprising 20 randomly sampled messages from each of the 72 accounts in a procedure similar to that of Starbird (2017). The following sections summarize results by each of the three collective action frames.

How do Hate Groups Diagnose the Problem?

On Facebook, *oppression* and *failure* are more popularly used than they are in Twitter (*oppression*: 22% versus 14%; *failure*: 15% versus 8%). On the other hand, *immorality* is more commonly used on Twitter than Facebook (27% versus 19%). Immorality frames appeared to be used to educate the audience about the target groups' stereotypically negative qualities. Derogating the out-group via *immorality* frames may also help to reinforce the hate group's identity (McNamee et al., 2010).

What Prognostic do Hate Groups Offer?

Comments that advocated for *hatred*, *violence*, or *discrimination* are more extreme, and use extreme language, and as a result such comments are more likely to be removed from the platform by content moderators. For that reason, it was not surprising that on both Facebook and Twitter, *hatred*, *violence*, and *discrimination* subframes were relatively less common. *Policy* frames were more commonly used across Twitter than in Facebook (25% versus 17%). Policy-related comments ranged from demanding a general political action from the President, to signing specific petitions. *Membership* messages, however, involve calls for direct association with the in-group. Facebook had relatively more *membership* calls compared to Twitter (29% versus 14%), asking the audience to join events, meetings, and web conferences organized by the group.

How do Hate Groups Motivate their Audience?

Fear was the most prominent motivator found on Facebook (27%), followed by *status enhancement* (11%). *Fear* appeals describing existential threats were commonly used to motivate like-minded audiences (McNamee et al., 2010). *Fear* provides a negative incentive to follow the solution, whereas *moral*, *status enhancement*, and *efficacy* offer positive motivation. Particularly, messages with *status enhancement* and *efficacy* attempt to maintain a positive self-image of the in-group. On Twitter, more messages contained the *status enhancement* category compared to Facebook. Further, other positive motivators (*efficacy* and *moral*) were also more frequent on Twitter compared to Facebook. Hate groups often strategically construct messages with self-valorizing views in order to strengthen their group identity (Duffy, 2003).

RQ2: Analyzing Information Sharing across Platforms

In order to address the second research question, analysis involved examining the nature of the URL links that appeared in the social media messages associated with the hate groups. The objective was to categorize the URLs into different types of content they usually host, which can indicate which information gets shared across platforms. After excluding Facebook posts and Tweets that contained links to other posts and tweets within the same platform, 12,290 links from Twitter and 11,926 links from Facebook reflected 1,021 distinct information types. In order to identify the type of information shared, we conducted inductive qualitative content analysis to categorize the nature of each URL, based on what content the websites primarily hosted and the descriptions that they provided (i.e., the "About Us" or equivalent page of each website). From these numerous content domains, further analysis organized them into five more meaningful categories: *streaming* (audio/video streaming, podcasts, radio shows), *promotion* (petition sign-ups, membership forms, merchandise, and links to various social networks), *information* (issue-specific news, information watchdogs, reports, and websites of concerned organizations), *opinion* (commentaries, opinion pieces, and personal blogs), and *news* (online newspapers and general news forums).

The findings show that sharing links in their social media postings provides a sizable opportunity for hate groups to redirect their followers toward their own websites and other extremist blogs. The articles to which links pointed often contained more toxic language and extremist propaganda than is typically presented on content-moderated mainstream social media.

Almost 50% of the links shared on Twitter led to general *news,* whereas less than 20% of Facebook links did. Instead, Facebook posts hosted more links to focused *information* websites (37%) and blogs (30%). Often, these domains hosted extreme views. For example, Facebook's most frequently linked domain, drrichswier.com, is a conservative blog citing Barry Goldwater, saying "extremism in the defense of liberty is no vice and moderation in the pursuit of justice is no virtue." Similarly, the next most popular links on Facebook pointed to theworldview.com and standinthegapradio.com, which host radio and talk shows with extremist attitudes. There were many references to right-biased *news* domains (according to mediabiasfactcheck.com). For example, breitbart.com and frontpagemag.com are extreme right biased, and foxnews.com is far-right biased. Almost 10% of Facebook links fell under the *promotion* category, hosting links to other social media sites, petitions, and membership forums, and promoting online merchandise. Links to various *streaming* websites, although present, were less popular in both Twitter and Facebook.

RQ3: How Framing and Information-Sharing Differ across Ideologies and Platforms

Investigating the nuances of framing and URL-sharing within individual ideologies took into consideration the Facebook and Twitter frames annotations. Combined with the types of information links, the research developed "domain networks": Graphs representing URL content domains co-shared within and across platforms. A domain network graph depicts URL domains where every domain constitutes a network node, connected to other nodes based on some predetermined criteria, such as number of common users and frequency of sharing. Previous research employing domain network graphs depicted the ecosystem of alternative news domains on Twitter (Starbird, 2017). Our research connected two domains (i.e., nodes in a graph) if they were shared by a hate group account, with edge weights representing the number of accounts that shared them.[2] Visualizations of domain co-sharing (i.e., shared only on Twitter, only on Facebook, or shared on both platforms) by the various ideologies – *White Supremacy, anti-Muslim, Religious Supremacy, anti-LGBT*, and *anti-Immigration* – appear in Phadke and Mitra (2020), with specific examples illustrating how the processes differed between every ideology. The findings regarding collective action *content framing* and website content/*information sharing* for two of those five ideologies – *White Supremacy* and *anti-LBGT* – follow.

White Supremacy

Content Framing: On both Facebook and Twitter, White Supremacy groups frequently discussed racial and political issues. However, their diagnostic and prognostic discussions varied. On Facebook, they complained how white culture is being oppressed (17.8%), for example, "If White Genocide is an unfounded conspiracy, why is it so heavily censored and suppressed?" On Twitter, messages primarily described how people of other races are immoral (17.64%) and inferior (16.2%), for example, "by debasing themselves they are acting entirely within their class interest retaining the very privilege they are criticizing." Messages advocating *discrimination* (4%), *hatred* (2%), and *violence* (2%) appeared only on Facebook, for example, "Say 'no' to their way of dress, 'no' to their entertainment, 'no' to their degenerate culture. To love all equally is not to love at all." Concerning motivational categories, Facebook had more *fear* appeals (14%), for example, "When America is no more, future generations are going to want to know who murdered our country," while Twitter contained more *status enhancement* (21.5%), for example, "Review: On Edward Dutton's RACE DIFFERENCES IN ETH-NOCENTRISM – And Why White Ethnocentrism Will Return."

Information Sharing: A mix of *news* sources, from alternative (rt.com, breitbart.com) to mainstream (nytimes.com), was prominently shared on Twitter (57%), whereas on Facebook there were more links to *promotion* domains (35%), such as those offering subscriptions to content creators' creation. Among these, Patreon.com and Subscriberstar.com are known to house extreme right-wing activists (Coulter, 2018). Other promotion domains include foreign and U.S. websites that host extremist books and literature (e.g., logik.se, kirkusreviews.com) and talk shows (thepoliticalcesspool.org). There were also links pointing to other social media platforms (gab, telegram, bitchute) emanating across both Twitter and Facebook. In the light of recent censorship of white nationalism on Facebook (Facebook, 2019), white supremacy hate groups seem to adapt by moving their online operations to alternative platforms that champion free speech and little content moderation (see also Walther, this volume). Figure 9.1 portrays information shared within and across both platforms.

Anti-LGBT

Content Framing: On both Facebook and Twitter, anti-LGBT groups discussed sexual and gender identity the most. However, there appeared relatively more discussions focused on the *immorality* of LGBT life on Twitter

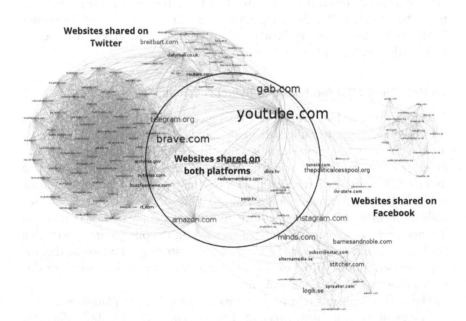

FIGURE 9.1   Information-Sharing Network by White Supremacy Groups

(34%). Facebook postings discussed how the LGBT agenda oppresses peo-ple with traditional values (23%), for example, "This legislation is specifi-cally designed to place 'sexual liberty' above 'Religious Liberty' and our First Amendment civil rights!" Similarly, there are more calls for *membership* on Facebook (37%) to join anti-LGBT groups in their rallies and seminars: "Come and meet like-minded people that are concerned about our coun-try. We want to restore honor, respect, civility, and hope for our children's future." Twitter hosted more demands for changes in *policy* through general social action (24%), for example, "The work we have to do is clear. We must train people to make them active in establishing a godly society, and that takes work, sweat, sacrifice." Twitter messages also promoted the *efficacy* (18%) of anti-LGBT policies and heightened social *status* (19%) achieved by following them: "Texas MassResistance pressure causes pro-LGBT church to cancel Drag Queen reading in public library. Antifa backs down! Another big win!" Facebook, however, mostly contained messages motivating by *fear*, warning about the effects of LGBT lifestyle on child development, religious liberty, and society (29%), for example, "If the 'Equality Act' becomes law, women and girls would instantly forfeit equality rights and opportunities gained over decades."

Information Sharing: Similar to other hate ideologies, anti-LGBT accounts also shared more *news* on Twitter (54%) compared to Facebook (34%). However, Facebook contained more links to *opinion* blogs (12%) and *informational* forums (26%) (e.g., resources for parenting such as fatherly.com, dadsguidetowdw.com, childdevelopmentinfo.com) compared to Twitter. Like the Religious Supremacy accounts, links to several websites in the *promotion* category host petitions (e.g., endbirthdayabortion.com, focusonthefamily.com).

Do Hate Groups Use Facebook and Twitter Differently?

It does appear that hate groups used the two platforms differently. Generally, they used Facebook to radicalize an already like-minded audience and used Twitter to educate a more ideologically diverse set of followers. On Face-book, *fear* was prominent as a motivating agent, a strategy that is common among hate groups to strategically recruit like-minded people (McNamee et al., 2010). Further, hate groups claimed to be oppressed, and they issued calls for *membership*, at a higher rate on Facebook compared to Twitter. On Twitter, hate groups' messages often focused on the out-groups, portraying them as *immoral* or *inferior*. This is a common strategy to imbue deliberate, negative perceptions of the out-group, regardless of how inaccurate or dis-torted those are (McNamee et al., 2010).

The analyses suggest that hate groups use social media platforms to pur-sue different goals in furtherance of their extremist agenda: Radicalization/recruitment and education/image control. Radicalization is associated with beliefs like being oppressed, suffering from failure of the system, or fear of extinction (McCauley & Moskalenko, 2008; see also Kruglanski et al., 2014). This rhetoric of *oppression-failure-fear* appeared to be more frequent on Facebook than on Twitter. Moreover, Facebook had more calls for *membership* and links to personal mailing lists and recruitment forums. The Facebook audience of hate group members or prospective members might be more susceptible to extremist radicalization and successful recruitment, compared to Twitter. Hate groups used Twitter predominantly to share news from various news media. Hate groups spread negative news that addressed (educated) the problems associated with the out-groups and that stressed positive aspects (image) of themselves (Douglas, 2007; Gerstenfeld et al., 2003; McNamee et al., 2010). They dehumanized out-groups by describing them as inferior or immoral, while presenting themselves with a positive image through *status enhancement* and effectiveness (*efficacy*) of their proposed solutions (e.g., "doing the god's work in fighting the LGBT mafia").

Characterizing Roles and News Sources in Online Extremist Movements

In addition to the extremist content stemming from the social media accounts of established extremist organizations, the landscape of online hate extends far beyond these sources. The participatory nature of social media encourages users to contribute to the dissemination of extremist information through simple actions such as liking and sharing content. Moreover, the nature of participation in online movements could be organic, with the users being unaware of the fact that they may be advancing an extremist movement. Therefore, to gain a deeper understanding of the participatory information-sharing dynamics within online extremist movements, research has endeavored to characterize various social roles that emerge within Facebook groups that espouse extremist ideologies, helping to understand the ecosystem of online hate.

A Facebook group is created by a number of Facebook users who establish a closed interaction space – that is, one that can be made available to specific members that the organizers invite and/or approve but is unavailable to the Facebook public (Facebook, 2023). According to the Southern Poverty Law Center, Facebook groups serve as the primary avenue for extremists to recruit new members and spread extremist propaganda (Hatewatch Staff, 2020). By sharing links from the websites of known extremist organizations, extremist groups and extremist accounts become participants in the extremist ecosystem on Facebook and operate as key players in sustaining and growing extremist movements.

Yet, not all groups and participating members are the same. In order to develop a better-informed assessment of the contributions they make to hate in social media, research examined how U.S.-based extremist accounts played different social roles in advancing extremist movements online. The study involved records from 4,876 extremist accounts that shared links from 289 SPLC-designated extremist groups, data that were obtained using Facebook's CrowdTangle API. Our study labels Facebook groups and pages as extremist accounts based on the general content shared by such groups and accounts. Further, the research described deduces roles played by Facebook groups and pages, and the roles' dynamics and influence, to understand the online participatory ecosystem of hate.

Participatory Activism and Extremist Movements

Previous research presents opposing perspectives on the effectiveness and the legitimacy of using the web and social media to encourage participation in social movements and activities. The terms "clicktivism" and "slacktivism" refer to users' superficial engagement in political action through low-cost activities such as liking or sharing the content in order to raise awareness (Rotman et al., 2011; Vromen, 2017). Writers on popular press comment that "clicktivism" or "slacktivism" is largely unproductive and ephemeral – an ideal type of activism for a lazy generation (Gladwell, 2010; Morozov, 2009; Wiebe et al., 2005). However, communication and political science scholars argue that such low-cost and low-risk participation is not only widespread but is also becoming a legitimate channel for political activism (Halupka, 2018). Specifically, Obar et al. (2012) interviewed advocacy groups and found that all the groups viewed online participation as an effective tool for civic engagement and collective action.

Researchers have mostly investigated participatory activism in the context of positive social change (see, e.g., Arda, 2015; Keller, 2012; Núñez Puente et al., 2017; Rahimi, 2016), empowering populations in social justice causes. However, antisocial movements, for example those advocating for terrorism and extremism, can also benefit from similar practices. Researchers have proposed a variety of theoretical roles that members may adopt in social movements (e.g., Edwards & McCarthy, 2004; McCarthy & Zald, 1977; Owen, 2019; Turner, 1969; Wahlström et al., 2018). What are the different roles played by extremist accounts in extremist social movements? How stable or transitory are these roles? And how influential are these roles in spreading mis- and disinformation? The research specifically focused on U.S. domestic extremism, such as *White Supremacy* and *anti-LGBT* movements (analyzed above) to identify a variety of roles through the lens of social movement theories.

Extremism, Social Movements, and Roles

Social movements are collective efforts to bring about a specific goal or ideology, and they emerge when the constitution and function of society are misaligned with the movement's goals (McCarthy & Zald, 2003). By this logic, extremist movements such as white supremacy become more active and aggressive when there is an increased racial diversity in the society (Zald & Ash, 1966).

It is difficult to adopt directly the theoretical taxonomies of roles in the literature cited above to the context of online extremist movements, as the roles are based on physical social movement participation and commitment (Owen, 2019; Rodan & Mummery, 2017; Wahlström et al., 2018), unlike online participation. Consequently, drawing on taxonomies and theories of social movement participation, this research derived a new taxonomy of roles for the online setting: *Solicitors, Educators, Flamers, Motivators*, and *Sympathizers*. Before discussing the constellations of behaviors that typify each role, the next paragraph summarizes the processes used to identify these roles. In order to identify roles in the extremist movements, the research drew on theories in social movement participation, which suggested three basic dimensions to investigate: *Drives for participation, engagement in the movement*, and *strategies of mobilization*. These three dimensions, and the computational features derived from them, formed the crux of the methodology for identifying roles in the extremist movements. Phadke and Mitra (2021) provide succinct literature and conceptual reviews of the three dimensions and related models. The first two columns in Table 9.2 summarize several relevant theoretical models, with central citations in the third column, and associated behaviors in the fourth column. The next step was to identify how occupants of these roles disseminate different types of information, such as extremist content, fake news, biased news, and conspiracies.

The analysis of roles involved *extremist accounts* – public Facebook pages and Facebook groups that share links pointing to extremist websites. The analyses also involved verifying the extremist websites; there were 289 websites hosted by extremist groups as denoted by the SPLC. For each website, they also note the extremist domain ideology type, such as *anti-Immigration, Religious Supremacy, anti-Muslim, White Supremacy*, and *anti-LGBTQ ideologies*. Analyses also involved parsing the sample of accounts into those that shared a significant number of links over time, and then content analyzing the posts to classify them as extremist, biased, fake news, or conspiracy-oriented. The sample contained 450,000 posts, as generated by 71,430 unique Facebook pages or group accounts. Further limiting the sample to those accounts that shared at least ten messages with links to an extremist website domain, the final number was 4,876 Facebook pages/groups (see Table 9.3 for descriptive statistics).

Finally, the data were reviewed for interpretive analysis by seven social psychology and social movement experts not related to the project. These experts labeled the roles and their descriptions. The author and the experts worked together to select the most descriptive label for every cluster of roles

TABLE 9.2 Features Used to Identify Roles in Online Extremist Movements on Facebook

Characteristics of Participation	Theoretical Models	References	Behavior	Operationalization
Drives for participation	Expectancy-value	Klandermans, 1984; Marx & Wood, 1975; Oberschall, 1973	Risk	% LIWC risk words (e.g., caution, crisis, failure)
			Reward	% LIWC reward words (e.g., benefit, bonus, award)
	Social psychology	Van Stekelenburg & Klandermans, 2013b Gamson, 1992; 22	Injustice	% MFD fairness words (e.g., parity, fair, justice)
			Achievement	% LIWC achievement words (e.g., accomplish, ability, attain)
		Simon & Klandermans, 2001	Group Identity	% LIWC we words (e.g., we, ours, us)
		Van Stekelenburg & Klandermans, 2017	Anger	% LIWC anger words (e.g., resent, argue, angry)
Engagement in the movement	Degrees of participation	McCarthy & Zald, 1977	% links from extremist domains	Ratio of links from extremist domains to total link posts
	Degrees of participation	McCarthy & Zald, 1977	Likes	Ratio of links from extremist domains to total link posts
	(popularity)		Shares	Proportion of likes on extremist links to likes on the rest of the link posts
			Comments	Proportion of comments on extremist links to comments on the rest of the link posts
	Trends in participation	Corrigall-Brown, 2011	Trend	Trend line fitted on the number of extremist links posts per month
Strategies of mobilization	Opinions	Valenzuela, 2013	Expressions of opinions	Proportion of extremist link posts containing opinion patterns; based on % LIWC thinking, perception, expression words
	Solicitation	Bromley & Shupe, 1980; McCarthy & Zald, 1977	Expressions of solicitation	Proportion of extremist link posts containing solicitation patterns (donations, invitations, policy advocacy words, based on % LIWC social and affiliation words)

TABLE 9.3 Descriptive Statistics for the 4,876 Extremist Accounts in the Dataset

Statistics (Per Account)	Min	Max	M	SD
Posts	71	932K	7,067	30,574
Link posts	23	78,571	1,614	3,915
Extremist link posts Engagement	10	5,129	207	528
Page likes	206	1.8 M	7,241	36,576
Group members	35	2.2 M	2,827	13,603

TABLE 9.4 Roles and the Corresponding Percent of Extremist Accounts in the Dataset

Role	% Frequency	Example Texts Used by the Accounts While Sharing Links from Extremist Websites
Solicitors	5.2%	"Sign here to demand her {Rep. Maxine Waters} immediate resignation" "Join us in signing thank you card for President Trump"
Educators	10.6	"Escaping from motherhood: how it destroys society" "We believe that we have the duty to instruct people in the truth of Tradition. Even if it destroys their party"
Flamers	18.4	"Genuine Christians know that homosexuality is an abomination before GOD!" "MURDERED in cold blood. Emergency: Gunfire, bodies, and BLM murderers"
Motivators	29.4	"Senator Dan Halls stands with us in a passionate commitment to strengthening religious freedom" "FREE SPEECH WINS!!! Supreme court rules pregnancy centers can't be forced to advertise abortion"
Sympathizers	36.4	"White South Africans petition Trump to allow them to migrate to the US" "A jihadi cult member running for Congress as Democrat from Alaska"

and associated behaviors. Table 9.4 presents the five roles played by extremist accounts and their typical behaviors.

Solicitors

These are the accounts that solicit participation from their readers for signing petitions, attending rallies, etc. On average, around 20% of their links came from extremist domains, and users posted extremist content fairly consistently over time. These accounts frequently used group identity language such as "we," "our," and "us," compared to other roles. One expert analyst mentioned: "These groups appear to be soliciting action for their hate. To some extent, they seem pretty keen on motivating action against the groups they hate."

Educators

Educators have a distinctively high amount of extremist content in their link sharing. On an average, 50% of their links came from extremist domains. Additionally, the extremist links posts received more likes and comments compared to other material on these pages/groups. They posted the extremist content with consistently high rates over time. According to one expert analyst, "they seem to take effort to make logical arguments. They are not necessarily showing anger toward other groups but are instead more focused on highlighting their own group's worth logically/analytically."

Flamers

These accounts tended to spew toxic and inflammatory content. Around 5% of their links belonged to extremist web domains, and the messages on the links and the link text itself often contained language suggesting anger and injustice. The extremist links posted on these accounts got a higher number of shares compared to the rest of the content. Immediately after looking through the posts, one evaluator commented, "These are clearly very strong, divisive and toxic posts."

Motivators

Around 7% of the links by motivators were from extremist web domains. The expert analysts pointed out that motivators used exceptionally positive language. While posting extremist content, they emphasized the achievements and rewards associated with extremist activities and exhibited the highest proportions of opinions. Experts noted that these accounts engaged in policy activism focusing on policies protecting and defending cultural and moral values. Experts also mentioned, "It almost looks like they are celebrating the in-group (people and organization involved in the extremist movement) and the sensationalized news about the in-group."

Sympathizers

These accounts posted extremist content links at the lowest rates (2% of their Facebook link posts) and sporadically over time. They also showed low engagement in terms of likes, shares, and comments on the extremist link posts. According to the experts, these groups were on the fringe of extremist ideology and might have been only slightly interested in extremist causes. One expert described sympathizers by saying, "They look more like general conservative interest groups."

Relations and Information-Sharing Influence among Roles

Although they tend to exhibit certain distinct clusters of activities and functions within the online presence of their respective hate groups, these roles are not isolated from each other. Indeed, additional modeling revealed how influential the different roles are in spreading extremist content, fake news, biased news, and conspiracy sources. *Influence* in this case refers to a measurable probability that a link posting by an occupant of one role affects a link posting by members of other roles in the future. An example of how different roles behave and influence one another appears in the case of an anti-immigration organization's effort to affect regional legal matters.

On June 10, 2018, ALIPAC – an anti-immigration political action organization (Shanmugasundaram, 2018) – put out a call for action to stop the amnesty deal for immigrants in California. This included calls for donations and participation to help support ALIPAC's operational costs. A link pointing to this call for action was posted on Facebook on the same day at 9:59 PM by a verified page managed by the president of ALIPAC. This Facebook page was also known for posting fake news from websites hosting plagiarized content (Kaplan, 2018). The analysis suggests that the poster is a *solicitor*. Three minutes after the initial post by page 1, another Facebook page – identified as *flamer* – posted the same link. Following the post by page 2, a *sympathizer* page (fringe supporter of the extremist content) as well as another recruiter page also posted the same link. Following these four link posts, another 32 pages posted the same link containing the anti-immigration group's call for action over the next three days.

The degree of cross-role influence can be seen against the baseline rates at which different roles tend to generate link postings for each type of information. Table 9.5 summarizes these base rates. Looking at the number of events, *sympathizers* made up the largest percent of link-posting events of all types of sources. This is not surprising, given that 36.4% of the accounts were *sympathizers*. Along the same lines, *solicitors* (who actively solicit participation by posting extremist links) and *educators* (who share the largest proportion of extremist links) contributed to a high percent of posting extremist links. Interestingly, *flamers* (accounts that often post inflammatory and violent content) were also among the highest in posting links from the fake news sources. Moreover, *motivators* (who focus on the efficacy of policy changes and use opinionated language) generated 23% of the biased

TABLE 9.5 Link Posting Activities by Various Roles

Source Type	#Domains Labeled	#Labeled domains Present in T1	#Events (Link Posts)	% Link Posts Made By				
				Solicitors	Educators	Flamers	Motivators	Sympathizers
Extremist	289	231	758	12%	28	9	5	44
Biased	133	94	1279	11	9	19	23	36
Fake	304	107	380	9	20	23	13	34
Conspiracy	154	68	936	20	20	10	21	29

Note: Example – *solicitors* contribute to 12% of the link posts from the extremist domains.

news postings. *Educators, solicitors,* and *motivators* all posted links from conspiracy sources with similar rates, while *flamers* posted the fewest and *sympathizers* the most.

Analysis of the relative influence attributed to posts from these different role occupants showed that some roles were more influential than others. Of the 289 extremist website domains that verifiably were linked by Facebook posts, *solicitors* and *educators* posted the largest proportion of links. However, solicitors and educators also generated significant influence on other roles, triggering the spread of extremist content by others. Among other roles, *flamers* generated greater influence than motivators and sympathizers. Overall, *solicitors, educators,* and *flamers* were the most influential in spreading links from extremist sources.

Types of News Sources Shared among Roles

That said, there were differences between roles in terms of the kind of linked information each role was more or less likely to share and the influence that sharing those information types had on occupants of other roles. A more fine-grained picture of information-sharing and influence emerges when different kinds of news sources are examined distinctly from one another. Additional analyses drew on the analytic typology provided by the Rand Corporation's "OpenSources" classifications,[3] and evaluations of particular news sites by mediabiasfactcheck.org, which describe the particular kinds of information distortions – *biased, fake,* and *conspiratorial* – associated with specific news sources.

Biased Sources

Biased news sources not only hold a very specific point of view but also present propaganda, decontextualizing information, and opinions as though they are facts. For example, 100percentfedup.com presents stories with extreme right-wing bias, and dailywire.com is strongly biased toward conservative causes and/or political affiliation. Overall, the influence of all roles was relatively lower when sharing links from *biased* sources. However, in comparison to other roles, *motivators* were more influential in triggering other roles to share information from biased sources.

Fake News Sources

Fake news sources fabricate information or grossly distort actual news reports. *Flamers* frequently posted links that were flagged as fake/misinformation by Facebook fact checkers, possibly with the intention of spreading hate and outrage. Both *educators* and *flamers* had greater influence on *solicitors* in spreading links from fake news sources than the other three roles. However, fake news sources had the lowest number of links and link posting events among all source types.

Conspiratorial Sources

Sympathizers were most influenced by conspiracy information from *solicitors* and *educators*, while *flamers* were susceptible to conspiratorial information sharing by *motivators*.

Discussion and Implications

For those who object to and detest online hate and extremism, it can be easy to view their perpetrators monolithically. Through their own in-group/out-group perspective, there is an *us* and a *them*, and *in-group members may* consider *them* to be undifferentiated "bad actors," bigots, or as some other category among whom there is no need to see any difference in who they are or what they do. This is not to argue that their objectives and behaviors are not objectionable or repugnant. In order to advance our understanding of how online hate operates, and the social processes that facilitate its propagation, it is important to recognize that participants in these online movements do different things by different means and that these differences are not random but rather are systematic social processes, involving collective action frames (diagnostic, prognostic, motivational), content domains (streaming, promotion, information, opinion, news), roles (solicitor, educator, flamer, motivator, sympathizer), information sharing (such as biased, fake, or conspiratorial sources), and interactions among all of these.

Inter-Platform Content Framing and Information Sharing

Understanding the patterns of the extremist dark side of social media in general leads to meaningful inferences about antisocial behavior, some of which may lead to offline violence (The Telegraph, 2015). Yet, failing to discriminate between different social media platforms is to ignore how hate groups envision and exploit them.

Frames, Content Domains, Roles, and New Sources

The first part of this chapter summarizes analyses applying collective action frames and shared links. By annotating the collective action frames embedded in Tweets and Facebook posts, as well as the links from these messages to other sites and services, research can refine the theoretical understanding of the hate groups' actions online. Scholars studying collective action framing state that messages rich with frames have a strong mobilizing potential (Snow & Benford, 1988). Such messages combined with information from various biased news sources, informational guides, and blogs can make for influential narratives of online hate.

The second part of the research summarizes our research on the identification of five functional roles (*educators, solicitors, flamers, motivators, and sympathizers*) in online extremist movements, and the differences between these roles in their influence in spreading links from four types of news sources (*extremist, biased news, fake news,* and *conspiracy*). As part of a long-standing approach to social movements of many kinds, scholars have connected the advancement of movements to the successful distribution of resources through its participants (McCarthy & Zald, 1977). Similarly, the operators of extremist accounts, enacting various roles, use social media to distribute information resources. For example, *educators* and *solicitors* dedicate a large proportion of their Facebook activity to distributing extremist content for educating and soliciting the readers into extremist movements. They also influence other roles in spreading information from extremist websites. By disseminating information through their Facebook accounts, attempting to educate readers about their agenda, and soliciting funds and participation in the movements, *educators* and *solicitors* create human and material resources (see McCarthy & Zald, 1977). By prominently sharing misinformation and using toxic language, *flamers* arouse emotional resources that create opportunities for public outrage and, eventually, collective action (Van Stekelenburg & Klandermans, 2017) to advance the hateful agendas of their extremist movements. This distributed system of online information mobilization – the distribution of various information resources through various roles online – can be compared to the process of participatory activism (Krona, 2019).

Theoretical Implications: Parallels between Theoretical and Online Roles

Some of the roles uncovered in this research correspond to the categories of participants identified in theoretical analyses of physical protest events and social movements, with some important exceptions. For example, the *educators* – accounts that primarily focus on distributing links from extremist domains – seem to correspond to *constituents*, as described by McCarthy and Zald (1977); constituents are primary distributors of resources. Similarly, *solicitors* – who actively solicit participation via donations and gatherings – correspond to *beneficiary constituents* (McCarthy & Zald, 1977) who stand to gain from the success, funds, and connections emerging from the movement. The *sympathizers'* category may be similar to *bystanders* – a group of third-party participants, as defined by Turner (1969) – who acknowledge grievances related to the issues of social movement and take a sympathetic stand. Two of the roles discovered to exist in online hate, however, do not resemble any of the theoretically described categories of prior, offline protests and movements. The *motivator* role seems specifically suited to the online setting, relaying positive news and successes related to extremist causes. *Flamers* also do not correspond to prior theoretical roles. The emergence of these new roles that characterize online participation in extremist social movements extends previous theories to incorporate the relatively novel social processes embedded in and facilitated by social media.

Practical Implications: Interventions for Online Extremism Engagement

The research reported here can also inform the design of interventions for countering extremism. Our results suggest that while account roles core to the extremist movements – *educators* and *solicitors* – tend to retain their roles, others are more likely to transition to different roles. For example, *flamers* and *motivators* become *sympathizers* with high probability. Flamers, motivators, and sympathizers also show more sporadic engagement with sharing extremist links compared to the educators and solicitors. A study by Siegel and Badaan (2020) revealed that targeted interventions against hate speech, such as sanctions on hateful messages, lead users to tweet less hateful content, especially if the individuals are less engaged with the hate speech in the first place. On the other hand, accounts that frequently see or produce hostile language are less likely to get deterred by sanctions and may even express backlash. Other researchers report that rather than conforming to the community norms upon receiving sanctions, the producers of hostile content are more likely to move to other platforms (Newell et al., 2016; see also Walther, this volume) or find creative ways of continuing their hate speech (Chancellor et al., 2016). Considering this, our results suggest that flamers, motivators, and sympathizers – accounts infrequently exposed to extremist content – might benefit most from targeted interventions designed to counter extremism. On the contrary, educators and solicitors may retaliate or relocate to alternate platforms in response to an intervention.

Limitations

This research has some limitations that are important to acknowledge. First, the dataset contained only U.S.-based extremist websites, most of which hold a far-right political ideology. This skew may not represent the political scenarios of other countries (e.g., Counter Extremism Project, 2020; Jungkunz, 2019). Second, it compiled extremist accounts based on the number of unique links they shared from known SPLC-designated extremist websites. While this is a common methodological choice made while choosing users/ accounts for studying social media activity, there are reasonable alternatives. Extremist accounts can be selected on the basis of the topics discussed in the posts or on other criteria. Third, observations about the influence of various roles in spreading information on Facebook were based on the posting of links to other websites. This approach does not account for other modes of information sharing, such as images, memes, screenshots, videos, and other forms, and how those might affect role dynamics.

Future Directions

Despite these limitations, this research reveals the information ecosystem of extremist movements among Facebook and Twitter in the first part of this chapter, and on Facebook in the second part. Indeed, extremist movements leverage different social media platforms toward different goals, and it is hoped that future research may extend the methods and findings described herein to extremist movements on other platforms or even across platforms. Future research using cross-platform studies of both content and information – such as the work reviewed in this chapter – may provide insights for building automated or semiautomated tools to detect potentially mobilizing hate narratives online.

Conclusion

The social processes associated with participatory activism seem to be advancing extremist movements through various collective action frames, website content types, account roles, and types of information shared. The existence of roles and the variegated patterns of influence they exert clearly demonstrates that there is a social order to online hate, involving a variety of social processes. Different kinds of actors do not draw in an unintentional manner from some undifferentiated black box of hate messages. They manifest social goals and objectives through a variety of social activities. Their aims, at least in the short run, have less to do with accomplishing real-world action but, rather, to educate, motivate, participate, and orchestrate the evolution of their social movement itself. That is, their efforts are both manifestations of, and efforts directed toward, the social processes that enable the expression and propagation of online hate.

Notes

1 This chapter integrates three related publications: Phadke and Mitra (2020, 2021) and Phadke et al. (2018), which provide extensive analytical and methodological details.
2 Removed from further analysis were edges with weights less than 2 and nodes that were shared fewer than five times or were connected with less than two other nodes.
3 https://www.rand.org/research/projects/truth-decay/fighting-disinformation/search/items/opensources.html

References

Arda, B. (2015). The construction of a new sociality through social media: The case of the Gezi uprising in Turkey. *Conjunctions: Transdisciplinary Journal of Cultural Participation*, 2(1), 72–99. https://doi.org/10.7146/tjcp.v2i1.22271

Auger, G. A. (2013). Fostering democracy through social media: Evaluating diametrically opposed nonprofit advocacy organizations' use of Facebook, Twitter, and YouTube. *Public Relations Review*, 39(4), 369–376. https://doi.org/10.1016/j.pubrev.2013.07.013

Beirich, H., & Buchanan, S. (2018). *2017: The year in hate and extremism*. Technical Report. Southern Poverty Law Center. https://www.splcenter.org/fighting-hate/intelligence-report/issues/2017-spring-year-hate-extremism

Benford, R. D., & Snow, D. A. (2000). Framing processes and social movements: An overview and assessment. *Annual Review of Sociology*, 26(1), 611–639. https://doi.org/10.1146/annurev.soc.26.1.611

Boydstun, A. E., Card, D., Gross, J. H., Resnik, P., & Smith, N. A. (2014, August). *Tracking the development of media frames within and across policy issues*. American Society for Public Administration Annual Meeting.

Bozarth, L., & Budak, C. (2017). *Social movement organizations in online movements*. https://papers.ssrn.com/sol3/papers.cfm?abstract_id=3068546

Bromley, D. G, & Shupe Jr., A.D. (1980). Financing the new religions: A resource mobilization approach. *Journal for the Scientific Study of Religion*, 19(3), 227–239.

Burston, A. (Chapter 2 this volume). Digitally mediated spillover as a catalyst of radicalization: How digital hate movements shape conservative youth activism.

Chancellor, S., Pater, J. A., Clear, T., Gilbert, E., & De Choudhury, M. (2016, February). #thyghgapp: Instagram content moderation and lexical variation in pro-eating disorder communities. In *Proceedings of the 19th ACM conference on computer-supported cooperative work & social computing* (pp. 1201–1213). ACM. https://doi.org/10.1145/2818048.2819963

Chau, M., & Xu, J. (2007). Mining communities and their relationships in blogs: A study of online hate groups. *International Journal of Human-Computer Studies*, 65(1), 57–70. https://doi.org/10.1016/j.ijhcs.2006.08.009

Corrigall-Brown, C. (2011). *Patterns of protest: Trajectories of participation in social movements*. Stanford University Press.

Costello, M., Hawdon, J., Bernatzky, C., & Mendes, K. (2019). Social group identity and perceptions of online hate. *Sociological Inquiry*, 89(3), 427–452. https://doi.org/10.1111/soin.12274

Coulter, M. (2018, December). PayPal shuts Russian crowdfunder's account after alt-right influx. *Financial Times*. Retrieved September 13, 2019, from https://www.ft.com/content/7c4285b2-fe2f-11e8-ac00-57a2a826423e

Counter Extremism Project. (2020). *Germany: Extremism & counter-extremism*. Counter Extremism Project. Retrieved January 14, 2021, from https://www.counterextremism.com/countries/germany

Donovan, J. (2019, March 17). Extremists understand what tech platforms have built. *The Atlantic*. Retrieved September 11, 2019, from https://www.theatlantic.com/ideas/archive/2019/03/extremists-understand-what-tech-latforms-have-built/585136/

Douglas, K. M. (2007). Psychology, discrimination, and hate groups online. In A. Joinson, K. McKenna, T. Postmes, & U.-D. Reips (Eds.), *The Oxford handbook of internet psychology* (pp. 155–163). Oxford University Press.

Duffy, M. E. (2003). Web of hate: A fantasy theme analysis of the rhetorical vision of hate groups online. *Journal of Communication Inquiry*, 27(3), 291–312. https://doi.org/10.1177/0196859903252850

Edwards, B., & McCarthy, J. D. (2004). Resources and social movement mobilization. In D. A. Snow, S. A. Soule, H. Kriesi, & H. J. McCammon (Eds.), *The Blackwell companion to social movements* (pp. 116–152). Wiley Blackwell.

Entman, R. M. (1993). Framing: Toward clarification of a fractured paradigm. *Journal of Communication*, 43(4), 51–58. https://doi.org/10.1111/j.1460-2466.1993.tb01304.x

Facebook. (2019, March). *Standing against hate*. Facebook Newsroom. Retrieved September 13, 2019, from https://newsroom.fb.com/news/2019/03/standing-against-hate/

Facebook. (2023, September). *Difference between public and private Facebook groups*. Retrieved September 17, 2023, from https://www.facebook.com/help/220336891328465?ref=hc_about&helpref=about_content

Gamson, W. A. (1992). *Talking politics*. Cambridge University Press.

Gerstenfeld, P. B., Grant, D. R., & Chiang, C. P. (2003). Hate online: A content analysis of extremist Internet sites. *Analyses of Social Issues and Public Policy*, 3(1), 29–44. https://doi.org/10.1111/j.1530-2415.2003.00013.x

Gladwell, M. (2010, September 27). Small change. *The New Yorker*, 4, 42–49. https://www.newyorker.com/magazine/2010/10/04/small-change-malcolm-gladwell

Goffman, E. (1974). *Frame analysis: An essay on the organization of experience*. Harvard University Press.

Guo, C., & Saxton, G. D. (2014). Tweeting social change: How social media are changing nonprofit advocacy. *Nonprofit and Voluntary Sector Quarterly*, 43(1), 57–79. https://doi.org/10.1177/0899764012471585

Halupka, M. (2018). The legitimisation of clicktivism. *Australian Journal of Political Science*, 53(1), 130–141. https://doi.org/10.1080/10361146.2017.1416586

Hatewatch Staff. (2020). *Facebook's strategy for taking down hate groups is spotty and ineffective*. Southern Poverty Law Center. Retrieved September 15, 2020, from https://www.splcenter.org/hatewatch/2020/04/07/facebooks-strategy-taking-down-hate-groups-spottyand-ineffective

Hewstone, M., Rubin, M., & Willis, H. (2002). Intergroup bias. *Annual Review of Psychology*, 53(1), 575–604. https://doi.org/10.1146/annurev.psych.53.100901.135109

Johnson, N. F., Leahy, R., Restrepo, N. J., Velásquez, N., Zheng, M., Manrique, P., Devkota, P., & Wuchty, S. (2019). Hidden resilience and adaptive dynamics of the global online hate ecology. *Nature*, 573(7773), 261–265. https://doi.org/10.1038/s41586-019-1494-7

Jungkunz, S. (2019). Towards a measurement of extreme left-wing attitudes. *German Politics*, 28(1), 101–122. https://doi.org/10.1080/09644008.2018.1484906

Kaplan, A. (2018). *The head of an anti-immigration PAC runs Facebook pages that share fake news from plagiarized sites.* Media Matters for America. Retrieved October 15, 2020, from https://www.mediamatters.org/facebook/head-anti-immigration-pac-runs-facebookpages-share-fake-news-plagiarized-sites

Keller, J. M. (2012). Virtual feminisms: Girls' blogging communities, feminist activism, and participatory politics. *Information, Communication & Society, 15*(3), 429–447. https://doi.org/10.1080/1369118X.2011.642890

Klandermans, B. (1984). Mobilization and participation: Social-psychological expansions of resource mobilization theory. *American Sociological Review, 49*(5), 583–600. https://doi.org/10.2307/2095417

Krona, M. (2019). ISIS's media ecology and participatory activism tactics. In M. Krona & R. Pennington (Eds.), *The media world of ISIS* (pp. 101–124). Indiana University Press.

Kruglanski, A. W., Gelfand, M. J., Bélanger, J. J., Sheveland, A., Hetiarachchi, M., & Gunaratna, R. (2014). The psychology of radicalization and deradicalization: How significance quest impacts violent extremism. *Political Psychology, 35,* 69–93. https://doi.org/10.1111/pops.12163

Lenz, R. (2013). *Following the White Rabbit.* Southern Poverty Law Center. Retrieved October 15, 2020, from https://www.splcenter.org/fightinghate/intelligence-report/2013/following-white-rabbit

Levin, B. (2002). Cyberhate: A legal and historical analysis of extremists' use of computer networks in America. *American Behavioral Scientist, 45*(6), 958–988. https://doi.org/10.1177/0002764202045006004

Marx, G. T., & Wood, J. L. (1975). Strands of theory and research in collective behavior. *Annual Review of Sociology, 1*(1), 363–428.

McCarthy, J. D., & Zald, M. N. (1977). Resource mobilization and social movements: A partial theory. *American Journal of Sociology, 82*(6), 1212–1241. https://doi.org/10.1086/226464

McCarthy, J. D., & Zald, M. N. (2003). Social movement organizations. In J. Goodwin & J. M. Jasper (Eds.), *The social movements reader: Cases and concepts* (1st ed., pp. 169–186). Blackwell.

McCauley, C., & Moskalenko, S. (2008). Mechanisms of political radicalization: Pathways toward terrorism. *Terrorism and Political Violence, 20*(3), 415–433. https://doi.org/10.1080/09546550802073367

McNamee, L. G., Peterson, B. L., & Peña, J. (2010). A call to educate, participate, invoke, and indict: Understanding the communication of online hate groups. *Communication Monographs, 77*(2), 257–280. https://doi.org/10.1080/03637751003758227

Morozov, E. (2009, May 19). The brave new world of slacktivism. *Foreign Policy.* https://foreignpolicy.com/2009/05/19/the-brave-new-world-of-slacktivism/

Newell, E., Jurgens, D., Saleem, H., Vala, H., Sassine, J., Armstrong, C., & Ruths, D. (2016). User migration in online social networks: A case study on Reddit during a period of community unrest. *Proceedings of the International AAAI Conference on Web and Social Media, 10*(1), 279–288. https://doi.org/10.1609/icwsm.v10i1.14750

Núñez Puente, S., Fernández Romero, D., & Vázquez Cupeiro, S. (2017). Online feminist practice, participatory activism and public policies against gender-based violence in Spain. *Feminist Theory, 18*(3), 299–321. https://doi.org/10.1177/1464700117721881

Obar, J. A., Zube, P., & Lampe, C. (2012). Advocacy 2.0: An analysis of how advocacy groups in the United States perceive and use social media as tools for facilitating civic engagement and collective action. *Journal of Information Policy, 2,* 1–25. https://doi.org/10.2139/ssrn.1956352

Oberschall, A. (1973). *Social conflict and social movements.* Prentice Hall.

O'Callaghan, D., Greene, D., Conway, M., Carthy, J., & Cunningham, P. (2013, May). Uncovering the wider structure of extreme right communities spanning popular online networks. In *Proceedings of the 5th annual ACM web science conference* (pp. 276–285). ACM. https://doi.org/10.1145/2464464.2464495

Owen, N. (2019). Chapter 1: The conscience constituent reconsidered. In *Other people's struggles: Outsiders in social movements*. Oxford University Press.

Phadke, S., Lloyd, J., Hawdon, J., Samory, M., & Mitra, T. (2018, October). Framing hate with hate frames: Designing the codebook. In *CSCW '18: Companion of the 2018 ACM conference on computer supported cooperative work and social computing* (pp. 201–204). ACM. https://doi.org/10.1145/3272973.3274055

Phadke, S., & Mitra, T. (2020). Many faced hate: A cross platform study of content framing and information sharing by online hate groups. In *CHI '20: Proceedings of the 2020 CHI conference on human factors in computing systems* (pp. 1–13). ACM. https://doi.org/10.1145/3313831.3376456

Phadke, S., & Mitra, T. (2021). Educators, solicitors, flamers, motivators, sympathizers: Characterizing roles in online extremist movements. *Proceedings of the ACM Conference on Human-Computer Interaction*, 5(CSCW2), 310 (pp. 1–35). ACM. https://doi.org/10.1145/3476051

Phillips, W. (2018, May). The oxygen of amplification: Better practices for reporting on extremists, antagonists and manipulators. *Data & Society*. Retrieved September 23, 2020, from https://datasociety.net/library/oxygen-ofamplification

Rahimi, B. (2016). Vahid online: Post-2009 Iran and the politics of citizen media convergence. *Social Sciences*, 5(4), 77. https://www.mdpi.com/2076-0760/5/4/77

Rea, S., Mathew, B., & Kraemer, J. (Chapter 8 this volume). 'Hate parties': Networked antisemitism from the fringes to YouTube.

Rodan, D., & Mummery, J. (2017). *Activism and digital culture in Australia*. Rowman & Littlefield.

Rotman, D., Vieweg, S., Yardi, S., Chi, E., Preece, J., Shneiderman, B., Pirolli, P., & Glaisyer, T. (2011). From slacktivism to activism: Participatory culture in the age of social media. In *CHI'11 extended abstracts on human factors in computing systems* (pp. 819–822). ACM. https://doi.org/10.1145/1979742.1979543

Schafer, J. A. (2002). Spinning the web of hate: Web-based hate propagation by extremist organizations. *Journal of Criminal Justice and Popular Culture*, 9(2), 69–88.

Shanmugasundaram, S. (2018). *Anti-immigrant roundup: 7/6/18*. Southern Poverty Law Center. Retrieved October 15, 2020, from https://www.splcenter.org/hatewatch/2018/07/06/anti-immigrant-roundup-7618

Siegel, A. A., & Badaan, V. (2020). # No2Sectarianism: Experimental approaches to reducing sectarian hate speech online. *American Political Science Review*, 114(3), 837–855. https://doi.org/10.1017/S0003055420000283

Simon, B., & Klandermans, P. G. (2001). Toward a social psychological analysis of politicized collective identity: Conceptualization, antecedents and consequences. *American Psychologist* 56, 319–331.

Snow, D. A., & Benford, R. D. (1988). Ideology, frame resonance, and participant mobilization. *International Social Movement Research*, 1(1), 197–217.

SPLC. (2019a, September). *Hate map*. Southern Poverty Law Center. Retrieved September 13, 2019, from https://www.splcenter.org/hate-map

SPLC. (2019b, September). *Ideologies*. Southern Poverty Law Center. Retrieved September 14, 2019, from https://www.splcenter.org/fighting-hate/extremist-files/ideology

SPLC. (2020a). *Alliance defending freedom*. Southern Poverty Law Center. Retrieved October 15, 2020, from https://www.splcenter.org/fightinghate/extremist-files/group/alliance-defending-freedom

SPLC. (2020b). *National vanguard.* Southern Poverty Law Center. Retrieved October 15, 2020, from https://www.splcenter.org/fighting-hate/extremistfiles/group/national-vanguard

Starbird, K. (2017, May). Examining the alternative media ecosystem through the production of alternative narratives of mass shooting events on Twitter. *Proceedings of the International AAAI Conference on Web and Social Media, 11*(1), pp. 230–239. https://doi.org/10.1609/icwsm.v11i1.14878

Stringhini, G., & Blackburn, J. (this volume). Understanding the phases of coordinated online aggression attacks.

The Telegraph. (2015, June 19). Charleston church shooting: Gunman kills nine in South Carolina – latest pictures. *The Telegraph.* Retrieved September 18, 2019, from https://www.telegraph.co.uk/news/picturegalleries/worldnews/11688917/Charleston-church-shooting-Gunman-kills-nine-people-in-South-Carolina.html

Törnberg, A., & Törnberg, P. (Chapter 5 this volume). From echo chambers to digital campfires: The making of an online community of hate within Stormfront.

Turner, R. H. (1969). The public perception of protest. *American Sociological Review, 34*(6), 815–831. https://doi.org/10.2307/2095975

Udupa, S., & Gerold, O. L. (this volume). 'Deal' of the day: Sex, porn, and political hate on social media.

Valenzuela, S. (2013). Unpacking the use of social media for protest behavior: The roles of information, opinion expression, and activism. *American Behavioral Scientist, 57*(7), 920–942.

Van Stekelenburg, J., & Klandermans, B. (2013a). Social psychology of movement participation. In D. Della Porta, B. Klandermans, D. McAdam, & D. A. Snow (Eds.). *The Wiley-Blackwell encyclopedia of social and political movements* (pp 1–6). Wiley-Blackwell.

Van Stekelenburg, J., & Klandermans, B. (2013b). The social psychology of protest. *Current Sociology, 61*(5–6), 886–905.

Van Stekelenburg, J., & Klandermans, B. (2017). Individuals in movements: A social psychology of contention. In C. Roggeband & B. Klandermans (Eds.), *Handbook of social movements across disciplines* (pp. 103–139). Springer.

Vromen, A. (2017). Chapter 1: Digital citizenship and political engagement. *Digital citizenship and political engagement* (pp. 9–49). Springer.

Wahlström, M., Peterson, A., & Wennerhag, M. (2018). "Conscience adherents" revisited: Non-LGBT pride parade participants. *Mobilization: An International Quarterly, 23*(1), 83–100. https://doi.org/10.17813/1086-671X-23-1-83

Walther, J. (Chapter 2 this volume). Making a case for a social processes approach to online hate.

Wiebe, J., Wilson, T., & Cardie, C. (2005). Annotating expressions of opinions and emotions in language. *Language Resources and Evaluation, 39*(2–3), 165–210. https://doi.org/10.1007/s10579-005-7880-9

Zald, M. N., & Ash, R. (1966). Social movement organizations: Growth, decay and change. *Social Forces, 44*(3), 327–341. https://doi.org/10.1093/sf/44.3.327

Zhou, Y., Reid, E., Qin, J., Chen, H., & Lai, G. (2005). US domestic extremist groups on the Web: Link and content analysis. *IEEE Intelligent Systems, 20*(5), 44–51. https://doi.org/10.1109/mis.2005.96

10

DETECTING ANTISOCIAL NORMS IN LARGE-SCALE ONLINE DISCUSSIONS

Yotam Shmargad, Stephen A. Rains, Kevin Coe, Kate Kenski, and Steven Bethard

Online discussions are fundamentally social. Participants are engaged audiences of the messages that other contributors post and are concurrently exposed to the social approval and disapproval (as seen in "votes") that those (and their own) messages receive. These two sources of social information are deeply intertwined – messages receive votes based on their contents (Rains et al., 2017), while votes shape the content that future messages contain (Shmargad et al., 2022). Posts and votes differ, however, in the kind of information that they tend to communicate. Information within a post often reveals the *descriptive norms* of a discussion setting, or signals of what other people do, while votes reflect the *injunctive norms*, or signals of what people ought to do (Cialdini et al., 1990). Because people rely on descriptive and injunctive information to guide their behavior (Rimal & Real, 2005), online discussion data are uniquely suited for the study of social norm formation and evolution, compliance, and deviance. Historical records of online discussions are often readily available, enabling a better understanding of online socialization processes at both the collective level (e.g., by tracking aggregate trends in posting and rating behaviors) and individual level (e.g., by analyzing a person's posting and rating behavior over time). Lapinski and Rimal (2005) label these two analytical levels *collective* and *perceived* social norms, respectively.

Using the lens of social norms can help to shed light on the various forms of antisocial commenting that are prevalent online, including incivility (Coe et al., 2014), trolling (Cheng et al., 2017), and online hate speech (ElSherief et al., 2018). These forms of commenting have been of increasing concern, with nearly a third of adults (and over half of those between the ages of 18 and 29) reporting they have been called an offensive name online

DOI: 10.4324/9781003472148-10

(Vogels, 2021). This increase in public concern has been met with an increase in research into the topic, with much of it focusing on the automated detection of antisocial commenting (Tontodimamma et al., 2021). One project that offers free access to several automated classifiers is called Perspective, which originates from Google's Jigsaw lab (Lees et al., 2022). We authors have built an additional classifier that identifies name-calling specifically (and it is available to others via the platform Hugging Face[1]; Sadeque et al., 2019; Ozler et al., 2020). Automated classifiers make it possible to detect text features such as name-calling at scale and to discover variations in their deployment across time and individuals (e.g., Rains et al., 2021; Rains et al., 2023a; Rains et al., 2023b).

This chapter is about how the Internet shapes social processes that foster the expression of incivility, hate, and other antisocial language on the one hand and how scientists study these processes on the other. We make a modest contribution to knowledge by analyzing antisocial commenting by both human-coded annotations and automated classification techniques in order to identify the extent that automated classifiers are suitable for the large-scale study of online (anti-)social norms. To do so, we replicated results from previous work that relied on human-coded annotations (Rains et al., 2017; Shmargad et al., 2022), here using automated classifiers instead of human coders. Our findings are mixed, with some classifiers more reliably replicating prior work than others. In general, however, there was a meaningful overlap between using human annotations and automated classifiers. To show how our framework can be applied to contemporary online discussions, we applied automated classifiers to discussions on Reddit and Twitter during the January 6th Capitol riots, and we compared the norms surrounding antisocial commenting across these two platforms. Using these multiple approaches, several important points became clear. First, that antisocial commenting is promoted through at least two social processes, one in which people mimic others and another in which people who get rewarded for antisocial messages subsequently generate more of them. Second, that automated classification is a measurement advancement that can aid in the study of both the collective and perceived norms surrounding antisocial commenting.

Social Norms in Online Communities

Theorizing about deviance from societal normative boundaries goes at least as far back as Durkheim's (1893) work on the topic – for more informal examples, you can go back as far as *The Epic of Gilgamesh* or Shakespeare for relevant discussions. Durkheim argued that deviance is a necessary, even beneficial, part of society because it clarifies the norms (thereby encouraging compliance), strengthens bonds among those reacting to deviance, and can lead to positive social change by challenging people's existing views. Lofland

(1969) clarifies the process by which deviance is socially constructed, becomes ingrained in a society's view of itself, and creates a dual process whereby deviants increasingly associate deviance with their own identity. Maratea and Kavanaugh (2012) update these classic sociological ideas to provide a modern understanding of online deviance, specifically. They point out that emerging information and communication technologies allow "scholars to study deviant subcultures that did not exist, or were too hidden to access, prior to the advent of the internet" (p. 107). As a site of contemporary deviance, online discussion threads thus represent a promising venue for investigating anti-normative behavior.

While incivility and other forms of antisocial commenting are sometimes conceptualized as deviance from socially accepted manners of speech (Jamieson et al., 2017), one would be hard pressed to find societal benefits for some of the speech that can be found online. And yet, in addition to the (sometimes circular) arguments about one's rights to freedom of speech, unsavory online language cannot be uniformly treated as "bad" as it can serve positive, even necessary, societal and democratic functions (e.g., Edyvane, 2020; Rossini, 2022). Such considerations, ethical in nature, are central to recent debates about how digital platforms should be moderating, and whether and when they should be censoring information that circulates on the web (Forestal, 2021). Proposed solutions, such as focusing only on the most extreme forms of commenting such as hate speech (Jiang et al., 2020) or paying special attention to the targets of such speech (Zampieri et al., 2019), showcase how politically fraught these considerations can become – particularly when automated methods are employed (Udupa et al., 2023). For example, Haimson et al. (2021) find that the people most likely to report that their posts were removed from online platforms were either ideologically conservative, transgender, or Black. The reasons provided for removal, however, varied substantially across these groups, with the latter two groups having more of their posts removed that either did not violate platform policies or fell under moderation gray areas.

Despite clarifying ethical nuances surrounding the censorship of antisocial comments and the groups that engage in or are targeted by such language, discussions of content moderation often ignore the underlying social processes that culminate in specific communication patterns. The work that exists often treats antisocial commenting as either a contagious process (Song et al., 2022), one in which particular people are drawn into contentious discussion (Bor & Peterson, 2021), or both (Kim et al., 2021). While their work starts to unpack the mechanisms behind antisocial behavior, they still leave much to ponder. Is such language always contagious or are there social contexts that are more conducive to mimetics? If specific people are primarily responsible for its spread, how does one become (or learn to respond to) such a person? These questions suggest a focus on social processes as critical forces impacting the expression of antisocial content. It is important to focus on both the relational drivers of behavior as well as a longer time window through which to witness the socialization of antisocial expressions take place. The very platforms often blamed for fueling antisocial behavior also provide such a relational and temporal view of human interaction and development.

Most traces of behavior generated by everyday online activity are intrinsically *relational* (Golder & Macy, 2014). For example, on Twitter alone, people share or *retweet* messages that others post, show approval of a post with a *favorite*, respond to a post with a *reply*, inform other users of their message with a *mention*, or *quote* a post by sharing it with additional commentary. On platforms such as Reddit and YouTube, people provide comments and videos, respectively, with *up* and *downvotes* to signal their approval and disapproval. While platforms may provide various ways for people to register their feedback about other users' posts, we refer in this chapter to clicks of approval or disapproval as *votes*. Votes can be said to be relational because they have meaning not just for voters but also for receivers of the vote, for audience members who can view aggregated statistics of votes, and for platforms that use votes to filter posts in and out of people's content streams via algorithms (Burrell & Fourcade, 2021). From the perspective of a researcher studying online behavior, votes are understood differently depending on whether the sender or receiver of the vote is the focus. For example, retweeting a message can be interpreted as a signal of homophily, or similarity, with the person who posted the message (Barbera, 2015). Receiving retweets, on the other hand, can imply that a message has resonated (McDonnell et al., 2017) and was influential in getting people to pay attention to the poster (Shmargad, 2022).

In addition to reflecting the relational aspects of human behavior, digital trace data are also inherently *temporal* in nature. For example, timestamps typically accompany post data that are collected from social media platforms, so that it is possible to construct sequential timelines among comments. For the study of antisocial commenting, the temporal nature of digital trace data can be used to understand macroscopic trends (Rains et al., 2021) on the one hand and microscopic dynamics (Shmargad et al., 2022) on the other. Rains et al. (2021) used a dataset of Russian troll tweets (Linvill & Warren, 2020) to study their use of antisocial commenting across different periods of the 2016 U.S. presidential election cycle. Shmargad et al. (2022) used the temporal nature of digital trace data to understand the dynamics of antisocial commenting as a discussion thread evolves. They found that anti-sociality is more likely after prior anti-sociality by other commenters as well as votes of approval for one's own antisocial commenting. These two applications of temporality – analyzing macroscopic trends and microscopic dynamics – can aid researchers in the study of the collective and perceived norms (Lapinski & Rimal, 2005) surrounding antisocial commenting, respectively.

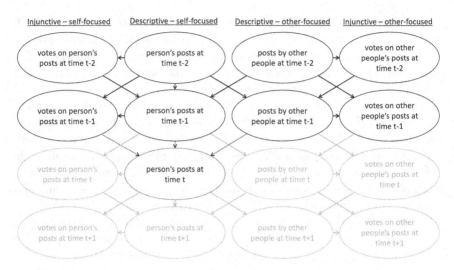

FIGURE 10.1   A Framework for Using Online Discussion Data to Study Socialization Processes

We build here on our prior work (Shmargad et al., 2022) to argue that the tone of online contributors' posts at a particular point in time depends in large part on two factors: The tone of other users' previous posts and the up or downvotes that they have seen posts receiving. These factors reflect the descriptive and injunctive norms, respectively, that users perceive. Each of these norms, in turn, has two further components: They can be either *self-* or *other-focused* (see Figure 10.1). One's *self-focused descriptive norms* are their perceptions of contributions they themselves have made in the past, while their *self-focused injunctive norms* are their perceptions of how those contributions were rewarded or penalized. One's *other-focused descriptive norms* are perceptions of the contributions others have made, while *other-focused injunctive norms* are perceptions of how those contributions were rewarded or penalized (either by the focal user or by others).

Figure 10.1 depicts in dotted lines the *immediate signals* that will inform an individual's posting behavior at a particular point in time. These are the signals that not only will matter but also represent what a first attempt at a test of our framework might look like. The total number of the votes, or clicks of approval and disapproval, reflect the aggregated feedback of other users. Because votes provide the person posting with feedback about what is and is not appropriate (i.e., self-focused injunctive norms), we might expect that a person will continue to post in ways that provide positive feedback and stop posting in ways that yield negative feedback. However, this is not always the case; for example, Cheng et al. (2014) show that negative feedback can backfire and increase the likelihood of future posts that also receive negative feedback. As such, the role that votes play in discouraging or encouraging particular behaviors, such as antisocial commenting, is an empirical question that our framework can help to address.

The extent that language in other people's posts will shape the language that is chosen by a subsequent user depends on various factors. Goldberg and Stein (2018) argue that the spread of information relies on the mental frames of the receiver, a process they call *associative diffusion*. In-group status (Rimal & Real, 2005), social tie strength (Bakshy et al., 2012), online anonymity (Kim et al., 2019), identity performance (Freelon et al., 2020), political influence (Shmargad, 2022), elite status (Rains et al., 2023b), and many other factors will likely shape how contagious a person's language might be. The content in another commenter's posts can be viewed as contributing to a descriptive norm because it represents what another user is doing. A subset of posts may also include injunctive information, however, and the large-scale extraction of such information is a worthwhile direction for future research. Moreover, the full set of posts that constitute the descriptive norms guiding a person's posting behavior at a specific point in time could be large and varied, and identifying the bounds of this evolving set is also an important research direction.

While votes provide people with quantitative measures of feedback, the text contained within a post is "unstructured data," and meaning must be extracted from posts by discussion participants and behavioral researchers alike. Automated ways for extracting meaning from text have increased both in number and ease of use, with the most recent advancements evident in the large language models (LLMs) that may represent the future of data annotation (Ding et al., 2022). The primary advantage of automated classification techniques is that one can process large amounts of text quickly and cheaply – which, for the study of socialization, implies that a broader set of people, discussions, and contexts can be studied. However, to be influenced by the behavior of another requires that discussant participants are able to extract information from another person's post (e.g., the presence of antisocial commenting) and use that information in their own posting decisions. For example, if a person does not pick up on a particular name-call (e.g., the capitalization of the R in democRat; see Sadeque et al., 2019), they may not take it as an insult and may thus not return in kind. To test the extent that automated techniques pick up on human interpretations, we compare human-coded annotations and automated classification techniques to study the collective and perceived norms surrounding antisocial commenting. This allows us to both evaluate the framework in Figure 10.1 and to validate the use of automated classification techniques in the detection of antisocial normative behavior.

Comparing Human Annotation to Automated Classification of Antisocial Commenting

Online Comments in The Arizona Daily Star

The data that we discuss in this section are similar to those analyzed in Coe et al. (2014), Rains et al. (2017), and Shmargad et al. (2022) and include all of the online comments made on news articles published in the online website for the *Arizona Daily Star* (*ADS*) over a three-week period in October and November of 2011. These news articles, along with their comments, were printed as PDF files, and the text of the comments was then manually annotated by human coders for five different measures of incivility (*name-calling, aspersion, accusations of lying, vulgarity,* and *pejorative speech*). The annotation process was designed to increase intercoder reliability. It began by having trained coders independently annotate the same set of comments, then discuss disagreements in their annotations, and finally to update a codebook that further clarified how annotations were to be made. When the coders reached sufficient intercoder reliability in their annotations, they then independently coded the actual comments on the *ADS* articles. Further details about the methodology, including intercoder reliability scores for the different measures of incivility and specific examples of each measure, can be found in Coe et al. (2014).

An independent research effort (Sadeque et al., 2019) developed an automated classifier using the coded data for name-calling, specifically, the application of which required the extraction of text from the comments in the original *ADS* discussion files. We use those data, which include the text of the comments in addition to information in the original dataset (e.g., comment numbers, counts of the down and upvotes that comments received). We thus had the human annotations of incivility alongside the comment text, the latter of which was prepared for automated classification. We applied our own classifier for name-calling to the comment text, which was built by Ozler et al. (2020) and trained on several annotated datasets in addition to the *ADS* comments. We also processed the text in the comments using Google's Perspective API (Lees et al., 2022) to obtain scores for several additional attributes, including *toxicity, severe toxicity, identity attack, insult, profanity,* and *threat*. The Perspective API also provided text attributes that were trained on a set of comments from *New York Times* articles, and we used these as well, given their similarity to our data.[2] These attributes include *attack on author, attack on commenter,* and *inflammatory language*. The various classifiers provided different measures of antisocial commenting, each of which was a possible candidate for the detection of normative behavior (i.e., for evidence of mimetics and/or response to social votes). Automated classifiers each provided scores between 0 and 1, and we converted these scores into binary variables using a threshold of .5.

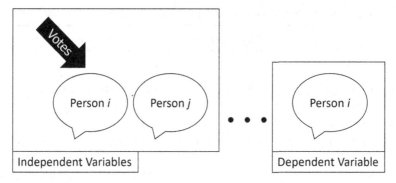

FIGURE 10.2   Organizing Comments into Triplets

To test the framework from the previous section (Figure 10.1), we adopted a data preparation strategy first outlined in Shmargad et al. (2022) to transform the comment data into triplets such that: (1) The three comments in a triplet were on the same news article, (2) the second comment in a triplet followed immediately after the first, (3) the first and second comments were authored by different contributors, and (4) the first and third comments were authored by the same contributor. This empirical strategy let us test how three factors highlighted in Figure 10.1 above – a person's prior comment, the votes that person's comment received, and another person's comment – contribute to the nature of a person's subsequent comment. Figure 10.2 depicts the empirical strategy that we adopted as a test of the framework in Figure 10.1. The votes that Person i received on their initial comment capture self-focused injunctive norms, while the presence of antisocial commenting in Person i's and j's comments captures self- and other-focused descriptive norms, respectively. Because this empirical strategy allowed us to investigate the (possibly interactive) effects of descriptive and injunctive norms, it could also be construed as a partial test of Rimal and Real's (2005) theory of normative social behavior (TNSB) according to Shmargad et al. (2022). (We leave the study of other-focused injunctive norms for future research.)

Collective Descriptive Norms in the Arizona Daily Star

Shmargad et al. (2022) used a single, collapsed measure of antisocial commenting, which was set to 1 for comments that included *name-calling, aspersion, accusations of lying, vulgarity,* or *pejorative speech,* and 0 for comments that lacked those message features. The classifier in Ozler et al. (2020) was trained on the *name-calling* annotations only, so that in addition to Shmargad et al.'s (2022) collapsed measure, we also defined two new measures – "name-calling" tracked the presence of name-calling, specifically, while "not name-calling" tracked the presence of any of the other incivility measures.

TABLE 10.1 Summary Statistics of Antisocial Commenting in the *Arizona Daily Star*

	All Comments			*First Comment in Triplet*		
	N	M	SD	N	M	SD
Annotated incivility	6,165	0.20	0.40	2,672	0.19	0.39
Name-calling		0.14	0.35		0.12	0.33
Not name-calling		0.09	0.28		0.08	0.28
Automated name-calling	6,121	0.14	0.35	2,620	0.13	0.33
Perspective API	5,998			2,534		
Toxicity		0.05	0.21		0.04	0.20
Severe toxicity		0.00	0.00		0.00	0.00
Identity attack		0.01	0.08		0.01	0.07
Insult		0.05	0.22		0.04	0.20
Profanity		0.00	0.06		0.00	0.07
Threat		0.01	0.08		0.00	0.06
Any perspective		0.06	0.24		0.05	0.22
New York Times	5,998			2,534		
Attack on author		0.10	0.30		0.10	0.30
Attack on commenter		0.22	0.41		0.25	0.43
Inflammatory		0.33	0.47		0.30	0.46

Note: M and SD values are in percent.

Table 10.1 includes summary statistics for these three measures as well as those obtained from the Perspective API and *New York Times* attributes. These statistics capture the *collective* descriptive norms surrounding antisocial commenting in this community. We include statistics for all comments, as well as for the subset of comments that started a triplet. The latter will serve as a useful comparison in the next section, where only comments that were included as parts of a triplet were classified for the presence of antisocial commenting. Table 10.2 includes definitions and examples of the various forms of antisocial commenting that we classified using automated methods.

Several observations in Table 10.1 are worth discussing. First, the rate of anti-sociality in comments that started a triplet did not deviate much from the rate across all comments. Since the focus later will be on triplets to provide a test of our theoretical framework, it is reassuring that these triplets did not begin in an atypically pro- or antisocial manner.[3] Second, the name-calling classifier successfully recovered the rate of name-calling that was coded by human coders (i.e., the means were identical or close). This result highlights the utility of classifiers that are trained on properly annotated data as a means of evaluating name-calling behavior at scale. Third, the scores obtained from

TABLE 10.2 Definitions and Examples of Antisocial Commenting in the *Arizona Daily Star*

Form of Anti-Sociality	Definition	Example
Name-calling	Mean-spirited or disparaging words directed at a person or group of people	"You ARE BREAKING THE LAW, you dopes."
Perspective API		
Toxicity	A rude, disrespectful, or unreasonable comment that is likely to make people leave a discussion	"Useful idiots!"
Severe toxicity	A very hateful, aggressive, disrespectful comment or otherwise very likely to make a user leave a discussion or give up on sharing their perspective. This attribute is much less sensitive to more mild forms of toxicity, such as comments that include positive uses of curse words	"Arizona voters are stupid and they get what they deserve by electing these scum sucking sleaze balls." (Note: This had the highest severe toxicity score, but at .45 did not meet the .5 threshold to be classified as such)
Identity attack	Negative or hateful comments targeting someone because of their identity	"Mexico sending more INVADERS to our nation."
Insult	Insulting, inflammatory, or negative comment toward a person or a group of people	"You are truly an IDIOT."
Profanity	Swear words, curse words, or other obscene or profane language	"Just build the damn mine already!"
Threat	Describes an intention to inflict pain, injury, or violence against an individual or group	"Every person on their death-bed should die in pain."
New York Times		
Attack on author	Attack on the author of an article or post	"Leave it to Tony to turn a 'news' story into a one-sided bleeding heart opinion piece."
Attack on commenter	Attack on fellow commenter.	"All of what you said just shows that you haven't grown up yet."
Inflammatory	Intending to provoke or inflame.	"Want a chance at a job, get rid of Obama, Pelosi, and the rest. Want a government handout like the OWS clowns, then vote for Obama. Simple enough."

Note: Definitions for the Perspective API and *New York Times* features were obtained from https://developers.perspectiveapi.com/s/about-the-api-attributes-and-languages. For examples of the *annotated* measures of incivility (i.e., name-calling, aspersion, accusations of lying, vulgarity, and pejorative for speech), see Table 1 in Coe et al. (2014).

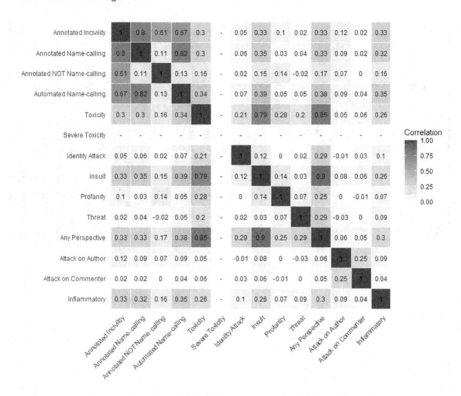

FIGURE 10.3 Correlation Matrix for Measures of in Online News Comments

the Perspective API measures were low for these data, with *severe toxicity* not appearing in any of the comments. This finding raises questions about the sensitivity of the Perspective measures. We thus also constructed a collapsed measure across the six Perspective API measures, which is 1 if *toxicity, severe toxicity, identity attack, insult, profanity,* and *threat* were present, and 0 otherwise. Using the collapsed Perspective API measure, only 6% of the comments included at least one of these forms of antisocial commenting, compared to 20% that included at least one of the incivility measures coded by Coe et al. (2014). Although the types of behaviors captured in the Perspective API appear broader, they are less sensitive to common forms of incivility. Finally, the rates of the *New York Times* attributes were higher than measures obtained with the Perspective API, with a third of the comments containing instances of *inflammatory language.* Figure 10.3 presents the correlation matrix of these measures of antisocial commenting.

Collective Injunctive Norms in the Arizona Daily Star

As previously mentioned, in addition to measures of incivility, the *ADS* dataset includes counts of the down and upvotes that comments received from other readers. Figure 10.4 presents a plot of the relationship between the

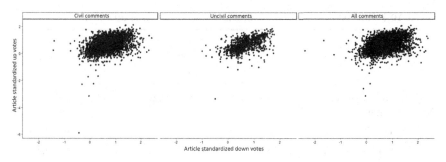

FIGURE 10.4   Log-Log Plot of Down and Upvotes after Article Standardization

down and upvotes that comments received. We standardize the number of down and upvotes for each article by subtracting the article-specific mean and dividing by the article-specific standard deviation. This controls for correlations across down and upvotes that result from some articles simply drawing more attention. We then transform the standardized down and upvote measures by taking a logarithm to remove skew. As we can clearly see in Figure 10.4, down and upvotes were highly correlated even after controlling for the specific news article, suggesting that comments frequently divided the community (i.e., a given comment received a proportional number of down and upvotes). These rankings thus reflect in- and out-group dynamics in a broad sense, some of which can be explained by partisanship (Rains et al., 2017). Papakyriakopoulos et al. (2023) show that discussions on forums with both up and downvote capabilities are less civic-natured than forums that only allow upvotes (though, notably, more civic-natured than forums that allowed neither up nor downvotes).

The next set of analyses relates the presence of antisocial commenting to the number of down and upvotes that comments received, which reflect *collective* injunctive norms around antisocial commenting in this community. Table 10.3 reports results for the various measures of antisocial commenting. Each coefficient was obtained with a multilevel model that included random effects for the news article and for the contributor who posted the comment. The random effects were included to remove variation from specific articles that drew more antisocial commenting or from people who were more likely to deploy antisocial commenting. We also included an additional control variable, the numerical order of the comment in the set for that article. As reported in Rains et al. (2017), comments that included incivility were more likely to draw both downvotes and upvotes. Interestingly, *name-calling* was primarily responsible for the increases in upvotes, while the other incivility measures were responsible for increases in downvotes. Among the Perspective API measures, only *insult* showed a positive relationship with upvotes. *Attacks on commenters* were associated with fewer upvotes, while *inflammatory language* was associated with more downvotes. Figure 10.5 portrays these effects.

TABLE 10.3 Effects of Antisocial Commenting on Downvotes and Upvotes

	N	Downvotes: Coefficient (S.E.)	Upvotes: Coefficient (S.E.)
Annotated incivility	5,665	0.65* (0.26)	1.20** (0.43)
Name-calling		0.34 (0.30)	1.16* (0.51)
Not name-calling		0.79* (0.37)	0.84 (0.55)
Automated name-calling	5,621	0.55 (0.30)	0.44 (0.50)
Perspective API	5,506		.
Toxicity		0.90 (0.56)	1.53 (1.03)
Severe toxicity		0.00 (0.00)	0.00 (0.00)
Identity attack		1.15 (2.78)	0.48 (2.55)
Insult		0.37 (0.51)	1.74* (0.95)
Profanity		0.76 (2.29)	1.80 (2.91)
Threat		2.21 (2.04)	–2.17 (2.38)
Any Perspective API	5,506	0.32 (0.45)	1.62* (0.85)
New York Times	5,506		
Attack on author		0.59 (0.36)	1.13 (0.59)
Attack on commenter		0.19 (0.25)	–1.26** (0.40)
Inflammatory		0.96*** (0.24)	0.69 (0.39)

Note: * p < .10, ** p < .05, *** p < .001.

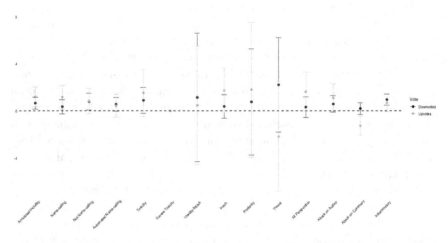

FIGURE 10.5 Effects of Antisocial Commenting on Votes with 95% Confidence Intervals

Perceived Descriptive and Injunctive Norms in the Arizona Daily Star

The final set of analyses in this section replicated Shmargad et al.'s (2022) on the effects of *perceived* descriptive and injunctive norms on the spread of incivility (Figure 10.2). The purpose of these analyses was to examine how community responses to incivility influence the degree to which it is perpetuated in online discussion. We used multilevel models with random effects for article and commenter and included control variables for the numerical order of the comment as well as the "gap" (i.e., number of comments) between the first and last comment in a triplet. Note that the triplets, as constructed, allow for several comments to occur between the first and last comment, so far, as none of these comments was contributed by the author of the first and last comment. We did not run the model for the six Perspective API measures separately (*toxicity, severe toxicity, identity attack, insult, profanity,* or *threat*) as they were not prevalent enough. Instead, we report results for a collapsed measure that tracked if any of these six Perspective API attributes were present (0 for no, 1 for yes). We do not report numerical estimates here but instead provide images of the marginal effects in Figures 10.6 and 10.7.

Figure 10.6 provides estimates for the human-coded measures of incivility as well as for the automated classifier for *name-calling*. The right panels depict the effects of downvotes while the left panels depict the effects of upvotes. The first row in Figure 10.6 replicates the results from Shmargad et al. (2022): The effect of incivility in another user's comment depends, in part, on the number of upvotes that a user's initial comment received. When the user was initially uncivil and received no upvotes, the presence of incivility in another user's comment decreased the likelihood of incivility in the initial user's subsequent comment. However, as the number of upvotes a user received increased, the effect of another commenter's incivility also increased. This implies that incivility was met with incivility when it was initially rewarded. Downvotes, on the other hand, did not influence the effect of another commenter's incivility.

When we break up the collapsed human-annotated incivility measure into two categories, *name-calling* and all other measures (*not name-calling*), the effect of proximate incivility increased as the number of upvotes increased for other incivility measures but not for *name-calling* itself. When the same analyses were conducted using the automated *name-calling* classifier (Ozler et al., 2020) rather than the human-annotated measures, results matched. The results suggest that the effect of other users' name-calling on one's own name-calling was not shaped by how many upvotes the initial name-calling received. This suggests that different forms of incivility may elicit different normative responses, with name-calling showing less sensitivity to mimetics and social rewards. The results (as also seen in Shmargad et al., 2022) replicate with the collapsed Perspective API measures (the presence of any

Annotated Incivility

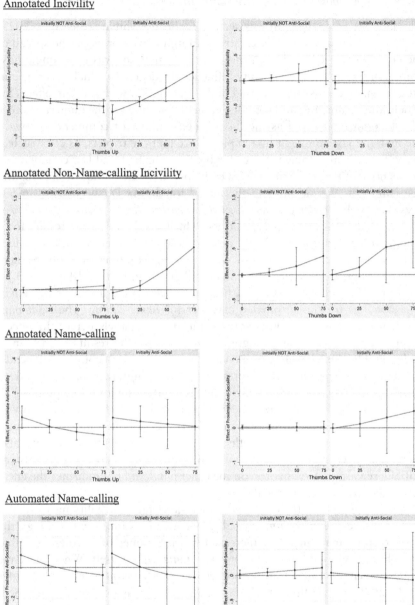

Annotated Non-Name-calling Incivility

Annotated Name-calling

Automated Name-calling

FIGURE 10.6 Testing TNSB with Human Annotation and Automated Classification of Incivility

All Perspective (Toxicity, Severe Toxicity, Identity Attack, Insult, Profanity, or Threat)

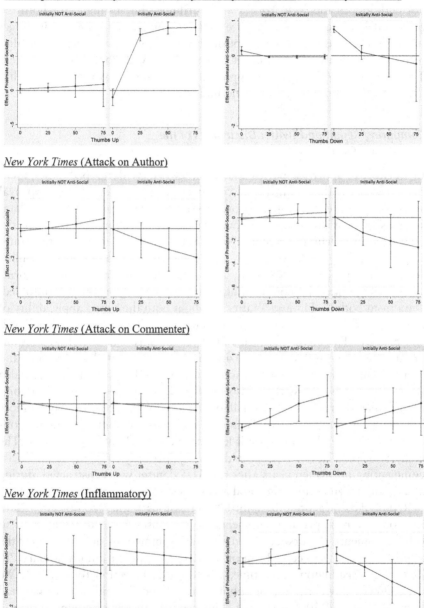

New York Times (Attack on Author)

New York Times (Attack on Commenter)

New York Times (Inflammatory)

FIGURE 10.7 Testing TNSB with Google's Perspective API and _New York Times_ Attributes

toxicity, severe toxicity, identity attack, insult, profanity, or *threat*) but not with any of the *New York Times* attributes. Interestingly, for both the collapsed Perspective API measure and *inflammatory language*, the effect of proximate anti-sociality was positive when a user's initial anti-sociality received no downvotes – an effect that went away as downvotes increased. The Perspective API thus picks up on forms of antisocial commenting that are sensitive to both descriptive and injunctive norms.

Comparing Reddit and Twitter Discussions of the January 6th Capitol Riots

In an effort to apply the norms-based framework we developed – the potential effects of others' antisocial commenting as well as social approval votes – to a more contemporary online context, we employed a novel dataset consisting of discussions surrounding the insurrection that followed the 2020 U.S. presidential election. The collective that raided the United States Capitol building on January 6th, 2021, was, in part, a product of online socialization processes (Ng et al., 2022). Given this, we looked for norms surrounding antisocial commenting as the events of January 6th unfolded. Data from both Reddit and Twitter highlight both the broad applicability of our framework as well as the nuanced understanding of social norms that it can provide. These two platforms differ in the way that social interactions are structured, with Reddit organizing discussions in topic-based forums and Twitter employing a network graph of follower relations. Moderation also works differently across these two platforms, with Reddit relying on community members and Twitter on algorithmic solutions. Norms may be more influential on platforms like Twitter, where out-of-community interactions are more likely and moderation is less specific to one's own community. The analysis of the Capitol riots provides an opportunity to examine antisocial commenting norms ten years after the *ADS* dataset was constructed, during an especially contentious time and across these different platforms.

Reddit data are organized into "submissions" and "comments." Submissions are prompts and comments are responses either to prompts or to other comments. We first collected all of the submissions that mentioned the word "Capitol" between 11 am on January 6th and 11 am on January 7th EST (i.e., Washington, D.C. time, where the insurrection took place). We then filtered down the set of submissions to include only those that had between 100 and 500 comments. This set reflects 3% of submissions and 9% of comments, respectively. This was done not only to constrain the amount of comment data we analyzed for anti-sociality on the one hand but also to ensure that (1) there were enough comments per submission to model submission-specific random effects and (2) all of the comments for each submission were obtained, as the Reddit API (which was used for data collection) only allows for 500 comments per submission to be collected. We then collected all of the comments posted on the submissions in our filtered set, organized the comments into triplets similar to those discussed in the previous section, and applied several automated classifiers of antisocial commenting (i.e., name-calling, toxicity, severe toxicity, identity attack, insult, threat, attack on author, attack on commenter, and inflammatory) to each of the comments in these triplets.

Data collection for Twitter proceeded in much the same way. Since tweet volume is much larger than that of Reddit submissions, we sampled one, ten-second interval per minute for the same 24-hour period and collected all of the tweets in these intervals that included the word "Capitol." We removed retweets and replies that matched our query (i.e., we constrained the data to original tweets) and filtered down the tweets to those that had between 100 and 500 replies, in order to be consistent with the Reddit data collection. The filtered set of original tweets and replies captures .3% and 17% of the respective totals. We then collected the replies to the tweets in our filtered set, created triplets, and processed the tweets in these triplets using the automated classifiers. One additional detail is that discussions on Reddit and Twitter are organized in tree-like threads rather than single-comment streams as in the *ADS* dataset. Our triplets thus reflect any three sequential replies in which the initial and final comments were made by the same user. Unlike the triplets constructed from the *ADS* dataset, we did not allow for a "gap" of multiple comments separating the first and third comment, as these are not well-specified in tree-like threads because each comment can split into separate sub-threads. In all, we analyzed 12,594 triplets on Reddit and 6,303 triplets on Twitter. Table 10.4 presents summary statistics for the three comments in each triplet.

Collective Descriptive Norms on Reddit and Twitter

These first set of analyses we report reveal the *collective* descriptive norms surrounding antisocial commenting on Reddit and Twitter. *Name-calling* was prevalent in these data, with 21% and 19% of the initial comments including name-calling on Reddit and Twitter, respectively (compared to just 13% in the *ADS* comments). Scores on the Perspective API measures were substantial, with 41% and 35% of comments on Reddit and Twitter including at least one of the six measures, compared to just 6% of the comments in the *ADS*. While these differences between the 2011 ADS dataset and 2021 Capitol dataset are notable, recent work acknowledges the limitations of the Perspective API for making comparisons over time (Pozzobon et al., 2023). The *New York Times* attributes' scores were not particularly high – in fact, *attacks on author* were less common than in the *ADS* analyses, at 5% and 2% for Reddit and Twitter, respectively (compared to 10% in the *ADS*).

TABLE 10.4 Means and Standard Deviations of Antisocial Commenting on Reddit and Twitter

	Initial Comment		Proximate Comment		Subsequent Comment	
	Reddit	Twitter	Reddit	Twitter	Reddit	Twitter
Name-calling	.21 (.40)	.19 (.39)	.20 (.40)	.18 (.39)	.18 (.38)	.17 (.38)
Perspective API						
Toxicity	.28 (.45)	.23 (.42)	.26 (.44)	.24 (.43)	.24 (.42)	.22 (.42)
Severe toxicity	.15 (.36)	.10 (.31)	.13 (.34)	.11 (.31)	.12 (.32)	.10 (.30)
Identity attack	.12 (.32)	.11 (.32)	.10 (.30)	.11 (.31)	.09 (.28)	.10 (.30)
Insult	.27 (.45)	.23 (.42)	.25 (.43)	.23 (.42)	.23 (.42)	.22 (.42)
Profanity	.19 (.39)	.13 (.33)	.17 (.37)	.14 (.34)	.16 (.37)	.13 (.34)
Threat	.19 (.39)	.14 (.35)	.17 (.37)	.13 (.33)	.14 (.35)	.11 (.31)
All perspective	.41 (.49)	.35 (.48)	.38 (.49)	.35 (.48)	.35 (.48)	.32 (.46)
New York Times						
Attack on author	.05 (.21)	.02 (.15)	.05 (.23)	.03 (.16)	.05 (.23)	.03 (.16)
Attack on commenter	.24 (.43)	.45 (.50)	.29 (.45)	.46 (.50)	.29 (.45)	.45 (.50)
Inflammatory	.41 (.49)	.33 (.47)	.37 (.48)	.33 (.47)	.34 (.47)	.30 (.46)

Note: Values are in percent.

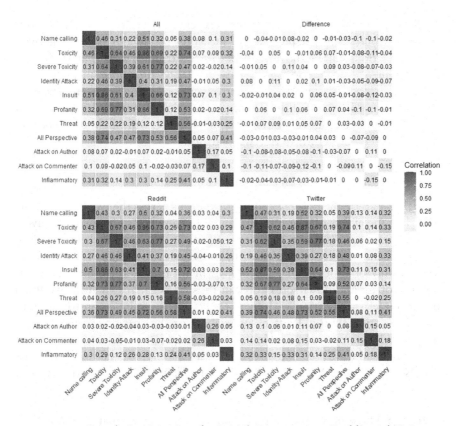

FIGURE 10.8 Correlation Matrices for Initial Comments on Reddit and Twitter

Antisocial comments were typically more prevalent on Reddit than on Twitter. One exception was *attacks on other commenters*, which occurred in a staggering 45% of initial comments on Twitter, compared to 24% of those on Reddit. Understanding the reasons for these cross-platform differences is beyond the scope of this chapter but is a worthwhile direction for future research.

Figure 10.8 shows correlations for these different forms of antisocial commenting. The bottom panels report correlations for Reddit comments and Twitter replies separately. The upper left panel includes both platforms together. Finally, the upper right panel includes differences in the correlations across the two platforms. The classifier for *name-calling* was consistently correlated with the Perspective API measures, aside from *threat*. This was not the case in the *ADS* comments, which featured relatively low rates of the Perspective API measures, in contrast to which comments on Reddit and Twitter frequently included *several* forms of antisocial commenting. Finally, there tended to be stronger correlations among the Perspective API measures on Reddit (more positive) and higher correlations between the *New York Times* attributes and Perspective API measures on Twitter (more negative). The correlations among the *New York Times* attributes were split, with Reddit showing a stronger correlation between *attacks on author* and *attacks on commenter*, and Twitter showing a stronger correlation between *attack on commenter* and *inflammatory language*. Multiple forms and variations of antisocial commenting were often used in harmony, with slight differences in co-occurrence rates between the two platforms.

Collective Injunctive Norms on Reddit and Twitter

Next, we analyze the *collective* injunctive norms across the two platforms by modeling the effects of anti-sociality on how many votes comments received. On Twitter, comments can be favorited (or not rated at all), while on Reddit, comments can receive down or upvotes (or neither). However, the Reddit API only provides a single "score," which captures the difference in the number of up and downvotes and can thus be negative. As such, we use a linear model specification with fixed effects for the submission (on Reddit) or conversation ID (on Twitter), as well as for the specific commenter. We do not include a control variable for the order of the comment, as this is not clearly defined for a tree-like thread structure. We report the results of these analyses in Table 10.5 and depict them in Figure 10.9. The name-calling

TABLE 10.5 Effects of Antisocial Commenting on Votes in the Initial Comments

Name-Calling	Reddit		Twitter	
	N	Coeff. (S.E.)	N	Coeff. (S.E.)
	2,982	4.91 (3.37)	4,939	−0.27 (1.42)
Perspective API	9,300		4,939	
Toxicity		6.73** (1.89)		−1.45* (0.76)
Severe toxicity		9.32*** (2.18)		−0.56 (0.58)
Identity attack		3.21 (2.87)		−1.30 (0.84)
Insult		8.54*** (1.99)		−1.71** (0.70)
Threat		0.13 (1.84)		1.65 (1.53)
Any Perspective API		6.16*** (1.72)		−1.00 (0.93)
New York Times	9,300		4,939	
Attack on author		−1.62 (2.14)		−0.02 (1.48)
Attack on commenter		−3.27* (1.71)		−2.82** (1.17)
Inflammatory		6.50* (2.83)		−1.04 (1.12)

Note: $* \ p < .10, \ ** \ p < .05, \ *** \ p < .001.$

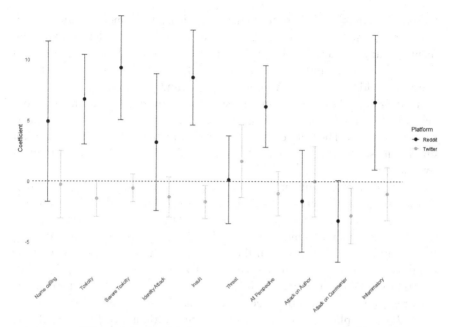

FIGURE 10.9   Effect of Antisocial Commenting on Votes across Reddit and Twitter

classifier annotated only about a third of the Reddit comments because many of them exceeded the default input length limitations of the tool.[4] This not only introduces bias in our analysis toward shorter comments but also makes the comparison to Twitter more apt. All of the Twitter tweets were coded properly as they tend to be shorter than Reddit comments. Several measures of anti-sociality were rewarded (i.e., received relatively more upvotes than downvotes) on Reddit, including *toxicity, severe toxicity, insult,* and *inflammatory language.* In contrast, *toxicity* and *insult* were associated with fewer votes (i.e., "favorites") on Twitter. *Attacks on other commenters* were consistently associated with lower social rewards on both platforms.

Perceived Descriptive and Injunctive Norms on Reddit and Twitter

We close this section with a set of analyses investigating the role of *perceived* descriptive and injunctive norms on the spread of antisocial commenting across the two platforms. While the previous analyses of collective norms focused on aggregate rates of antisocial comments and their associated social rewards, an analysis of perceived norms investigates instead the effects on individuals' postings due to their exposure to antisocial commenting and associated rewards within a conversational thread. We modeled the outcomes, or dependent variables, using several of the antisocial features that were used in the previous analyses, above, but as they appeared in the final triplet comment. We tested whether antisocial comments resulted from a statistical interaction between (1) anti-sociality in the triplet's initial comment, (2) anti-sociality in the proximate comment, (3) the number of votes of approval that the initial comment received, and (4) whether the comments were on Reddit or Twitter. A multilevel modeling procedure specified a random effects variable representing the submission number (on Reddit) or conversation ID (on Twitter), as well as a random effects variable representing each contributor. The full numerical results are available from the first author upon request, but the marginal effects depicted in Figure 10.10 reflect definitive patterns.

Across a range of antisocial features, proximate anti-sociality on Reddit was associated with a greater likelihood of anti-sociality in the final comment. However, we found no effects of votes on Reddit, and the rate of anti-sociality in a Redditor's final comment did not differ due to anti-sociality in that user's initial comment. On Twitter, on the other hand, the rate of anti-sociality in the final comment was regularly associated with anti-sociality in prior posts as well as votes that a triplet's initial comment received for anti-sociality. This result suggests that the theory of normative social behavior (Rimal & Real, 2005) applies to Twitter's dynamics more than Reddit's. The theory predicts an interaction between descriptive and injunctive norms (in this case, between proximate anti-sociality and votes for initial anti-sociality). *Insult* on Twitter, in particular, appears partially caused by such an interaction effect and, to a lesser extent, so do *severe toxicity, identity attacks, profanity*, and *threat*. An unexpected finding was that, on Twitter, votes for initial anti-sociality were associated with *lower* rates of subsequent *name-calling* and *inflammatory language*, suggesting a possible satiation effect whereby rewards for anti-sociality filled a need that no longer must be met, a threshold effect, providing an interesting direction for future research.

To summarize, we found notable differences between Reddit and Twitter in the constitution of norms surrounding antisocial commenting. At the collective level, discussions on Reddit tended to feature higher rates of antisocial commenting than Twitter, except for *attacks on commenters* which were greater on Twitter. These aggregate descriptive norms are useful for understanding the kinds of language that users are exposed to on the two platforms, albeit at a very abstract level. Rewards for antisocial commenting were more common on Reddit than Twitter, suggesting that (collective) injunctive norms are more favorable to anti-sociality on Reddit. However, when shifting from collective to perceived norms, a slightly different picture emerges. In particular, while votes for anti-sociality were more common on Reddit, they may be more *influential* on Twitter. Being rewarded for antisocial comments on Twitter increased a contributor's likelihood of repeating antisocial behavior, while the same rewards did not produce additional antisocial messaging on Reddit. Injunctive norms surrounding anti-sociality

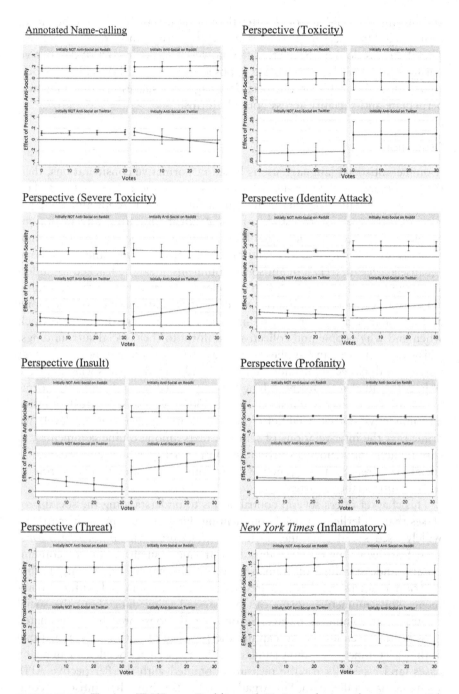

FIGURE 10.10 Testing TNSB on Reddit and Twitter during the January 6th Capitol Riots

are thus more incendiary on Twitter than Reddit, possibly due to the afore-mentioned differences in their interaction structure or moderation practices. The platforms do not appear to differ, however, in the impact of descriptive norms – on both platforms, being exposed to antisocial language is associated with higher rates of antisocial language use, suggesting that mimetics perpetuate anti-sociality across both platforms.

Discussion

If online antisocial language use is based in normative considerations, then the combination of online discussion thread data and automated text classification techniques together is the equivalent of a microscope and telescope (i.e., macroscope) for the study of social norm formation and evolution. A microscope because individual-level behavior can be tracked over time to study the formation and evolution of perceived norms, and a telescope because aggregate trends in antisocial commenting can be tracked to understand the formation and evolution of collective norms at scale. By providing behavioral researchers with a rich set of *relational* artifacts as well as a long and granular *temporal* frame, online discussion data can be used to track when and why people and collectives conform to their social surroundings. This study validates and applies text-based classification methods to uncover normative dynamics that underlie the use and spread of antisocial language online. In addition to distinguishing between collective and perceived norms at the analytical level (Lapinski & Rimal, 2005), we also separate descriptive and injunctive norms (Cialdini et al., 1990) at the measurement level. We argue that the inter-relations of series of texts among online comments can capture descriptive norms surrounding anti-sociality, while the allocation of social votes reflects the injunctive norms and that both can play a role in fueling antisocial comments.

This chapter offers several contributions to understanding the social processes that underlie antisocial commenting. First and foremost, it maps the widely used social scientific constructs, *descriptive* and *injunctive norms*, onto features of digital trace data that are increasingly useful for contemporary understanding of human behavior. In particular, we argue that descriptive norms can be measured using the text contained within a comment, while injunctive norms can be assessed using data about the social "votes" that comments receive. Second, we demonstrated how automated classification techniques can capture the presence of antisocial commenting within a comment, yielding similar results as human-coded data in many cases (and especially for the measures obtained with the Perspective API). Using human-coded data, Shmargad et al. (2022) show that antisocial commenting is sensitive to descriptive and injunctive norms, and we show here, using comments from the online *Arizona Daily Star,* that the Perspective API

(Lees et al., 2022) can be used to replicate these findings. Finally, we analyzed the collective and perceived norms around antisocial commenting as the January 6th Capitol riots unfolded and showed how these differed across the social media platforms Reddit and Twitter. While antisocial language was more likely to be rewarded on Reddit than Twitter, rewards were more influential for the spread of antisocial language on Twitter. The presence and influence of antisocial norms can thus vary widely across sociotechnical contexts.

The broad theoretical approach we introduce, which delineates self- and other-focused signals of descriptive and injunctive information available in online discussion data, can be used in a variety of ways that go beyond the analyses that we present. One direction worth pursuing is the adoption of a longer time window of individual-level behavior (e.g., Rains et al., 2021) and the social contexts from which it emerges. In contrast, the temporal dimension we study here is short and focuses more on the dynamics of comments in a single thread. A longer view of how an individual's contributions change over time could yield new knowledge about how antisocial personalities develop (Bor & Peterson, 2021) and, more importantly, knowledge about when and why people evolve *out of* antisocial patterns. This will help to inform moderation policies that are less myopic than those that focus on the removal of specific comments, and to provide more sustainable solutions for how we might design public spaces that yield the kinds of discussions (and deviance) that achieve a balance between individual and collective ambitions, thereby being more accommodating to the inherent social processes that underlie online posting and commenting.

New applications in automated text analysis are likely to propel even more advances. Text similarity techniques such as TF-IDF (Bail, 2016) could be used to measure the extent that one's posting behavior conforms to or deviates from their previous posts or from other people's posts on the same discussion thread. Large language models, such as those created by OpenAI, can be used to construct more nuanced annotations and interpretations of text that are then applied at scale.[5] For example, a large language model can be prompted to detect whether or not two sequential comments are in agreement or disagreement, which can be an important moderator in addition to social votes for whether descriptive norms are propagated. This could provide more contextual information that can be used to investigate both moderators and catalysts of antisocial language spread. The validation of such language models for large-scale annotation is an important direction for future research.

Despite the aforementioned advantages of these new data sources and text classification techniques, there of course remain many barriers to their successful application in social science research. The findings we report here suggest that automated classifiers, and especially those obtained with the Perspective API, can be used to generate similar behavioral findings as human annotations *on average*. There will, however, inevitably remain variation in how people interpret the contents of online messages and incivility in particular (Kenski et al., 2020). One risk of the kinds of automated techniques we deploy is that, by providing central tendencies in text interpretation, they remove variation in human interpretation, especially infrequent or extreme content, that may very well be informative sources or sites of social deviance. Finally, we note that people do not live their entire lives online, and there is an enduring variation across (as well as within) people in their engagement with online platforms. Our framework should thus be viewed as a starting point for incorporating online discussion data into the study of anti-sociality, and we encourage the concurrent investigation of multiple platforms, offline activities, and other measures obtained through more traditional instruments such as interviews and surveys.

Notes

1 Retrieved November 22, 2023, from https://huggingface.co/civility-lab
2 More information on the attributes from the Perspective API, including those trained on the *New York Times* comments, can be found here: Retrieved November 22, 2023, from https://developers.perspectiveapi.com/s/about-the-api-attributes-and-languages
3 That the rate of anti-sociality in comments starting a triplet does not differ substantially from that of comments in general should not be viewed as evidence for a lack of social influence. This is because early comments will not necessarily start a triplet, as the triplets we constructed have the particular structure that allows for a test of our framework (that is, they originate and end with the same commenter with a different commenter sandwiched between them). For example, if the identities of the contributors of a string of comments are 1234546, then there will only be one applicable triplet (454) and it will not be found at the beginning of the set.
4 Upon further investigation, we discovered that the default input length limitations can be circumvented with additional code. However, a complete reanalysis of the data was not possible at the time of this writing.
5 More information about OpenAI's API can be found here: Retrieved November 22, 2023, from https://platform.openai.com/overview

References

Bail, C. A. (2016). Combining natural language processing and network analysis to examine how advocacy organizations stimulate conversation on social media. *Proceedings of the National Academy of Sciences, 113*(42), 11823–11828. https://doi.org/10.1073/pnas.1607151113

Bakshy, E., Rosenn, I., Marlow, C., & Adamic, L. A. (2012). The role of social networks in information diffusion. In *Proceedings of the 21st international conference on world wide web* (pp. 519–528). ACM. https://doi.org/10.1145/2187836.2187907

Barbera, P. (2015). Birds of the same feather tweet together: Bayesian ideal point estimation using Twitter data. *Political Analysis, 23*(1), 76–91. https://doi.org/10.1093/pan/mpu011

Bor, A., & Peterson, M. B. (2021). The psychology of online political hostility: A comprehensive, cross-national test of the mismatch hypothesis. *American Political Science Review, 116*(1), 1–18. https://doi.org/10.1017/S0003055421000885

Burrell, J., & Fourcade, M. (2021). The society of algorithms. *Annual Review of Sociology*, 47, 213–237. https://doi.org/10.1146/annurev-soc-090820-020800

Cheng, J., Danescu-Niculescu-Mizil, C., & Leskovec, J. (2014). How community feedback shapes user behavior. *Proceedings of the Eighth International AAAI Conference on Weblogs and Social Media (ICWSM)*, 8(1), 41–50. Association for the Advancement of Artificial Intelligence. https://doi.org/10.48550/arXiv.1405.1429

Cheng, J., Danescu-Niculescu-Mizil, C., & Leskovec, J. (2017). Antisocial behavior in online discussion communities. *Proceedings of the Eleventh International AAAI Conference on Web and Social Media (ICWSM)*, 9(1), 61–70. Association for the Advancement of Artificial Intelligence. https://doi.org/10.48550/arXiv.1504.00680

Cialdini, R. B., Reno, R. R., & Kallgren, C. A. (1990). A focus theory of normative conduct: Recycling the concept of norms to reduce littering in public places. *Journal of Personality and Social Psychology*, 58(6), 1015–1026. https://doi.org/10.1037/0022-3514.58.6.1015

Coe, K., Kenski, K., & Rains, S. A. (2014). Online and uncivil? Patterns and determinants of incivility in newspaper website comments. *Journal of Communication*, 64(4), 658–679. https://doi.org/10.1111/jcom.12104

Ding, B., Qin, C., Liu, L., Bing, L., Joty, S., & Li, B. (2022). Is GPT-3 a good data annotator? arXiv. https://doi.org/10.48550/arXiv.2212.10450

Durkheim, E. (1893). *The division of labor in society*. The Free Press.

Edyvane, D. (2020). Incivility as dissent. *Political Studies*, 68(1), 93–109. https://doi.org/10.1177/0032321719831983

ElSherief, M., Kulkarni, V., Nguyen, D., Wang, W. Y., & Belding, E. (2018). Hate lingo: A target-based linguistic analysis of hate speech in social media. *Proceedings of the Twelfth International AAAI Conference on Web and Social Media (ICWSM)*, 12(1). Association for the Advancement of Artificial Intelligence. https://doi.org/10.48550/arXiv.1804.04257

Forestal, J. (2021). Beyond gatekeeping: Propaganda, democracy, and the organization of digital publics. *Journal of Politics*, 83(1), 306–320. https://doi.org/10.1086/709300

Freelon, D., Bossetta, M., Wells, C., Lukito, J., Xia, Y., & Adams, K. (2020). Black trolls matter: Racial and ideological asymmetries in social media disinformation. *Social Science Computer Review*, 40(3), 560–578. https://doi.org/10.1177/0894439320914853

Goldberg, A., & Stein, S. K. (2018). Beyond social contagion: Associative diffusion and the emergence of cultural variation. *American Sociological Review*, 83(5), 897–932. https://doi.org/10.1177/0003122418797576

Golder, S. A., & Macy, M. W. (2014). Digital footprints: Opportunities and challenges for online social research. *Annual Review of Sociology*, 40, 129–152. https://doi.org/10.1146/annurev-soc-071913-043145

Haimson, O. L., Delmonaco, D., Nie, P., & Wegner, A. (2021). Disproportionate removals and differing content moderation experiences for conservative, transgender, and black social media users: Marginalization and moderation gray areas. *Proceedings of the ACM on Human-Computer Interaction (CSCW)*, 5, 1–35. https://doi.org/10.1145/3479610

Jamieson, K. H., Volinsky, A., Weitz, I., & Kenski, K. (2017). The political uses and abuses of civility and incivility. In *The Oxford handbook of political communication* (pp. 205–218). Oxford University Press. https://doi.org/10.1093/oxfordhb/9780199793471.013.79_update_001

Jiang, S., Robertson, R. E., & Wilson, C. (2020). Reasoning about political bias in content moderation. *Proceedings of the 34th AAAI Conference on Artificial Intelligence*, 34(9), 13669–13672. Association for the Advancement of Artificial Intelligence. https://doi.org/10.1609/aaai.v34i09.7117

Kenski, K., Coe, K., Rains, S. A. (2020). Perceptions of uncivil discourse online: An examination of types and predictors. *Communication Research*, 47(6), 795–814. https://doi.org/10.1177/0093650217699933

Kim, J. W., Guess, A., Nyhan, B., & Reifler, J. (2021). The distorting prism of social media: How self-selection and exposure to incivility fuel online comment toxicity. *Journal of Communication*, 71(6), 922–946. https://doi.org/10.1093/joc/jqab034

Kim, K. K., Lee, A. R., & Lee, U. (2019). Impact of anonymity on roles of personal and group identities in online communities. *Information & Management*, 56, 109–121. https://doi.org/10.1016/j.im.2018.07.005

Lapinski, M. K., & Rimal, R. N. (2005). An explication of social norms. *Communication Theory*, 15(2), 127–147. https://doi.org/10.1111/j.1468-2885.2005.tb00329.x

Lees, A., Tran, V. Q., Tay, Y., Sorensen, J., Gupta, J., Metzler, D., & Vasserman, L. (2022). A new generation of perspective API: Efficient multilingual character-level transformers. In *Proceedings of the 28th ACM SIGKDD conference on knowledge discovery and data mining (KDD 2022)* (pp. 3197–3207). https://doi.org/10.1145/3534678.3539147

Linvill, D. L., & Warren, P. L. (2020). Troll factories: Manufacturing specialized disinformation on Twitter. *Political Communication*, 37(4), 447–467.

Lofland, J. (1969). *Deviance and identity*. Prentice-Hall.

Maratea, R. J., & Kavanaugh, P. R. (2012). Deviant identity in online contexts: New directions in the study of a classic concept. *Sociology Compass*, 6(2), 102–112. https://doi.org/10.1111/j.1751-9020.2011.00438.x

McDonnell, T. E., Bail, C. A., & Tavory, I. (2017). A theory of resonance. *Sociological Theory*, 35(1), 1–14. https://doi.org/10.1177/0735275117692837

Ng, L. H. X., Cruickshank, I. J., & Carley, K. M. (2022). Cross-platform information spread during the January 6th Capitol riots. *Social Network Analysis and Mining*, 12(1), 133. https://doi.org/10.1007/s13278-022-00937-1

Ozler, K. B., Kenski, K., Rains, S. A., Shmargad, Y., Coe, K., & Bethard, S. (2020). Fine-tuning for multi-domain and multi-label uncivil language detection. *Proceedings of the Fourth Workshop on Online Abuse and Harms*, 28–33. https://doi.org/10.18653/v1/2020.alw-1.4

Papakyriakopoulos, O., Engelmann, S., & Winecoff, A. (2023). Upvotes? Downvotes? No votes? Understanding the relationship between reaction mechanisms and political discourse on Reddit. *Proceedings of the 2023 CHI Conference on Human Factors in Computing Systems*, 549, 1–28. ACM. https://doi.org/10.1145/3544548.3580644

Pozzobon, L., Ermis, B., Lewis, P., & Hooker, S. (2023). On the challenges of using black-box APIs for toxicity evaluation in research. arXiv. https://doi.org/10.48550/arXiv.2304.12397

Rains, S. A., Harwood, J., Shmargad, Y., Kenski, K., Coe, K., & Bethard, S. (2023a). Engagement with partisan Russian troll tweets during the 2016 US presidential election: A social identity perspective. *Journal of Communication*, 73(1), 38–48. https://doi.org/10.1093/joc/jqac03

Rains, S. A., Kenski, K., Dajches, L., Duncan, K., Yan, K., Shin, Y., Barbati, J. L., Bethard, S., Coe, K., & Shmargad, Y. (2023b). Engagement with incivility in tweets from and directed at local elected officials. *Communication and Democracy*, 57(1), 143–152. https://doi.org/10.1080/27671127.2023.2195467

Rains, S. A., Kenski, K., Coe, K., & Harwood, J. (2017). Incivility and political identity on the internet: Intergroup factors as predictors of incivility in discussions of news online. *Journal of Computer-Mediated Communication*, 22(4), 163–178. https://doi.org/10.1111/jcc4.12191

Rains, S. A., Shmargad, Y., Coe, K., Kenski, K., & Bethard, S. (2021). Assessing the Russian troll efforts to sow discord on Twitter during the 2016 US election.

Human Communication Research, 47(4), 477–486. https://doi.org/10.1093/hcr/hqab009

Rimal, R. N., & Real, K. (2005). How behaviors are influenced by perceived norms: A test of the theory of normative social behavior. *Communication Research*, 32(3), 389–414. https://doi.org/10.1177/0093650205275385

Rossini, P. (2022). Beyond incivility: Understanding patterns of uncivil and intolerant discourse in online political talk. *Communication Research*, 49(3), 399–425. https://doi.org/10.1177/0093650220921314

Sadeque, F., Rains, S. A., Shmargad, Y., Kenski, K., Coe, K., & Bethard, S. (2019). Incivility detection in online comments. In *Proceedings of the eighth joint conference on lexical and computational semantics (SEM 2019)* (pp. 283–291). Association for Computational Linguistics. https://doi.org/10.18653/v1/S19-1031

Shmargad, Y. (2022). Twitter influencers in the 2016 US Congressional races. *Journal of Political Marketing*, 22(1), 23–40. https://doi.org/10.1080/15377857.2018.1513385

Shmargad, Y., Coe, K., Kenski, K., & Rains, S. A. (2022). Social norms and the dynamics of online incivility. *Social Science Computer Review*, 40(3), 717–735. https://doi.org/10.1177/0894439320985527

Song, Y., Lin, Q., Kwon, K. H., Choy, C. H. Y., & Xu, R. (2022). Contagion of offensive speech online: An interactional analysis of political swearing. *Computers in Human Behavior*, 127, 107046. https://doi.org/10.1016/j.chb.2021.107046

Tontodimamma, A. Nissi, E., Sarra, A., & Fontanella, L. (2021). Thirty years of research into hate speech: Topics of interest and their evolution. *Scientometrics*, 126, 157–179. https://doi.org/10.1007/s11192-020-03737-6

Udupa, S., Maronikolakis, A., & Wisiorek, A. (2023). Ethical scaling for content moderation: Extreme speech and the (in)significance of artificial intelligence. *Big Data & Society*, 10(1). https://doi.org/10.1177/20539517231172424

Vogels, E. A. (2021). *The state of online harassment*. Pew Research Center. https://www.pewresearch.org/internet/2021/01/13/the-state-of-online-harassment/

Zampieri, M., Malmasi, S., Nakov, P., Rosenthal, S., Farra, N., & Kumar, R. (2019). Predicting the type and target of offensive posts in social media. In *Proceedings of the 2019 conference of the North American chapter of the association for computational linguistics: Human language technologies* (pp. 1415–1420). Association for Computational Linguistics. https://doi.org/10.18653/v1/N19-1144

11

UNDERSTANDING THE PHASES AND THEMES OF COORDINATED ONLINE AGGRESSION ATTACKS

Gianluca Stringhini and Jeremy Blackburn

In the middle of the day, on an early summer Sunday in 2016, an anonymous user on 4chan's Politically Incorrect Board (/pol/) posts a link to a music video on YouTube which portrays the romantic story between a young female pop star and an African American man. The poster, outraged by the fact that the singer is normalizing interracial relationships, says "she's blatantly burning coal right in front millions of kids. When will this degeneracy end?" and urges others on the board to manifest their outrage too. Soon after, other anonymous users start piling on in the 4chan thread, posting racist comments about the pop star and the actor in the video, wondering why they hate America, and worrying about young girls following her example. At the same time, the anonymous users start posting hateful and harassing messages on the YouTube page where the video appears, in a coordinated attack.

It is March 2020. On /pol/, a bored high school student forced to attend school remotely posts the link to the Zoom room for his English lecture: "Anyone wanna crash our online lesson?" Shortly after, a mob of anonymous trolls storms the meeting room, shouting profanities and slurs, hijacking the share screen function to display pornography to the horrified teacher and students, and changing their profile names to those of other students in the class to make it more difficult to be identified and kicked out. The shocked teacher is helpless and resorts to ending the Zoom call to avoid further disruption. Meanwhile, the attackers head back to the original thread on /pol/, posting screenshots of the meeting and reporting about what they did: "Anyone heard me farting?" "HAHAHA that was great." Other messages celebrating the hilarity of the situation soon follow.

These are just two examples of *coordinated aggression attacks*. As part of our work studying polarized online communities for the past decade, we

DOI: 10.4324/9781003472148-11

have seen hundreds of similar instances, and we have developed automated systems to identify these attacks and collect data about them. In this chapter we discuss what coordinated aggression attacks look like, analyze the phases that attackers follow while carrying them out, and discuss common themes observed in our data. We focus on attacks originating from 4chan's Politically Incorrect Board (/pol/) as previous work has shown that this site and its devotees are particularly active in this practice (Hine et al., 2017). We look at attacks targeting YouTube videos and online meeting rooms (e.g., Zoom and Google Meet), as they appear particularly frequently on the 4chan platform (Hine et al., 2017; Ling et al., 2021).

Like previous research on networked harassment, we find that online aggression is a social activity (Marwick, 2021), in accord with the *social processes* theme of this volume. Unlike previous work that identified attackers selecting their targets within the same platform (Lewis et al., 2021), we find that attackers usually target victims on secondary platforms. Like previous work, we find that online aggression attacks often appear to be motivated by misogyny and racism (Antunovic, 2019; Tynes et al., 2018). At the same time, we also find that disruption for the sake of it (and for its "entertainment" value) is often the focus of these attacks, particularly in the case of coordinated attacks against Zoom meetings (i.e., *Zoombombing*). In these instances, we find that inflammatory language like racist and hateful speech is an *efficient tactic* to cause havoc instead of being the apparent *focus* of the attack. Similarly, while hurting the victim is the apparent goal in some instances, many attackers seem to be motivated by some perverse enjoyment in unleashing chaos; that is, they do it "for the lulz" (for amusement, for laughs; see Phillips, 2015). This resonates with previous work studying the underlying psychological elements of online attackers, which found that trolls often act for the sake of enjoyment (Buckels et al., 2014).

Contrary to previous work on networked harassment (Marwick & Caplan, 2018), we find that coordinated harassment is not only made up of explicitly hateful content but also that, often, attackers attempt to cause disruption by pretending to be legitimately concerned parties in the conversation. This *concern trolling* is designed to bait real users into conversations that have the goal of shutting down legitimate discussion and potentially lure them into endless arguments (DiFranco, 2020).

We also discuss important challenges faced by the research community and by practitioners when trying to mitigate coordinated online aggression and online hate activity in general.

The rest of the chapter is structured as follows: First, we present our methods, comprising computational techniques that we developed that detect coordinated attacks and the synchronization of indicators that exemplify them, and we describe our data that illuminate the activities that comprise the attacks. We then identify the phases by which coordinated aggression attacks evolve and show some examples and general themes that we have observed. Next, we dig deeper into these themes, discussing, for example, what might be the attackers' motivations as well as the minimal influence of anonymity on attacking behavior. Finally, we discuss challenges and opportunities for researchers and practitioners working toward mitigating coordinated online harassment, including the unintended consequences of deplatforming.

Detecting Coordination

Methods and Data

This work is the culmination of over a decade's worth of effort to understand the *modus operandi* and motivation of coordinated online attackers. To identify social media posts and threads that call for coordinated online aggression attacks, we use a combination of quantitative and qualitative techniques. However, before continuing, it is important to discuss a component of our research efforts that usually goes unreported: Our data collection systems.

We have developed tools to automatically collect data from a variety of social media platforms (e.g., 4chan, Reddit, Twitter, and YouTube). Since 2016, we have collected billions of social media posts (Baumgartner et al., 2020; Papadamou et al., 2020; Papasavva et al., 2020). Building these types of reliable and robust systems is as much of an art as it is an engineering exercise. For example, consider that 4chan is an ephemeral platform: By design, posts expire and are deleted. What this means is that, in practice, we must design a system that collects all data, not just data that we think is relevant or available at the time of collection. To complicate things further, the process that controls when a post is deleted is driven by activity on the site, as opposed to being a preordained expiration date. In practice, this means that our systems must be dynamic and adapt to changes in user activity.

Over the years, we have arrived at an extensible and powerful crawler construction toolkit of programmatic building blocks that enable the rapid development of new crawlers. A crawler is an automated, continuous data collection system that dynamically adjusts a variety of parameters related to the data collection process itself. For example, a crawler for 4chan must regularly discover new content that needs to be collected while at the same time being robust with respect to the ephemeral nature of 4chan as well as the typical errors that occur when dealing with large-scale data traversing the Internet. One of the key insights behind this toolkit is that social media platforms, regardless of difference in affordances, have a lot in common, at least when it comes to data collection. For example, most social media platforms have rate limits that we must work within. That is, we are only able to make requests for data a certain number of times per second. Even for platforms that do not have strict rate limits, we aim to be neutral observers and thus do our best to minimize the impact our crawlers might impose on the systems' performance. To this end, we have built a relatively complicated, reusable rate limiting subsystem. When writing new crawlers, we simply hook into our rate limiting subsystem, instead of having to write custom code for every crawler we build.

In addition to our crawler construction toolkit, we have, over the years, developed a robust architectural software architecture design (a "pipeline") that we build our crawlers around (see Figure 11.1 for a high-level overview). This architecture treats the crawling process as a series of jobs. For example,

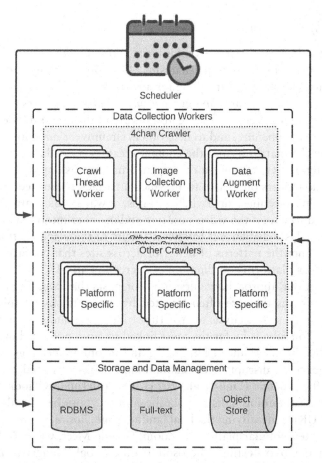

FIGURE 11.1 Software Architectural Design ("Pipeline") of Crawler Processes

one job could be collecting all the posts made in given 4chan thread, and another job could be collecting the images the posts link to. Once the crawling process is broken up into different logical jobs, we can then use a scheduler to independently control how and when each job is executed. Because each job is independent, we can run many instances of the same type of job concurrently. That is, we can collect the posts from several threads at once, while at the same time collecting images from other threads. Furthermore, we can adapt to changing conditions (e.g., more or less posting activity) by adjusting when a job is scheduled to run. As an added bonus, this architecture, while being "cloud native" and scaling to multiple worker servers, also scales down to run on cheap computer hardware, making it suitable for rapid development and testing before deployment into our production environment.

Detecting Synchronization

Coordinated aggression attacks take place through traceable collaborative activities and coordination mechanisms. Our observations indicate that attackers usually start a post calling for an attack, within a certain platform, and that this post generates an *aggregation thread* where users partaking in the attack elsewhere return to share insights about the raid, provide feedback about what is happening, and to help others circumvent mitigation steps put in place by the platforms and the content creators. Coordinated aggression attacks often target content on other platforms. For example, the inception of an attack appears on 4chan, from which an attack is directed at YouTube videos, online meetings, or Twitch streams, toward which attackers have been invited to harass the video's creator and/or other meeting participants. Our data analysis challenge is to identify many of these aggregation threads and to decipher the patterns of behavior across sites that confirm and illustrate the cross-platform coordination of aggression attacks.

As part of our approach, we first look for posts that contain links to secondary platforms that are often targeted by these attacks. In this chapter, we limit our present analysis to YouTube videos and links to online meetings, since YouTube is by far the most linked to from polarized online communities like 4chan (Hine et al., 2017), and to online meetings because of the emergence of disruptive Zoombombing attacks observed early in the COVID-19 pandemic (Ling et al., 2021). For YouTube, we look for social media posts containing links to youtube.com or youtu.be. We also expand shortened URLs, identifying the final landing page. For online meeting tools, we identify ten popular platforms (Zoom, Google Meet, Cisco Webex, Jitsi, Skype, Citrix GoToMeeting, Microsoft Teams, Google Hangouts, Bluejeans, and Starleaf) and look for links to those platforms (e.g., zoom.us). Since Zoom meetings can also be shared by ID instead of by links, we also look for posts that include a meeting ID and potentially a passcode for a Zoom meeting, even without an explicit link.

Of course, most posts containing a link to a YouTube video or to an online meeting platform are not calling for a coordinated aggression attack. To further refine our investigations, we use two different techniques that we developed in our previous work (Hine et al., 2017; Ling et al., 2021).

In the case of YouTube videos, we have access to both the thread on 4chan that called the attack and to the publicly visible user-generated comments that were written in the YouTube videos' pages. By analyzing the timing of the comments posted on the video pages, we observed that the number of comments on YouTube increases immediately after the link to a video is posted on 4chan. Additionally, since 4chan threads are ephemeral, the thread discussing a certain video will be visible to other users only for a limited time, and we observed that comments spike during the lifetime of the thread and die off after the thread is removed. However, while this pattern is indicative of an increased activity on YouTube generated by 4chan, the phenomenon is not unique to aggression attacks. On the one hand, we expect that most content linked on social media will generate an increase in activity on the linked platform (Kujur & Singh, 2016). What is unique about coordinated aggression attacks, on the other hand, is that attackers use the thread that calls for the coordinated attack as an aggregation point; they post comments related to the attack in real time, reporting back, for example, on their actions and the outcomes of them (Hine et al., 2017). Based on this observation, comparing the timing of the posts made in the initial thread and in the attacked YouTube video's page shows specific cross-correlational timing patterns: Attacked videos show a higher degree of synchronization with the 4chan thread that linked to it, compared to videos that were linked on 4chan for purposes other than coordinated aggression. The strongest possible synchronization would occur when someone posts a comment on YouTube and instantly reports back on 4chan about what they just did. Obviously, this seldom happens, but we expect synchronization to be stronger for videos that are being attacked than for videos that are not being attacked, where people are just posting more innocuous comments without much coordination going on.

To further enhance confidence that videos that see a high synchronization in their comments to the 4chan thread that links to them indicate a coordinated aggression attack, we ran the following experiment. For each of the 19,568 YouTube videos linked on 4chan in our dataset (Hine et al., 2017), we first calculated the lag of their comments in YouTube with the comments on the 4chan thread. Then, for each comment in the YouTube videos, we determined whether it contains hate speech by looking up its words against Hatebase.org, a crowdsourced hate speech lexicon (discontinued now but still available when this analysis took place). We considered a comment to contain hate speech if one or more words in it appeared in the Hatebase lexicon. Our results indicated that a lower lag was associated with more hateful comments, showing that the cross-correlation metric is a good indicator of coordinated aggression attacks (Mariconti et al., 2019). Manual analysis of the 4chan threads that included links to those videos confirmed that they were indeed calls for coordinated aggression.

In the case of threads calling to attack online meetings (e.g., Zoombombing), we cannot apply the same techniques adopted for YouTube video pages, since we do not have access to the meetings (and the concept of persistent comments does not really apply in this context). For this reason, to identify threads calling for Zoombombing, we apply a qualitative approach: Four annotators performed thematic coding, identifying which threads are likely calls for attacks, and resolving disagreements through discussion (Ling et al., 2021). We find that identifying these kinds of threads is easy for trained annotators, who achieve perfect agreement (Cohen's $\kappa = 1.0$). In total, we identified 123 online meetings that were disrupted through calls for coordinated online aggression on 4chan, in addition to 428 YouTube videos, accounting for 551 confirmed calls for coordinated aggression attacks.

What Attackers Do and How: A Taxonomy of the Phases of Online Coordinated Attacks

Our study of the social process surrounding coordinated online aggression between 4chan's /pol/ and their targets on secondary platforms has allowed us to discover and describe several phases that these attacks go through. We identify five phases that characterize coordinated aggression attacks: (1) Call for attack, (2) preparation, (3) execution, (4) reporting back, and (5) wrap up/celebration. This section analyzes these phases in detail, identifying differences and commonalities between the attacks that target YouTube videos and those that target online meetings. Later in the chapter, we further analyze different themes that emerge from our data.

Call for Attack

As illustrated in the two examples at the beginning of this chapter, a coordinated aggression attack begins with a user starting a new thread in which the user calls for the attack. This initial post both identifies the target and makes it known to other members of the community, and the thread that evolves from that post serves as an aggregation and discussion point for the further phases of the attack. The post containing the call for attack usually comes with a link to the online resource to target and a short message. This message can be a clear indication of what the user wants others to do (e.g., "My English class, come in and trolley for a while"), an inflammatory message designed to enrage other users and encourage them to join (e.g., "God fucking dammit! She's blatantly burning coal right in front millions of kids. When will this degeneracy end?"), or a dog whistle (e.g., "You know what to do") designed to evade content moderation, which often forbids these calls for attacks. In many cases, the call for attack only contains the external resource (e.g., the YouTube link) and a picture of the victim (e.g., a female influencer), which, we have observed, are often enough for /pol/'s users to understand what is wanted of them.

In some cases, the attacker posts some details about the victim(s) with the goal of encouraging others to pile on and target them based on their gender, sexual orientation, race, etc., as well as making the purpose of the attack more explicit (e.g., "Anyone wanna join our online lesson? Our teacher is Black. Its gonna be in 20 mins," "we must invade this class of lib shills!," "What's your opinion on this kosher conservative?").

In other cases, however, the calls for attack offer no indication of the specific qualities of the victims. In those cases, instead, the goal of the attack seems to be the attack itself. The presence of these types of attacks suggests that coordinated aggression is sometimes performed in order to provide some entertainment value ("for the lulz") which transcends the aim of causing harm to the victims (e.g., "if you want to come fuck with my apartment complexes yoga class be my guest. It's also being recorded so have at it"), giving an easy distraction to the person calling for the attack from the mundane tasks of daily life (e.g., "Feel free to fuck with my working meeting. Bored as fuck").

Perhaps surprisingly, we have found that most calls for attacks are not planned ahead of time but are called for in conjunction with events that are happening in real time or in the near future (e.g., scheduled Zoom meetings). Even those that do not target real-time content are carried out shortly after the call is made, although this might be a particular characteristic of 4chan threads, which are ephemeral in nature, which persist for 47 minutes on average (Hine et al., 2017) and make it challenging to elaborate long-term plans.

Finally, it is important to note that any issues or resentments between the user that called for the attack and the victim are not always disclosed. In fact, we have seen instances of failed calls for attack where the response from other users is not just unenthusiastic or even subdued but quite explicit statements that they are not interested in participating in attacks that directly benefit the caller (e.g., we're "not your personal army.")

Preparation

Before an attack, offenders often coordinate to improve their effectiveness. We often see anonymous users post additional information about the victim on the coordination thread, which goes beyond aspects of the particular resource being attacked such as their YouTube video. The additional information may include personal information (i.e., doxxing) or the victim's other social media handles. In many instances, attackers spend considerable effort posting offensive comments about the victims on the original 4chan thread, either to further motivate the attack or for the enjoyment of other attackers, rather than to use as ammunition against the victim, since the victim will probably never see them (an important point emphasized by Walther, this volume). In the case of Zoombombing, the person who called for the attack is often an insider, who also provides additional information to help other attackers stay under the radar and to make it difficult for the meeting host to identify them and kick them out. For example, attackers are often instructed to adopt certain names, which belong to the legitimate students of the remote class being attacked, so that the teacher will have a hard time identifying who is a real student and who is an attacker and will allow the attack to continue for a longer time.

Execution

When an attack starts, attackers will carry out their disruptive activity. We find that these actions are often disjointed, and we do not observe much coordination between attackers with respect to the specific hateful content they post. Actions seem to have the goal of maximizing chaos and disruption and potentially to harm the victims. This is in contrast with other types of trolling activity, like state-sponsored trolling, where multiple attackers coordinate closely to build arguments and sow discord in online groups (Saeed et al., 2022).

The way in which the attack is carried out largely depends on the affordances offered by the target platform. On YouTube, attackers post hateful comments below the video that they are targeting. With online meeting platforms, they make use of the variety of modalities that are available to them, from annotating on-screen content, to screaming audible obscenities through the microphone, to taking over the screen-sharing function and showing pornography. During the attack, we observe that attackers frequently ask others to perform certain actions to maximize disruption, for example, to perform lewd acts on camera (e.g., "Someone join with their dick out and make this interesting. I'm bored"), show pornography (e.g., "Someone can also print out a hardcore pic and hold it up for screenshot "), or shout profanities (e.g., "use your damn mic"). These requests are usually not targeted at any particular victim but seem to be encouraged due to their efficiency in shocking legitimate participants, which in turn is more entertaining to the attackers. There are certain relatively standardized tactics that become specialized for the given platform of an attack, and these tactics align with the overall strategy of achieving chaos, in large part simply for its entertainment value.

Reporting Back

Coordinated aggression attacks are not unidirectional. As we have explained, the thread that called for the attack tends to become an aggregation point that attackers use to discuss the attack itself, how it is unfolding, and eventually (as we will discuss) to celebrate and congratulate each other. We have observed many instances of attackers reporting back in the original thread about the disrupting actions that they just carried out, indicating that the social gratification surrounding coordinated aggression itself, more than harming a victim, might be their goal (see also Walther, 2022).

The attackers often write about their victims in the thread. In the case of Zoombombing, this can span from general remarks (e.g., "There's a couple of lookers, a couple of old ones too," "he's probably the kind of teacher who sits reverse on a chair and is up to date with the cool kids") to gender-based attacks (e.g., "that is definitely a he"). In the case of YouTube, where the attack activity is more asynchronous than in an online meeting, attackers often post hate speech in the original thread on /pol/ in addition to commenting on the video's page itself. These comments are often unsavory (e.g., "She looks like her face is made of solidified candle wax"), misogynistic (e.g., "Casting couch reject"), or homophobic (e.g., "He likes dicks in his cereal").

In addition to comments about the victims, we find that attackers often report back about what they themselves just did or about what happened in the attack. This is more common for Zoombombing than for YouTube attacks, which, we hypothesize, is due to the different level of openness and persistence between the two platforms: While hateful comments on a You-Tube videos are there for everyone to see forever, disruptive activities in an online meeting are only visible to those that are participating in the meeting at that moment, and any evidence of them is gone once the meeting ends. Attackers targeting online meetings often report back about what they did (e.g., "I hopped in and told them I was spanking one out," "I earraped all of them lol") or discuss notable events in the meeting (e.g., "someone started farting and the class was just dying of laughter," "Who is roleplaying the pope?"). This is usually done through text, but sometimes attackers even include screenshots from the secondary platform showing their contributions to the attack itself, providing more vivid testimony of their disruption.

When executing coordinated aggression, attackers have to deal with the legitimate owners of the resources that they target, who (sensibly) try their best to end the attack and reduce harm. In the case of YouTube attacks, hateful messages are often caught and removed by the platform's moderation system, whether it is in real time or after the fact. In the case of Zoombombing, attackers often must deal with a meeting host who actively tries to defend the meeting, who is usually trying to figure out what is going on and how to regain control of the call. We have observed many posts from attackers discussing how they had been kicked out of the Zoom room (e.g., "He banned me the second I joined and got my video set up," "Tried to join as Nate Higgers and got removed again wtf"). Again, due to the private and ephemeral nature of online meetings, these threads become the only testimony to show the broader community that the attack happened at all and are the only way that attackers can signify to their community that they carried out a successful attack.

The fact that this hate is shared among like-minded peers on /pol/ and is not directly visible to the victims (unlike comments on the video or direct actions in the online meeting) might once again indicate that these hateful activities are aimed at building social capital within the community, exceeding the wish to cause harm, orchestrated to gain recognition from their peers and enhance their status within the group.

Wrap up/Celebration

When the attack has concluded, we find that attackers often continue discussion in the original /pol/ thread. They often congratulate each other over a job well done (e.g., "Class ended. Good raid boys," "Good job you got my class cancelled"). As we will discuss later in the chapter, this is an essential element of the camaraderie aspect that characterizes coordinated aggression attacks. The other anonymous users usually react with hilarity and giving "high fives," often praising specific attackers (e.g., "You will be remembered").

Themes from the Observed Attack Threads

In this section, we dig deeper into some of the common themes that we have observed in the instances of coordinated aggression attacks. We find tension between the anonymous nature of 4chan and the need for attackers to receive recognition for their nefarious actions. In fact, we find that the main reason why attackers seem to be carrying out coordinated online aggression attacks is to feel part of and contribute to a community and to enjoy themselves. In this setting, reporting back to the 4chan thread about the outcome of an attack and celebrating each other become key in enjoying the fruits of their labors. While certainly causing harm to the victims, the harm caused to the victims is often secondary, a sort of collateral damage (see Walther, this volume). We also find that 4chan's /pol/ board is not a monolith, but rather that its users have different sensibilities and goals. As such, calls for attacks often fail, with users openly disagreeing with the practice of coordinated aggression as a whole or with the chosen victim.

The Impact of Anonymity on Coordinated Online Aggression

4chan epitomizes the concept of anonymous platforms. While most platforms require accounts for users to post content, there are no accounts whatsoever on 4chan. This means that it is not possible for outside parties or even for the users of the platform to know who posted what, aside from a temporary identifier that is given to each user in threads to identify different parties in the conversation. After the thread is gone from view, these identifiers lose any meaning, and the same user posting on a different thread will get a different identifier (Hine et al., 2017).

Prior research has argued that anonymity facilitates online hateful activity (Lapidot-Lefler, 2012; Rohlfing, 2014), and we tend to concur. Being completely anonymous allows attackers to be almost entirely free from consequences; other users will not be able to identify the perpetrators of coordinated aggression attacks and hold them accountable for their actions. The absence of accounts also makes it harder for the platform to suspend a particular user (although tightly policing the platform is not practiced in 4chan to begin with).

Even where accounts do exist, such as on YouTube, attackers often create throw-away accounts, whose suspension is more of a nuisance than a deterrence, let alone a solution. The main pain point in losing such a social media account is that any reputation associated with that account or connections built over time is also lost. In the case of coordinated aggression attacks, it is more appropriate to think of participation as hobby. Attackers just want to have fun. Considering that 4chan caters to the "gamer" demographic in general, we speculate that having to create a new account is not terribly dissimilar to having to create a new character in a free-to-play video game.

The case of Zoombombing is slightly different, because the hosts of online meetings often have the ability of mandating that participants are logged in, sometimes even restricting participation to only users within an organization (e.g., those with a university email account) (Ling et al., 2021). If set up this way, online meetings become protected from the kind of aggression attacks that we describe in this chapter. This is not feasible for all meetings, though, since some gatherings need to be open to the public. Also, our study looked at online meetings at the beginning of the pandemic, when the entire world was forced to move activities online, and is therefore a testimony about what happens when abrupt technological changes are forced on people without adequately preparing them. Most hosts of online meetings had no training, or indeed any clue, about how to secure their meetings, opening them to attacks.

Anonymity can also be a double-edged sword for attackers, because without explicit accounts, it is not possible for them to later claim credit about their actions and build their reputation among other haters. There is no concept of likes, follows, or retweets on 4chan. For this reason, attackers go out of their way to make sure that their nefarious actions are recognized and celebrated by the community. As a side effect of anonymity, actions are what is celebrated on 4chan, rather than who performs them. It is almost as if the community is a hive mind, and faceless attackers are celebrated for their contribution in carrying out the greater goal of causing havoc. When a thread eventually dies, so do any relationships its users might have forged. In turn, this means that the full richness of these fleeting relationships must be savored quickly, before they are lost to the ether forever. Unlike most social media platforms, and indeed the human experience in general, relationships on 4chan are *explicitly* ephemeral and, in this way, is a rather unique social process. This, along with anonymity, exposes a facet of what it means to be a social creature that is seldom experienced in the real world. On the Internet, nobody knows you're a dog, but on 4chan, they don't know or care. You shared the experience. That's enough.

This lack of persistent fame can be reconciled when considering how /pol/ (and 4chan at large) has a (mostly) unwritten lore, akin to an oral tradition. Things like screenshots of threads that are later posted in other threads as well as spreading to mainstream media, having direct knowledge of previous successful attacks, an ability to share this knowledge with (and potential direct the actions of) future attackers, etc., are thus likely to serve as proxies for some of the ways that social capital is spent in scenarios with long-lasting relationships. While it is not possible to keep track of who did what when carrying out an attack, the actions of attackers can become part of the community's culture (see DeKeseredy, this volume).

Coordinated Aggression as a Form of Camaraderie

Previous notions of networked harassment considered attacks to be a one-way street, with attackers directing hate toward their victims presumably with the exclusive goal of causing harm (Marwick, 2021; Snyder et al., 2017). This assumes that once the attack is done, people will just move on and stop discussing it.

Our results, however, paint a different picture: The social process of carrying out a coordinated aggression attack seems to be as important or perhaps even more important than the harm it causes (see also Walther, this volume). Attackers pile messages on their victims on the 4chan thread, too, but this is for the other aggressors to see and further comment upon, as those messages are never expected to reach the victim to cause additional harm. In the case of Zoombombing, we observe that attackers often report back about what they did during the attack and provide each other advice on how to be more successful in disrupting the meeting, making the practice of aggression look like a form of bonding. Its purpose is to be part of a community and to see oneself as a successful member of it. This resonates with previous work that observed that harassers on social media are motivated by earning approval and praise from their peers (Marwick & Caplan, 2018; Walther,

2022). Our work shows that approval seeking explicitly manifests in 4chan threads, where even though attackers are essentially finished once they have executed the attack, they are as much interested in celebrating the harm they caused as they were in causing it.

Concern Trolling

Traditional definitions of networked harassment consider explicit hateful or otherwise harmful activities toward a victim like hate speech, doxxing, and revenge porn (Marwick & Caplan, 2018). This is reflected in our data, where we see attackers directing hateful speech toward their victims. However, coordinated aggression does not have to be explicitly hateful to cause disruption. In our work, we find that attackers of YouTube videos often express what looks like legitimate concern about a sensitive topic, with the goal of baiting the content creator into replying to them or luring unwitting users into a conversation that could later be derailed by the attackers.

We often observe our attackers post YouTube comments, raising concerns about censorship and free speech (e.g., "What a joke! Everyone you don't agree with is a Nazi," "Luckily there are places on the Internet where free speech still exists") or generic comments designed to attract responses by other users (e.g., "I'm shocked this video is still up," "he must be proud of himself"). These comments look completely harmless, but they take on a completely different meaning when viewed not in isolation but rather as part of a larger coordinated aggression attack. Identifying these comments as potentially harmful is very hard (if not impossible) to do for a human, but our automated techniques (which look for synchronization of seemingly unrelated comments) can help expose them.

Victim Targeting as a Vehicle for Disruption

Coordinated aggression attacks against YouTube videos are usually directed at the video's creator, who is often singled out because of their gender, race, sexual orientation, or political opinion. We find similar elements in Zoom-bombing attacks, where the person calling for the attack sometimes points out demographic elements of the victims and participants in the targeted meeting (e.g., "Hurry hurty join and yell. Teacher is black"). We also observe instances of participants joining online meetings and commenting on specific traits of the meetings' participants ("Is the teacher Jewish?," "That is definitely a dude").

Analyzing the discussion on the 4chan thread, however, one gets the impression that these expressions of hate against women, queer people, and racial minorities are primarily used as a tool to maximize disruption; the harm it causes to the victims is just a secondary goal, where the primary one is the enjoyment of the attackers' mischief. Hate speech and slurs are easy vehicles for laughter and have a strong shock factor and are therefore likely to cause a vehement response by victims, which in turn increases enjoyment among the perpetrators, who go back to the 4chan thread to make fun of it (e.g., "have you seen their face?").

Premediated or Opportunistic?

Perhaps motivated by this need for instant gratification, we find that coordinated aggression attacks are rarely premeditated, but are assembled *ad hoc*, spontaneously in real time. In the case of online meeting, the calls are made to target meetings that are either already in progress or that are about to start. In fact, we only found one instance calling for an attack on a live streamed political rally scheduled for a later time (i.e., formally planned), and we have no indication that the attack was successful. In the case of YouTube, attackers could potentially post their hateful comments at any point in time, but we observe a tendency for attackers to stick together and post their comments in waves, correlating with the lifetime of the 4chan thread. This might be a side effect of 4chan threads being ephemeral: If the thread is not available anymore, attackers no longer have a reference to the target. It could also mean that what attackers are after is the social camaraderie that comes with attacking a victim together and that sending hateful comments in isolation outside of the time when the attack is supposed to happen is less social and unentertaining.

Short Attention Span

Most of the Zoombombing attacks that we observed are not very long lived. This seems to be the case for several reasons. First and foremost, if an attack does not immediately provoke a response from other attackers or victims, attackers deem any additional effort a waste of their time; this is a form of entertainment, and if the attack does not provide instant gratification, attackers will move on and find a different victim. There are plenty of other online interactions on which to spend energy. Second, even when a response does come from victims, and attackers get something interesting to report back on the 4chan aggregation thread, the responses might cease being "entertaining" at some point. In that case, attackers might lose interest and move on, to look for more rewarding targets.

Another interesting aspect that we observe is that the community does not seem to keep a collective "memory" of past attacks, possibly because threads on 4chan are ephemeral. For this reason, we sometimes see the same YouTube videos being picked as targets multiple times, perhaps because they are easy targets that provide a high entertainment value.

Not Your Personal Army – NYPA

From our description and analysis, it might appear that coordinated online aggression works like a perfectly oiled machine, with attackers collaborating to deliver harm and disruption with great effectiveness. While this is often the case, we observe that users on /pol/ are far from uniform and do not always act upon calls for coordinated attacks. For the Zoombombing threads in our dataset, we find that 46 out of 123 calls for attack did not receive any further replies, likely becoming moot. This can be explained by the fact that most calls for Zoombombing attacks are made for meetings that are happening in real time, and there might not have been any user on the /pol/ board looking for that kind of thrill at the time. From a theoretical perspective, this aligns with the Routine Activities Theory framework of environmental criminology, where a suitable target and a motivated offender need to converge for a crime to happen (Miró, 2014). With Zoom meetings having a short duration and the median thread lifetime on /pol/ being 47 minutes (Hine et al., 2017), it is plausible that many potential attackers would not see the call for attack in time to act upon it. Note that we could not perform a similar analysis for the calls for attacks against YouTube videos since the cross-correlation method that we used to extract the threads needs more than one post per thread to work.

In addition to calls for Zoombombing that never receive a response, we find 20 cases where /pol/ users actively refuse to participate in an attack, calling it unethical, or simply insulting the person who called for it instead (e.g., "Your teacher works hard to give you an education and this is what you give them," "I'm too lazy. And disagree with your morals you are in college you want us to troll other people who are having to spend their own money to attend school to do better in life"). In one case, an anonymous user stated opposition because of disagreement with the choice of the victim ("No because your teacher looks young and hard working so fuck you. Post a Boomer teacher"). A common phrase that we encounter in this setting is "NYPA – not your personal army," indicating that the user who is calling for the attack should handle their dirty work instead of asking for help on the /pol/ board. This shows that not all /pol/ users are motivated to carry out coordinated aggression attacks or enjoy the entertainment factor of it, giving us a glimpse at a more variegated set of motivations and interests than one might have originally anticipated. We find similar opposition messages posted in calls for attacks against YouTube videos, too (e.g., "must suck to live a life of impotent rage over shit that doesn't matter like music videos how much of a fucking loser are you, OP?")

Challenges in Automatically Moderating Coordinated Aggression Attacks

We conclude this chapter by discussing potential challenges that we identified in effectively moderating coordinated aggression attacks. We first discuss the fact that the coordinated behavior studied in this chapter is not unique to online hate, and that 4chan's Politically Incorrect Board has in the past carried out coordinated operations to subvert the actual functionality of Internet Platforms. We then reason about deplatforming, which is a popular countermeasure against online hate but could have potentially unintended consequences, creating new safe havens for attackers to coordinate and carry out inter-platform attacks. Finally, we discuss the challenges in dealing with concern trolling, stemming from the fact that the content moderation process developed by social media companies is geared toward identifying and blocking explicit hate.

Coordinated Attacks Can Go beyond Harassment

This chapter showed that the coordination by anonymous users on /pol/ plays an important role in the success of coordinated aggression attacks. The same social dynamics are at play in other endeavors embarked on by /pol/ users, which go beyond targeting a single victim or a small group but have the more ambitious goal of subverting the entire order of online platforms.

In mid-2016, Jigsaw, a Google-affiliated nonprofit focusing on sociotechnical issues, announced the development of a machine learning tool to detect toxicity. 4chan's /pol/, being a nexus of online toxicity, was understandably alarmed. Instead of taking this threat sitting down, /pol/ participants devised a response they called "Operation Google." The idea was to use words like "Google" and "Skype" in place of racial slurs when posting online. While this might seem like an odd response, it is a form of attack known "data poisoning" in computer security circles (Fang et al., 2020; Si et al., 2022). The core idea is that machine learning models are trained on large amounts of data, and that by using innocuous words like "Google" and "Skype" instead of actual slurs, a model to detect toxicity would learn that "Google" and "Skype" are toxic themselves.

This operation resulted in a massive spike in the use of replacement words on /pol/ for about a week, at which point, for some reason, they returned to their normal levels. When looking for an explanation within the empirical data, we saw that there was almost no adoption of the replacement words outside of 4chan itself. When looking at posts, qualitatively, we discovered that 4chan users themselves decided that Operation Google was not a success. Even in response to its initial proposal, users had lamented that it was dumb and destined to failure. This is a strong indication that while trolls' swarming behavior might make it look like they operate as a hive mind, there is dissent even down to the level of whether or not a particular campaign is worth pursuing in the first place.

Also in 2016, Microsoft released an artificial intelligence chatbot called Tay, which was designed to learn from its audience and reply to queries on Twitter (Neff & Nagy, 2016). The users of /pol/ took it upon themselves to hijack the bot and turn it racist. Through online coordination similar to the ones observed in the attacks described in this chapter, 4chan users managed to teach the bot to state that the Holocaust was made up, and to post other inflammatory statements, forcing Microsoft to take it down only 16 hours after its release.

At the time of writing this chapter, /pol/'s users are targeting the new technological frontier of artificial intelligence in the forms of large language models (Wei et al., 2022) and vision models (Khan et al., 2022). The developers of these models have put safeguards in place to prevent them from generating hateful and racist content (Shen et al., 2023). However, it is possible to circumvent these restrictions by either issuing specific requests (i.e., prompts) (Shen et al., 2023) or finding words that, albeit harmless, generate a toxic response (Si et al., 2022). This can be done due to the fact that these models are trained on huge real-world datasets from the Internet and are therefore bound to contain explicit or implicit hate. This type of attack on large language models, even at small scale, has only recently become a focus of the computer security research community (Shen et al., 2023; Si et al., 2022). At the time of this writing, however, building AI models to defend against this type of attack appears to be a Sisyphean task. We believe that we will witness successful attacks against these models being orchestrated by /pol/ and similar communities not just in the coming months but also for the entire deployment lifespan of current state-of-the-art large language model architectures.

These examples show that research into online hate should continue studying the social dynamics of polarized communities on /pol/, not only those geared toward harassment but also those that have a different goal.

Dealing with Deplatforming

A common solution against aggressors is to suspend their accounts, and we have seen platforms like YouTube and Twitter adopt this solution often. This makes sense when the attackers and their victims reside on the same platform; suspending someone's real account makes it difficult for them to keep operating. In fact, previous work on networked harassment operated under this assumption that attackers would both be members and perpetrators in the same online community (Marwick, 2021).

However, our analyses show that these attacks are often orchestrated on platforms where moderation is virtually nonexistent, and as we have mentioned, the accounts that attackers must use to post and cause harm on mainstream platforms like YouTube are usually throwaway ones. In this context, suspending the accounts that are used to deliver the attacks on the secondary platform would merely be a nuisance to the attackers, who could regroup and create new ones. Account suspension would have a very limited effect.

Another popular countermeasure adopted by platforms against online hate is deplatforming, where entire communities are suspended (Buntain et al., 2023; Chandrasekharan et al., 2022). Following assumptions in previous work on networked harassment, suggesting that attackers operate within a single online platform, deplatforming should work, and in fact research shows that this mitigation strategy reduces hate speech on the original social media platform (Jhaver et al., 2021). However, our research has found that deplatformed communities do not disappear but rather migrate and create their own platforms, out of the eye of moderators (Horta-Ribeiro et al., 2021). After these migrations, we have found, although the size of the community decreases, remaining users become more active and more toxic (Horta-Ribeiro et al., 2021). This raises the question of whether these *communities*, rather than specific *platforms*, become safe havens for aggressors, providing a place for aggregation and as the origination point for further coordinated aggression attacks, similar to what we have seen in /pol/. Another way to conceptualize this is that social processes are distinct from their technological platforms.

Dealing with Concern Trolling

"Do not feed the troll" is a popular adage (Center for Countering Digital Hate, 2019), but it becomes challenging to live by this when the line between what is trolling and what is legitimate activity becomes almost indistinguishable. *Concern trolling* is designed to make attackers appear like concerned users, and victims themselves. This type of trolling is difficult to identify even by a trained eye, as it is not easy to distinguish between complaints made in good versus bad faith. This impairs the effectiveness of content moderation, which has been designed to identify explicitly hateful content or other explicitly prohibited content such as nudity and calls for violence (Karabulut et al., 2023). More research is needed to better understand concern trolling and to develop suitable approaches to identify it and block it on social media platforms.

We have been personal victims of this type of attack, when trolls faked being concerned about a particular topic or discussion point but with the goal of causing harm. For example, trolls have sent emails to university administration in which they pose as transgender people and claim that our work is transphobic. Concern trolling exploits the tendency of humans to believe or be moved by others who are espousing a view that they already held. In this specific example, the troll was exploiting the administration's presumed desire to protect a marginalized group. Universities are not well equipped to deal with this type of malicious activity and neither are online platforms.

Conclusion

Online hate in the form of coordinated aggression attacks has become one of the core threats enabled by the social media. Instant communication, where physical distance is meaningless, and anonymous communication, where users are unidentifiable, have provided unheard-of opportunities to reach out and *hurt* someone. Moreover, the same tools used to cause harm act as a force multiplier for attackers, enabling them to easily share tactics and celebratory feedback. In this chapter, we leveraged our years of experience exploring fringe online communities to look at the phases followed by attackers when carrying out online aggression stemming from 4chan's Politically Incorrect Board and analyzed themes and challenges that emerge from our data.

We found that although online hate targeted toward one or more victims is one of the prevalent themes, attackers seem to be motivated by the camaraderie resulting from the social process of online aggression in and of itself. In addition to posting explicit hate, they record testimony on the 4chan threads calling for the attack about the disruptive activities that they took elsewhere, for the perusal and enjoyment of other anonymous users on the platform. This also indicates that attackers are looking for social approval, provided in part when attacks often terminate with a collective celebration of the havoc that was caused.

While studying two forms of coordinated aggression attacks, targeting YouTube videos and online meeting rooms such as those on Zoom, we find that although the two types of attacks share many commonalities, they also present differences, mostly due to the different time constraints of the two platforms (i.e., asynchronous versus synchronous) and because of the different level of openness (i.e., public versus private settings). In particular, attackers targeting online meetings appear even more compelled to come back to the 4chan thread and post evidence of what they have done to disrupt the meeting, which otherwise would not be visible to other users who did not take part in the attack.

This work paints a multifaceted overview of coordinated aggression attacks on 4chan and identifies a set of open challenges in moderating them. We hope that these challenges will serve as an inspiration for other researchers studying online content moderation and will help the identification and development of more effective moderation practices.

Acknowledgments

This work was partially supported by the National Science Foundation under Grants CNS-1942610, CNS-2114407, CNS-2114411, CNS-2247867, CNS-2247868, and IIS-2046590.

References

Antunovic, D. (2019). "We wouldn't say it to their faces": Online harassment, women sports journalists, and feminism. *Feminist Media Studies, 19*(3), 428–442. https://doi.org/10.1080/14680777.2018.1446454

Baumgartner, J., Zannettou, S., Keegan, B., Squire, M., & Blackburn, J. (2020). The Pushshift Reddit dataset. *Proceedings of the AAAI International Conference on Web and Social Media, 14*, 830–839. https://doi.org/10.1609/icwsm.v14i1.7347

Buckels, E. E., Trapnell, P. D., & Paulhus, D. L. (2014). Trolls just want to have fun. *Personality and Individual Differences, 67*, 97–102. https://doi.org/10.1037/e520722015-006

Buntain, C., Innes, M., Mitts, T., & Shapiro, J. (2023). Cross-platform reactions to the post-January 6 deplatforming. *Journal of Quantitative Description: Digital Media, 3*. https://journalqd.org/article/download/4030/2985

Center for Countering Digital Hate. (2019, September 16). *Don't feed the trolls: A practical guide to dealing with hate on social media.* https://counterhate.com/wp-content/uploads/2022/05/Dont-Feed-the-Trolls.pdf

Chandrasekharan, E., Jhaver, S., Bruckman, A., & Gilbert, E. (2022). Quarantined! Examining the effects of a community-wide moderation intervention on Reddit. *ACM Transactions on Computer-Human Interaction (TOCHI), 29*(4), 1–26. https://doi.org/10.1145/3490499

DeKeseredy, W. S. (Chapter 4 this volume). Misogyny and woman abuse in the incelosphere: The role of online incel male peer support.

DiFranco, R. (2020). I wrote this paper for the lulz: The ethics of Internet trolling. *Ethical Theory and Moral Practice, 23*, 931–945. https://doi.org/10.1007/s10677-020-10115-x

Fang, M., Cao, X., Jia, J., & Gong, N. (2020). Local model poisoning attacks to Byzantine-Robust federated learning. In *29th USENIX security symposium (USENIX security 20)* (pp. 1605–1622). https://www.usenix.org/system/files/sec20summer_fang_prepub.pdf

Hine, G., Onaolapo, J., De Cristofaro, E., Kourtellis, N., Leontiadis, I., Samaras, R., Stringhini, G., & Blackburn, J. (2017). Kek, Cucks, and God Emperor Trump: A measurement study of 4chan's politically incorrect forum and its effects on the web. *Proceedings of the AAAI International Conference on Web and Social Media, 11*, 92–101. https://doi.org/10.1609/icwsm.v11i1.14893

Horta-Ribeiro, M., Jhaver, S., Zannettou, S., Blackburn, J., Stringhini, G., De Cristofaro, E., & West, R. (2021). Do platform migrations compromise content moderation? Evidence from r/the_donald and r/incels. *Proceedings of the ACM on Human-Computer Interaction, 5*(CSCW2), 1–24. https://doi.org/10.1145/3476057

Jhaver, S., Boylston, C., Yang, D., & Bruckman, A. (2021). Evaluating the effectiveness of deplatforming as a moderation strategy on Twitter. *Proceedings of the ACM Conference on Human-Computer Interaction, 5*(CSCW2), Article 381. https://doi.org/10.1145/3479525

Karabulut, D., Ozcinar, C., & Anbarjafari, G. (2023). Automatic content moderation on social media. *Multimedia Tools and Applications, 82*(3), 4439–4463. https://doi.org/10.1007/s11042-022-11968-3

Khan, S., Naseer, M., Hayat, M., Zamir, S. W., Khan, F. S., & Shah, M. (2022). Transformers in vision: A survey. *ACM Computing Surveys (CSUR), 54*(10s), 1–41. https://doi.org/10.1145/3505244

Kujur, F., & Singh, S. (2016). Social networking sites as a multimedia tool for brand popularity – an exploratory study. *Indian Journal of Science and Technology, 9*, 45. https://papers.ssrn.com/sol3/papers.cfm?abstract_id=2951553

Lapidot-Lefler, N., & Barak, A. (2012). Effects of anonymity, invisibility, and lack of eye-contact on toxic online disinhibition. *Computers in Human Behavior, 28*(2), 434–443. https://doi.org/10.1016/j.chb.2011.10.014

Lewis, R., Marwick, A. E., & Partin, W. C. (2021). "We dissect stupidity and respond to it": Response videos and networked harassment on YouTube. *American Behavioral Scientist, 65*(5), 735–756. https://doi.org/10.31235/osf.io/veqyj

Ling, C., Balci, U., Blackburn, J., & Stringhini, G. (2021). A first look at zoombombing. *Proceedings of the IEEE Symposium on Security and Privacy, 42*, 1452–1467. https://doi.org/10.1109/sp40001.2021.00061

Mariconti, E., Suarez-Tangil, G., Blackburn, J., De Cristofaro, E., Kourtellis, N., Leontiadis, I., Serrano, J. L., & Stringhini, G. (2019). "You know what to do": Proactive detection of YouTube videos targeted by coordinated hate attacks. *Proceedings of the ACM on Human-Computer Interaction, 3*(CSCW), 1–21. https://doi.org/10.1145/3359309

Marwick, A. E. (2021). Morally motivated networked harassment as normative reinforcement. *Social Media+Society, 7*(2). https://doi.org/10.1177/20563051211021378

Marwick, A. E., & Caplan, R. (2018). Drinking male tears: Language, the manosphere, and networked harassment. *Feminist Media Studies, 18*(4), 543–559. https://doi.org/10.1080/14680777.2018.1450568

Miró, F. (2014). Routine activity theory. In M. Miller (Ed.), *The encyclopedia of theoretical criminology* (pp. 1–7). Wiley-Blackwell. https://doi.org/10.1002/978111 8517390.wbetc198

Neff, G., & Nagy, P. (2016). Talking to bots: Symbiotic agency and the case of Tay. *International Journal of Communication, 10*. https://ijoc.org/index.php/ijoc/article/view/6277

Papadamou, K., Papasavva, A., Zannettou, S., Blackburn, J., Kourtellis, N., Leontiadis, I., Stringhini, G., & Sirivianos, M. (2020). Disturbed YouTube for kids: Characterizing and detecting inappropriate videos targeting young children. *Proceedings of the AAAI International Conference on Web and Social Media, 14*, 522–533. https://doi.org/10.1080/14680777.2018.1450568

Papasavva, A., Zannettou, S., De Cristofaro, E., Stringhini, G., & Blackburn, J. (2020). Raiders of the Lost Kek: 3.5 years of augmented 4chan posts from the politically incorrect board. *Proceedings of the AAAI International Conference on Web and Social Media, 14*, 885–894. https://doi.org/10.1609/icwsm.v14i1.7354

Phillips, W. (2015). *This is why we can't have nice things: Mapping the relationship between online trolling and mainstream culture.* MIT Press. https://doi.org/10.7551/mitpress/10288.003.0015

Rohlfing, S. (2014). Hate on the internet. In N. Hall, A. Corb, P. Giannasi, & J. Grieve (Eds.), *The Routledge international handbook on hate crime* (pp. 293–305). Routledge. https://doi.org/10.4324/9780203578988-25

Saeed, M. H., Ali, S., Blackburn, J., De Cristofaro, E., Zannettou, S., & Stringhini, G. (2022, May). Trollmagnifier: Detecting state-sponsored troll accounts on reddit. In *2022 IEEE symposium on security and privacy (SP)* (pp. 2161–2175). IEEE. https://doi.org/10.1109/sp46214.2022.9833706

Shen, X., Chen, Z., Backes, M., Shen, Y., & Zhang, Y. (2023). "do anything now": Characterizing and evaluating in-the-wild jailbreak prompts on large language models. arXiv preprint arXiv:2308.03825; https://doi.org/10.48550/arXiv.2308.03825

Si, W. M., Backes, M., Blackburn, J., De Cristofaro, E., Stringhini, G., Zannettou, S., & Zhang, Y. (2022, November). Why so toxic? Measuring and triggering toxic behavior in open-domain chatbots. In *Proceedings of the 2022 ACM SIGSAC conference on computer and communications security* (pp. 2659–2673). https://doi.org/10.1145/3548606.3560599

Snyder, P., Doerfler, P., Kanich, C., & McCoy, D. (2017, November). Fifteen minutes of unwanted fame: Detecting and characterizing doxing. In *Proceedings of the 2017 Internet measurement conference* (pp. 432–444). https://doi.org/10.1145/3131365.3131385

Tynes, B. M., Lozada, F. T., Smith, N. A., & Stewart, A. M. (2018). From racial microaggressions to hate crimes: A model of online racism based on the lived experiences of adolescents of color. In G. C. Torino, D. P. Rivera, C. M. Capodilupo, K. L. Nadal, & D. W. Sue (Eds.), *Microaggression theory: Influence and implications* (pp. 194–212). Wiley. https://doi.org/10.1002/9781119466642.ch12

Walther, J. B. (2022). Social media and online hate. *Current Opinion in Psychology*, *45*, 101298. https://doi.org/10.1016/j.copsyc.2021.12.010

Walther, J. B. (Chapter 2 this volume). Making a case for a social processes approach to online hate.

Wei, J., Tay, Y., Bommasani, R., Raffel, C., Zoph, B., Borgeaud, S., Yogatama, D., Bosma, M., Zhou, D., Metzler, D., Chi, E. H., Hashimoto, T., Vinyals, O., Liang, P., Dean, J., & Fedus, W. (2022). Emergent abilities of large language models. arXiv preprint arXiv:2206.07682. https://arxiv.org/abs/2206.07

12

BACKGROUND SCHOLARSHIP AND A SYNTHESIS OF THEMES IN *SOCIAL PROCESSES OF ONLINE HATE*

Ronald E. Rice

This volume began with the observation that prior research on online hate research falls into four areas: Describing the prevalence and extensiveness of online hate, summarizing forms and content of online hate (its typical content in terms of symbols, lexicons, and discourse), assessing online hate's effects on victims (whether as targets or observers), and analyzing the individual attributes of and influences on online hate propagators (Walther, 2, and Tong, 3).

This book specifically examines the fourth focus: The *(social) processes that motivate and propel individuals and groups to generate, coordinate, and propagate hate messages online.* Not only is this perspective different than and complementary to the other major foci, it also fills a critical gap in the literature about the causes that lead to, promote, and shape online hate in the first place and reinforce and disseminate it in the second place. Further, the other three approaches generally do not open up the theoretical underpinnings about the creation and gratifications of online hate and therefore provide little direct basis for the development of specific and effective mitigation strategies rather than brute force punishments, removals, and account suspensions that may incur boomerang effects and make the problems associated with online hate even worse.

A comprehensive view of online hate research deserves some mention of the history of, and alternative methodological approaches to, its study, as well as highlighting the cross-cutting trends and themes within this collection. So, this chapter describes the outside and the inside of the book's research. That is, it summarizes what has been going on in other popular and scholarly literature, outside of these chapters, and then it attempts to summarize and synthesize various aspects of the scholarship that emerge within and across these chapters, offering a general model and descriptions of the

DOI: 10.4324/9781003472148-12

overlapping landscapes that these chapters have mapped, methodologically, thematically, etc.

Each chapter focuses on one or several such social processes and provides extensive, focused coverage of the relevant literature. This chapter steps back a bit, first briefly noting the growth not of online hate per se but, rather, of coverage of the topic by books, print news, and academic research. This background then provides context for an integrated review of themes across the chapters in *Social Processes of Online Hate*, which is also not about the prevalence of online hate but, rather, the arguments and evidence about the role of social processes in online hate posting. The first section provides an overview of the growth in coverage of online hate in books, news, and research articles. The second explores the main themes of the book. That analysis synthesizes an overall social processes model: Propositions, affordances, concepts, and theory related to the model and chapter results supporting the model. It also briefly summarizes contexts for social processes that emerged in previous chapters, related to perpetrators, venues, targets/victims, mechanisms, and effects. And it highlights three of the main methodological themes of the chapters: Content analysis, big data, and lexical and computational approaches. The chapter ends by noting some challenges and interventions.

Coverage of "Online Hate" in Books, Print News, and Academic Articles

With the rise of online hate (summarized by Tong, Chapter 3) came growth in coverage of the phenomenon, including descriptions of its perpetrators; digital sources; motivations; types; effects; and attempts to regulate, manage, or counter it. The increased attention to the issue is summarized here, to situate our studies on the social processes of online hate within the phenomenon of its increasing coverage corresponding to its increasing prevalence.

Books

To find when online hate first appeared in books and how its appearance has increased since then, Google Ngram Viewer (https://books.google.com/ngrams/info) was searched using "online hate," "Online hate," and "Online Hate" (i.e., case insensitive). This analysis is highly constrained, however. First using only these two words limits related results (however, "online anti-semitism" or "online Islamophobia" did not return any books). Second, currently Ngram Viewer only includes digitized Google books, and only through 2019; third, it only considers Ngrams that occur in at least 40 books. The first entry appeared in 1991 (however, as any of the terms appeared in at least 40 books, the first actual date is unknown). While the appearance of "online hate" slowly increased and plateaued through 2010, its frequency has been rising quickly since then (see Figure 12.1).

Table 12.1 summarizes several books that deal with the notion of online hate. These works tend to presume that the prevalence and harm due to online hate provide sufficient justification for intervention by technology companies and legislative requirements on those companies. The list is of course limited, as it includes only recent books and those with a title or summary containing the words "online hate."

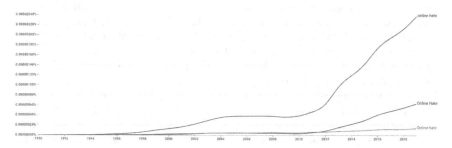

FIGURE 12.1   Growth in Occurrence of "online hate" in Google Books

Note: Using Google Ngram Viewer.

TABLE 12.1 Several Recent Books about (Primarily) Online Hate

Assimakopoulos, S., Baider, F. H., & Millar, S. (Eds.). (2017). *Online hate speech in the European Union: A discourse-analytic perspective.* Springer Nature. https://library.oapen.org/bitstream/handle/20.500.12657/27755/1/1002250.pdf
This open-access volume is a product of the European Union co-funded C.O.N.T.A.C.T. (Creating an On-line Network, monitoring Team and phone App to Counter hate crime Tactics; http://www.reportinghate.eu) program on hate crime and hate speech in several EU states. The book relies primarily on analyzing online comments to news reports, discourse analysis, corpus linguistics techniques, and semi-structured interviews to illustrate the kinds of messages and their contents that Europeans encounter in online hate messages. Its primary arena is political discussions that are hostile and that sometimes turn toward racism, anti-LGBTQ, and bullying. Using discourse analytic methods, it offers the authors' interpretations of hate messages and the meanings of interview comments with targets and observers of hate messages.
Barker, K., & Jurasz, O. (2018). *Online misogyny as hate crime: A challenge for legal regulation?* Routledge.
Barker and Jurasz focus on legal aspects of online misogyny (see Ging & Siapera, and Richardson-Self, in this table; and DeKeseredy, and Udupa & Gerold, this volume), in particular in the EU, England, and Wales. They note that legal approaches overlook foundational causes of and ways to prevent online abuse, since legal approaches emphasize punishment. Chapters consider legal and feminist approaches to online misogyny, the way that social media heighten misogyny, the challenges and complexities of regulating online communications, hate crimes and legal limits, and implications for law and regulation.

(Continued)

TABLE 12.1 (Continued)

Citron, D. K. (2016). *Hate crimes in cyberspace*. Harvard University Press.

This volume archives a number of harrowing anecdotes in which specific individuals were attacked virtually and threatened physically. These attacks focused primarily on women and often involved rape fantasies, explicit photographs, and reputation-damaging lies. Based on these incidents, the author frames cyberharassment as a matter of civil rights law, promotes advocacy, and provides recommendations for readers to take political action. Its strong point is its description of online hate as a rippling-out from one to many among coordinated aggressors (c.f. chapters by Udupa & Gerold, Burston, Rea et al., Phadke & Mitra, and Stringhini & Blackburn, this volume) rather than individual actions – that is, a social process.

Daniels, J. (2009). *Cyber racism: White supremacy online and the new attack on civil rights*. Rowman & Littlefield.

With insightful analyses of the allure of Twitter and other platforms to white supremacists, Daniels' book is easy to read and illustrates the offensiveness of online racism. The book focuses on formally organized movements and the online activities associated with long-standing offline organizations such as the KKK and neo-Nazi groups moreso than a focus on ordinary individuals – that is, on more social processes (cf. Burston). Further, it reveals direct linkages from the print-only era, such as printed publications, to online sites.

Donovan, J., Dreyfuss, E., & Friedberg, B. (2022). *Meme wars: The untold story of the online battles upending democracy in America*. Bloomsbury Publishing.

Meme Wars focuses on the cartoons, images, and electronic posters (memes) created by amateur users and professional political campaigns, generally by groups hating the media and liberal government, to ridicule opponents, encourage virality, promote ideologies, and recruit participants. In particular, it analyzes the case of the evolution and migration of the "Stop the Steal" conspiracy movement from online to offline through the epidemic influence of memes.

Ging, D., & Siapera, E. (Eds.). (2019). *Gender hate online: Understanding the new anti-feminism*. Palgrave Macmillan.

Ging and Siapera take a processual look at online misogyny, grounded in a feminism perspective (see Barker & Jurasz, and Richardson-Self in Ging & Siapera, and DeKeseredy, and Udupa & Gerold in this volume). This involves the diffusion of online misogyny, technological affordances that facilitate or constrain it, how cross-cultural appropriation of it has diverse effects in different cultures (such as India, Pakistan, and Russia), and how women may resist such activity and take back online spaces in the virtual world. The 13 chapters explore theorizing about techno-capitalism, digital gender politics, and consent; provide case studies of transcultural, race, revenge porn, and ideological news sites; and discuss ways in which women respond, resist, and experience online gender hate.

Herz, M., & Molnar, P. (Eds.). (2012). *The content and context of hate speech: Rethinking regulation and responses*. Cambridge University Press.

Herz and Molnar focus strictly on law and policy in the context of different nations' definitions and protection of free speech with respect to online hate. For example, what are the tradeoffs and boundaries among freedom of speech, control of hate speech, and concern over different social groups? To what extent does criminalizing hate speech generate benefits or harms in different contexts? How does or might international case law apply to hate speech?

(Continued)

TABLE 12.1 (Continued)

Keipi, T., Näsi, M., Oksanen, A., & Räsänen, P. (2016). *Online hate and harmful content: Cross-national perspectives.* Routledge.

This book elucidates features and affordances of social media platforms that facilitate the spread of online hate messaging, such as easy access, anonymity, vast content, and freedom from time and geography. It also describes negative effects of online hate, particularly for young people, using cross-national survey data to report effects of online hate on well-being, self-image, trust, and relationships. It relies on several theories from criminology, social psychology, and sociology, especially social identification (in-group/out-group) theory in a way that does acknowledge that theory's strong limitations in this domain (as does Walther's chapter in our volume).

Marantz, A. (2020). *Antisocial: Online extremists, techno-utopians, and the hijacking of the American conversation.* Penguin Random House.

This is a fascinating examination of the deliberate creation and targeted placement of disinformation into social media within a larger narrative describing how professional political campaign operatives maximize damage to political opponents. It is not focused on hate as much as on politics and so-called fake news. It discusses the by-now familiar argument that the initial vision of the Internet as a means of freedom, democracy, civil discourse, and participation has been corrupted as a source for alt-right, white supremacist, extreme, propagandistic, and rapidly diffused political content.

Mitts, T. (2022). *Moderating extremism: The challenge of combating online harms.* (under contract, Princeton University Press.)

Mitts suggests an insightful approach to online aggressors, which is consistent with some of the perspectives in our volume. Mitts argues that online antagonists who have their postings removed and/or their accounts suspended escalate their anger and adopt various evasion strategies, rather than desist, leading to an increase in velocity of hate messaging as hate posters migrate across social media platforms. Mitts develops a "theory of digital resilience" which strongly argues that the main reason for recidivism through platform migration is the variation in social media platform content moderation policies and procedures. Essentially, what she calls "dangerous organizations" evolve or migrate to online niches that are more supportive of online hate.

Phillips, W. (2016). *This is why we can't have nice things: Mapping the relationship between online trolling and mainstream culture.* The MIT Press.

Phillips is a classic source on the subject of trolling, akin to hate messaging. Phillips situates the emergence of trolling as a subcultural phenomenon, originally among computer programmers, which accompanied the development and evolution of the early Internet. She looks at online hate as one form of intentional disruption by cynical and lonely cybergeeks against "normies" – normal people who are ignorant about how technology works (and the companies who exploit their ignorance) – who are easily unsettled by uncivil taunting behavior. Phillips shows that trolling and hating are not only a sport or leisure activity, and thus a social process, but also mirror in some ways socially dominant cultural tropes concerning gender roles (similar to Richardson-Self's argument, below), success, and entitlement and are related to sensationalist media.

(*Continued*)

TABLE 12.1 (Continued)

Richardson-Self, L. (2021). *Hate speech against women online: Concepts and countermeasures*. Rowman & Littlefield.

This volume focuses on online misogyny. It theoretically develops and explicates the surrounding "social imaginary" (patterns of interconnected symbols that bound interpretations of the world, social beliefs, and narratives) that both foster this hate speech but which is also strengthened and reproduced by that hate speech (in some ways similar to the approaches of Ging and Siapera, noted above, and DeKeseredy, this volume). Importantly, online hate speech is not typically interactive or communicative with the targets, as the hate speech is intended to silence or dismiss the targets, and not intended to initiate discussions or debates with them. The author asks how can these social beliefs be resisted and repelled, and how can counter and positive imaginaries and alternative norms be developed and implemented? Richardson-Self suggests six conditions for such re-imaginings.

Simi, P., & Futrell, R. (2015). *American Swastika: Inside the white power movement's hidden spaces of hate* (2nd ed.). Rowman & Littlefield.

Simi and Futrell concentrate on formally organized white power movements – hate groups such as neo-Nazis and KKK chapters – that have offline bases. Their research methods include case studies, first-person accounts, and interviews. The book focuses on how members of these organizations recruit members offline (through conventional media including roadside billboards and music festivals) as well as online, and how these groups plan and commit violence in the physical world. The work stands in contrast to informally organized social networks that reside entirely online (as analyzed by chapters by Törnberg & Törnberg, Udupa & Gerold, Stringhini & Blackburn, and Shmargad et al., in our volume).

Strippel, C., Paasch-Colberg, S., Emmer, M., & Trebbe. J. (Eds.). (2023). *Challenges and perspectives of hate speech research*. Digital Communication Research, 12. Open Access. https://www.digitalcommunicationresearch.de/v12/

This valuable and free resource with 26 chapters presents three distinct parts. The initial seven chapters focus primarily on the first of the three approaches to online hate that Tong describes (this volume) – what is the content and shape of online hate messaging. The analyses consider different social schisms within specific nationalities (Brazil, India, Lebanon, Nigeria, and Poland). The second group of chapters approaches definitions of different types of messaging/content that are related to online hate, in terms of various social inequalities that have led to them and different kinds of harms they are presumed to effect (described in critical/societal rather than empirical terms). The third section explains, applies, and critiques a variety of methodological approaches to the analysis of online hate messaging.

Udupa, S., Gagliardone, I., & Hervik, P. (Eds.). (2021). *Digital hate: The global conjuncture of extreme speech*. Indiana University Press. Open Access. https://publish.iupress.indiana.edu/system/resource/4/3/c/43cf237a-65c7-4c5e-9807-4290125ff2a8/attachment/6cdcbd08b6e30d0debc93b36de8a002b.pdf

The chapters in this excellent, edited compendium focus on the content and shape of online hate messaging as those messages appear in different nationalities. The essays focus on distinctive incarnations of content, and how those forms of hate discourse evoke cultural significance in different contexts around the world such as India, Denmark, Islamophobia in China, Bolivian immigrants in Chile, Pakistan, Germany, Indonesia, and Turkey. The discussions are embedded on assumptions that hate messaging is a modern-day incarnation of colonialism and racism. The collection evokes cultural anthropological themes of exploitation and dominance.

(Continued)

TABLE 12.1 (Continued)

Wachs, S., Koch-Priewe, B., & Zick, A. (Eds.). (2021). *Hate speech – Multi-disziplinäre Analysen und Handlungsoptionen* (Hate Speech – Multidiscipli-nary analyses and options for action. Theoretical and empirical approaches to an interdisciplinary phenomenon). Springer VS. https://pub.uni-bielefeld.de/record/2957520

This book treats hate speech generally but also has chapters specifically about online hate. All but 2 of the 18 chapters in this edited book are in German. The first section includes models, research, and theories of hate speech from disciplinary perspectives of communication and media, linguistics and speech, pedagogy and psychology, and computer science. The second section offers four chapters on effects and potential prevention of, mitigation of, or responses to, hate speech, especially online.

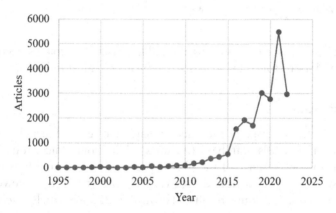

FIGURE 12.2 Growth in News Coverage of "online hate"

Note: Using Nexis Uni.

News Coverage

A search for "online hate" in news articles in Nexis Uni (which includes over 17,000 news, business, and legal sources, with coverage beginning in 1995) revealed a few such news stories with the term initially, but then a rise in 2009 and rapid growth from 2017 on (see Figure 12.2), with 21,691 entries as of this writing.

Prevalent topics in 2009 included debates between advocates of free speech versus regulation of online hate, and which regulatory agency has how much power to do so; reporting the rise in online hate posting; venues (web, Facebook); and a variety of specific instances and targets. In 2017, news emphasized calls for more general societal responses; the European Union's criticisms of and agreements with Internet platforms; platforms' responses with new actions or features; more regulations, legislation, and legal actions against online hate; the rise in online hate incidents and support for online

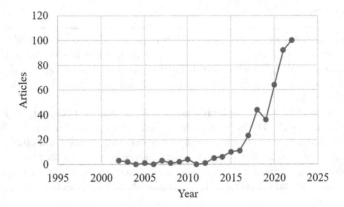

FIGURE 12.3 Growth in Academic Articles Referring to "online hate"

Note: Using ProQuest Social Sciences Database.

hate, especially associated with Brexit and the Trump campaign/election; and recommendations for individuals to help protect against online hate.

Academic Articles

To portray the coverage of the issue in academic research articles, the Pro-Quest Social Sciences Database (includes 22 bibliographic databases) was searched for the presence of the phrase "online hate" in any location (e.g., title, abstract) in peer-reviewed articles. (As with the Ngram viewer, using only these two words limits results.) Through 2022, 408 articles included the phrase, with growth beginning in 2013, accelerating in 2017, and even more in 2020 (see Figure 12.3). Articles published in 2017 investigated the criminalization of online hate speech, online victimization, and confronting online extremism. Articles from 2020 covered psychological influences on online hate, experiences of online hate by different minority or nationality groups, challenging or counter-strategies to deter online hate, relationships of social media use to acceptance of hate speech, and textual or rhetorical analyses.

Many academic books and articles include comprehensive reviews of relevant literature. Among the most relevant ones, Castaño-Pulgarín et al. (2021) assessed 67 studies that were published between 2015 and 2019 on the extent to which the Internet and social media may facilitate hate speech, cyberhate types, and triggers such as terrorism. Online hate speech, they found, focuses on gender, racism, politics, and religion and is often motivated by a variety of respective ideologies. The article also reviewed methodological approaches in prior studies. Common methods used to analyze online hate included grounded theory, discourse analysis, thematic analysis, computational methods, and network analysis, with most studies using a combination of methods. They conclude that "there are many theoretical gaps on the explanation of this behavior and there are not enough empirical data to understand this phenomenon and its relation with the use of Internet" (p. 2).

Tontodimamma et al. (2021) also describe the growth in research on the topic, using a different approach. They overview prior analyses of research (especially detection and identification of hate speech by automated computer-based analyses). Then, using knowledge mapping, topic modeling, and bibliometric data, they analyze 1,614 academic publications over 30 years (1992–2019) in the Scopus database, using a broad range of terms to describe the components, topics, and trends of online hate research. The analysis reveals two phases, with slow growth in publications from 1992 to 2010, and more rapid growth from 2010 to 2019. Using keyword co-occurrence, Tontodimamma et al. (2021) identify three clusters of concepts: (1) Religion and politics: Hate speech related to religion, human rights, democracy; (2) the social sphere: Hate speech related to the more common and unfortunately familiar topics such as Islamophobia, racism, gender, misogyny, radicalization, censorship, freedom of speech, and holocaust denial, on YouTube, Facebook, etc.; and (3) methods: Deep machine learning, text classification, sentiment analysis, and social network analysis. The authors note a slight shift over the years from more general themes to more technical and analytical emphases.

Waqas et al. (2019) used a broad and diverse set of search terms and combinations in titles, abstracts, and keywords to identify research publications on online hate and their foci, indexed in the Web of Science core database. Their queries yielded 3,371 articles with 33,721 non-self citations. Analyses revealed clusters of articles (each with multiple sub-clusters) in four domains: Cyberbullying; sexual solicitation and intimate partner violence, including seeking social support; deep learning and automation (cyber defense, neural network learning); and extremist and online hate groups (recruitment, discourse, misogyny, Islamophobia).

Themes in *Social Processes of Online Hate*

Within this background of increased attention to online hate, in books, the press, and research articles, employing a variety of analytic methods, little previous research took a decidedly social explanatory approach. The contributions to this volume, in contrast, have a common focus on how interactions and relationships among online hate producers facilitate their socially organized hate behavior. Nevertheless, the chapters also present considerable variation in the form, emphases, and contexts of those behaviors. One goal of this final chapter is to organize, synthesize, highlight, and identify the main themes and foci of the chapters that collectively offer and largely support a model of the social processes of online hate.

A Social Processes of Online Hate Model

Walther's chapter (Chapter 2) clearly sets the stage, and the other chapters elaborate or extend the underlying theme and concepts of a model of the social process of online hate. The following sections set out to advance the model in several ways: To present a set of propositions about the role of social processes, identify the range and importance of social media affordances in facilitating or constraining those processes, highlight concepts and theory related to the model, and summarize results supporting the model.

Propositions

The book's arguments offer the following propositions:

- A focus on individual behaviors and solutions is incomplete and ineffective, theoretically and practically. While theories of social identity and out-group derogation play a large part in the social process proposed here, they do not sufficiently identify, focus on, or analyze social interactions and gratifications. Diverse and continued interaction among perpetrators is a key process in the creation and dissemination of online hate (Chapter 2).
- A primary purpose of online hate activity is to engage in social processes and activities with, and receive social approval from, fellow perpetrators, in addition to complementing or, even in place of, antagonizing or harming victims. Social gratifications (such as approval), entertainment, connectedness, support, visibility and sharing of fellow perpetrators' content and actions, and identity development are all key social processes. The act of interacting and sharing opinions and ideologies among hate posters and their admirers may be sufficient motivations (Chapters 2, 5, 8, 11).
- Perpetrators share in-group symbology, post to venues accessible to fellow actors, and engage in behaviors that may not be seen by or even involve "targets" (Chapter 6).
- Analyzing social and emotional processes is crucial for understanding online hate (Chapter 5).
- Perpetrators occupy different social movement roles to provide different information resources, in varying ways, across different social media platforms (Chapter 9).
- Social processes of descriptive and injunctive norms, represented in different social media features and measures (such as "votes"), shape the type of antisocial messages posted and comments received (Chapter 10).
- Some kinds of online hate attacks are more or less coordinated, reflecting social interactions and collective action (Chapters 8, 11).
- The affordances of digital/social media also play a complex role in facilitating or constraining online hate content and social processes (Chapter 2; see next section).

Affordances

A complementary but perhaps underemphasized aspect of the social processes argument is that various affordances (features, capabilities, multi-model content, options, restrictions) of different social media platforms and discussion forums both facilitate and constrain particular social processes. Table 12.2 lists the features specifically mentioned in the chapters, grouped (loosely applied) by a common set of affordances. Rice et al. (2017) reviewed various

TABLE 12.2 Digital Media Affordances Facilitating Online Hate Mentioned in Chapters

Awareness
- Advertising and monetizing nature of many websites reinforces content that attracts and engages attention, such as extremist content and misinformation
- Filter bubbles and echo chambers limit exposure to diverse opinions and information
- Online platforms have fragmented boundaries and decentralized leadership of formerly organized movements, bypassing the role of face-to-face interactions, public gatherings, and visual artifacts
- Recommender algorithms that can funnel polarizing content to stimulate interest or reinforce group ideology
- Structuring of online interactions (topic forums, follower relations)

Editability
- Allows mashed-up memes combining a range of satire, insult, and denigration
- Content moderation by users, algorithms, platform monitors
- Digital tools and platforms allow the creation and distribution of deepfake pornography, often used for misogynist hate postings
- Memes, with photo, video, gif, and text, perhaps familiar enough to be referred to by a catchphrase
- Open architecture and open source promote evolution and adaptation of online affordances; that is, some sites, apps, and platforms are more structurally editable or customizable than others
- Tailoring content and information-sharing to specific and diverse segments of both supporters and targets, such as on Facebook and Twitter

Pervasiveness (including accessibility)
- Bottom-up influence from users instead of or in addition to control by formal organizations or platforms leads to greater access by and diversity of strategies and actors
- Creating social media or chat groups, designated channels, or playlists helps organize, maintain, and increase accessibility of content in multiple ways
- Crowdfunding to generate resources for otherwise not publicly supported actions and content increases access
- Doxxing and public publishing of a target's personal information
- Financial incentives or monetizing (such as on YouTube) for producing extremist or hateful content, which increases pervasiveness of content
- Flexibility and access also pose challenges to authoritarian figures and governments
- Globalized access to otherwise specific and localized hate groups

(Continued)

TABLE 12.2 (Continued)

- Hate can now be expressed and diffused by orders of magnitude more compared to offline exposure and remain online, vastly increasing the pervasiveness of hate
- Networked harassment, where perpetrators find and collaborate with others to target an individual; also brigading, dogpiling, overloading
- Online multi-player video games commenting can foster online hate groups and recruitment
- Social media have provided an immense array of spaces supporting all kinds of views, including the normalizing of hate toward women and racial or ethnic groups
- Using links and forwarding hashtags to disseminate content across sites
- Variations in hate content restrictiveness or supportiveness across platforms facilitating migration
- YouTube's "Super Thanks", which allows commenters to make instant donations to a channel operator
- Zoombombing, hijacking video meetings

Searchability (including association)
- Hashtags, serving both as reference links to as well as representations of ideas and actions, increasing likelihood that both targets and fellow hate perpetrators can find the content
- Indexing by search engines allows interested users to find content and sites promoting online hate
- Tweets that can be followed or forwarded/retweeted
- Use of @usernames in tweets to direct content to, and refer others to, targets

Self-presentation (including others' feedback, likes, etc.)
The chapters describe and analyze a broad array of ways that users can manage their online presentations, others can provide signals of social approval/disapproval of one's or a group's presentations, a user or group can indicate or refer to their status or influence, and which can portray and strengthen collective group identity. These include: Comments, embedded hashtags, emojis, favorites, followers, friends, hearts, likes, quotes, reply, retweets, sharing, votes (up/down), etc.

Visibility (including anonymity)
- Anonymity (voluntary or platform-imposed) and pseudonymity, shielding the perpetrators; allows perpetrators to delete or abandon accounts and set up new accounts without the identification of the same actor, making it difficult to sanction or suspend users
- Encryption and private group messaging limit visibility for out-groups
- Exposing hate content to others who did not seek or want it, intentionally or not
- In VR, display of both verbal and nonverbal behaviors directed toward a target, or satirizing/offending an identity, including virtual touching and spatial harassment
- Inclusion of visual, auditory, and textual hate symbols and phrases
- Messages or screen grabs that document and make visible victims' distress over trolling, baiting, and provocation incidents
- Multiple media modes, such as images, stickers, video, sound, and pop-ups, enhance the visibility of specific content

(Continued)

TABLE 12.2 (Continued)

- Opportunistic Zoombombing, via image, text, audio, video
- Persistent visible user comments on YouTube video pages
- Posters can easily expose their thoughts to others
- Posting within private groups
- Some postings are ephemeral and disappear in a short time (e.g., 4chan; most video meetings)
- Threaded conversations make visible relationships among comments, replies, posters, and rationales

---

Note: Affordances from Rice et al. (2017), expanded here as noted in parentheses.

conceptualizations of and debates about affordances, leading to this definition of media affordances: "relationships among action possibilities to which agents perceive they could apply a medium (or multiple media), within its potential features/capabilities/constraints, relative to the agent's needs or purposes, within a given context" (p. 109). Here, we apply the six affordances identified as having reliable and valid measures: Awareness, editability, pervasiveness (including accessibility), searchability (including association), self-presentation (including feedback, likes, etc.), and visibility (including anonymity). While Stringhini and Blackburn (Chapter 11) explicitly distinguish social processes from their technological platforms conceptually, the processes and platform affordances are nonetheless highly interrelated.

Each affordance is illustrated by an example of how that affordance (features, capabilities, or aspects of digital media) fosters or shapes social processes of online hate. *Awareness*: Recommender algorithms funnel polarizing content to stimulate interest or reinforce group ideology. *Editability*: Digital tools and platforms allow the creation and distribution of deepfake pornography, often used for misogynist hate postings. *Pervasiveness*: Creating social media or chat groups, designated channels, or playlists helps organize, maintain, and increase the accessibility of content in multiple ways. *Searchability*: Indexing by search engines allows interested users to find content and sites promoting online hate. *Self-presentation*: Votes, likes, follows, etc., provide signals of approval of the identity or status of a poster or a group. *Visibility*: Messages or screen grabs that document and make visible victims' distress over trolling, baiting, and provocation incidents.

Concepts and Theories Related to the Model

The chapters introduce, advance, and apply a variety of concepts and theories that also support or help explain the social processes of online hate. The section highlights those contributions, generally ordered by chapter. The range of such concepts and theories underscores the heuristic value of the social processes approach: There are many facets of such social processes, and research can continue to enhance our understanding of them through complementary concepts and theories.

Tong (Chapter 3) presents a relational taxonomy of online hate, categorizing it by private/public and by one-on-one/many-to-one/group or intergroup-level. DeKeseredy (Chapter 4) applies male peer support theory to the case of the incelosphere, helping to explain incels' motivations and support for, and engagement in, abuse of women and in other forms of misogyny. Males provide support to peers in fostering abusive attitudes and behaviors. In particular, charismatic leaders with prototypical hegemonic masculine qualities attract and sustain their peers.

Although a common explanation for online hate invokes the concepts of "echo chambers" and "filter bubbles" where users passively find themselves with like-minded others, and their views and networks are reinforced through algorithmic notifications, news, and recommendations (Chapters 5, 6), Törnberg and Törnberg (Chapter 5) eschew these receiver-oriented approaches. They invoke deeper social processes by applying Durkheim's community formation theorizing, especially the importance of rituals in creating group identity. Thus, one way to understand the enduring nature of the Stormfront site is to frame their online behaviors as "digital campfires" – an in-group space for extremists to discuss and share identity, feel a sense of belonging and support, and defend their group and ideological boundaries, again reflecting a social process approach to online hate. One form of ritual is the use of "subcultural literacy" or terms, jargon, memes, and symbols understandable only by insiders. Another is to interpret events and events in ways that reinforce the group identity and ideology, even when counter to external objective reality. Participating in such rituals creates "collective effervescence" (Collins, 2014), strengthening the community.

Udupa and Gerold (Chapter 6) craft a theory about the interrelationship of political aggression, consumption of porn, and speech act theory, as a way to describe and explain particularly sexualized online hate, especially of Muslim women by young Hindi males, reflecting Islamophobia, and larger sociological forces of objectification, digital image manipulation, and patriarchal political norms. This form of online hate embeds the Manosphere, more general than the incelosphere as discussed by DeKeseredy (Chapter 4). Burston (Chapter 7) and Phadke and Mitra (Chapter 9) apply social movement theory to social media platforms, arguing that online hate groups are often a part of social movements and, as such, engage in familiar movement strategies and goals. In particular, Burston (Chapter 7) introduces the term "digitally mediated spillover," a social process whereby members of one online movement introduce their ideologies, culture, and networks into another online group or an offline group. This spillover involved three phases of (successful or unsuccessful) radicalization. His analyses of three conservative college groups show that the notion of digitally mediated spillover provides a better explanation than "entryism," which is an intentional and organized strategy to send extremists to conservative college groups to groom right-wing candidates for Congress.

Phadke and Mitra (Chapter 9) conceptualize online hate groups as social movement organizations, which frame their communication to legitimatize their behavior, recruit members, work toward develop shared perspectives on needed social change, and motivate others to engage in that change. They content-analyze a wide range of Facebook posts and Twitter tweets to identify three types of collective action framing, five ideologies, five sources of information sharing, and five social roles. Then they show how content is shared across these categories, to understand how hate groups attract and redirect their followers, in different ways across the two platforms. Theoretically, they refer to three dimensions of social movement participation, each motivated by specific theoretical models (for participation, engagement, and mobilization), to derive the social roles and indicators of each based on online content and platform features.

Rea et al. (Chapter 8) develop the concept of "hate parties," whereby the activity on fringe sites inspires sharing of links to YouTube videos, where members extend the hateful rhetoric of those videos and then migrate to other sites to continue and elaborate their discussions. Their unique contribution appears in their discovery that participants in hate conversations carry on their discussions across multiple platforms simultaneously, opportunistically choosing the platforms that allow more extreme and offensive hateful language, in order to evade content moderation in any one particular platform. Again, this conceptualization rejects the traditional conceptualization of online hate as unidirectional attacks on specific targets for nonstrategic purposes. Like DeKeseredy (Chapter 4) and Udupa and Gerold (Chapter 6), Rea et al. also refer to larger sociological and economic forces as influences on the nature of social media and the prevalence of online hate.

Shmargad et al. (10) turn to foundational social norms theory to understand the magnification of antisocial comments in response to preceding norms and sanctions in a large set of comments to an online newspaper and discussions in Reddit and Twitter about the January 6th Capitol riot. They explicate the theory to identify four types of perceived social norms: Self-focused or other-focused, by descriptive or injunctive. Moreover, they develop sophisticated measures of each based on content and relational and temporal usage data. Stringhini and Blackburn (Chapter 11) also develop a temporal approach to online hate, identifying the stages through which coordinated cross-platform online attacks progress: Call for attack, preparation, execution, reporting back, and wrap up/celebration. Social processes are fundamental to each of these stages. For example, a "call for attack" may be motivated by the goal of amusement, as well as by racism and misogyny. They argue that "coordination" may be too strong a word, with its implications of planning and instrumentality; rather, applying routine activities theory, Stringhini and Blackburn explain that many such attacks are an unplanned convergence of the content or individual in a YouTube video, a perpetrator on another (perhaps fringe) site trying to inspire others to post aggressive comments (whether to disrupt a system or a zoom meeting) and then returning to enjoy the process (if successful).

Chapter Evidence Supporting the Model

Throughout the book, authors provide various forms of results (here, in the form of summary results) illuminating or supporting the social process of online hate model. Membership in, or the ability to comment on other members' posts on, hate sites may require explicit commitment to the cause, not only protecting the group from outside disapproval but also underscoring group identity and connection (Chapter 3). Male peers influence others, via social psychological and sociological processes, to abuse women (Chapter 4). The language of new entrants to online groups quickly converges to content, memes, discourse, jargon, and emotions from veteran group members, indicating semantic and collective social influence. Members of Stormfront provide support to each other for their experiences, marginalization, and beliefs (Chapter 5).

Hindu posters are embedded in a "close web of actors" or clusters of users, strengthening their resilience in spite of online or legal disciplining (Chapter 6). Rating of "online auctions" is a collective, participatory activity, a "social interaction episode," which reinforces those bonds (Chapter 6). They also share in the performance of male homosociality, manhood, masculinity. Resonating with Walther's argument, much content on the online auctions and related sites involves humor and a sense of fun, at least among the perpetrators (Chapter 6). Stringhini and Blackburn highlight that the purpose of many coordinated online attacks seems to be primarily for entertainment. Burston (Chapter 7) similarly describes how online hate activists celebrated and laughed for successful antagonization of feminists and undocumented immigrants.

Rea et al. (Chapter 8) also describe how antisemitic comments on YouTube videos were often intended for fellow perpetrators, not the video creator or the target in the video. Further, social interactions among such actors occurred within and across platforms, a form of "continuous conversation" or "hate party." Stringhini and Blackburn (Chapter 11) also remark on how much of a coordinated attack process is not directly visible to a target, again emphasizing how such behavior is intended for fellow perpetrators. These actors intentionally link information across multiple sources and sites, creating a "participatory ecosystem of online hate" (9). Phadke and Mitra note that "sharing links in their social media postings provides a sizable opportunity for hate groups to redirect their followers toward their own websites and other extremist blogs." Further, two of the five social movement roles they identify in online hate groups are explicitly social. *Solicitors* motivate other users to engage in action and use group words such as "we" and "us." *Motivators* highlight and celebrate the accomplishments of fellow actors and protect and defend group values. Shmargad et al. find that online contributors tend to imitate prior posters and are reinforced by approval "votes," supporting the theory of normative social behavior, there, in terms of fostering antisocial content (Chapter 10). Cross-platform raids (Chapter 11), along with collective action and networked harassment, are informally coordinated, rather than individual or random attacks. Posters or disseminators of harassment may return to the originating site or aggregation thread to congratulate each other and boast of their actions (Chapters 2, 11). Interestingly, Stringhini and Blackburn (Chapter 11) also note that not all fellow members will engage in, or even support, some attacks and Zoombombing, indicating diverse social norms.

Contexts for Social Processes of Online Hate

The chapters consider a variety of online hate or harassment perpetrators, and how they aim at a wide range of targets or fellow perpetrators, directly or indirectly, individually or collectively, through many venues on multiple topics using diverse mechanisms with a range of effects, all supported by, and providing contexts for, social processes. The following sections summarize the extensive range of instances of the contexts of social processes of online hate noted by the authors: Perpetrators, venues, targets/victims, topics, mechanisms, and effects. Thus, comprehensive analyses of the social processes of online hate could identify additional instances of these contexts and assess how the combinations of the contexts manifest online hate in different ways.

Perpetrators

The many online perpetrators in the chapters include (but are not limited to): ALIPAC, anti-LGBTQ+ advocates, anti-Semites, Aryan Nations, conservative youth organizations carrying out campus-based extremism, conspiracy theorists, cyberstalkers, Goyim Defense League, Hindu "trads" (staunch traditionalists who have sought to revive practices deemed as "properly" Hindu), incel movement, Leather Apron Club, Liberty Bell Publishing, male supremacist movements, male entitlement proponents, misogynists, neo-Nazis, professional influencers who explicitly promote online hate, racists, religious supremacists, "toxic technocultures" or "leaderless, amorphous" cultures of hate, trolls, (explicitly self-labeled) "White Christians," white nationalists, white supremacists, and so on.

Venues

The Internet in general and social media in particular facilitate the production and dissemination of online hate, enabled or constrained by each medium's affordances (see above). Windisch et al.'s (2022) review noted how the Internet and various platforms can disseminate hate speech and connect users sharing those perspectives, whereby such content and interaction become normalized, leading to radicalization and intergroup violence. Table 12.3 lists the numerous online hate venues mentioned in the chapters. The major platforms are well known and apply multiple and changing approaches to minimize online hate (e.g., Facebook), while others engage in only minimal monitoring and management (X, formerly Twitter), while still others are explicit shelters for and even foundational sites for some online hate groups (e.g., Stormfront).

TABLE 12.3 Venues for Online Hate Mentioned in the Chapters

2channel	Minds
4chan	online gaming
8kun	Parler
BBSes	Poal
Bitchute	Reddit
Bluejeans	RightToBe
Clubhouse	Rumble
cozy.tv	Secret
Facebook	Skype
Facebook group chat	Starleaf
Facebook Messenger	Stormfront
Facebook page	Telegram
Fascist Forge	Telegram Chat Worlds
Gab Social	The incelosphere
Gab	The Manosphere
Gettr	The Metaverse
GitHub	TikTok
Google	Truth Social
GroupMe	Twitch
Instagram	Twitter
Internet	virtual reality or virtual worlds
Internet communities	Whisper
Iron March	Wimkin
Jitsi	Win
LBRY	Y Combinator's Hacker News forum
livestreaming	YouTube
messaging apps	Zoom
MeWe	

Targets/Victims

The chapters consider many types of targets/victims. These include: Race/ethnicity (Asian Americans, Blacks, Hispanics, people of color), sex and sexual orientation (bisexuals, gays, lesbians, queer, women, and women in gaming), nationality and citizenship ("illegals," immigrants, Mexicans, people with strong accents), religion (Jews, Muslim male "rivals," Muslim women, other specific religions), disability, as well as online bystanders/unintentionally exposed individuals. As Tong (Chapter 3) reviews, and the sources in the section on Coverage identify, many others are targets as well, for an extensive range of reasons and perceived provocations.

Topics

The topics of the online hate analyzed in these chapters are also extensive. They include: Anti-Black racism, anti-immigrant racism, antisemitism, conspiracy theories, discrimination, education/image control, gender, hatred (of particular targets), Holocaust denial, identity attack, immorality of LGBT life, "invaders" (immigrants), Islamophobia, misogyny, nationality or national origin, political beliefs, race/ethnicity/culture, races as immoral or inferior, radicalization/recruitment, religious beliefs, sexuality, violence, and whites (as a threatened race).

Mechanisms

The chapters note a host of mechanisms through which perpetrators engage in online hate. These include: Accusing a target of lying, attack on commenter, casting aspersion, concern trolling, cyberstalking, doxxing, group linking to and commenting on YouTube videos, hashtags, hate parties, inflammatory language, insult, memes, name-calling, networked harassment, nonconsensually sourced women's images, online auctions, pejorative speech, profanity, revenge porn, threat, toxicity, and vulgarity. Each of these may facilitate different aspects of social processes, leading to different effects for both perpetrators and targets/victims and shaped by different platform affordances.

Effects

While the chapters in this book highlight the various motivations, attractions, and social processes that facilitate online hate, they do so in the context of a critical presumption: That online hate has negative effects or influences on its targets, its perpetrators, or both. The authors note a wide variety of such effects. For *perpetrators*, these include: Becoming active perpetrators of hate or being recruited to hate groups themselves, becoming desensitized, gratification such as entertainment and social support, in-group cohesion and identification, increased willingness to use and actual involvement in radical ideology-based violence, mobilization, and normalization of hate.

For *targets/victims*, these include: Being terrorized, collateral damage (where the main intent was not necessarily to harm specific individuals but who were nonetheless negatively affected such as unintended observers or passive bystanders), disruption of/or chaos/havoc in online activities (e.g., online meetings or school classes), harm to an individual's reputation, increased problems with relationships, increased social isolation, offline aggression/violence/murder, terrorist attacks, victims' mental and emotional states (anger, anxiety, depression, fear, sadness, shame, stress, trouble sleeping, and difficulty concentrating on everyday activities), and withdrawing from online interaction.

Method

Each of the chapters includes their own reviews of data sources and collection, research design, and analytical methods relevant to their studies. This section identifies three main types of data and analytical methods used by the authors to describe, explain, analyze, and test their respective aspects of the social processes of online hate model. They include content analysis, big data, and lexical and computational analyses. Other methods are also used, such as ethnography (Chapter 7) and image analysis (Chapter 6). The methods here are a subset of the broad range of methods reviewed by Castaño-Pulgarín et al. (2021) noted above and Strippel et al. (2023). One of the implications of the range of methods used by the chapters is that insights can be gained from a variety of methods and that computational analysis of big data and qualitative approaches can complement each other (Chapters 5, 6, 9, and 10).

Content Analysis

Though computational lexical approaches (see below) do analyze content, here we use the term to refer to manual, reliable human coding of content to categories, whether a priori, emergent, or a combination. Such content analysis has considered explicit or implicit hate speech, Islamophobic and anti-immigration attitudes, identification of target groups, etc. Content analysis may be applied not only to words but also to symbols (such as the ampersat @), other information (usernames), and particular terms to identify individually targeted tweets as hate messages (Chapter 3).

Udupa and Gerold (Chapter 6) developed coding typologies for gender-based themes (homophobic, threats to Hindu masculinity, and safety of Hindu women, etc.) and for general themes (primarily religious). Phadke and Mitra (Chapter 9) generated a multistage coding scheme, beginning with annotating a small sample of tweets based on both a priori and emergent coding, leading to 13 codes within three collective action frames. Stringhini and Blackburn (Chapter 11) took a more interpretive approach to identify discussion threads invoking online attacks. Several of the researchers compared human coding/annotation with automated classifiers to establish reliability and validity so that the computer-based tools could be applied to large-scale data, and that subtle differences in content identification can be documented (Chapter 10).

Big Data

Many studies of online hate collect and study "big data," or large sets of content, threads, links, etc. (for some reviews, see Chapters 3 and 10). Such large-scale data allow for analyses of changes over time, comparisons across types of content and platforms, and detection of specific roles and sources. Several of these chapters report on their own big data (Chapters 8, 9, 10, and 11). For example, Rea et al. (Chapter 8) assessed over 3 million comments and nearly 1.5 million replies to locate and identify what they call "hate parties." Phadke and Mitra (Chapter 9) analyzed large numbers of Twitter tweets, Facebook messages, links from those to the same and other platforms, extremist accounts, and extremist groups, showing how hate groups promote their interests in interlocking webs of selectively sourced news posts, comments, and memes. Shmargad et al. (Chapter 10) described how streams of data can be parsed into three-message triplets to detect over-time changes in antisocial commenting in large-scale discussion threads during the January 6th Capitol riots, showing how prior postings and the levels of social approval they beget affect later one. Stringhini and Blackburn (Chapter 11) analyzed "billions" of social media posts to show how perpetrators coordinate online aggression attacks.

Lexical and Computational Analyses

The big data available from social media and other online media not only provide increasingly robust and sophisticated opportunities for analysis but also require appropriately scaled and parameterized computational tools. Researchers may apply meaning, linguistic, and speech dictionaries (a lexical approach), or train algorithms to infer reliable meaning (a machine learning approach, whether supervised or unsupervised), or develop and standardize multiple stages (pipelines) in such analyses.

The chapters refer to and specifically apply some of these tools, including ADL's antisemitism classifier the Online Hate Index (OHI), CrowdTangle

API, custom-built classifier and modular pipeline, evaluations of particular news sites by mediabiasfactcheck.org, Google's Jigsaw lab's Perspective, Hatebase.org (no longer operational), recent large language models, Reddit API, the Rand Corporation's "OpenSources" classifications, and YouTube data API, etc. (Chapters 8, 9, and 10). Several of the authors, such as Törnberg and Törnberg (Chapter 5), and Phadke and Mitra (Chapter 9), combine one or more computational tools with qualitative/interpretive methods.

Challenges and Interventions

Challenges, tensions, and limitations pervade the study of online hate. While not the focus of this book, a crucial dimension of the online hate phenomenon is how to deal with it, with the chapters and much other literature suggesting and evaluating various interventions.

Challenges

Perhaps the most central challenge, for researchers, policymakers, and online discussion boards and social media platforms, is defining "online hate" itself. Tong (Chapter 3), as do others (e.g., Arora et al., 2023; Baider, 2020; Hietanen & Eddebo, 2023; Siegel, 2020; Srba et al., 2021), remarks on the wide variation and ambiguities in terms (such as antisocial norms, cyberhate, extreme speech, extremism, incivility, online aggression, online hate, toxicity) and definitions of online (and offline) hate. However, as Tong concludes:

> At their core, many of these terms highlight that hate – both online and offline – is a form of communication that promotes denigration or harm against targets based on their stigmatized, identity-based characteristics.
> (p. 38)

This vagueness in terminology makes it difficult to generate accurate comparisons, prevalence, or effects.

A fundamental tension in dealing with online hate is between protection from hate speech and protection of free speech (Chapters 3 and 10). The balance between the two takes a wide range of forms depending on national and regional ideology and politics (see, e.g., Benesch, 2023). The expression of speech that is deemed unacceptable in some contexts may even serve valuable civil and political functions in others, such as allowing dissent and identifying disagreement.

There are many problems and obstacles in obtaining and using big data. Different platforms provide different levels and types of access to their content. Limits and formats of platform content and research tools may not correspond (Chapter 10). Different platforms constrain the amount and type of content that can be collected in any one attempt. Stringhini and Blackburn (Chapter 11) note the particular challenges of collecting 4chan content because it is by design not only completely anonymous but also ephemeral, with posts being automatically deleted quickly.

The chapters also mention various challenges and limitations of the lexical and computational approaches. For example, the meaning of some content may be ambiguous or misleading in isolation but revealed only in the context of a threaded conversation, shared symbology and terms, or measured synchronization with other actions (Chapter 10). Arora et al. (2023) and Srba et al. (2021) provide extended discussions of such challenges, such as constantly changing forms and implicitness of such content; diffusion across platforms; distinguishing hate speech from offensive, abusive, socially unacceptable, or protected content; difficulties, harm, and ambiguities of manual coding; analyzing multilingual or minor language content; integrating context; passive, sarcastic, or satiric hate speech; understanding machine learning algorithms; and the need for effective, especially real-time, mitigation mechanisms.

Interventions

Researchers, computer and data scientists, tech companies, policymakers, legislators, and the public all have varying suggestions for responses and interventions (see, e.g., Barker & Jurasz, 2018; Herz & Molnar, 2012; Mitts, 2022; Richardson-Self, 2021; Wachs et al., 2021). Based on a systematic review, Blaya (2019) explained and critiqued three key intervention approaches toward cyberhate (legal, technological, and educational through the empowerment of the individuals such as through counter-speech) but found few evaluations of those interventions. Siegel's (2020) comprehensive review of online hate includes a detailed section on interventions intended to combat online hate speech and their effectiveness.

A number of interventions receive mention within this book's chapters as well, and as they appear, they are supported or challenged on the basis of the social processes that they may implicate. One explicit and common intervention is to suspend an account or deplatform (remove) it. As described in several chapters, one problem with content moderation and suspensions is that users and groups can migrate to more lax platforms (Chapters 2, 6, 8, and 9). Indeed, some sites have no moderation and are supportive of "hate speech" and may even moderate or filter out oppositional content (Chapter 3). Most deplatforming attempts are aimed at an individual or group of users, or specific content, rather than on the social processes underscored in this book. Because of the interdependent and interrelated social aspects of online hate, interventions need to take into account cross-platform coordination and relationships within and across comment threads (Chapter 8). Though not much discussed in the literature, perpetrators, accounts, or groups may be *re-platformed*. For example, although still exceedingly popular, with the change in ownership and name, X (formerly Twitter) has relaxed or removed constraints on misinformation (climate change, COVID-19 and vaccines, grooming, Russian state media, Trump, war, etc.) and hate speech (slurs, neo-Nazi, antisemitic, etc.) (Myers et al., 2023). Myers et al. list 19 articles or reports reporting increases in these problematic message types after reducing such limitations.

Beyond human and AI content monitoring and deletion, more delayed and reactive approaches include restricting, quarantining, suspending, and deplatforming (banning or removing users and accounts; see Trujillo & Cresci, 2022). Mitts (2022; Rae et al., Chapter 8; Walther, Chapter 2) notes how restricting, blocking, removing, and deplatforming may not have a substantial effect, as posters go to other platforms or online groups that do not moderate hate content, or may even support (e.g., Gab Social), though these platforms have relatively less reach and membership. Unfortunately, even interventions such as counter-narratives can boomerang: A review and study by Poole et al. (2021) found that dense interconnected right-wing networks and platform affordances limited the effects of counter-narratives and even stimulated the perpetrators to intensify their voices. Deplatforming may be considered an individually oriented approach, rather than a social processes approach – that is, it targets the individual user or content.

However, underlying the general deplatforming approach lurk various larger social processes. Van Dijck et al. (2023) provide a deep and systemic analysis of the technical, social, and infrastructural aspects and implications of *deplatformization*. They distinguish between deplatforming and deplatformization. Deplatforming "simply" removes and bars single offenders (individuals or groups), though it is often part of a phased increasingly stringent approach (warnings, flagging, removal of content, quarantining, restriction, temporarily suspension, banning). Deplatformization moves beyond content moderation, taking a more integrated ecosystem approach, attempting to limit such actors to the online fringe by preventing them from accessing infrastructural resources. These may include banning associated accounts and groups from a specific platform, removing platforms from online app stores, demonetization, disabling analytics, removing links to mainstream sites and platforms, denying advertising and commercial transaction services, limiting the use of domain name services, implementing algorithms that demote their content, etc. There is no one consistent set of deplatformization practices across providers, however. The concept of deplatformization expands our awareness of the broader interconnections among not only perpetrators' venues but also with the background infrastructural resources and legal landscape. These may be considered large social and economic processes involving sites, platforms, service providers, and financial actors. Deplatformizations, while being substantial and responsible responses to online hate also raise questions of Internet neutrality, control by tech companies over access, what constitutes sufficiently unacceptable or illegal content and acceptable and allowable governance processes (Van Dijck et al., 2023).

The online hate interventions literature is vast and is not the focus of our chapters. However, several of the authors do refer to possible actions. An intriguing approach is "shadow banning," where a user's posts are set by the platform to be not visible to anyone else, removing reinforcement from other users and preventing linking to those posts (Chapter 2). Tong (Chapter 3) reviews other interventions. One is preventing entry to users from extremist or raiding sites or via external links (Chapter 8). Another is engaging in (collective) counter-speech (perhaps generated through AI social bots), designed to influence bystanders and undecided users. Tong further discusses how some active viewers have attempted to reappropriate or reclaim hashtags, memes, phrases, or slurs. There has been, of course, extensive pressure on social media companies to more actively monitor and moderate, but they are somewhat free of responsibility for the content as legislated in section 230 of the United States' Communications Decency Act (3; see also Kosseff, 2019).

Tech companies have implemented a variety of changing techniques to prevent, identify, flag, remove, or punish online hate, with varying levels of effectiveness (Chapter 3). These include extensive and rapid evaluation of content as it appears, using both algorithms and human monitors. Using human moderators is not only inefficient and subjective but also imposes substantial harm on the workers who are continuously exposed to such content (Chapter 3). Yet Stringhini and Blackburn (Chapter 11) feel that AI models to confront online attacks will not be able to stay ahead of the evolving hate process and are often even subverted themselves. Identifying, moderating, and removing hate content are difficult because of perpetrators' deliberate use of metaphor, misspellings, slang, symbols, and contextual material designed to evade content detection schemes (Chapter 8). Also, perpetrators can also create and abandon accounts, avoiding tracing and suspension.

DeKeseredy advocates for more fundamental societal changes, such as changing gender and sexuality norms, changing access to women's health resources, and fathers modeling behavior of "well-meaning men" (Chapter 4). He particularly argues that interventions should target incelosphere accounts, sites, and platforms.

A perhaps even more subtle issue is that most platforms survive based on either direct advertising or sale of user information, so even hateful content can attract attention and generate revenue for the perpetrators (Chapter 8).

Conclusion

This chapter and this book end with the underlying goal explained in the Introduction (Walther & Rice, this volume). The motivations for this book are to conceptualize, analyze, and interpret a crucial yet understudied aspect of online hate: the social processes generating, reinforcing, shaping, and diffusing that content. The chapters focus on diverse contexts, platforms, data, methodologies, and processes of online hate. They are groundbreaking, thoughtful, well-justified, rigorous, and detailed. The elements of these chapters as synthesized here (social processes, contexts, methods, and challenges and interventions) not only provide broad and deep insights into and analyses of such social processes but also offer a rich foundation for further research into, and interventions about, online hate.

Acknowledgments

I am exceptionally grateful for Dr. Joe Walther's detailed, insightful, and challenging comments, edits, and questions on prior versions of this chapter.

Note

For parsimony, chapter authors are either referenced explicitly or by their chapter number (2–11) as listed in the References. Other authors are referenced as usual.

References

Arora, A., Nakov, P., Hardalov, M., Sarwar, S. M., Nayak, V., Dinkov, Y., Zlatkova, D., Dent, K., Bhatawdekar, A., Bouchard, G., . . . & Augenstein, I. (2023). Detecting harmful content on online platforms: What platforms need vs. where research efforts go. *ACM Computing Surveys*, 56(3), 1–17. https://doi.org/10.48550/arXiv.2103.00153

Baider, F. (2020). Pragmatics lost? Overview, synthesis and proposition in defining online hate speech. *Pragmatics and Society*, 11(2), 196–218. https://doi.org/10.1075/ps.20004.bai

Barker, K., & Jurasz, O. (2018). *Online misogyny as hate crime: A challenge for legal regulation?* Routledge.

Benesch, S. (2023). Content moderation needs auditing at scale, starting with Israel and Palestine. *University of the Pacific Law Review*, 54(4), 604–611. https://scholarlycommons.pacific.edu/uoplawreview/vol54/iss4/6

Blaya, C. (2019). Cyberhate: A review and content analysis of intervention strategies. *Aggression and Violent Behavior*, 45, 163–172. https://doi.org/10.1016/j.avb.2018.05.006

Burston, A. (Chapter 7 this volume). Digitally mediated spillover as a catalyst of radicalization: How digital hate movements shape conservative youth activism.

Castaño-Pulgarín, S. A., Suárez-Betancur, N., Vega, L. M. T., & López, H. M. H. (2021). Internet, social media and online hate speech. Systematic review. *Aggression and Violent Behavior*, 58, 101608. https://doi.org/10.1016/j.avb.2021.101608

Collins, R. (2014). Interaction ritual chains and collective effervescence. In C. von Scheve & M. Salmela (Eds.), *Collective emotions: Perspectives from psychology, philosophy, and sociology* (pp. 299–311). Oxford University Press. https://doi.org/10.1093/acprof:oso/9780199659180.003.0020

DeKeseredy, W. S. (Chapter 4 this volume). Misogyny and woman abuse in the incelosphere: The role of online incel male peer support.

Herz, M., & Molnar, P. (Eds.). (2012). *The content and context of hate speech: Rethinking regulation and responses*. Cambridge University Press.

Hietanen, M., & Eddebo, J. (2023). Towards a definition of hate speech – with a focus on online contexts. *Journal of Communication Inquiry*, 47(4), 440–458. https://doi.org/10.1177/01968599221124309

Kosseff, J. (2019). *The twenty-six words that created the internet*. Cornell University Press.

Mitts, T. (2022). *Moderating extremism: The challenge of combating online harms*. (under contract, Princeton University Press. (under contract))

Myers, S. L., Thompson, S. A., & Hsu, T. (2023, October 28). Swirl of vitriol and false posts. *The New York Times*, (B1, B6, B7). https://eeditionnytimes.pressreader.com/the-new-york-times/20231028

Phadke, S., & Mitra, T. (Chapter 9 this volume). Inter-platform information sharing, roles, and information differences that exemplify social processes of online hate groups.

Poole, E., Giraud, E. H., & de Quincey, E. (2021). Tactical interventions in online hate speech: The case of # stopIslam. *New Media & Society*, 23(6), 1415–1442. https://doi.org/10.1177/1461444820903319

Rae, S., Mathhew, B., & Kraemer, J. (Chapter 8 this volume). "Hate Parties": Networked antisemitism from the fringes to YouTube.

Rice, R. E., Evans, S. K., Pearce, K. E., Sivunen, A., Vitak, J., & Treem, J. W. (2017). Organizational media affordances: Operationalization and associations with media use. *Journal of Communication*, 67(1), 106–130. https://doi.org/10.1111/jcom.12273

Richardson-Self, L. (2021). *Hate speech against women online: Concepts and countermeasures*. Rowman & Littlefield.

Shmargad, Y., Doe, K., Kenski, K., Rains, S., & Bethard, S. (Chapter 10 this volume). Detecting anti-social norms in large-scale online discussions.

Siegel, A. A. (2020). Online hate speech. In N. Persily & J. A. Tucker (Eds.), *Social media and democracy: The state of the field, prospects for reform* (pp. 56–88). Oxford University Press. https://doi.org/10.1017/9781108890960

Srba, I., Lenzini, G., Pikuliak, M., & Pecar, S. (2021). Addressing hate speech with data science: An overview from computer science perspective. In S. Wachs, B. Koch-Priewe, & A. Zick (Eds.), *Hate speech – Multidisziplinäre Analysen und Handlungsoptionen* (Hate speech – Multidisciplinary analyses and options for action. Theoretical and empirical approaches to an interdisciplinary phenomenon). (pp. 317–336). Springer VS. https://doi.org/10.1007/978-3-658-31793-5_14

Stringhini, G., & Blackburn, J. (Chapter 11 this volume). Understanding the phases of coordinated online aggression attacks.

Strippel, C., Paasch-Colberg, S., Emmer, M., & Trebbe, J. (Eds.). (2023). *Challenges and perspectives of hate speech research. Digital Communication Research*, 12. Open Access. https://www.digitalcommunicationresearch.de/v12/

Tong, S. T. (Chapter 3 this volume). Foundations, definitions, and directions in online hate research.

Tontodimamma, A., Nissi, E., Sarra, A., & Fontanella, L. (2021). Thirty years of research into hate speech: Topics of interest and their evolution. *Scientometrics*, 126, 157–179. https://doi.org/10.1007/s11192-020-03737-6

Törnberg, A., & Törnberg, P. (Chapter 5 this volume). from From echo chambers to digital campfires: The making of an online community of hate within Stormfront.

Trujillo, A., & Cresci, S. (2022, November). Make Reddit great again: Assessing community effects of moderation interventions on r/The_Donald. *Proceedings of the ACM on hHuman-cComputer iInteraction*, 6, (CSCW2), 1–28, Article 526, pp. 1–28 (November). ACM. https://doi.org/10.1145/3555639

Udupa, S., & Gerold, O. L. (Chapter 6 this volume). "'Deal'" of the day: Sex, porn and political hate on social media.

Van Dijck, J., de Winkel, T., & Schäfer, M. T. (2023). Deplatformization and the governance of the platform ecosystem. *New Media & Society*, 25(12), 3438–3454. https://doi.org/10.1177/14614448211045662

Wachs, S., Koch-Priewe, B., & Zick, A. (Eds.). (2021). *Hate speech – Multidisziplinäre Analysen und Handlungsoptionen* (Hate Speech – Multidisciplinary analyses and options for action. Theoretical and empirical approaches to an interdisciplinary phenomenon). Springer VS. https://pub.uni-bielefeld.de/record/2957520

Walther, J. B. (Chapter 2 this volume). Making a case for a social processes approach to online hate.

Walther, J. B., & Rice, R. E. (Chapter 1 this volume). Introduction to social processes of online hate.

Waqas, A., Salminen, J., Jung, S. G., Almerekhi, H., & Jansen, B. J. (2019). Mapping online hate: A scientometric analysis on research trends and hotspots in research on online hate. *PLoS One, 14*(9), e0222194. https://doi.org/10.1371/journal.pone.0222194

Windisch, S., Wiedlitzka, S., Olaghere, A., & Jenaway, E. (2022). Online interventions for reducing hate speech and cyberhate: A systematic review. *Campbell Systematic Reviews, 18*(2), e1243. https://doi.org/10.1002/cl2.1243

INDEX

Note: Page numbers in *italic* indicate a figure and page numbers in **bold** indicate a table on the corresponding page.

Printed in the United States
by Baker & Taylor Publisher Services

Printed in the United States
by Baker & Taylor Publisher Services